Choosing Single Motherhood:

The Thinking Woman's Guide

Mikki Morrissette

Be-Mondo Publishing
Minneapolis, MN 55408

Janice —
Happy to have
you as part
of the
discussion!
Mikki

Direct all requests, corrections and comments to author
at www.ChoosingSingleMotherhood.com.

Book and cover design: Mary Leir

First edition, September 2005
ISBN: 0-9772042-0-0

Dedicated

to Sophie and Dylan

who make everything possible

TABLE OF CONTENTS

STAGE 3 – IS IT FAIR TO THE CHILD?

STAGE 4 – CHOOSING THE METHOD

STAGE 5 – DAY-TO-DAY PARENTING

STAGE 6 — THE LEGACY OF CHOICE

ACKNOWLEDGEMENTS

As with my two children, I am solely responsibly for creating, fine-tuning and delivering this labor of love to the wider world—yet I could not have done it alone. There are so many people who enabled this book to happen, starting with agent Theresa Park who encouraged me to pursue the idea over a year-long development process....designer Mary Leir who gave so much of her time to create the website and look of the book...my parents (and Sherry) for giving me the child-free time to write...Sophie and Dylan for finding ways to amuse themselves as I pressed forward.

In a book with so many different sources, covering so much territory, it is impossible to list every one of the resources that helped educate me. But I would like to single out a few of the therapists, child experts and social scientists who offered time for consultation and chapter reviews. I am particularly grateful to Richard Weissbourd for his thoughtful critiques, to Stephanie Coontz for her inspiration, to Kyle Pruett for his balanced advice, and to Michael Gurian for his spiritual wisdom. Elaine Gordon, Joann Paley Galst, Diana Greenwald, Carole Lieber Wilkins, Lois Gilman, Amanda Baden and Charlotte Patterson gave me helpful insight during the process. Andrew Vorzimer and Jody DeSmidt offered time for legal discussion. And the wonderful resources provided by the Donor Conception Network and Diane Allen of Infertility Network were invaluable.

Most of all, I am in debt to every single woman who shared her story with me—on the record, off the record, anonymously, or for attribution. Starting with Jane Mattes, the founder of Single Mothers by Choice...including Wendy Kramer, co-founder with her son of the Donor Sibling Registry...and ending with the Thinkers and Choice Moms who offered to review chapters to keep me focused on answering the right questions in an effective way. Especially Renai Gallagher, who I have never met but who was as generous with her feedback as a good friend.

And, last but not least, I would like to thank Dave for showing up to remind me that life never turns out quite the way you planned it.

INTRODUCTION

ABOUT THE AUTHOR, ABOUT THE BOOK

When I was a little girl, I spent more time playing tag and shooting baskets than taking care of dolls. In junior high school I was more interested in starting a school newspaper and doing "Roots" research than in cooking and sewing classes; I consistently earned my lowest grades in home economics.

In high school I launched another school newspaper and worked as a sports reporter at the community paper. I did very little babysitting. My best friend was a gay male, and I generally spent my weekends four-wheeling and playing poker with seven guy pals. I had my share of swooning over dark-haired boys with slight builds, but I dated only two boys and had no desire to attend prom.

In college, I still had primarily platonic male friends. I became sports editor of the University of Minnesota newspaper, worked in the press box of Minnesota North Stars hockey games, sometimes wrote about the team for the Associated Press, and dabbled in sports broadcasting.

In sum, I tended to be a tomboy, with no daydreams of marriage and children and domestic life. My dream instead was to work in magazine journalism, so I moved to New York City when I was 22. I knew one acquaintance there—someone I'd met when he was covering a swim meet for *Sports Illustrated* during my internship with U.S. Olympic Swimming. When I was 25, we married. Seven years later we divorced. At 36, after dabbling in boyfriends and falling in love once, I met someone who would enable me to fulfill my new dream, the one that had started growing in me about becoming a single mom. My daughter Sophie was born in May 1999.

A few years later I decided Sophie should have a sibling, and the same donor was used to help me get pregnant again. Five months after I succeeded, I met a guy I fell in love with. He and my daughter were in the delivery room when my son, Dylan, was born in January 2004.

Women You Will Meet in This Book

Maybe my story isn't typical, but one thing I've learned as a journalist is that no story is typical. Over a three-year period, I talked with more than 100 single women about their stories and why, generally in their 30s and 40s, they decided whether, when and how to become a mother. I largely met an incredible group of intelligent, professional, emotionally together women.

Some of these women were Thinkers—the term used by Jane Mattes, founder of the Single Mothers by Choice organization, to describe women considering single motherhood. Some were Tryers, and had taken steps to conceive or adopt. And many were Choice Mothers—my term, used throughout this book, for women who consciously and responsibly chose single motherhood after asking serious questions about what the lifestyle might mean for herself and her child.

> *I define a* **Choice Mom** *as someone who proactively seeks to become a nurturing mother on her own.*

Some of the women I talked to had more passion for career moves and hobbies than for men. Others were serial daters who never found anyone they wanted to have a child with. Some were lesbians with no intention of marrying. Others were open to the idea of wedded bliss, someday—just not in time to satisfy their urge for a child.

Women like Brooke, a former model and current television reporter. To be honest, I was stunned when I sat down with her. She is a tall, thin blonde with poise and obvious intelligence, and I wondered, despite myself, why *she* wasn't married. She explained that she had held on to her dream of finding a husband until she approached her 40s and hadn't yet found the man she wanted to settle down with. After being a "deep thinker" for a year, she learned that she'd be losing lenient fertility health benefits. She organized a girl's night to vote on which of her five potential anonymous donors she should choose. A few weeks after we talked, she confirmed that an insemination had worked. She is now a Choice Mom.

I talked with women like Dona, the Alabama mother of a 16-year-old son. When she decided to keep her child, in a conservative community, after an unplanned pregnancy with a man she did not want to marry, "My friends thought I'd lost my mind. Now they're all divorced with kids, and think I was the smartest one of them all." An obviously strong-willed woman, Dona told me, "My attitude is that life is an adventure. Of course there's going to always be tough times. Some days I don't want my baby to grow up, other days he doesn't grow up fast enough. But you can let

Choosing Single Motherhood © Mikki Morrissette

things drive you crazy or let it go. In the end, we've been lucky, being able to spend more time together than most parents and kids do. We've had it very special."

Janet, a university professor in Utah, says with utmost confidence that her daughter "has a really great situation in her life. A mother, grandparents, aunt and uncle who adore her. An amazing community around us. She's like a princess in our synagogue. More than 100 people came to her baby-naming ceremony. She has a great deal of security in her life. Maybe someday she'll mourn the absence of a father, but probably not. I'm here to support her if she does."

*"I feel like whatever her questions and concerns are,
I might not get the words right every time, but I will find
the words to explain why I did what I did to have her in my life."*

I learned the amazing story of Diana, who adopted a 13-month-old neglected child. Years of Choice Motherhood later, her daughter had become a top student at an Ivy League college, and had parlayed curiosity about the differences between her adoptive mother's Jewish background and her own Puerto Rican roots into a passion for understanding other cultures. She was described by a former teacher as someone who is "open to the world, open to explore new, challenging ideas, and open to learn about life far from her milieu, while listening closely to her inner voice. She shows a maturity that is rare for most students her age and is not cowed by anyone."

Why This Book?

As the conversations continued, I began to realize how common were the concerns of these women—particularly Thinkers, who were hungry for insight from experienced Choice Moms. All too often, as mothers yielded to the busy schedules of school-aged children, their collective wisdom disappeared from online discussion groups and single mom get-togethers. There were many pioneering Choice Moms who had guided their children from infancy, through the budding awareness of childhood, through rebellious teenage years, into young adulthood. But their advice—as well as the perspectives of their children—was not readily available to the growing audience either.

An unknown number of women in their 20s, 30s and 40s contemplate this choice each year. It's impossible to get a good approximation, since so many women decide *not* to pursue single motherhood, but **my estimate is that more than 50,000 single, unpartnered women end up choosing "yes" to motherhood each year!** My number is based on the following:

1. More than 100,000 single women aged 30-44 give birth each year, based on a 2002 U.S. Census report.[1] [Another report revealed that 134,000 unmarried women between the ages of 35 and 50 gave birth in 2001, based particularly in New York City, Chicago, Detroit, Los Angeles, Philadelphia, Boston, Miami, Dallas, Seattle and San Francisco, in that order.] One study indicates that roughly half of these women are living with a partner, which leaves us with about 50,000.[2]

2. Yet industry speculation is that there are about 30,000 anonymous donor inseminations each year, and roughly one-third of the clients are single women—which gives us only 10,000. [Note: Single women account for *nearly half* of the business at California Cryobank, one of the world's largest sperm banks, which ships about 2,500 ampules of sperm each month. Some places have more limited work with single clients, so one-third is a safer estimate.]

3. Based on my conversations with Choice Moms, anonymous donor insemination is a more common method to motherhood than using a known donor. So I would not go above another 10,000 for the known option, despite the fact that we might have 50,000 unpartnered women in their 30s and 40s giving birth each year. The gap might be made up of women who accidentally conceived.

4. **To be conservative with what we know, it is reasonable to expect that 20,000 single women each year give birth to a child, using sperm from an anonymous or known donor, after proactively choosing to become a mother.**

5. Industry speculation also is that there are roughly 125,000 adoptions each year, and an estimated *one-third* are with single parents. [Note: At one New York adoption agency, one-quarter of its clients are not married. Another reported that during the previous five years, 15 percent of its adoptions were with single clients.] **Conservatively, 30,000 single women adopt each year.**

No matter what the number, today's growing numbers of Thinking women could benefit from comprehensive, up-to-date information about the implications of this choice, as well as the perspectives of experienced Choice Moms and Choice Kids.

As a journalist who made the decision to become a Choice Mom, twice, I wanted to get a closer look at this lifestyle and how it affects our children. I wanted to share what I was learning, first- and secondhand, about the realities (and myths) of Choice Motherhood. I wanted to talk to experts who had specialized insight into child development, identity issues, and legal concerns. I wanted to dig up and summarize some of the excellent resources already out there.

The result of my quest was this book, which ended up covering much more material than I originally anticipated. Among other things, we will look at the faces behind the trend—real women who are making this decision and what concerns them as

Choosing Single Motherhood © Mikki Morrissette

they contemplate the choice. (Note: throughout the book some of the names have been changed.) We will consider advice and wisdom about the common questions Thinking women struggle with: *Can I afford to do this? Should I adopt, use anonymous donor insemination, or find a known donor? How do women handle the stress of solo parenting?*

Although I wrote the book to answer typical questions of Thinkers, Choice Moms also will benefit from some of the advice. The four chapters in Stage 5 walk through practical and emotional issues Choice Moms face with their growing children.

Although I kept my focus narrowed to issues of concern to single women—rather than the many lesbian couples and gay men who are turning to this option—I could not ignore some of the political and policy issues that affect many of us (in particular, see Chapter 15).

Although the material is written for a U.S. audience, I know from emails I have received from women in other countries that many of our concerns are universal.

How the Trend Began

During the 1980s and 1990s, as more women entered their 30s with financial and emotional security of their own creation, child-rearing without a mate seemed like the logical step for many. Some of them accidentally got pregnant and felt empowered enough to not have an abortion or make an adoption plan. Others felt their commitment to a career was cheating them out of a personal life, and opted to fill in the blanks by creating their own family. Still others, coming of age in a divorce culture, saw Choice Motherhood as a positive alternative to putting a child through the traumas of an unstable marriage.

In essence, the pioneers of Choice Motherhood grew up feeling more entitled to creating their own destinies than previous generations of women did.

"Twenty years ago middle-class women believed it took a man to have a child, but that's no longer true," said Rosanna Hertz, chair of the women's studies department at Wellesley College, to a *Newsweek* reporter in 2001.[3] Hertz, a social scientist studying aspects of Choice Motherhood for a book to be published in 2006, said it was hard to find women to interview when she started in the mid-1990s, but "now they're all over—next door, at the playground, in your kid's classroom. They've become a normal part of the terrain."

*In previous lives, Hertz said, women would have settled
by marrying Mr. Almost Right, but today settling can mean
having the baby even if you can't find the husband.*

As I talked with Mattes I could detect her surprise at the way things have changed
since she became a single mother in the early 1980s. "Now nearly everyone I talk
with knows of at least one person—a neighbor, a cousin, a coworker—who has
become a single mother by choice."

When Mattes chose to become the unmarried mother to her son, the decision was
a much lonelier one to make. It was more subject to disapproval and scorn than it is
today. That's why she formed the SMC organization (www.singlemothersbychoice.
com), where Thinkers, Tryers and Mothers find support.

IMPACT OF THE WOMEN'S MOVEMENT

BY VALERIE S. MANNIS
excerpted from Adoption Quarterly [4]

Said Pamela: "I think the social changes of the last couple of decades and the
history that led up to them made it possible for me to do this. I have the job.
I have the income. And even though I don't know any other single mothers
who've done this—I knew of them, but I don't know them personally—just
knowing they're out there in a sense makes it feasible. And in a sense, they've
also made it necessary, because in an earlier age I would have married one of my
early boyfriends and had children when we were young."

Why the Trend Is Growing

When TV character Murphy Brown decided to become an unmarried mother in
1992, the sitcom caused a national stir, thanks partly to public denunciation of the
message by Vice President Dan Quayle. But ten years later, "Friends," "Frasier,"
"Will and Grace," "Sex and the City," and other popular shows embraced the
lifestyle option with little fanfare. In 2005, several networks and cable channels
began rolling out drama and reality shows featuring single women, fertility clinics,
and sperm donors.

One reason for the popularity is that there are increasing numbers of single
professional women working in large cities across the country. Particularly in

places like Los Angeles and New York, untraditional households are simply more acceptable.

Yet even women I talked to in Kansas and Florida and Arizona were turning to the option as a way to fulfill a traditional dream of having children. Family-oriented women in their early 30s were aware of biological deadlines, thanks partly to books and articles pointing out how quickly fertility can decline after the age of 35. For them it was simply too important to become a mother than to wait for an opportunity to start a family with a husband who might not show up in time. Also, pioneers of Choice Motherhood have largely been successful in raising well-adjusted children, which has helped legitimize the option, sociologist Jane Bock pointed out to the *Boston Globe* in 2002.[5] And the image of single motherhood expanded from that of welfare-dependent teenagers to include strong, empowered women, from Jodie Foster to Angelina Jolie.

High rates of divorce in the 1970s and 1980s made single parenthood common. A woman raised by a lone parent because of divorce can be less intimidated by the choice—and in some cases, not willing to risk that trauma with her own child. According to the *Newsweek* article, "For many women, the barrier to marriage may be that they care too much about it, not too little, and they want to get it right. If they can't find the perfect soulmate of their dreams, they'd rather stay single. Others are the adult children of divorce, who don't want to make their own offspring suffer the pain of watching a parent leave."

National Public Radio commentator Lori Gottlieb wrote in *The Atlantic Monthly* about her own decision to become a Choice Mother in 2005.[6] "Unlike women a decade or two our seniors, we took it for granted that we could do anything we wanted," she said. "The way my generation sees it, if you're not forced to compromise, why should you? But sometimes we forget that if you don't choose anything, eventually you're left with nothing."

Every woman's story is different about how they came to a point in their lives when Choice Motherhood seemed like the decision it was time to make. One single woman I talked to had been married eight years before divorcing. When she was growing up, her parents had a high-conflict marriage, made more difficult because of alcoholism. She hadn't had a relationship with her mother for 10 years. Her sister had gotten pregnant when she was 18, and her daughter, then 13, had a father who was an unhealthy influence in her life. This no-nonsense woman knew that she did not want to put a child through the same conflicts.
Yet she realized her dating had gotten off track. "Every man I dated I was looking

at as potential father material for my child, not as a partner for myself," she told me. "I pushed them away by wanting to be a mom so bad. I wanted to fast forward everything to know if it was going to work."

Some women believe it is more responsible to have a child alone than to get married for the sake of having a child. Others feel that if they earn money while being a good parent the lack of partner should make no significant difference. And still others wonder what they can do to make up for the lack of a father in the home.

The Goals of This Book

America's sense of family identity continues to evolve so rapidly that we rarely take time to understand what it means for our children. Reproductive technologies and the overwhelming needs of international adoption and foster care agencies are making the "conventional" family harder to define. Court battles about paternity and child support are challenging the definition of "parent." Popular culture is portraying diverse families on TV and movie screens. Yet children today still pick up on the fact that large segments of society prefer the "biological mom, dad and kids" model. What impact, really, can Choice Motherhood have on our children?

Some of the concerns we will explore in this book include:
 • What research says about the influence it can have to grow up with a single parent, how and when to answer a child's "daddy" questions, and the potential identity issues of adopted, transracial and donor-conceived children.
 • The politics of choice, including the simmering debate about how children —and society, by extension—are affected by fatherless homes.
 • How grown children of pioneering Choice Mothers feel about the way they were raised and the impact it has had on their life.

Whether you are a Choice Mom, are a Thinker contemplating single motherhood, or are simply curious about the faces behind the trend, the intention of this book is to offer an in-depth look at the reasons women make this choice, as well as the obstacles, politics and psychology they confront along the way. Although I tend to be encouraging, the purpose is not to promote Choice Motherhood as a lifestyle for everyone—it is not the right decision for many to make. Rather, the goal is to offer an honest and realistic picture of what the lifestyle is and is not, so that all Choice Kids are raised by mothers who have consciously prepared for the challenge.

— *Mikki Morrissette, August 2005*

Choosing Single Motherhood © Mikki Morrissette

STAGE 1

TYPICAL INNER CONFLICTS

I was one of the lucky ones. Before I became a Choice Mom, I was oblivious to the issues that many Thinking Women face. I didn't worry about whether I could afford it because I had a high-paying job. I didn't worry about whether I could handle the stress of solo parenting because I assumed that I could handle anything. I didn't grieve the fact that I was embarking on motherhood without a lifetime partner because I had never been a fan of convention.

So I was lucky—at the start, anyway. Ignorance can be bliss.

Shortly after I got pregnant I started to freak out about whether I would actually *like* being a mother. Maybe I'd been foolish to think it was the logical next step of my life…maybe I was supposed to stay solo, traveling and writing and having experiences as a lone wanderer in the universe. Wouldn't my life stop if I was locked inside four walls changing diapers and, ohmigod actually *preparing* three meals a day, and helping someone else turn into a person who had experiences? *Bump*

After my daughter was born, in that first year of often lonesome, scary motherhood I discovered many moments of sadness that I wasn't sharing her development, and mine, with someone else. My local friends were single and childless, with no real interest in being part of my motherhood journey. My family was literally a thousand miles away. I didn't have a childhood dream of "husband, wife and kids" to grieve, but I found myself grieving something I couldn't even define. *Bump*

After three months of unpaid leave, I was ready to return to my well-paid job—only to learn that I was being "eliminated." *CRASH*

Talk about a rude awakening to the realities of life.

In hindsight, I'm happy I was oblivious to how much my life would change until it did. After talking to more than 100 women about their struggles in reaching this decision—and their struggles *after* —I understand how lucky I was to avoid many of the typical concerns before Sophie was born.

Alhough I had no regrets about being a Choice Mom, my hard won lessons about the bumps in the road made it more difficult to make a decision the second time. It took about two years of inner debate to choose "yes" before Dylan was born.

Today's Choice Mothers feel less stigma about their decision than did pioneers of the 1980s. But that doesn't mean it's an easy choice. Women today tend to focus less on whether having a child will be seen as "legitimate" for her and the child, but on whether the decision itself is a legitimate one: *Is this the right decision for me to make? Will I have the strength and energy to be a good mother? Do I have the financial, emotional and support resources to pull it off? Should I wait a little longer to see if life turns a new corner?*

If you're struggling with some of the typical "should I?" conflicts, the next three chapters have been written to help you through.

"Am I Single Mom Material?" looks at some of the most common reasons women hesitate as they contemplate this choice.

"Can I Afford It?" explores the number one issue of concern, based on results of an informal survey I did in 2003 of members of the Single Mothers by Choice network.

"Grieving the Childhood Dream" includes personal stories of women who came to this decision reluctantly, having dreamed for years of raising children with a lifetime partner.

NOTE: These are very common concerns. While the material here is ultimately reassuring—so many women have addressed them and gone on to Choice Motherhood—there are many more women who have chosen "no" because of these questions. Listen closely to yourself.

Choosing Single Motherhood © Mikki Morrissette

CHAPTER 1

AM I SINGLE MOM MATERIAL?

One morning when I was visibly pregnant, riding to work on the subway, I ran into an acquaintance who congratulated me on my courage for becoming a single mother. She was a highly paid corporate lawyer in her early 40s and had considered but rejected the idea of Choice Motherhood for herself. As she stood squeezed between the elbows of fellow commuters, she told me she was too "tightly wound" to take care of a child without a partner.

I confidently told her that I had always loved a challenge. But I didn't tell her about the night, a few weeks after my pregnancy test was positive, when I melted down in my small New York City living room, feeling isolated, panicked, and completely unsure about whether I had what it would take to be a good mother.

She would never know about the moment, a few days after returning from the hospital with my newborn girl, when I wearily watched my mother diaper Sophie yet again, after I'd finished nursing yet again, while my father prepared dinner yet again, and I wondered how I would ever manage alone.

She would never hear me internally disparage my parenting skills in comparison to others, as I saw the patience a friend had with the monotony of her preschooler's play, or as I admired the playful water-balloon-throwing spirit of another mom.

You could have the confidence of Joan of Arc, but no matter who you are there will be many moments wondering if you have what it takes to be a Good Mother. And you will have worries and fears no matter where you are in the process, whether you are thinking about the choice—*should I wait? go ahead? or is remaining childless okay for me?*—or whether you are in the middle of a pregnancy or adoption, or well into the realities of taking care of an infant, toddler or teen.

Although only you can decide whether you have the temperament to handle the inevitable stresses of being a Choice Mother, remember that doubts about your strength, energy and patience are natural. In this chapter we examine typical situations when these doubts occur, and how women have persevered in the face of sometimes overwhelming emotions about their ability to be a good parent.

The Before Time: Can I Handle It?

Some women want a child more than anything, and wonder even in their 20s why they have to wait for a husband. Others, 40-ish, wonder if they want a child simply because they feel they are supposed to, or worry that the desire will come after it's too late to do anything about it. But most women I've talked to fall somewhere in between: *I'd like a child, I'd like a husband, I'm in my 30s and not sure if I should wait and hope my situation changes.* Or, *I know I want to do this—the question is how?*

The fears of any woman who considers motherhood are largely the same, whether she is married or not: Do I have the "right" personality to handle it? Am I too selfish to take care of someone else? Will I regret not having the time, money, or energy for spontaneous nights out? Am I ready to commit myself to nurturing a child for 18 years? Have I taken care of my baggage? If I've never had a burning desire to take care of a child before, can I trust my motives now?

These questions take on added significance for the single woman because of the lack of a back-up parent who can help balance daily life and perceived character weaknesses. As one Thinking woman told me frankly: "I can be selfish and domineering. Best of all worlds would be to have a partner so my personality impact is diluted on the child and he/she doesn't have to bear my moods alone."

For women who do hope to find a partner someday, it is daunting to consider that it tends to be more difficult to date after a child comes. It's not impossible (see Chapter 3 for more)—some women report that the shifting of priorities seems to make it easier to find someone—but odds are that parenting will replace partnering in the Choice Mother's future.

Many women (I was one) have very little experience taking care of young children and have no way of knowing if it's the right role for them. Some women have tested themselves with volunteer work with youth-oriented organizations and babysitting friends' kids.

One Choice Mom I know had an unusually difficult time deciding whether she had the inner resources to become a mother. She had been sexually abused as a child and never had been able to develop a trusting relationship with a man. She didn't think she would be comfortable having the physical exams necessary for insemination. "Even if I adopted, I was very concerned that my fear of men might be passed on to a daughter, or indeliberately taken out on a son," she told me. "Would my inability to be physically touched leave me unable to nurture my child?"

In the end, with the support of family and friends, she conceived a daughter through anonymous insemination and discovered that "all my fears were unfounded. I had no trouble bonding with my child." When we talked, she was considering having a second. "The one thing I have learned is that I do have a tendency to exaggerate the potential pitfalls," she said, "and that life does somehow manage to go on despite all the potholes in the road."

Do I have the proper motivation?

Many women wonder if the reasons they want to have a child are "good enough" to warrant going ahead. Some realize they wish to replicate the loving relationship they had with a parent. Others understand they don't want to grow old alone—they see how happy their parents are to have kids and grandkids around them. Or they see the lonesome aunt and want to avoid a similar fate.

But being able to say out loud that you want to fulfill a human need for family and companionship isn't easy. Wanting to nurture a child in order to make yourself happy sounds selfish to some people. But it's generally the same reason a married person might give if asked. The difference is that most married people aren't asked why they want to be a parent.

Knowing you will need to justify to others your decision to have a child can make single women question whether they deserve it— can they sell their right to self-fulfillment?

My conversations with Choice Moms reveal, however, that justifying your decision to others is much less important after you have a child. As long as your child is happy, that's the only person whose opinion matters. *(We'll deal with your child's happiness with your decision in future chapters.)*

Am I too selfish?

Not surprisingly, this is a big question for many single women who have become accustomed to doing things how they want to, when they want to. It was certainly one of my big questions before I gave birth. My social life had begun slowing down already because of my professional life, so I wasn't put off by the idea of being at home so much. But I wondered how I'd handle being at the mercy of a child when I hadn't had to mesh with anyone else's life since leaving my marriage six years earlier. As soon as Sophie was born, however, I didn't want to be apart from her. She stayed with me every moment that we were in the hospital, and we were nearly inseparable until she started preschool. Which is not to say that I didn't covet my alone time. I felt liberated each time I walked the streets of New York City solo in that first year while Sophie was home with the babysitter: nothing but my backpack and a subway token…how free!

These days it still feels refreshing every time I go out with friends sans children. And I don't mind if someone else feeds or diapers or plays with them, to give me a break. But whenever we've been apart for any length of time I am eager to see them as soon as I walk in the door.

It does take a leap of faith, however, to trust that the changes in your social life will seem worth it. When you're on the other side of motherhood, it can be daunting to think you'll be stuck inside four walls after the baby comes. As Amy told me when she was a Thinker, she was reluctant "to give up the life I have now. No more spur-of-the-moment weekends away, no more theater subscriptions, no more long dinners out, no more peace and quiet when I close my door."

After motherhood, there are solutions to break the monotony of a more sedentary life. Some mothers arrange for a scheduled night out every few weeks—any more can seem like a hassle for a busy mom, any less doesn't give the mental break she might not realize she needs. Another advantage of the scheduled night is that babysitters can be lined up in advance.

As one woman said, before her daughter was born she "went out about four times a week. Since then, it's not so much that I can't go out, but I am so tired that I'm very happy reading a book, taking a long bath, or watching a movie. I go out about once a month now. This has been such a learning experience for me. I miss the freedom of jumping in my car and going wherever I please. Most of my friends don't come around as much anymore now that the novelty of me having a baby has worn off. It's bittersweet, but I do feel I know what's truly important now."

You will miss your freedom, sometimes for months at a time when your child is going through a particular stage. And it's important to know that dating—and developing long-term relationships—likely will be more difficult. But parenting is a "transformative experience," one therapist told me, that typically triggers unanticipated changes in individual values and priorities. When I talked to Amy after she had been a Choice Mom for more than a year, she said, "Yes, I do

　　　　　　　　Choosing Single Motherhood © Mikki Morrissette

occasionally miss the spontaneity, but I don't at all miss the solitude and I never, ever doubt I did the right thing."

From: A TYPICAL THINKER

I've been thinking for nearly 12 years. Something in me just seemed to "know" that I was going to end up going this route. I keep hoping that Mr. Right will come around. But I will be turning 35 soon, and the time seems to be ticking a bit faster these days. At some point fairly soon I know that I will have to stop thinking and hoping and just do it. I feel like I am waiting to just wake up one morning and know that it is right.

For the past few years I have been constantly trying everything I can think of to meet men: meeting new friends and networking, telling everyone I know that I want to meet someone, Match.com, Fastdating, etc. Along the way, I have met some wonderful men (and many, many duds!). But none that I felt I could be happy with for the rest of my life.

I'm not as concerned about finances as many others. I am fortunate to have an excellent job, home, etc. However, I also know that could change any day. It's a little nerve-wracking knowing that there is no one to depend on for an income should I lose my job and have a baby to take of.

I am concerned about being fair. I'm very concerned about how I will answer everyone's questions at work, neighbors, etc. And I am concerned about how others would act toward my future child—and how my child would do without a father.

My biggest concern though is not all these questions. I guess I know in my heart that we will just figure them out as we go along. My challenge is knowing when I have waited for Mr. Right long enough.

I wish God would send me a sign—and a very obvious one!

Is it fair to the child?

When I asked a group of women who were considering Choice Motherhood what their greatest hesitation was, a large number of them reported that they were concerned about the impact it would have on a child to grow up without a father. This is a good reaction for any potential mother to have. Ultimately the greatest gift of motherhood is the grace that comes from thinking first and foremost about another human being. In the end, it is that kind of commitment and dedication to your child that will make the biggest difference in his or her life.

Carol consulted with everyone she could think of before becoming a mother. She discussed it with a priest, a rabbi and a minister. "I thought they might say it wouldn't be appropriate or that every child needs a father, but they all basically said the same thing: that I was bringing a child into this world who would be loved and cared for by a mother who felt the most important thing was to love and show others love."

Even Carol's highly conservative brother approved of her decision to go ahead before her fertility declined. "That really shocked me."

She said she worried that she might hurt her child psychologically or emotionally by not providing him with a father, but an adopted male friend convinced her that continuous love and honesty would make her child feel blessed. "He said my child might wonder about his donor dad, but he'll know he was so wanted by his mom— and this is what will be most important."

[We'll discuss the important issue of fathers, and your child's inevitable daddy questions, in upcoming chapters.]

Do I have enough resources to be a good single parent?

This is a very important question, and one we'll get into more as the book develops. We're not simply talking about finances—although that's a big enough question in the early stages that it's the topic of our next chapter.

We're also talking about emotional and community resources. Who will help you raise your child? You'll need a stronger network than you have now. Many of your single friends won't end up being there after you become a mom. You will need mentors and male role models for your child. You will need community ties to help you alleviate stress, to give your child wider experiences, to provide spiritual growth. You will need family or neighbors to help in emergency situations. You will need good child care options that won't make you feel so guilty about working. You will need to connect with other single mothers for empathy. And you will need to expand your resources as soon as you can, so you know where to turn when you're too busy or tired to figure it out.

Choosing Single Motherhood © Mikki Morrissette

JUGGLING CONGRESS, ADOPTION NOT EASY
BY MALIA RULON, THE ASSOCIATED PRESS (2005)[1]

Rep. Deborah Pryce was all jitters. The highest-ranking Republican woman in Congress never breaks a sweat when she presides over committee hearings or takes questions from reporters at weekly House leadership briefings.

But three years ago, Pryce received a phone call from an adoption agency that a 3-day-old girl could be picked up immediately. There was one catch: The baby's 17-year-old black birth mother wanted to meet her. "I was terrified," Pryce said. "I didn't want anything to stop this from happening, and she didn't know I was white ... she didn't know how old I was, she didn't know that I was single."

Pryce, 53, arrived at the hospital after years of struggle. She and her husband had tried for a decade to have a child, weathered a failed adoption attempt, then lost their adopted daughter, Caroline, to cancer at age 9. Heartbroken and at odds over whether to adopt again, Pryce and her husband divorced in 2002.

Then came the call. Pryce and the birth mother spent 45 minutes together, taking turns holding the child. Now, 3-year-old Mia Denine Pryce zooms around her mother's suburban Columbus home in bumblebee outfits, singing the "Star Spangled Banner" and "America the Beautiful."

Pryce packs her schedule each week so she can fly home to Ohio and spend several days with Mia, who stays with a family friend while Congress is in session. "I can't say it's easy," Pryce said. "But you can make things work if you have enough love in your heart and the desire to see it happen."

A therapist I consulted for this chapter suggested that any woman considering Choice Motherhood needs to ask herself these questions:
- Do I have stability in my life (financial, familial, emotional, supportive)?
- Do I have realistic expectations about motherhood?
- Have I considered health issues in becoming pregnant?
- Can I be flexible and roll with the punches?
- If something happens to me, temporarily or permanently, who would take over?

Transitioning to Motherhood

It's one thing to contemplate your ability to parent when you're a single woman. It's quite another to be stabbed with fear when you're pregnant or on your way to pick up an adopted child. Yet it is extremely common for women to panic when their life is on the verge of changing. One woman I know had dreamed of having a child for more than 10 years. In her mid-30s, she decided to conceive, gave herself six months before inseminating, and got pregnant on her first attempt. Two months later,

---

JOURNAL EXCERPT

SINGLE MOMS EXPLAIN THEIR CHOICE
DR. VALERIE S. MANNIS[2]
edited excerpt by permission of author

The author of this journal article interviewed 10 Choice Mothers about why they felt comfortable going ahead with their nontraditional choice. All but one had college degrees, five earned more than $50,000 a year, five had been divorced, two had abortions in the past. Their children were aged 5 to 12 at the time of the interviews. The women had become mothers between the ages of 37 and 45.

Cara: "My pastor is married and has two adopted children from Paraguay. Whenever I played with her children she said, 'You have to adopt a baby.' And I said, 'No, you have to have two parents. Single women can't adopt babies. I couldn't handle it.' I always assumed I would get married and have lots of children, but I dated men who never wanted to make a commitment. When I was 39 I read an article in *Ladies Home Journal* about all the abandoned children in China, and that China lets single women adopt, and it just seemed like the right decision. I read the article on a Sunday afternoon and by Tuesday had contacted a social worker and started the process. My first appointment was December 1994 and by May 1995, I was on an airplane going to China."

Kenna decided to go forward with an unplanned pregnancy after doing a formal cost/benefit analysis. A professional in a demanding field, she needed to consider how she would handle the responsibility.

Dawn decided not to use artificial insemination and instead adopted two children from China. "My friends really supported [donor insemination], and they asked, 'why can't you do it?' I said it was emotionally too hard. I wouldn't know anything

---

hormones were in full force and she was "scared to death."

One woman's panic was triggered by certain events: making her first clinic appointment, during each insemination process, when she discovered she was pregnant, various points in the pregnancy, even after her child was born when she thought about the immense responsibility of being a parent. But she also reported profound confidence that her decision to become a mother was the right one.

about the father. When the child asked, "What was my Dad like?" all I would be able to say was on this piece of paper. I grew up with the concept that you had a father and mother. When they're abandoned [as in China], you're not consciously making that choice to say you're not going to have a father. Instead, you try to give them a better life than they could have had."

While women welcomed not having the hassle of a spouse, they showed the strains of being the only parent as their child matured. Amidst the most glowing descriptions of happiness, these women are often quick to say, "it's tough." They didn't interpret this duality as a contradiction; it is simply the way things are for them.

Dawn: "It's not a cake walk. There are a lot of downsides to being a single mom. But I think the plus sides far outweigh them. I try to focus on the good, because if you focus on the bad you're going to get overwhelmed real easy. If you're not set up with a good support system, you've got to reconsider your decision to do it."

Ellie: "I don't think people understand how difficult it is. My days start at 5 a.m. Last night I worked until 11 p.m. [Here in describing how difficult it was to do everything required of her, the mother was so overcome with tears she could not go on for some minutes.] . . . my family's been very supportive but I don't think they realize what they have and how much easier it is for them. Cooking, cleaning, laundry, keeping the house up. Emotionally I'm on a rollercoaster. I feel guilty when I'm at work. I feel guilty when I'm at home. I feel guilty that he doesn't have a father."

In a society dominated by powerful institutions that speak of a traditional family consisting of a married man and woman, it is informative to hear the stories of women who are consciously constructing their own new families and who are supported in this by those who love them.

After You've Become a Mother

Motherhood is filled with intense moments. Sophie can sit in her room singing *"Frosty the Snowman, was a tolly holly snow,"* earnestly sharing her muddled lyrics with her dolls, and it makes my heart burst with pride at how cute she is. Then I discover she's scrawled permanent red marker over the bedroom wall.

One Choice Mom talked about how astonished she was at the depth of love she felt for her child. But she also remembered going through an extremely painful time in her life, when she wanted to withdraw from the world and cry, yet the requirement of being Mom was to play and talk about nonsensical subjects. "You just do it."

After 9/11, when I witnessed the devastation 20 blocks away and on the TV screen, it was astonishing to have a clueless two-year-old dancing like normal in the living room. When I was in the middle of an emotional interview with a Muslim teenager who saw the tragedy from his school, Sophie loudly interrupted with an urgent message. "Come and look," she proclaimed. "I've gone poo-poo in the potty." She was so proud and insistent that I had to put my interviewee on hold while I dutifully followed her into the bathroom. Yet although the dichotomy of her world and mine during that emotional time was disconcerting, it helped me much more than watching continuous news coverage would have.

The dark days

Any mother, single or not, needs to be prepared for the rough moments. Sometimes they come because the child is stressed. Sometimes they come because the mother is stressed.

One mother complained of more than a year of stubborn behavior she endured from her daughter—trying every trick she could to survive—until in the end the phase lifted. In hindsight, she realized there was nothing she could have done differently, except try to be patient that "this too shall pass."

Karyn used to get upset with her son's tantrums and "no" attitude. One particularly difficult weekend, she said, she locked herself in the bedroom several times. "He would scream, beg, plead, and say everything he thought I wanted to hear. Then I'd see his little fingers crawl under the door, desperately reaching for some sort of contact. I would go over to touch them, and that diffused things so that I would come back out—until ten minutes later, when the whole thing would repeat itself." As a coping mechanism, she sent e-mails to friends with older kids. "It turns out, we're normal."

Choosing Single Motherhood © Mikki Morrissette

"Sometimes it's boring to be a parent, sometimes frustrating. But never for a moment, even with the memory of that weekend, do I doubt this life is good."

Every mother will have dark moments, sometimes for unbearably long stretches of time. And every mother will have moments of profound joy. The difficult thing for many Thinkers is having faith that she will be able to balance the bad with the good, that she won't snap hysterically, that it will all be worth it in the end.

BOOK EXCERPT

IN PRAISE OF SINGLE PARENTS

BY SHOSHANA ALEXANDER[3]

In this interesting book, a single father is quoted as saying:

"In my twenties, before I became a father, I was a very self-absorbed person. What got thrown into sharp relief for me as a single father—and of course every mother knows this too—is that it isn't always a lot of fun to take care of kids. It's a lot of giving and giving and giving. When I pick my kids up, there's no woman to do seventy percent of it, or, as is more likely in the typical marriage, ninety percent of it. When my boys are with me, I do one hundred percent of the giving.

"But as the weeks and months and years have gone by, I have begun to realize something. I *like* this. It has given me an anchor and a focus. I think when you have a child, something happens to you that is beyond words, if you allow it. I think my spiritual life is infinitely richer now because of being with them. It's understanding sacrifice, not in some dark, self-negating sense but in a deeply enriching way."

Final Thoughts

One of the things—honestly—that I got down about when I was pregnant was how much time I'd have to spend shopping. Yet now that I'm a mom, I love picking out new things for my kids.

Of course, that's not the most stressful test of my ability to be a good Choice Mom. But my point is, all mothers do find strength and joy in little—and big—things they never felt before.

Children interfere with your sleep, privacy, savings, career ambitions, errand-running, love life, travel destinations. Yet there is no way to anticipate the rewards of being a mother until you are one, because so much of parenting transcends the simple tasks of taking care of another human being.

A capable woman can be a capable mother. All of us have faced obstacles, down periods, crabby times and low moments. Yet we all find ways to persevere. We seek support from others, devise creative solutions, chill out behind closed doors, or treat ourselves to a much deserved night out or pampering session. Our children learn from our example about how to deal with frustrations they will inevitably feel.

Parenthood is always a juggling act, balancing time and energy and finances and emotions with your child's—and your own—natural good and bad days. There are serious issues that you need to face if you decide to become a Choice Mom, which we will cover in upcoming chapters. But if you are motivated enough to continue reading this book, being a good mother is not likely to be one of your issues.

FROM: THE AUTHOR'S JOURNAL

It's a Wednesday night and I've just snapped at Sophie, who didn't deserve it. She was jumping and hovering while I was trying to read the newspaper and I was annoyed at not having my personal space. Rather than asking her to give me space—which she probably would have ignored out of three-year-old incomprehension—I yelled at her to "leave me alone…can't you just leave me alone?" She takes these occasional outbursts in stride now, which makes me feel horrible. Her general cheeriness in contrast to my night-time crabbiness makes me feel momentarily inadequate as a parent. Is this unusual short-temperedness of mine showing up now because I'm stressed and not aware… an inevitable result of being a single parent… or a byproduct of simply being a parent?

Thursday night. I yell at Sophie for not cleaning her room, despite at least six requests in the last few hours, and dramatically scoop up everything on her floor — dolls, toys, clothes, books, movies — and whisk them "away." I ignore her cries, commanding that

BOOK EXCERPT

THE MYTHS OF MOTHERHOOD
BY SHARI THURER[4]

The briefest glance at history will dispel any notion that there is one correct way to mother. Your grandmother may have bottle-fed your father on a rigid schedule and started his toilet training when he was the tender age of three months, practices generally regarded as ridiculous today. Yet he managed to grow up. Youngsters tend to survive their parents' bungled efforts. The nervousness parents feel about their adequacy will dissipate when decent people are encouraged to mother in their own decent way.

if she can't take care of her things then she's not responsible enough to have them. Is this discipline that I've done? Or nasty-mother torture?

The next night, she and I make a special dessert for company. The next night…I'm teaching Sophie how to use chopsticks at a sushi bar after watching an OmniMax movie about chimps. The next day…we're exploring African art at a local museum. The next night…she's sitting with me at a reading of a Jon Hassler story, fidgety but doing her darnedest to follow this "grown-up" event. The next night…I get teary as I walk into Sophie's preschool with other parents about to watch her first "dance" recital. The next night…she's excitedly bouncing to the beat on my lap as we watch professional skaters in an ice show. She of course nods off on the way home and I carry her three flights up to bed where she curls sweetly into a cherub ball and I sit and watch her sleep, unable to take my eyes off her face.

After my inadequate moments of motherhood, we've had a week of wonderful togetherness and joy as mother and child.

CAVEAT: MOTHERHOOD IS NOT PROVISIONAL
From: Nicola

There are profound joys of Choice Motherhood, but it is important to remember that no one can pick their child's temperament, skills and attitude. When you say yes to parenthood, you say yes to everything, as this story reminds us.

Although I strongly believe in the autonomy of women to make the choices that are right for them, I have been distressed to hear single women say, "I couldn't cope on my own with a child who has a disability."

Although some may be speaking from experience and a real sense of themselves, I want to ask: Will you be able to cope with a child who barely sleeps for the first two years? Will you be able to cope with a child with cerebral palsy or autism or one of the other disabilities for which there is no prenatal testing and which may not be diagnosed for months or even years? Will you be able to cope with a child who is of a temperament you don't warm to (very timid, very loud, very sporty, very bookish, whatever)?

I believe that becoming a mother requires a degree of commitment to a child that is in no way provisional. I also know from experience that the fundamentals of parenting (offering love, security, boundaries, guidance, planning, teaching etc.) are the same for any child, of whatever ability. It is only the detail that is different.

I am the single mother by choice to two special needs children. My daughter, age 8, has Down Syndrome. I didn't do any of the testing you can do when you're pregnant, partly because she was a much-wanted baby, conceived by donor insemination, and I knew I would never terminate.

A few months after my daughter's birth, my father asked me if I would want her to take a magic drug to get rid of the Down syndrome, if the drug were to ever exist. We looked at each other and were both surprised to find ourselves saying, "No!" Her DS is part of who she is. She is a wonderful, funny, determined, warm little girl who loves to dance and ride and swim, plays her own CDs in her room, argues with (and loves) her brother, tells me to calm down when I get ratty, is cheeky, moody, interested in everything, loves to dress up for parties.

Last night she went to a party and scorned my advice that the other girls would

Choosing Single Motherhood © Mikki Morrissette

be wearing jeans, insisting on a pink party dress and a sequined purse. I was right, but she was not fazed. When I asked her what the others thought about what she was wearing, she said, "They loved it," firmly, and that was the end of that. Temperamentally, she's a lot like me! I can't imagine her being someone else, which is what she would be if she didn't have DS.

I look at my daughter's beautiful face and it hurts to know that one day she will realize that many people feel so strongly about who she is that they kill babies because they are like her. That sounds brutal, but I can't imagine how that will make her feel.

As someone who has valued intellectual activity above everything else, the irony of having a child with learning difficulties is not lost on me. If I was a religious person, I would be tempted to think it was a special test/blessing. I'm not, so I think that we've both been lucky. My daughter has a mom who really loves her and is interested in knowing how best to help her, and I have a daughter I adore and whose achievements make me just as proud as if she was top of her class.

When I tried to get pregnant a second time, the genetic counselor urged testing. I realized that for me it felt wrong to have some kind of checklist—this child would be acceptable, this would not. If I was going to have another child, I would need to do so feeling that I would love and care for him/her no matter what.

After two miscarriages, when I was pushing 41, I decided, with some difficulty, that it was time to stop. A few years later I adopted my son—who was diagnosed with Noonan syndrome—when he was three. His features include learning and behavioral difficulties, heart problems, an extroverted charming personality, short stature, and curly hair.

My son is the bravest little boy I know. At three, he said goodbye to everyone he'd ever known (including the birth parents and brothers he was seeing weekly) and crossed the country to a new life. For months, he never cried. He tested me out a lot, wrecked the house, attacked his new sister, did unspeakable things—some of which were just that he's a BOY. It took my daughter and I a few months to recover from the maelstrom of male energy that hurtled into our little enclave.

Adoption of a toddler is hard at the beginning partly because you don't love them but you have to pretend to. With an older child you could talk about it, but with a three-year-old you just have to pretend and wait for the feelings to grow. What is heartbreaking, of course, is that the child is doing just the same. It is wonderful when you can both relax because it has become real.

I would a million times rather be a mother to a child with special needs than not be a mother at all. If I had not become mother to my daughter, I'm sure I would not have gone on to adopt. I simply wouldn't have had the confidence to feel that I could persuade someone else that I could raise a child.

I love being a mom, and really enjoy my children. I feel as though I'm in a club that I never particularly wanted to join, but now I'm here it feels rather exclusive and special. I'm pretty sure my daughter feels the same way about having DS—that it's the other people (including me) who are outsiders, not her and her friends with DS. And that's the other thing you never know about unless it happens to you—the huge, warm community of parents, friends, groups, teachers, etc. of people with disabilities.

I would say that my two are in no way more difficult to raise than, say, a ferociously bright child who was demanding. And certainly I would find it harder to parent a child who had difficulty with affection.

My son needs a lot of help calming down and being the best person he can be, but he also soaks stuff up like a sponge. When he came, he had very little vocabulary (just "water" for a drink, a river, the sea, a pond). I think his foster parents had never read to him at night. A few weeks later, we were reading how the Gruffalo was in a "deep, dark wood" when he said, "That's not a wood, it's a forest!" There is so much pleasure in seeing little people develop and grow.

It isn't about what difficulties they have, it's about how they manage them. And if I'm going to get all philosophical, I guess I think that's what all of us are doing in life — trying to do the best with what we've got and what happens to us. I do think I've been lucky.

The one thing you can say for certain about becoming a mom is that nothing is certain. You don't know how you'll feel, how you'll react, what your child will be like, what life will be like a year, ten years, twenty years down the line. It's a big leap in the dark for anyone and that may feel more frightening when you're taking it on your own. But of course, you're not on your own, and whatever happens, as a woman with the courage to take this step, you'll be able to find the resources you need, even if the outcome is very far from what you expected.

Choosing Single Motherhood © Mikki Morrissette

CHAPTER 2

CAN I AFFORD IT?

Ask 50 women—as I did—what their primary concern is/was before becoming a Choice Mom and half of them will tell you it relates to money. *"Can I afford to do this?"* is the logical question of many. (*"Can I afford NOT to do this?"* is the emotional counterpart of others.) *"How much should I save before pursuing motherhood?"* *"What happens if I lose my job?"*

Ask those same women how much money they need in order to feel secure and you'll get a different answer from each one.

Mary, in her late 30s, lives in a medium-sized city on the East Coast. She has some debt, is trying to get a down payment together for her own home, and says she needs to have $15,000 in the bank before she'll begin trying to become a mother. Another woman in the same area has a different yardstick. She won't think of becoming a mother until she has an annual income of $60,000. Still others intend to become mothers with only a few thousand in the bank, a salary in the mid-20s, and a modest level of debt. Their desire to parent is so great that they believe they'll find a way to make it work with what they have.

Everyone has a different comfort zone when it comes to money. It tends to drive my mother insane that I don't have a conventional job. She grew up poor, worked at the same place for more than 25 years, and believes there is no such thing as financial security. But I have largely been self-employed for 15 years, have never had credit card debt, don't spend beyond my means, and own a nice home that provides rental income and is my retirement investment. I'm comfortable living this way.

The last time I had a full-time job was the three years prior to my daughter's birth. The nearly six-figure salary is what enabled me to feel confident that I could afford to become a Choice Mom. But a few months after Sophie was born, my job was eliminated. So much for financial security.

Darla is another woman who thought she had her ducks in a row. She was in a low-paying, dead-end job when she started thinking about becoming a Choice Mom.

Over a five-year period before giving birth to her son, she took computer science classes and worked as a software developer. Things were going great—until her company closed down her unit. After eight months of fruitless searching in the IT field, her severance pay was gone and her unemployment compensation and savings were dwindling.

"I finally took an entry-level job at a big company located a couple miles from my house. Money is really tight, but we're making it. I'm hoping that I can eventually move into an IT job within the company," she told me. "My point is that I waited until I was in good shape financially to have my child, but now I'm not much better off than I was before. You just have to deal with what comes."

> *"Maybe those people who say that 'if you wait until you're financially well-off to have a child, you'll never have one' aren't as far off the mark as I always thought they were."*

Most Choice Mothers who responded to a survey I sent out to 100 women reported a salary of more than $60,000, generally related to their post-graduate education. But just as with two-income families, it can be difficult to stretch existing funds— whatever they might be—for child care, recreation, education, and basic expenses.

Yes, you need to have money for health insurance, a safe home, and healthy food in order to be a responsible Choice Mom. However, there is no magical formula and no magical amount that will enable single motherhood to become a reality with no bumps on the road. You cannot plan for everything.

What you can do is assess—honestly—your current financial picture, and then determine if you can make things happen as a Choice Mom while maintaining your own comfort zone. Some women sit down with a financial advisor, who typically will ask you to determine your current net worth, track your income and expenses, estimate your future spending and saving, create a cash reserve, take care of debt, and set aside funds for emergencies.

If you're the type that doesn't even balance your checkbook (that's me) you do need to make an assessment of your spending habits before you can go any further.

Once you have a realistic sense of who you are as consumer and bread-winner, you will be ready to understand what you can and should do in order to afford responsible Choice Motherhood.

Choosing Single Motherhood © Mikki Morrissette

Check Your Spending Habits

AnnaMarie got pregnant on her first insemination try. During one low night of panic she considered terminating the pregnancy because she hadn't had time to save the money she thought she needed.

"I was irrational and obsessive about the finances," she told me, five years after her child was born. "A very dear friend set me straight. He told me to look at my single life, with all the eating out, the movies, the expenses of socializing, traveling, entertaining myself. He reminded me about my parents, who raised 12 children on only one salary. I spent the next several months taking a good hard look at cutting my out-of-pocket expenses. I was amazed at how much money I had set aside in no time flat. It has been tight, but I've been able to make it without outside help."

Living on the same income with a child does not have to be difficult. Often your money doesn't have to stretch further, it simply goes into different categories. Many women report that they spend less as a mother than they did as a single person—they have less interest in expensive travel, shopping, restaurants and entertainment. A lazy afternoon becomes playtime with child rather than mall cruising. A wintry day is spent making snowmen instead of shushing down the slopes.

As AnnaMarie found, once she cut out happy hours with co-workers and other forms of avoiding loneliness and blowing off steam, she was saving at least $100 a week. "I also shopped my insurances—all of them. Many people don't do this," she said. "They take their company's insurance, or the insurance company their realtor recommends. I shopped my homeowners, health, dental, life and car insurance, and did better in a couple areas. I called credit card companies and demanded they lower my interest rates or I'd close my accounts. I got a home equity line of credit to get a lower rate and moved some balances, stretched the payments out for a longer term.

"Mainly I put myself on a strict budget for things like groceries, clothes, shoes, etc. for the first time in my life. I went to Hair Cuttery for $10 cuts, and began coloring my own hair after my daughter was born. It took some time and discipline, but it was worth it."

Like AnnaMarie, when I was a single New Yorker, I regularly spent $100 each week at restaurants and bars without blinking. I had five magazine subscriptions, paid for standard cable, rented at least one video each week, and went to the movie theater a few times a month. I easily dropped $200 each year at the bookstore.

After Sophie was born, I stopped reading magazines, dropped to basic cable (I do miss Comedy Central), started using Netflix, rarely saw movies in the theater, and made library visits. Because of my new life, I ended up saving about $800 year on entertainment alone!

When I was single, I made it a point to visit a different country each year, and reached my goal of spending time in all 50 states. It was an expensive passion. Although I want both my kids to love travel—Sophie visited four other countries and 20 states in her first five years—my travels have slowed down significantly now that I have two children and am working only part-time.

Do I miss travel? Yes, but I'll get back to it someday, with and without kids in tow. An inexpensive visit to friends and family in other states will do for now. In the meantime, I live frugally. I don't spend much on clothing or shoes. I get my hair cut for $11. I notice which gas station is cheapest. I buy used music CDs. I invite friends over to drink a decent merlot for $6/bottle. And life is perfectly happy.

Anticipate Your Baby-Shopping Habits

Some women find great satisfaction in being bargain shoppers: using coupons, buying and selling on Ebay, seeking out consignment shops, flea markets, thrift stores, factory outlets, garage sales, and discount grocery stores like Sam's Club and Costco. As a mother of two on a limited budget, I find that I've become a much smarter consumer than I used to be.

When Sophie was born, work colleagues and friends chipped in on new big-ticket items: stroller, glider chair, pack 'n play. In fact, the portable playpen, with foam inserts, worked as her crib until she was ready for a bed. I used a hand-me-down high chair, bought all of her clothes at a consignment shop, and didn't have space for many toys—which was fine, since she preferred boxes, digging into drawers, dancing, trying on my clothes, and playground sandboxes during the first few years. Not anticipating then that I would have a second child, I sold what I could as soon as she outgrew it.

Although I wasn't extravagant in Sophie's early years, I am finding even greater resources for Dylan. I had no maternity leave pay, bigger medical bills because of weaker health insurance coverage, and no work colleagues to shower me with big gifts. His crib, bouncer chair, jumper, swing, exersaucer, and bassinette were free hand-me-downs, most of them from one generous Choice Mother. The baby monitor, breast pump, bottles, and most of his first-year clothes were gifts. His stroller came from a thrift shop. I don't use a changing table or fancy high chair. My only significant purchase for his first year was an infant car seat, and then a convertible one after he outgrew the first one at nine months.

I buy bulk diapers at Costco. When he used formula, I bought generic brands at Target or Walgreens. Instead of buying Gerber's baby food, I made my own. When he was an infant, a day's worth of Gerber's pears cost nearly $1. Instead, I bought pears in bulk, boiled them, pureed them, froze them, and fed him for two weeks for about $6. I'm no Earth Mother, and I don't like cooking. But even I managed to save money that way.

If money is an issue, you'll learn how to shop differently. And you'll discover that the $100 crib meets the same federal safety guidelines as the $600 one. That your infant doesn't notice if something is old or new. That a generic diaper works too. That your baby eats just as well from a $15 portable seat as from a pricey high chair that tilts, swivels and adjusts. That your toddler doesn't know the difference between a $3 toy and a $30 one. That your preschooler thinks a cousin's hand-me-down bicycle is just as cool as a store-bought one.

Honestly, my infant son preferred a piece of crinkly paper to the $4 wrist bands I bought him. And my daughter spent far more time drawing and coloring than using her $50 LeapFrog device.

Up until the age of 15, I wore hand-me-downs that my parents—both decently paid and loving—got from friends. When I was older, I rejected most of them because of the conservative styling, but there were usually one or two items in the bag that were funky enough for my tastes. I never resented my parents for bringing the bag home.

Having money to spend on your child doesn't mean you need to. If money is tight but you're prepared to bargain shop for daily essentials, your child won't suffer.

Determine Child Care Costs

Daily essentials are one thing, but child care is something else entirely. Any working mother without a retired relative to depend on will report that her primary expense is child care. And this is a non-negotiable item in which bargain-basement pricing is not the goal. No one should enter into motherhood until they know they can afford reliable child care.

The average annual cost for child care, according to the Nation's Network for Child Care Resources and Referral, is $6,750 for infants, $4,750 for preschoolers, and $3,500 for school-aged children.

When I was living in New York City with Sophie, I spent one-third of my income for her babysitter. When work was slow I used the $10/hour sitter three days a week, for a minimum of 25 hours. When work was flowing I used the sitter more.

Tips: FINDING CHILD CARE

Type in "child care referral" to launch an online search and you'll find good resources. An excellent starting place is the Nation's Network of Child Care Resources and Referral (*www.naccrra.net*), which represents more than 850 resource centers throughout the United States. One of its goals is to help families find affordable, quality child care, by offering lists of licensed daycares in every region, tips about choosing a provider, funding options, and much more. To find the CCR&R in your community, call Child Care Aware at 1-800-424-2246 or look it up online at *www.childcareaware.org*.

Another great resource is referrals from other moms. I found Sophie's babysitter simply by mentioning my need to a mother I didn't know, who was using her only two days per week. It was an invaluable referral, as she turned out to be Sophie's second mother for three years—and they maintain contact years after we've left New York. Consider researching early and getting on waiting lists—although most centers won't put your name on a list until the child is physically present.

It's easy to assess personality/philosophy in a simple phone conversation.

Typical questions to consider:

  • How long have the kids been with the same provider?
  • What is the maximum number of kids cared for?
  • How old are the current kids?
  • How are meals offered, and what do they consist of?
  • Is this a job, or does the provider seem to love kids?
  • How much communication does the provider generally have with parents?
  • What is the provider's parenting and disciplining philosophy?
  • How often is the TV used as a babysitter? (Consider pop-in visits.)

Choosing Single Motherhood © Mikki Morrissette

Primarily to save on child-care expenses, we moved to Minnesota, where I cut the babysitter expense in favor of free family and friends for the odd nights out, and enrolled her in tax-deductible preschool three days a week at roughly $4,500 per year. The average day care center would have cost me about $225/week. The average home-based care would have cost about $150/week. While writing this book, I found someone to live in our house for free in exchange for 20 hours per week.

- Are there regular art projects and preschool learning programs?
- How up-to-date is the baby furniture and toys?
- Does the price include food, formula, diapers?
- What are the hours, vacation and holiday schedules?
- What are backup plans for provider illness and vacation?
- Are you expected to pay for certain provider holidays, or weeks that care is not actually offered?
- What is the policy for sick kids?
- How flexible will the provider be in emergency situations?
- Are fees charged for late pickups?
- If it's home-based, are there pets?
- Is there a fenced-in outdoor play area?
- Is outdoor play a daily occurrence?
- What is the policy during rainy and winter months?

Ask the provider to describe a typical day. Is the provider someone you feel comfortable with as a "second parent"? When you visit with your child, be sure to notice how well-behaved and enthusiastic the kids are. What is hanging up on the walls? What kinds of toys and games are around?

If the provider has no space, ask for recommendations and critiques of others in the area. Verify the license with the county and check about any complaints that have been lodged. Above all, Choice Moms and daycare providers recommend "going with your gut" on whether the place is the right fit for your child. If something doesn't seem right to you, pay attention to that.

Always identify a backup babysitter if you are using home daycare. Unlike child care centers, the home provider usually requests paid holiday and vacation days regardless of your schedule.

In my case, I consider it easier and more fulfilling mom-wise to work part-time from home and make ends meet rather than pay for full-time care. My parents are willing caretakers in the summer months (they live six months in Arizona), but I don't ask them to step in more than a few days a week.

Many moms don't have the luxury of working flexible hours with family sitters. One woman I know spent $8,000 annually for full-time care for her preschooler (more in the infant year). After her child entered the free public school system, she was still spending $4,000 for summer care, after-school programs, and camps.

The only way to estimate this expense is to make calls in your area, since costs differ significantly by region. Check the range of costs with nanny agencies, want-ad listings, daycare centers, church and school sitting services, preschools, and home care listings. And call many sources. Daycare prices in particular can vary considerably from place to place, and might be significantly more expensive than licensed home care. And don't forget to ask if they are closed for long holidays and in the summer, if they shut down for school breaks that your employer doesn't recognize, if they only allow toddlers to attend a few days a week for part-time hours—anything that will affect your schedule or expenses.

Many mothers end up switching child care providers for various reasons—child is unhappy, provider is quitting, your job site moves—so don't assume you'll stick with one option until kindergarten begins. That's why fully exploring your options and determining price ranges is important, before you need it.

If the dollars are more than you can afford to spend, ask yourself these questions:

- Are you willing to move in order to use cheaper (or free) family and friends?
- Are you able to launch a babysitting co-op with neighborhood families?
- Can you convince your company to open an inexpensive care center?
- Can you work flexible hours at home and hire a supervised "mother's helper?"
- If you really love kids and are open to a career change, could you run your own daycare center, or work at a preschool for reduced or free tuition for a few years?
- Can you share an in-home nanny with another mom?
- Can you offer room and board to a local college student in exchange for sitting?
- Are you willing to change jobs to allow for more flexible or part-time status?
- Can you supplement income by taking in a renter or doing a home-based craft?
- Can you move to a less expensive area to reduce your housing costs?
- Can you find a better-paying job?

Choosing Single Motherhood © Mikki Morrissette

Reduce Debt

Many women report that the most important thing they should have done before having a child was to get credit-card debt under control. I've managed to be a freelance writer and home owner with up-and-down income, whereas single friends with no children struggle to make down payments on property or live paycheck to paycheck, simply because of mounting credit problems.

If you are drowning in debt, take care of that first. Pay attention to the interest rates, as AnnaMarie did, and switch to a less costly credit card company. Or open a home equity line of credit, if that's an option for you, and get a lower rate to pay off those cards. (And while you're at it, make sure you're with a bank that doesn't nickel-and-dime you with monthly fees.)

WHAT MOTHERS SAY ABOUT MONEY

I surveyed Choice Mothers about how money issues affect their daily lives. Here's a sampling of what they said:

"If I had enough of it I would stay home with my daughter and not have to deal with DAYCARE!"

"Finances have some impact, because of course we have little of it. But I never had much to begin with and am not materialistic, so it doesn't have a huge impact."

"It took a tremendous amount of money during the Trying Phase (between $600 to $1000/month). I was able to come up with that money...and now that money goes to daycare."

"If my income were higher I would go out and adopt a second child tomorrow!! I had to live partially out of savings until my daughter entered kindergarten to pay for the full-time daycare expenses. I congratulate myself that I haven't had to tap into savings since last summer. But I also haven't saved an additional dime for either retirement or college, I need to buy a car in two years, and I'm finding that summer child care seems to run about double what daycare cost."

"Now that my children are getting older, financing all of their extra-curricular activities (piano lessons, gymnastics, swim team, preschool, etc.) is a juggling act."

Calculate Taxes, Insurance and House Costs

I won't pretend that by the time you're reading this anything I write about finances and taxes will be current. But children aren't simply a financial debit—you win some decent tax deductions as well. As head of a household with a dependent, you qualify for a few tax breaks, including a child care credit and a child tax credit.

Based on 2004 data from the U.S. Department of Agriculture, the typical family spends $134,000 to $270,000 to raise their child from birth to age 17, depending on income level. Housing is the single biggest expense, followed by food, transportation, clothing, health care, child care/education (not including college) and miscellaneous. Writer Jeff Wuorio contributed a helpful online story to MSN Money website about these typical expenditures, strategies for cutting costs, and tax tips for the average family. (His story, titled "Raising Your Quarter-Million Dollar Baby," is available at http://moneycentral.msn-ppe.com/content/CollegeandFamily/ Raisekids/P37245.asp)

Note: The USDA survey is helpful, but no substitute for doing your own research. The child care number in that survey alone is the average price paid by families—the highs and lows divided in half—including those who have free help. Remember that your circumstances will vary considerably based on geographic location, child care arrangement, and health insurance variables.

Geography makes a big difference in many ways. Where you live usually is more important than the size of your house. As one Choice Mom told me, her small house in a good school district costs the same as a large house in other areas of her city.

If you lived somewhere else, would you be paying less in utilities, real estate taxes, homeowners insurance, mortgage or rent—or more? These are the big-ticket monthly expenses that are hard to trim. If a move might be in your future—so your child can attend better schools or you can find a better-paying job—check county records, documents at open houses, and your friendly insurance broker for numbers.

Other questions to explore, preferably with a financial advisor:
- How much more will you be paying for health insurance with a dependent, including premiums, deductibles and copays? If you got laid off, or became self-employed, do you know what this insurance would cost you?
- Does your employer offer a pretax dependent care benefit? (If so, take it.)
- Especially if you plan the insemination route, will your out-of-pocket medical expenses add up to 7.5% of your income? [Doctor fees, prescribed drugs, hospital fees…some people even deduct the cost of sperm, although this is a gray

area.] If you meet the minimum requirement for itemized deductions, you can realize additional tax savings.
• What would it cost, based on your income, to get disability insurance?

Consider Long-Term Issues

If you intend to invest in real estate before becoming a mother—as several women I talked to did—make sure to get a good house inspector before you buy any property. The furnace, plumbing and other maintenance can be damaging. Especially for houses that are more than 40 years old.

As one Choice Mom discovered after her house of 15 months sprung a leak, the repair was not, as she hoped, a $250 fix but a whopping $10,000 overhaul. When she read the fine print on her inspector's report—the inspector who said her roof would be fine for years—she learned that he disavowed any reliable knowledge of roofing matters.

A friend bought quickly, and paid for it later with costly plumbing repairs. She took the previous owners to court for failure to disclose, and lost that battle as well.

Before beginning her quest to become a mom, Teresa put together a plan with a financial advisor to reduce her debt and buy a house. "So I had a pretty solid grip on my financial situation and goals," she told me. "I did not have substantial savings, but I knew that if I waited until I could afford a child, I would never have one. Instead I decided to look at how I would afford it if I had one. I created a pre- and post-baby budget, started saving as aggressively as possible, refinanced my house, and set up a home equity line of credit. I made a list of other potential income sources I could consider if needed. I bought additional life insurance.

> *"I know my financial situation is not ideal, but neither was the one I grew up in, and I know my son and I will be just fine. The greatest financial burden will be daycare, and that's a short-term financial obligation, not unlike taking on a mortgage or grad school tuition, which I have done in the past."*

In my case, when Sophie was conceived I thought I was financially set. I had a high-paying job at a strong company, was well-respected by my clients, colleagues and most of management. I contributed to a 401(K), had great benefits, was able to pay off my mortgage (thanks to the sale of property bought in my 20s), and intended to set aside money every year.

Of course it was extremely unnerving to lose my job just as I was preparing to return to full-time work, a few months after my paid maternity benefits had ended. Although we eventually worked out a good severance package, I no longer had a long-term plan, and for five months pre-package I was very nervous about money. But I returned to the mantra that had carried me through many prior years of freelance struggles: *The universe will provide.* And it has.

In hindsight, losing that job was the best thing that could have happened to me. Instead of being locked into a job with long hours and a boss that didn't want me to return, I was free to relocate to Minnesota, sell my 700-square-foot New York apartment and buy a seven bedroom house for the same money (which provides me with rental income), publish a novel, write this book, have the space and time for a second child, spend five quality years with Sophie, and meet the man who would become my husband (himself not much better financially than I am).

THE COST OF CONCEPTION

Many Choice Mothers choose to inseminate with an anonymous donor. This generally costs less than adoption, but the numbers add up. If you are considering this route, investigate your insurance coverage and create a game plan for covering the expense. Barring fertility issues, there are two primary methods. The least expensive method is **intracervical insemination**, which can be performed at home or a doctor's office, when the sperm is placed inside the cervical opening with a speculum and syringe. **Intrauterine insemination** uses a catheter to place sperm inside the uterus, tends to have a higher success rate, but can only be performed by a doctor. Here are a few ballpark numbers:

• Intrauterine insemination generally costs $300 to $700. This does not include fertility drugs; the cost of preparing, shipping and storing frozen sperm; consultations, bloodwork and physical exams. The success rate is roughly 15 percent using frozen sperm. Often these expenses are not covered by insurance. One Midwest clinic charges $200-300 for initial consult, $37-90 for nurse practitioner visits, $160 for follicular ultrasounds, $38 for a pregnancy test, $69 for an estradiol lab test, and $138 for each insemination (2 per cycle).

• Sperm generally costs between $200 and $400 per vial. In most cases, you will need two vials per cycle. On average, it takes about six cycles to get pregnant. Many insurance companies won't cover this expense—although one woman I know used her company's health care spending account to pay for sperm, using

Choosing Single Motherhood © Mikki Morrissette

I may have sacrificed five easy retirement years down the road, but in my mind these early years with my kids are more important than the years I'll have after they leave home. I do have a large investment in my real estate property, which I expect to tap into when it's needed. And I intend for my kids to earn scholarships or financial aid to help pay for college.

If I could do it all—make lots of money from home on a part-time basis—I certainly would. But right now I'm focused on short-term needs and goals, and I have the courage to trust that I'll maneuver whatever sharp corners I need to along my path.

I realize that many of you—perhaps the majority of you—cannot live in such a precarious way. That's why every woman needs to determine her comfort zone and respect it. If it's important that you take advantage of earning years so you can retire comfortably or that you offer your child summer camp and costly music programs

---

a simple, unitemized laboratory receipt. Other typical fees, using the costs of one sperm bank as an example, include: registration ($100), long profile ($11), audiotaped interview ($25), storage ($300 for a year), delivery ($100 overnight).

- Expenses increase significantly for women requiring assistance in fertility. The combination of the fertility-enhancing drug Clomid, (roughly $50/month), ultrasound monitoring, a trigger shot and sperm, cost one woman $900/month in out-of-pocket expenses—and that's with insurance covering another $900/month. Insurance is more likely to cover if infertility is proven.

- In vitro fertilization involves removing eggs from your ovaries, fertilizing them with sperm in a laboratory, and putting the resulting embryos in your uterus. Roughly 30 percent of these attempts succeed. The procedure usually costs between $8,000 and $15,000. One clinic reports an average cost of $9,000 for IVF, including office visits, injections, bloodwork, monitoring, embryo freezing, lab fertilization, hospital costs, and physician time, with average medication costs as $2,700 per cycle. Another clinic offers women under 35, who meet weight requirements, three fresh sperm and three frozen sperm cycles for $15,000, with cycle monitoring at $3,000 to $5,000. This does not include consult, drugs or infertility work-up fees.

- One woman reported that it cost her about $1,100 per cycle to try to conceive. Her silver lining? She felt confident that if she could afford that, she could eventually afford child care.

as well as a top-quality education, then you should acknowledge that and figure out how to make it happen.

And therein lies the reason the answer to "Can I Afford It?" depends entirely on you, not the advice and numbers that worked for someone else. Your standard of living and ability to handle financial stress are uniquely yours. Assess your personality honestly as you consider these questions:

• How long could you survive financially if the economy took a downturn and you lost your job? Are there family and friends you could turn to in an emergency?

• After you've covered the fixed costs of basic necessities—home, car, food, clothing, household, child care—what else is in your budget? How much are you paying for cable, subscriptions, cell phone, Internet connection, entertainment? Would you be willing to trim them if it meant being able to afford to have a child?

• Is being able to afford treats for yourself and loved ones essential to your peace of mind? Do you find that you feel more energetic and happy when you have money, or does money have very little to do with your times of inspiration and joy?

• Do you tend to be optimistic about the future? Are you confident about your ability to earn money and be resourceful about spending it? Do you tend to do whatever it takes to make ends meet?

• Does the thought of sacrifice, or doing without material goods, depress you?

• Can you save a few thousand for emergencies and have the wherewithal to not touch it?

• Are your financial concerns related to trying to offer what you never had as a child, or to provide at least as much as you were given?

It comes down to priorities and values. Know what yours are.

Ultimately, living and working in high-paying New York City, my home for 18 years, was less important to me than being able to enjoy community living near family in Minnesota. I would never have believed it possible before I had Sophie, but after she was in my life, moving was the logical next step and it didn't hurt a bit. Many Choice Moms I've talked to, in fact, have made similar big moves in order to make a better life for their child.

Choosing Single Motherhood © Mikki Morrissette

HOW DOES YOUR INCOME COMPARE?

According to a 2004 Current Population Report, based on U.S. Census Bureau data, the median income of men who worked full-time, year-round, was $40,668 in 2003. The median income of the comparable group of women was $30,724. "Median" means half make above that amount, half below.

Golden Rules

If having a child is important to you, you will make it work and your child will love you for the commitment you bring to parenting. But:

1. **Make sure you know what you're prepared to do if a drastic change is required.** Even though I'm optimistic about money matters, I have had years of training as a poor, self-employed writer—and always had a modest security blanket in the bank.

2. **Understand what things cost in your neighborhood.** Make educated choices about how you will save and how you will spend.

3. **Determine whether you can create a loving environment while making ends meet.** If you need to sacrifice a responsive environment because of career goals, then maybe it's not the right time to become a parent.

Said one woman, "I had two working parents. But there were the years when my father was unemployed and my mother's secretarial salary, our savings, and the kindness of our extended family supported us. And those years were just as good as the 'wealthier' years, because what was important was not whether we took vacations or had new clothes, but that we loved and supported each other in all ways."

Said another woman, "I grew up without a computer, cell phone, cable TV, microwave, TV in my bedroom, VCR, designer clothes. I went to school, dressed like most other kids, and joined extracurricular activities. What I would have liked more of as a child was my parents' attention and love."

And yet another woman indicated that her pursuit of "enough" money cost her years in fertility. In hindsight, she said, she wishes she hadn't waited so long to try to conceive as it ended up costing her the ability to give birth.

New mother Rae told me she thinks the real question women need to ask is "Can I afford to wait?" Because of the cost of fertility drugs and procedures many 'older' women have to take, she decided to conceive in her mid-30s. She also decided to move ahead because her mother was healthy and available for child care, and she didn't know if that would be the case if she waited.

Final Thoughts

If the affordability of parenthood seriously concerns you after reading this chapter, be sure you understand why. Maybe there is a threshold income or savings that you require in order to feel comfortable, and flirting with poverty is not an option. Figure out what it is, preferably with the help of a financial adviser, and see if you can make it happen.

Maybe you believe that a few years paying off debt, or saving for a down payment on a home, or building that cushion, or finding what you need for fertility treatments or adoption, is worth waiting for. Your child will benefit from your excellent planning skills.

But also consider whether there is something else holding you back. Do you think it's vital that other things happen first: getting the house you never had, the house you *did* have, a husband, a higher-paying job? Is the absence of the "perfect" picture bothering you? Don't let money be the excuse if the ailment is elsewhere. People can spend a long time in pursuit of the "right" amount of money simply because they aren't taking steps to accomplish what actually will make them happy.

Have you ever known someone who made a list of goals and methodically reached them, only to end up still feeling discontented? Someone who got the right job, found the spouse, moved into a nice house, had kids, but still woke up with a major midlife crisis...or plunged into an affair...or dreamed eternally about "someday." People with lots of money still get divorced and still raise unhappy kids. If something is off balance in your life, money won't cure it. And neither will kids. Or a second wage-earner.

Examine your core and what you require to maintain it. Then and only then will you be able to determine whether you can afford to be a Choice Mother.

Choosing Single Motherhood © Mikki Morrissette

CHAPTER 3

GRIEVING THE CHILDHOOD DREAM

For anyone who grew up imagining herself raising a family with a loving partner by her side, giving up the traditional childhood dream of a glorious wedding followed by babies can be very difficult. Single motherhood can feel like a decision of "no other choice" rather than of choice: *if I can't find a man in time, I have to do this on my own or miss my opportunity to become a mother.*

Many women become serial daters, wading through men quickly and methodically in order to find someone "in time." Some become hopeful daters, confusing any potential relationship with the urgency that this be The One. Still others tell themselves the dream doesn't matter after all—men are generally pigs and relationships usually fail.

Some women have the benefit of perspective, having been married and divorced—perhaps because they married primarily in order to have kids, without having a deeper foundation. They don't intend to make the same mistake again.

Others find themselves in love with a man who doesn't want children, often because he has older ones of his own from a previous marriage. These women are faced with having to decide if they can give up their dream of having a child of their own, or give up their life partner.

And still others are in relationships with men who are ambivalent about having children. It becomes a question of 'how much longer should I wait for him before I do something else?'

Many women report that their criteria for finding Mr. Right has changed dramatically. A man who likes kids suddenly seems to have everything a woman needs—for a while.

Even if we think we've given up the dream, it still can be hard to retain equilibrium as men come into our path when we're considering Choice Motherhood. *Should I not date at all to avoid confusion? What if I go out with this guy and we hit it off?*

Should I tell him I'm thinking of becoming a single mom? Would this put a strain on the relationship and end it? Should I postpone my plans without telling him anything? Or would I regret it if the relationship didn't work out? Is it wrong to let him get involved without telling him what my hopes are? But when is it too soon? And when is it too late?

In the end, there are no right answers to any of these situations. This is a highly emotional place to be. The only solution is to buckle up and take the ride—letting your gut be your guide—and not jump off prematurely. If you're not sure whether to become a Choice Mom, take the time to waffle and don't rush to resolve your discomfort. Don't shut yourself off from dating if it interests you. There is no script for how you're supposed to do anything, and there is no reason to stop walking toward any of your goals. When the situation is right, you'll know what to say or do.

Most women, accustomed to success and being able to make things happen, never imagine themselves to be in this position. Revising the fairy tale can be a difficult process. But as the stories of the women featured in this chapter reveal, if you remain honest with yourself, the passages through grief, anger, sorrow and acceptance can lead you to many different resting places.

Case #1: Living With Grief

Judy admitted that she was "insane" in her 20s, involved in "not great" relationships. She entered therapy in her 30s. For five years she chose not to date. She eventually emerged as emotionally healthy and centered. She never became a serial dater, and never dated to find a father, but only if she legitimately wanted to be with a certain person. Once she unexpectedly got pregnant with a man who was "not the right man, and on his way out." She never regretted the fact that the pregnancy didn't lead to a birth. Some of her friends who once thought she was too picky ended up divorced. Others lamented being "stuck raising my kids with this #$@$ who has the morals of a flea."

When Judy was 40, she had no partner. Childlessness was not an option for her—so that much was clear. She visited her doctor for fertility testing, got involved with the Single Mothers By Choice (SMC) network, and knew she was taking steps she needed to realize her dream of having a child. But emotionally she was in pain, having a difficult time letting go of her longing to have a child with a partner, and struggling to embrace what felt like the overwhelming challenges of Choice Motherhood. She wavered between sadness and anger, and was concerned that she would never end up in another relationship if she became a mother.

She considered the choice for years. "I thought the reason I was stuck was because of my fear of affording it and being able to manage it all on my own. But in therapy it became clear that the real reason was that I couldn't let go of the dream. I'm becoming a single mother by default, not by choice. I'm blessed to have the choice and all that crap, but it's been a big struggle. I want the total package. I'm afraid that if I choose this path I'll never find the time to date. I don't like the fact that I won't have someone going through the challenges and excitement of pregnancy with me. And I keep asking myself, 'who's going to want me?'"

Through it all, she fought with her emotions. "How did I get here? At 40, this isn't where I wanted to be." The fantasy of the right man coming along 'in time' was gone. "I was grief stricken."

Judy also was angry. "If I'd come from a healthier family, I wouldn't have had to spend the first 35 years of my life getting my act together. Once I got to a good place, I wondered where all the men in a good place were. And I was ticked off at the biology of it all. Men didn't want women who were approaching 40. They wanted women under the age of 34. I was automatically knocked out of the vision of any man who wanted biological children. It's a frustrating system."

She recognized that if she waited to completely let go of the grief she would never be a mother. "There would never be a day for me when I had peace and total acceptance of the road ahead." She didn't want to stay stuck, so she decided to allow herself to continue to feel the grief and become a Choice Mom anyway. She took the leap into Trying.

Case #2: Choosing to Wait

Dev, too, was weary of the emotional pendulum: *I should become a single mother; I should not become a single mother.* For months she was comfortable with her decision to go ahead, but then she was confronted, strongly, by doubt, telling her it was too difficult to raise a child alone, that only the model of two parents worked for her.

She attended meetings of the local SMC network, did journaling, went through fertility tests, and planned everything but the donor she would use. Then, at the age of 38, she met a guy and felt enormous relief. "Now I don't have to do that," she thought.

The relationship didn't last, but she never felt inspired to pursue Choice

Motherhood again. When we first talked, it had been two years since she'd gotten off the path. "I feel that a man will come eventually. I want to let life unfold. Two years ago I was taking control of my life, my business, my spiritual journey. I was planning and pushing so hard. Now I think I'm more realistic about what single motherhood would mean. It would be a lot of work, emotionally, financially, physically. I think the biggest factor is that the process would be overwhelming and lonely, and I wouldn't have anyone to share that with me."

Childlessness was an option for her. So she decided to wait for a situation that appealed to her.

Case #3: Getting Focus

Cheri is from a conservative state where Choice Motherhood is rare. She wanted the traditional family, met someone she thought might be The One while in her 30s, and cried every night after it ended. When she recovered, she started dating "fast and furious," including time with some "real flakes."

When she refocused, she could see that the dream that she would have it all— husband, home and kids—was putting a timer on her relationships, and derailing many of them in the process. Her priority, she realized, was to be a mother. So she developed a plan to do that first. She continued dating, was upfront about her plans for Choice Motherhood when it seemed appropriate, and felt good about herself. "I knew where I was going."

The process was difficult, however. A few months before her plans for insemination were to start, she began dating someone she liked. She wondered if she should put her plans on hold. But when her next cycle started, she was in the doctor's office getting bloodwork done—and she kept going. "I'm glad I decided not to wait."

If she had approached Choice Motherhood intellectually, Cheri believes she never would have moved forward, primarily because of financial reasons. But the emotions of the first painful break-up helped her realize what she wanted in life—motherhood—and she listened and acted. When we talked, she was 25 weeks pregnant.

Having time gives us a chance to see what our motivations are—to get clarity on our priorities—just as it's easier to see the truth in someone else's life than in our own. Of course, if we had time on our hands, many women wouldn't be making this

        Choosing Single Motherhood © Mikki Morrissette

decision in the first place.

Desire for a Partner

Eventually the regret and remorse about timing can be confronted, learned from, and used as a launch pad to action. But women whose childhood dream is based on a deep desire for a partner, as opposed to a vision of how life should play itself out, seem to have fewer options for controlling their destiny. There is great power in making your priorities known to yourself, but sometimes the universe doesn't bless us how or when we think it should.

It's important to recognize and respect what your true values are. If having a partner is important to you, don't pretend it's not. It is often a defense mechanism to consider ourselves lucky to be without a partner, as if all men are unworthy and all relationships are doomed.

I used to be that woman. Once upon a time I insisted to a therapist that I could never be in a real, full-time relationship because it forces you to compromise and lose your identity. And not long ago, I sat in a friend's kitchen and proudly declared that I was such an independent spirit that I didn't want a man in my life, even if it would make it easier to raise two children.

But after I took care of my needs, dealt with baggage, made choices, and grew into my independent skin more fully, I met someone who had recently done the same.

I strongly believe that a relationship can add to our existing life. But only when we have met our own needs first. The question for all of us to answer is: Do we need the man before having the child, or not?

Getting to the Roots

It's hard to hear the inner voice when you have such a life-changing choice to make. The wrong man can look "good enough." The decision can seem impossible to make. In talking with many women who are grappling with the childhood dream, it seems the ones who have trouble reaching a decision about whether to become a Choice Mother are stuck for one of three reasons.

1. Timing — They know they want to be a mother, wish there was a father, and ultimately are stuck emotionally—with anger, sadness, depression—because of the unfairness of timing. *"Why can't I meet the right man before it's too late?" "I know I can adopt, but it's not fair that I have to do this alone." "What if the right man is around the corner and if I wait a little longer I'll be able to do this the 'right' way?"*

2. Desire for a partner — They want to be a mother, but they deeply want to share the experience with a life partner. For logistical, emotional and/or financial reasons, they want to have the husband/father in the picture and aren't sure if being a mother alone is enough. Some fear that becoming a Choice Mom will limit their options for finding a mate in the future.

3. Wanting to offer a father — They want to be a mother, but worry that it is selfish to deny their child a father. This type of guilt is common and normal, said one Los Angeles-based therapist who frequently counsels single women.

It sounds obvious, but only when you know what your true goals are can you decide what to do. As I mentioned in the previous chapter, I had no idea when Sophie was born that it would lead me to eventually leave New York City, where I had loved living for 18 years. But I knew I didn't want to work simply to make ends meet, that it would be good for both of us to be near extended family, and that I'd never afford a second child unless I moved. It became an unexpectedly simple decision to move to Minnesota once I really examined my priorities.

Question yourself
If you're struggling with the childhood dream, ask yourself these questions to get a deeper understanding of what your issues really are.

Is it more important to you to have a parenting partner for your sake, or for the sake of your child? If your conflict about proceeding without Mr. Right has more to do with providing a father for your child, see Chapter 7.

Are you dating men in order to find a partner, or to find a father? If you are dating primarily to have a child, then maybe you need to take a step back and try an alternate route. As one therapist told me, "Choosing a man for the purpose of having a father for a child will not sustain a marriage."

What is it about the childhood dream that you want the most? Is it the intimacy of an adult relationship, the support of a parenting partner, the legitimacy of a socially acceptable family life, or the seed to create life? Think deeply about what ranks number one for you.

Is having a child an attempt to combat loneliness? A child can add richness to our life, but does not make us feel "whole." That needs to come from within.

What is it that appeals to you the most about the two-parent model? Was your family life great with a dad so you'd hate to have a child miss that? Or was your childhood lousy and you're not sure you want to single-handedly be responsible for forming someone else's childhood? Determine what you think you lose emotionally in a one-parent family structure. For example, will you miss combining genes with a beloved partner?

If you could magically have the child without a partner—and no financial, moral, logistical or emotional burdens—would you? If you truly don't see a family life being complete without a man in it—or you being happy as a mother without also being a mate—pay attention to that. On the other hand, if your concerns are primarily about handling parenthood alone, then maybe it would help to widen your perspective and look to others for support. Talk to them: maybe the man can come later, after you've built a support network and established logistical solutions. *[See Chapter 11.]*

Once you specifically know what it is that you are grieving, it will be easier to confront it and move on to whatever decision is right for you.

Controlling the Clock

When it feels like the biological clock is ruling our lives, it can make anyone feel angry or depressed that something so important seems to be out of our control.

Some women find it easy to regain that sense of control in their lives by moving toward Choice Motherhood. They have a confidence that, whatever the timing, they will eventually find the right man, without deadline pressure. There might be many temporary relationships before we find the permanent one, but only a dwindling amount of time to have that permanent child.

The philosophy that carries other women is that there are lessons to be learned from every step of the journey and that as long as you are honoring your needs, the "package" you want will follow, maybe in a form you hadn't expected. My story is an illustration of this.

Case #4: My Story

Much to my surprise, when I was five months pregnant with my second child, I met my "Mr. Right." The man I would marry. The man who unexpectedly changed the complexion of the family life I had set up for myself.

Psychologically I was "ready" to meet him. I had made my own decisions about having kids, was happy about my choices, was making ends meet in an okay fashion, and had a solid support network around me. I had created a warm home environment with a good friend, who had moved in to my house with her son—my daughter's best friend since the moment they met on a playground.

Although I rarely dated after Sophie was born (and was a reluctant dater before), I knew I would marry again someday. I didn't care when it happened. I presumed it would be after my kids were grown and I had the time and interest to look.

I was on a boat cruise, enjoying a beach bonfire, when I met Dave. Although we didn't talk long, I knew there was something about him that I liked. After discovering his last name and finding his address in the phone book, I wrote him a letter. I laid all the cards on the table: I was pregnant (it wasn't noticeable yet) with a young daughter, looking for male role model material and friendship. Was he interested in becoming better acquainted? He laid his cards on the table in an email response: He was a widower with a teenaged son and a special needs daughter with aggression issues who required a lot of his energy. Yes, he needed more time being with an adult to balance out all the time he spent being dad.

We met over drinks. Two days later, he invited Sophie and me over for a family dinner. Everything clicked and within days, it seemed, we were in love. Six months later he proposed after a hot-air balloon ride. Bing, bang, boom.

In hindsight, do I wish I had waited to conceive again so that Dave and I might have had a child together?

Not at all. I was just shy of my 42nd birthday when Dylan was born, which for me was plenty late enough in life to be undergoing the last trimester of pregnancy and tending to an infant again. Dave's vasectomy years earlier made it unlikely for us to conceive. He was willing to undergo a reversal, but ultimately we both felt satisfied that I have my kids and he has his kids. Our job has been to attempt to share a family life together—for various reasons, in two separate homes—and squeeze in as much alone time as we can.

Choosing Single Motherhood © Mikki Morrissette

When we are on the present-day side of timing, we have no idea what's in store for us on the future side. If I had been childless when I met Dave, not only would I have missed the wonderfully "exclusive" four years that Sophie and I shared, but I likely would have been step-mom only, because of his vasectomy and teenaged children.

If we had met even six months earlier, when I was trying to conceive, I likely would have put those plans on hold—and precious Dylan wouldn't be in my life. Or I would have brought an urgency and confusion to our dynamic that would have derailed the relationship. Or been so focused on my goal that I wouldn't have noticed Dave. He and I met when the timing was just right.

The moral of my story: I believe things happen
when they do for a reason. We can't foresee any of it.

It's important to deal with grief about timing, but don't get stuck thinking there is only one way to end up with what you want. It might not happen the way you envisioned it, but the door doesn't shut on having relationships.

On the other hand, most women I talked to for this book remained single while raising their children, without regrets. In fact, none of the Choice pioneers told me they wished they'd had a partner, although a few said they wished they had had a second child.

There are lots of doors to choose from if you keep walking. Some of them include a partner. Some do not.

Setting Goals

Dr. Joann Paley Galst, a New York City-based therapist who reviewed several chapters in this book, counsels many single women who are contemplating motherhood. She knows that many of them are not ready. As she shared with me, "Parenthood, whether single or within the context of a couple relationship, is not for everyone. For a single woman, if she is actively grieving the loss of the dream of a partner along with parenthood, and if a child might be a reminder of this loss, rather than embraced as a gain to one's life, the woman may not yet be ready for single motherhood."

Forget, for a moment, the deadline pressure of age. If it's the connection with a mate that feels most important to you in your gut, then keep focused on finding Mr.

Right. If as a result you don't end up having a child, yes there will be regret—but like everything in life, there are options (adoption, foster care, travel, hobbies, volunteerism, activism). There is no one path to fulfillment.

If that feels hollow to you—if you want the mate but also want the child—then keep giving serious thought to having the child now and finding the partner later. Do the work you need—emotionally, financially, logistically—to reach this goal.

If you become a Choice Mother, you might not have time and energy and inclination to date for a few years, or you might meet men who don't click with your child and vice versa, or you might decide you don't want to spoil the family dynamic you've built by adding a new person to the mix. But if you're open to meeting a man, being a mother won't make you off limits.

Ellen is one Choice Mom who met her husband while in the process of adopting her second child. "It took a lot of dating to meet a good guy," she told me. "It was hard to fall in love with him. I was so involved with my son [her first Choice Child], I just wanted things to be perfect for him." One thing that helped a lot, she said, was that her future husband brought a present for her son on their first date.

And here's another interesting turn-of-events story to share with you that makes the point that life happens in mysterious ways...

Case #5: When You Keep Walking

After the break-up of a 13-year-old relationship, Paley moved to another state and bought a house with land in a more rural area where she could tend to the misfit collection of dogs she loved. She was happily single when she met a recent divorcee, fell in love, and made plans to marry. Eventually he realized he wasn't ready to commit to having another child and a brood of animals, and called off the wedding.

Despite a lifetime of loving relationships, Paley discovered, like Cheri, that it wasn't the dream of being married that she missed, but the dream of being a mother. After months of soul-searching, she realized she could have the child without the man, and felt a sense of empowerment by separating the baby dream from the relationship dream. She began to pursue Choice Motherhood.

Sounds simple in summary, but it was a gut-wrenching process.

Choosing Single Motherhood © Mikki Morrissette

"It took me a number of months to recognize the damage and pain that the relationship actually caused me," she said. "I'm pretty tough and smart and independent and capable, even about emotional stuff, and I thought I was okay. But I was wrong. A part of me died. That part of me was The Dream. I don't know how I'll ever believe again. With him, for the first time, I had let myself believe that the dream was possible. The wedding was planned, the invitations sent, I had my gown—now boxed up in the closet."

Over time, however, she felt liberated. She shared these thoughts with me: "From here on in, I can evaluate future relationships with men for who they are and what they can offer my child and myself, not based on whether he can fulfill my dream of marriage and a baby. Maybe I'll still dream of marriage after my baby is born. Maybe I'll just want a solid relationship with someone. Maybe I'll still be too hurt and jaded to believe again for a really long time. But the one thing I will have believed in will have been myself, my life and my ability to bring a beautiful child into this world who I can raise in a stable, loving home and with whom I can share my knowledge, my experiences and the magic that life shows us."

The interesting twist to this story is, after an emotional miscarriage with a child conceived with an anonymous donor, Paley married her ex-fiance a few months after we talked, and became pregnant with their child.

"None of this invalidates what I felt or the direction my life was likely to take," she said. "I would still be an SMC in an instant, without any reservation. Both are uniquely wonderful life choices that would have made me happy and complete. Things just changed, and he and I were able to work things out. Some would say I got lucky. I know I am blessed, but not because I have a husband and have recaptured that elusive dream. I feel I am blessed because I have found a life, whatever it may be, that works, that is fulfilling and I get a baby, too!"

Finding Your Path

A cataclysmic event like a break-up can awaken the senses to what we want. If you've had the *benefit* of being dumped just when you thought you were about to reach the childhood dream, ask yourself what you miss about the man. Maybe he made you feel warm and loved, until he stopped. Maybe the sex was great. Maybe he made you laugh. Maybe he took you to great restaurants. Maybe it was great to snuggle and listen to music together.

Someone else can come along to provide those things again someday. Keep looking for that next door to open.

But if what you miss most is the dream of sharing the joys of motherhood with someone, then ask yourself if the sharing is as important as the having. Would it be okay to have a close friend massage your shoulders through the last months of pregnancy, or a parent travel with you to China to bring home your baby girl? Could family members share the first gurgles and smiles and steps with you? Can that too-bad-he's-gay buddy help you paint the nursery?

If you don't have that kind of support network, with or without a partner you must develop them before you have a child. As we discuss in many chapters of this book, a support network helps immeasurably—more than one partner ever could. I have had a few good friends, one tremendous babysitter, supportive parents, and a baby-loving sister-in-law to help in spurts over the years, and can't imagine succeeding as well as I have without any of them.

> *As Galst said, "A woman who is isolated, without a solid support network for herself, may be too insular to offer her child an adequate sense of security in the world outside of the nuclear family. And it may be just too tough for her to go it alone."*

To be honest, it does feel good to have Dave along for the ride with my second child—at least part-time, as it is—starting with Dylan's first major kicks in the womb. He was by my side, holding my hand and taking pictures like a proud papa, when Dylan was born. I'll always remember how sweet it was to share my second night in the hospital with him, when he arrived with chocolate and champagne and we snuggled until 2 a.m. to the sounds of the hospital's "nature sounds" loop on the television. I couldn't have picked a more thoughtful man to share with me the last trimester of pregnancy, the pain and fear and excitement when contractions began, the blurriness of late-night feedings.

But it meant as much to me to hear Sophie squeal with delight when Dylan poked his head out. (I had taken drugs this time, so I was oblivious to pain and was not screeching irrationally.)

The incredible four-plus years of one-on-one bonding with Sophie had started in those first moments alone in the hospital after she was born, when I was tired and a little lonely, but mainly fascinated with this new being I had created and was now responsible for. I didn't need sleep—or snuggling or chocolate or champagne—so much as to have her always by my side so I could look at her non-stop. The experiences of both births were extremely different, yet both were wonderful. And certainly the experience of being Sophie's mother has been no less powerful because of the absence of a mate in the first years—quite the opposite.

There are times when I feel sad about the way my relationship with Sophie is changing. One night, shortly before her brother's five-month birthday, she asked if she and I could do something together, just the two of us, not Dave, not Dylan. It was a sweet moment. Of course, I was disappointed in myself that she'd had to ask, although I was happy she was able to articulate that she was missing something.

But change is constant. With or without Dave and an extended family, when she watched her brother Dylan come into the world our bond was permanently affected. And before I know it, her increasing circle of friends soon will mean even less mother-daughter intensity.

My point is, a partner—a sibling, a job—does make a huge difference in the level of interaction you have with your child. There is a positive and a negative, a yin and a yang, to everything. A partner can be a tremendous plus to having a child, but there will be negatives as well. Just as adding a child to your life will have regular ups and downs. (In one day I can spill over with love for the child that is Sophie, and be infuriated with the child that is Sophie.)

Don't think that having a partner is the one ingredient that would make motherhood complete, because—much as I love Dave—life can be simpler in many ways without one. Parenting skills, disciplining methods, communication patterns and energy levels, to name a few, differ greatly between adults, causing friction no matter how much they love each other. As one married friend told me, she finds motherhood much easier when her husband is traveling on business.

A Choice Mom of three sometimes fantasizes about how nice it would be to have an extra income and a father in the home for her children, but she knows that the compromise involved in bringing another adult into the family would be tough for her to do. Only five years into Choice Motherhood, she said, "I've outgrown the desire to be married."

It can be difficult (or less desirous) to find a partner after children. And it is sometimes impossible to have children after finding a partner. Analyzing which possibility would make you feel worse is sometimes the only way single women can move on.

Final Thoughts

Staying in a bad marriage in order to have children, or remaining childless, are legitimate choices—as is becoming a Choice Mom when what you really want is a partner first. But don't "settle" for a choice because you're afraid that half the dream is the best you can do.

Don't use your grief as a crutch either, because no one gives you back the time you spend waiting. Every setback, every disappointment, every emotion, ultimately can be used as a way to assess your priorities.

Judy, the woman we met earlier who decided to become a Choice Mom despite her grief, kept walking—and became pregnant on her seventh insemination attempt.

Dev, the woman who decided not to become a Choice Mom, kept walking too. A few years later, when I talked to her a second time, she was engaged to a man with two children and they were talking about having a child together. "It was really helpful for me to speak with you, as it reaffirmed my desire to parent with a partner," she said. "I believe that setting my intention very clearly and directly helped to bring this dream into reality."

I couldn't have planned a better way to make the major point of this chapter:

Life reveals itself in ways you cannot control or predict, so allow yourself to mourn that plans are not going according to schedule, but don't let it stop you from moving. Life has surprises in store for you if you just keep walking.

Choosing Single Motherhood © Mikki Morrissette

STAGE 2

GAUGING COMMUNITY REACTION

"Good mother" came to have a precise meaning. You know her well,
for she has lingered all these years in the background of our domestic values.
She is most assuredly not Murphy Brown or Mia Farrow or Hillary Rodham
Clinton. She is, rather, properly married, faithful, subservient, modest,
a woman who puts aside her own desires to rear and inspire her children.
She is part of our mental furniture: the doormat.
— by Shari Thurer, The Myths of Motherhood (1994)

Today there is much greater acceptance of Choice Motherhood than there was 20 years ago. Yet many Choice Mothers and Thinkers still feel the bite from those who feel they are wrong to bring a child into a fatherless world, and that children who are raised in this environment are less likely to learn proper values and more likely to grow up as behaviorally troubled members of society.

In **"Will My Community Accept Us?"** we hear from women who have faced or feared disapproval from family, friends, fellow churchgoers and other important members of their local network. Much of the opposition is based on a belief that a child's right to have two parents is more important than a woman's desire to parent, and that by purposely depriving a child of a father the mother has made a selfish or immoral choice that should not have been hers to make.

In **"Revisiting the Murphy Brown Debate"** we return to the national conversation Vice President Quayle launched in 1992 about Choice Motherhood when he decried the "Murphy Brown" TV show for mocking the importance of fathers. We consider the arguments of prominent voices who have echoed concerns about raising fatherless children.

[We will examine the arguments in detail in the next section.]

CHAPTER 4

WILL MY COMMUNITY ACCEPT US?

"Lack of community acceptance can really hurt because it can be a painful mirror for a woman's feelings of loss."
—Jody, a Thinking Woman

All of us have our own definition of which circles of community mean something to us. For some, it includes only the inner sanctum of friends and family. Others would include in that list neighbors, co-workers, fellow church-goers, playground parents, clients or customers. Sometimes the opinions of social acquaintances, people in the doctor's office, and distant relatives affect us. Or the wider network of people in our hometown, strangers on the street, society in general. Maybe even the viewpoints of people in the news.

If you become a Choice Mother, you must be prepared to expect everything from strong, vocal criticism of your choice to a low level of disapproval. No matter how tight and supportive your circle, it can still rattle you the first few times you read headlines that declare how damaging it can be for a child to grow up in a single-parent home. Or hear the disparaging comments of those who believe it is immoral to raise a child without a father. Or see the upraised eyebrow of a client or boss who clearly disapproves and who you fear might now look at you in a different light. Or listen to your mother tell you that if you lost weight it would be easier to find a husband.

It's one thing to make a choice that some sociologists and policy-makers frown upon, but it's quite another when those critical of Choice Motherhood include members of your own community. Many women get full support from loved ones and colleagues who understand their strengths and self-sufficiency. Many do not.

Most of us have trouble—at least initially—dealing with even that one person who doesn't understand why you would consider this choice. Sometimes the criticism can come out as shrill opposition; other times as a disappointed murmur.

Choosing Single Motherhood © Mikki Morrissette

AnnaMarie is from a Catholic family of 12 kids. "It was hard for my mother and father to accept this decision. They felt I should play the cards I was dealt. Not having a mate was my hand. But I could see the sad example of my maiden aunt, who never married and never had kids, although I know she loves children.

"My mother actually asked me if I had had a psychological evaluation before I was inseminated. I asked her if she had one before she got married and pregnant at age 19. I mean come on! Who gets to decide if I'm fit to be a good parent but me? At age 37 I felt I was bound to be a better parent than lots of people."

"Although they love my daughter [now 5] and support me,
I know deep down they feel my decision was not the best.
My father still thinks my daughter has gotten a raw deal.
I don't think he can see her or our family as whole."

"I tell him I see couples arguing about who is right and which way to go with parenting issues and styles. My married sisters are always complaining about how little their husbands contribute to the household beyond finances. For me, it's easier and less stressful, and I think that reflects on my child."

When Ellen announced her pregnancy, her mother said, "That's the worse news I've heard in a long time." Her father, on the other hand, was supportive. And her sister, who was in the process of divorcing, said, "It's better not to have any partner than to have the wrong one."

Another woman told me that a close friend—also single, childless and in her 40s—tried to talk her out of Choice Motherhood. "I think her view is due to her being conservative, some stubbornness, and being generally averse to risks. She worries about everything going wrong. She lives near her family and shares an office with her dad. Closeness to family is a good thing, but she's not very independent."

One woman said her sister didn't talk to her for six months because she didn't approve of the decision to become a single mother. But after her sister's son was diagnosed with cancer, the two re-opened communication, *except* "about this hugely important thing in my life. It is a great sadness for me."[1]

Another woman told me her Jewish background emphasized that "family is the most important thing in your life," and that having children fulfills the command to "be fruitful and multiply" rather than to satisfy a "man/woman dynamic." Initially her grandmother was opposed, but after she realized the child would be her first great-grandchild she softened.

Many women find that there is less opposition after the child is on its way—say, in the second trimester of pregnancy or after a green light on adoption—rather than when the idea is a concept some might see as preventable.

One woman who grew up Catholic on a family farm had nine supportive siblings living in the area. Only her father expressed concern about her pursuit of single motherhood, right up to the day she left for the airport to pick up her daughter in China. When she returned home there was a messsage from her father saying he would like to see his granddaughter. "From that time on, he'll call, see how she's doing—he's been wonderful! He's been probably more support for me in a lot of ways than anyone since we've gotten home."[2]

Others recognize that sometimes loved ones simply need time to accept and embrace what for them seems to be a decision out of the blue. But many women recognize that their decision will be criticized no matter what.

Dora is an elementary school teacher in a conservative town. "My principal told me that I could not bring my baby into the building when I came in for my check while on maternity leave. I had two colleagues say to my face something about 'immoral' and 'your scandal.' Another colleague spread a rumor that a parent requested not to have her child in my class."

Dora's mother was equally as unsupportive. When she met her grandchild for the first time, her comment was, "How do you know he doesn't have AIDS?"

Others in her community have been more encouraging. Such as the aunt who said, "Most people are supportive of another person's good fortune." And the student's parent who said, "You finally have one that you don't have to send home at 3:15!"

Although many women will be faced with a stray friend or relative who opposes Choice Motherhood, for women in conservative communities, or who adhere to religions that disapprove, the challenge is far greater.

As Cindy told me, "I have been very concerned about what the Christian community and my church will think. I have read that Christians are against anonymous donor insemination, even for married couples, and I have been told that it is wrong for me to even consider being a single parent. I also have been told that being pregnant and single will affect my ability to be witness to other Christians

Choosing Single Motherhood © Mikki Morrissette

because others will assume I am having sex outside of marriage. I worry that my child and I won't be able to find a supportive church, and I wonder how other Christian parents will treat him/her."

Some women report that criticism of their decision leaves them re-questioning their choice, such as the woman who told me of the nurse who said no doctor in their small town would help her get pregnant by insemination because it is morally wrong for a single woman to bring a child into the world.

"I felt I had come to a crisis," she recalled. "Was it fair to bring a child into a community that was so close-minded?"

She talked to people she respected but didn't know in a close way, such as a 70-year-old co-worker and "an old male friend that I rarely see anymore but that I know would tell me the truth even if I didn't want to hear it. Basically they all felt that if I went into this responsibly and thoughtfully, I and any child would be okay."

"You Are Selfish"

Several months before my daughter was conceived, I told a good friend of my interest in becoming a Choice Mom. He surprised me with his very vocal opposition to the idea. "How can you purposely bring a child into the world knowing they won't have a dad? That's selfish. You're thinking only of yourself, not the child."

As our impassioned debate unfolded over dinner, he went on to say that adopting was morally better than purposely making a life, but even then I'd be putting the child into a disadvantaged situation.

His reaction is a common one among those who are opposed to Choice Motherhood. The roots of this argument are based on the idea that a child's right to have two parents is more important than a woman's desire to parent, and that by purposely depriving a child of a father the mother has made a selfish choice that should not have been hers to make. Some of these critics believe that it is less selfish to choose an already existing child—preferably one from a foreign orphanage—whose prospects for a good life are already weakened.

A male acquaintance of mine—a divorced father of two—also thinks it's selfish for a woman to choose this lifestyle for her child. It's a difficult way to raise kids, he said, and shortchanges everyone involved. He, too, is against the idea of a single woman giving birth, finding it more redeeming to at least adopt a needy child.

While I understand that some people think of it that way, many Choice Mothers agree that giving up time, money, freedom, and an independent lifestyle to raise another human being is not a selfish act. Any good parent, married or not, enters into the task with the "selfish" desire to experience the highs that come from unconditional love for a child—knowing the lows that come with it. The world needs more kids who were raised by a loving person who actively chooses parenthood.

That is, in fact, why I refer to it as Choice Motherhood. Those who make this choice are actively choosing to parent (and reading this book, among others, because they want to make a responsible decision and effort). It is not a choice that is made lightly. As one Choice Mother pointed out, it is more selfish—and harmful—to marry a man you don't love in order to build a family.

Another woman suggested, "With the divorce rate over 50 percent, your odds of becoming a single mother are greater than your odds of staying married. So is it selfish to have children in a marriage knowing that statistically you are likely to divorce, thereby destroying the family that your child has come to know? Aren't children better off, or at least as well off, with only one parent than starting off with two parents and having that family ripped apart?"

Why the Opposition?

What can be seen as an almost natural next step for a woman accustomed to being on her own can be a terrifying prospect for anyone else. Often the strongest opposition comes from married people who find child-rearing to be a difficult process. Many of them entered into it without as much thought as Choice Mothers tend to give, and cannot imagine taking it on single-handedly.

Sometimes these parents are full-time caregivers, and cannot understand why or how anyone could juggle motherhood and a job. Or they expected their spouse to share child-rearing duties, rather than considering it "babysitting," and are angrily entrenched in thinking that no one should handle the responsibility alone. Or they have very supportive mates who are engaged with the kids and cannot relate to approaching parenthood any other way.

Others run head-first into a person's religious beliefs. This opposition tends to see

Choosing Single Motherhood © Mikki Morrissette

Choice Motherhood as an immoral act that goes against God's plan. I expected my strongly Catholic grandmother and great-aunt to hold this view, but was pleasantly surprised to learn that both considered children to be gifts from God, irrespective of the method by which they arrive.

One of the first (among few) social scientists to study Choice Motherhood is Jane Bock, who in 2000 published a journal article titled, "Doing the Right Thing: Single mothers by choice and the struggle for legitimacy."[3]

She wrote that Choice Mothers interviewed over a two year period often made significant changes in their lives for the benefit of their child—arranging their careers so they could spend more time at home, or moving to an ethnically diverse neighborhood so their adopted child wouldn't stand out.

The mother generally feels her choice is morally acceptable if she can answer yes to questions such as: Can I afford a child? Do I have the skills to be a competent parent? Do I have the kind of job that will permit me to handle motherhood and work? But religious grounds often played a large role in deciding whether others would consider their choice to be morally acceptable.

One interesting similarity Bock noticed among the women she interviewed who were comfortable with their choice was that the majority of them were Jewish. Among Reform Judaism, the discussion tends to be focused not on the legitimacy of the child, but on the motive for having the child. Said one, "We are very traditional women…the idea of not having children is not okay."

A single Orthodox Jewish mother of three, quoted in *Hadassah Magazine,*[4] said, "It's precisely because religious women are steeped in family values that they want children and seek ways to have them. By 35, I realized I had dragged out relationships that were not appropriate because of my desire to have children."

Another woman quoted in the article, who was a Holocaust survivor, became a pioneering Choice Mother when she was in her 40s. "My whole family was destroyed in the Holocaust and I felt there must be continuity for our family."

Liberal Protestantism also tends not to concern itself with questions of legitimacy, Bock reported. "Instead, it focuses on the moral or ethical components of decision making."

On the other hand, a Catholic woman she talked with said her priest refused to baptize her baby with others during mass, insisting instead that a private ceremony would be more appropriate. Since Catholicism defines any child conceived out of wedlock as illegitimate, and anything that replaces marital intercourse as a method to conception as "morally illicit," one single woman did not tell her Catholic parents of her pregnancy until the eighth month.

> *One woman Bock met had a clever comeback for those who opposed her decision on moral grounds: "Jesus was the product of donor insemination!"*

Bock reported that most of the women she talked with sought guidance from friends, relatives, therapists, and religious leaders before making their decision about whether or not it was "right" to become a Choice Mom. "With the exception of those exposed to Roman Catholic doctrine, little concern focused on the legitimacy of the child. Instead, concern was more focused on whether living in a single-parent household would affect the child's psychological or emotional well-being."

What can you do?

Whatever the reason for non-acceptance of the decision to pursue Choice Motherhood, it is usually based in the person's own deep-seated experiences and values—and biases. It generally isn't productive to try to convert them to your perspective on the subject. Often the best you can do is agree to disagree and move forward.

As an extreme example of this, who among us would expend the time or energy trying to change the viewpoint of the following letter-writer to *Newsweek*, who was complaining in 2001 about the Choice Motherhood trend?

> *I read with alarm your piece on the cover of the latest issue, "Unmarried, With Children." What are we celebrating here? The right of an adult to choose a lifestyle that is demonstrably harmful to her offspring? The right of an adult to intentionally disadvantage the next generation to pleasure herself? Every child has a mother and a father. That is the nature of biology. Our adulteration of the prescription laid forth by biology for a stable and healthy next generation has served us horribly over the last 30 years, and threatens to undermine the very fabric of our society. Feminism has managed to instill in the mainstream American Woman that she has a right to disadvantage children for her own pleasure—a disgusting, immoral and unethical position. It is high time that we stopped "supporting all kinds of families."*

Although most people around us are not as acidic, even the less passionate nay-sayers

Choosing Single Motherhood © Mikki Morrissette

generally are speaking from their own ingrained perspective. Just as many Choice Mothers have strong opinions about whether a donor should be called "daddy," for example, or whether a 66-year-old Romanian woman should have been allowed to give birth, there are lines drawn for some who believe that Choice Motherhood should never be an option.

In the end, there are only a handful of approaches you can take to deal with someone who disagrees with you (about anything):

1. Arm yourself with facts *(some of which appear in later chapters of this book)* and attempt to address their concerns logically;

2. Listen to their concerns, let them know you hear them, and move on respectfully without engaging in battle (returning with emotionally based fire makes people think they've hit a nerve and are therefore "right");

3. Come to a mutual agreement that you'll never share the same viewpoint but that you have the right to make your own choices about your life, just as they do about theirs;

4. Fight endlessly about the issue;

5. Take flight and surround yourself with supportive allies.

Nicola, the Choice Mother of two, offers this advice: "Often you have to let other people know how to behave towards you and yours. About becoming a single mom, I would always get the words in first and say, 'I know not everyone would think it was the right thing to do, but it has been right for me.' There's really not much that someone can say to that. I've acknowledged their possible disapproval and declared that it's not relevant to me. Very few people make negative comments after that, but since I've already said it's okay if they do, it doesn't seem to matter."

It might not seem satisfying to accept that some people don't approve of you—and it often can be more stressful with silent dissenters, as opposed to the vocal ones who get it out in the open—but focus instead on those who do approve of you.

And always keep in mind that moral values vary with time, place and person. Remember the story of Amina, the woman in Nigeria sentenced in 2002 to be stoned because she had a child out of wedlock? Was that decision more "right" than that of those who eventually overturned the sentence? Rules change because they aren't based on absolutes. Choice Motherhood is not morally "wrong" unless you think it is, no matter who disagrees with you.

Diane told me, "Maybe some would call it denial, but I think it's best for me to simply ignore any naysayers. There's no point in absorbing the negativity of others. I am an emotionally strong person and most likely wouldn't be considering this as an option if I wasn't. I truly, truly believe that it is not the number of parents, or the type of family that contributes to a healthy child. I truly believe that it is the care, love, honesty, respect, that the child receives while growing up that sculpts who

MORAL VALUES, ONCE UPON A TIME
BY MIKKI

My ancestor Hannah Duston was kidnapped by Indians with her newborn and her midwife (coincidentally an ancestor of my ex-husband). This was 17th century Haverhill, Massachusetts, when tribes were rewarded by Canadian settlers for bringing them white slaves.

Early in the journey north, one of the Indians horrifically killed Hannah's baby girl to stop the crying. Days later, Hannah organized other kidnapping victims for the late-night killing of their captors, and returned home with the scalps as proof. In a ceremony at the Boston Commons, her husband was awarded bounty money for his wife's heroism—values being what they were—and Hannah returned to the simpler life of mother and wife. She eventually was lauded in history books, and a statue with her likeness was erected as the first memorial for an American woman.

Ironically, also in the Boston Commons, Hannah's younger sister Elizabeth was hanged for bearing twins out of wedlock. Cotton Mather, the fundamentalist preacher of his day, shamed her publicly as an example of someone who "consorted with the devil." The babies' father denied the charges and went on to father other twins in town—values being what they were.

Although unmarried mothers are no longer hanged—and men are less blatantly rewarded for the courage of women in their lives—much of the basis for rejecting Choice Motherhood has its roots in old-fashioned values that are based on economic worth.

As Mary Ann Mason wrote in her book *From Father's Property to Children's Rights*:[5] "For most of our history, well into the twentieth century, the worth of children they will be as an adult. Choice Mothers understand that they are a universe within themselves and by using whatever resources they can put their hands on they will be able to provide their children whatever they need to grow up healthy."

Why Do We Care?

Jody is a Thinker who had some interesting comments to share about why it matters what other people think about this choice.

was seen primarily in terms of economic, not emotional, value. Fathers, recognized as the economic heads of the household and the supervisors of their children's labor, were granted paramount rights to custody and control of their children. Mothers, who had no economic power or responsibility, had no right to custody as long as the father was alive. Custody disputes, which usually occurred only if the father died, were often determined practically by considering who could support the child (mothers often could not) or which relative needed the child's labor."

In fact, she wrote, only if the birth occurred within the legal institution of marriage was parenthood of consequence. "Children born out of wedlock were considered *filius nullius*—or child of no family—allowing neither the mother nor the father custodial rights. Such children were usually put out as apprentices to another family."

Orphanages and foster homes weren't yet available, so even if the mother was alive, courts would apprentice the children to masters, who had similar rights and obligations as biological fathers. "As children's labor became less useful (replaced in large part by waves of new immigrants), and mothers gained more rights, parenthood was turned on its head. Children became emotional, rather than economic assets. Parents were encouraged to have fewer children and to put more effort into raising them, as opposed to having many children who would serve the parents. In this new sentimental perspective, the mother was increasingly identified as the nurturer and educator, replacing the centrality of the father as taskmaster."

It wasn't until the late 1800s that most states passed legislation declaring that a "bastard child" was a member of his mother's family (not his father's). However, even through the Progressive era, unwed mothers were considered unworthy mothers and were given little help in supporting their children.

"Many women spend a good number of years truly believing and trying to get the childhood dream to come true for them," Jody suggested. "Being a single mother is not how most of us were raised, and is not what society tells us is 'right.' First you are a failure for not getting married, then you are a failure for bringing a child into the world in what some see as a 'disadvantaged' position. Or you are a cautionary tale about the price women pay for being 'too' successful."

> *"Since most of us tend to be independent women who have been successful at what we do, as time goes by and we fail to have a family in the traditional sense, it's hard to accept that we're not viewed as a 'successful achiever' anymore."*

The reflection of others tends to push the self-esteem button that is already within us. If we're confident in our choice, we don't usually care whether others agree. But when there is a nagging voice in our head—placed there, or of our own making—telling us we aren't as 'perfect' as we should be, the sound of everyone who echoes that notion, whether in a shout or a whisper, can affect us deeply.

As Jody put it, "Society tends to be more comfortable with women as victims, of divorce or whatever, rather than assertively making their way in the world or doing it their own way. They are viewed by some as being selfish, having too much fun to settle down, not accepting that they can't have it all, being too picky to marry, being too successful."

Community disapproval can be even harder for women who are considering Choice Motherhood as the only remaining option for having children. It can be hard to defend your choice if it is not something you're particularly happy about doing.

Helping the Child

Although acceptance of Choice Motherhood grows every year, largely because of the success stories and the inevitable trends in women's lives, sharp criticism from any corner can still do damage, if not to the woman, then to her child, at any age.

Anyone who decides to become a Choice Mother must be prepared to give her child tools for coping with anyone who disapproves of the family structure, such as:

> • Keeping the lines of communication open so he/she feels free to share with you something that was said at school;

Choosing Single Motherhood © Mikki Morrissette

• Showing the pride and confidence you feel as a loving parent;

• Not apologizing for choices you have made while acknowledging that life might not always be perfect;

• Making an effort to bring other role models and single parents into your network.

Remember too that many of the most inquisitive and blunt questions will likely come from other children—your child's young cousins, schoolmates, neighbor kids.

Although the harsh community reaction to Dora and her son, now a second grader, subsided with time ("I guess I'm 'old news'") she does talk about it with him when needed. "He and I have a wonderful rapport and talk things through when they come up." After his music teacher made an inappropriate comment, she wrote a letter of complaint—rather than letting it slide—and pointed out to him that some people have trouble accepting families that are not 'traditional,' then explained what that meant.

She has protected him by cutting off contact with her disapproving mother. "So far so good. He is delightful and hasn't seemed to have any problems. He's successful at school, popular, well-behaved—and the joy of my life. He's been worth everything!"

Dora recently added to their family by adopting. Her son went with her to Russia and was involved in the adoption process. "He's very proud of this and feels a special protectiveness of his sister."

Final Thoughts

As you consider this choice, and how support—or lack of it—affects your resolve, consider taking these steps:

1. Define who in your community means the most to you;

2. One-by-one, ask yourself if the rejection of this person or that group would derail your intent to have a child;

3. Consider how you react when these people have a different viewpoint than yours.

4. Reflect on why this person's or that group's disapproval would affect you. What self-esteem button would it push?

Answering these questions won't make the disapproval go away, if it ends up being there in the first place (and quite often we are surprised at who understands and who does not), but it can help you sort out feelings logically before the emotions of a particular dynamic kick in.

And remember: Typically a Choice Mother doesn't encounter as much resistance when the product of her "selfish" or "immoral" act grows into a happy and well-adjusted child. The Choice Mom who is proud and positive usually disarms even the most judgmental critics.

Although the friend who criticized my choice has never disparaged my daughter's existence in my life—and was named one of her guardian options—I've never forgotten his words. Or the pointed comment from a family friend that "every child wants two parents." Or the shock from a traditional couple that couldn't believe I'd do something so crazy. Or the accusations of an acquaintance who belittled the Choice lifestyle as a dangerous trend that Hollywood celebrities were ushering in "as if it was a good thing."

So yes, down deep under my determined nature, I might have cared a little about what other people thought of my choice. But I don't today—and in fact I haven't heard disapproval from anyone for having a second child, perhaps because my daughter is obviously happy, smart and well-behaved.

> *Every day that I spend with my children, I am happily secure that my conservative but open-minded brother was right when he said, in his thick Minnesota drawl after he learned I was pregnant with Sophie, "The kid's going to have an interesting life."*

And security, after all, is what enables us to have a thick skin with our detractors.

CHAPTER 5

REVISITING THE "MURPHY BROWN" DEBATE

When loved ones and members of a community raise eyebrows at the choice to raise a child in a single-parent home, the concern often is based on a basic philosophical debate about what children need in order to grow up strong and whole. The central aspect of that debate is whether having both biological parents married and living in the same household will resolve problems that affect society at large.

On the one hand, as Barbara Dafoe Whitehead wrote in a powerful *Atlantic Monthly* article in 1993:[1]

> *"If we fail to come to terms with the relationship between family structure and declining child well-being, then it will be increasingly difficult to improve children's life prospects, no matter how many new programs the federal government funds. Nor will we be able to make progress in bettering school performance or reducing crime or improving the quality of the nation's future work force—all domestic problems closely connected to family breakup. Worse, we may contribute to the problem by pursuing policies that actually increase family instability and breakup."*

But if raising strong children is the goal, Stephanie Coontz wrote in a 2002 *American Prospect* article, "Nostalgia as Ideology," the method should be to support parents on a global scale.[2]

> *"The most constructive way to support modern marriages is to improve work-life policies so that couples can spend more time with each other and their kids, to increase social-support systems for children, and to provide counseling for all couples who seek it. But many in the center-right marriage movement resist such reforms, complaining that single parents and unmarried couples—whether heterosexual or of the same sex—could 'take advantage' of them."*

In this chapter, we will start to examine Choice Motherhood as seen from the perspective of sociologists and policy-makers, starting with a walk through recent history. Although much of the information excerpted here is more than 10 years old—and is based on research done with children of divorce, rather than Choice households—many of the "moral values" arguments today against Choice Motherhood are rooted in this material.

The Choice Imperative

Whitehead pointed out in her *Atlantic Monthly* article that in the 1950s most Americans believed that parents should stay in an unhappy marriage for the sake of the children. But in the 1970s, divorce for the sake of parents' happiness began to take precedent, and the taboo against out-of-wedlock childbirth "collapsed."

She understood why some people choose an alternative path. "For some unmarried women, nonmarital birth is a way to beat the biological clock, avoid marrying the wrong man, and experience the pleasures of motherhood," Whitehead wrote. But she also cautioned: "What contributes to a parent's happiness may detract from a child's happiness. All too often the adult quest for freedom, independence, and choice in family relationships conflicts with a child's developmental needs for stability, constancy, harmony, and permanence in family life."

Whitehead implied that it is a mistake for society not to frown upon anything but the two-parent model. "There is virtually no widespread public sentiment for re-stigmatizing these classically disruptive behaviors. On the contrary, the prevailing opinion is that we should accept the changes in family structure as inevitable and devise new forms of public and private support for single-parent families." She added that advertising and Hollywood have defended and celebrated divorce and single motherhood by fashioning the raw material of life "into a powerful fantasy of individual renewal and rebirth."

Whitehead reported that 34 million Americans tuned in—35 percent of the TV audience—on the night in 1992 that TV character Murphy Brown became an unwed mother. Not only did the public tune in, but advertisers did not tune out, she said, contributing to the lack of backlash against this statement of new family values.

The Quayle Controversy

It was not the content of the "Murphy Brown" show that generated controversy, but

Choosing Single Motherhood © Mikki Morrissette

the brief comment of then-Vice President Dan Quayle during a 45-minute speech.[3] His intention at a San Francisco talk was to discuss a recent trip to Japan, but Quayle decided to talk about values instead, since riots in Los Angeles had recently erupted when white police offers were acquitted on abuse charges in the beating of black motorist Rodney King.

The infamous passage was: "Bearing babies irresponsibly is, simply wrong. Failing to support children one has fathered is wrong. We must be unequivocal about this. It doesn't help matters when prime time TV has Murphy Brown, a character who supposedly symbolizes today's intelligent, highly paid professional woman, mocking the importance of fathers by bearing a child alone and calling it just another lifestyle choice."

Newspaper reporters initially paid little attention to the Murphy Brown reference, but the sound bite was too tantalizing for television news to ignore—and a public controversy was borne. Quayle was labeled as sexist by some, and out of step with the times by others.

As Quayle explained later, his criticism was not against single mothers, but against the attitude that "fathers are irrelevant. Fathers are dispensable. Fathers don't need to be around. We don't even have to know who the father is." He indicated he was trying to make the point that society seemed to be embracing the idea that fathers are not important anymore.

In the next few lines of his speech, Quayle said: "I know it is not fashionable to talk about moral values, but we need to do it. Even though our cultural leaders in Hollywood, network TV, the national newspapers routinely jeer at them, I think that most of us in this room know that some things are good, and other things are wrong. Now it's time to make the discussion public."

Whether Quayle's intention was a simple one or not, the commentaries by people who agreed with his premise took another step with it. Some of them began compiling evidence to indicate the "wrongness" of single motherhood—that a family without a father produces children who are a burden on society.

The Debate

A few years after the Quayle controversy erupted, sociologist David Popenoe published a book called *Life Without Father: Compelling New Evidence That*

Fatherhood and Marriage Are Indispensable for the Good of Children and Society.[4]
He started the book by writing about how more people in society are deciding
fathers are unnecessary, that unwed motherhood is a woman's right, and that single-
parent families are as good as two-parent families. "I hope to convince you…that
the evidence is strong: Fathering is different from mothering; involved fathers
are indispensable for the good of children and society; and our growing national
fatherlessness is a disaster in the making."

Like many Choice Mothers, I do not dispute the point that good fathers are
important, or that the absence of a father has an impact on a child. In Chapter 7 we
will discuss how fathers tend to differ from mothers, and the benefits that involved
fathers can bring to their children. But in this section, which focuses on community
reaction to Choice Motherhood, we explore the argument faced by many Thinking
Women: that they are contributing to a fatherless society and, by extension, denying
their children that which would make them whole and productive citizens.

Popenoe concludes his book by saying: "One can think of many reasons for
such declining child well-being, including the growth of commercialism and
consumerism, the influence of television and the mass media, the decline of religion,

---

BOOK EXCERPT

MOTHERING THE RACE
BY ALLISON BERG (2001)[5]

Dan Quayle's censure of Murphy Brown, delivered in response to the violence
provoked by the acquittal of four white police officers in the beating of Rodney
King, a black Los Angeles motorist, deflected attention from real race and class
conflicts onto a fictional mother, who became both symptom and cause of a
nationwide crisis of values.

Specifically, Quayle saw in Murphy Brown's unwed maternity an example of
the "breakdown of the family structure," which was, in his view, responsible for
the "lawless social anarchy" represented by the April 1992 riots in Los Angeles.
Ignoring both the immediate cause of the riots—the legal exoneration of the
police officers' violence—and the obvious race and class differences between
Murphy Brown and the inner-city teenagers whose reproductive choices he
feared she might influence, Quayle equated single motherhood with social
anarchy.

Choosing Single Motherhood © Mikki Morrissette

the widespread availability of guns and addictive drugs, and the decay of social order and community relationships in neighborhoods. None of these reasons should be dismissed. But the evidence is now strong that the loss of fathering from the lives of children is one of the most prominent reasons of all."

Although he indicates that "surprisingly few studies have actually examined the effects on children of fatherlessness, independent of all other effects," he points out that "almost anything bad that can happen to a child occurs with much greater frequency to the children of divorce and those who live in single-parent families."

Whitehead's View

Whitehead's *Atlantic Monthly* article was perhaps the most comprehensive, compelling and persuasive response to the Quayle controversy. She wrote that the optimistic view of family change rested on three bold new assumptions: a woman can afford to be a mother without also being a wife; divorce and other family disruption does not cause lasting harm to children; diversity in family structure makes America a better place. The bulk of the article consisted of Whitehead dispelling each of these assumptions, using extensive research by others to support her views.

Point #1: Single Motherhood leads to instability

To dispel the notion that single mothers are successful as sole breadwinners, Whitehead largely used the 1986 book, *Single Mothers and Their Children*, written by Sara McLanahan and Irwin Garfinkel,[6] for proof that even single mothers who are not poor are not financially secure. "Single parenthood forces many women to be on the move, in search of cheaper housing and better jobs. This need-driven restless mobility makes it more difficult for them to sustain supportive ties to family and friends, let alone other single mothers."

She wrote that the rate of moves for single mothers is about a third higher than the rate for two-parent families. And that the composition of the household is likely to change, with boyfriends and babysitters moving in and out. "All this uncertainty can be devastating to children," Whitehead wrote. "Anyone who knows children knows that they are deeply conservative creatures. They like things to stay the same. So pronounced is this tendency that certain children have been known to request the same peanut-butter-and-jelly sandwich for lunch for years. Children are particularly set in their ways when it comes to family, friends, neighborhoods, and schools."

She includes numbers from the McLanahan book to point out the dangers of this instable environment on children, such as: "Among white families, daughters of single parents are 53 percent more likely to marry as teenagers, 111 percent more likely to have children as teenagers, 164 percent more likely to have a premarital birth, and 92 percent more likely to dissolve their own marriages. All these intergenerational consequences of single motherhood increase the likelihood of chronic welfare dependency."

Author Comment

A girl who gets pregnant at 16 might be more likely to come from a one-parent home than a two-parent home, but that doesn't mean that a girl in a one-parent home is more likely to get pregnant at 16 than not. Or that the girl is incapable of making any other choice. Or that her parent is powerless to influence her in any other way.

If the formula of life was that simple, no 16-year-old girl in a two-parent home would ever get pregnant, no parent would ever take a promotion to a job in a different state for fear of destabilizing a child's environment, and every family would be guaranteed a salary to keep them in comfortable middle class so that adolescent issues could be avoided altogether.

I do not question that many of our troubled youth come from troubled family backgrounds where there is a lack of attention and love. But a Choice household is not inherently a troubled environment. As we will read in more detail in the next chapter, Choice Mothers do not fall into the same category as the single mothers that largely figured in McLanahan's research.

Most Choice Mothers I interviewed have moved at least once, but the end result was to improve the lives of their children by moving to a better neighborhood, a better school district, a bigger home—not, as was the case with most of McLanahan's families, to settle into a less expensive community, which tends to have inadequate school opportunities.

Most Choice Mothers and Thinkers I have talked to earn more than $40,000 a year and have completed college. In fact 34 of 64 respondents in a survey I randomly sent out earned more than $60,000 (55 above $40K), and 42 had post-graduate degrees.

The instability of single parent families that Whitehead wrote about in 1993 is not a factor for most Choice households. The point to remember from her commentary, however, is that offering a stable environment is important for any child.

Choosing Single Motherhood © Mikki Morrissette

Point #2: Family disruption is to be avoided

Although Whitehead's article focuses on the trauma to children of divorce, and doesn't specifically discuss families who have no vacating father in the home to begin with, it's worth briefly exploring some of the concerns here, since they are sometimes mixed in with arguments against Choice households.

Whitehead discussed the research of Judith Wallerstein, director of the California Children of Divorce Study—a pioneering investigation of the long-term psychological impact of family disruption on middle-class children. Before divorce these kids were reportedly living in stable homes, and post-divorce they were generally free of severe poverty.[7]

Five years after divorce, Wallerstein's research indicated that more than a third of the children experienced moderate or severe depression. At ten years a significant number of them, as young men and women, were troubled, drifting and underachieving. At fifteen years, many of them were around the age of 30 and struggling to establish strong love relationships of their own.

"In a reasonably happy intact family," Wallerstein wrote, "the child gravitates first to one parent and then to the other, using skills and attributes from each in climbing the developmental ladder." In a divorced family, children find it "harder to find the needed parent at needed times." Children who are very young when their parents divorce seem to suffer the most, which is attributed to the lack of this kind of developmental process early in childhood.

Whitehead points out that Wallerstein's research was criticized because it was based on a small clinical sample [author's note: of young people who came to her center looking for help] without also studying children who came from intact families. But other, smaller studies have reported similar findings.

Author Comment

Numbers can be useful to indicate patterns and trends, but variables can lead to different outcomes. The quality and quantity of the sample is important, and a control group must be measured to determine if, in fact, a particular group deviates significantly from the norm. That's why Wallerstein ran into trouble with her divorce study. Pioneering and ambitious as it was, talking only to kids who came in looking for therapeutic help does not represent the kids of divorce who do not seek advice. And, absent a control group from non-divorced households, the results don't tell us how those kids differed from most kids growing up in America today.

As Whitehead included in her article, researcher Nicholas Zill has found, "The majority of young people from disrupted families have successfully completed high school, do not currently display high levels of emotional distress or problem behavior, and enjoy reasonable relationships with their mothers."[8]

There are real stories of success in most divorced households—as well as most Choice households.

Critics of single parenthood tend to:
1. Focus on the less successful stories as the norm, and
2. Group divorced and Choice households together—
even though in Choice homes there is no disruption, no trauma
of separation and conflict, and no breakdown of family structure.

Those are two very good reasons why the statistics of single parenthood do not apply to Choice Mothers. In Chapter 6 we will look deeper into actual stories of single-parent homes to find out the legitimate concerns that Thinking Women should be aware of.

Point #3: Diversity is destructive

Whitehead's final point is that the proliferation of diverse family structures has led to greater poverty, rising crime rates, and declining school performance. She indicates that if everyone came from a stable two-parent household these social issues could be better avoided.

As she points out, more than 70 percent of all juveniles in state reform institutions come from fatherless homes. Controlling for income, many studies indicate that boys from single-mother homes are significantly more likely than others to commit crimes.

A single-parent home has less money and time invested in the child's upbringing. Partly as a result, she wrote, "The great educational tragedy of our time is that many American children are failing in school not because they are intellectually or physically impaired, but because they are emotionally incapacitated. In schools across the nation principals report a dramatic rise in the aggressive, acting-out behavior characteristic of children, especially boys, who are living in single-parent families."

According to McLanahan's research, Whitehead said, there are three important benefits to a two-parent home, even in "intact families who would not win any

Choosing Single Motherhood © Mikki Morrissette

'Family of the Year' awards" :

1. Children share in the income of two adults. *[Author's note: she doesn't mention whether families with stay-at-home moms suffer from the lack of two incomes.]*

2. Intact families provide a stable authority structure, rather than allowing the children to make decisions or accept responsibilities they are not ready for.

3. There is a stability of household personnel, rather than bringing new adults into the family, such as stepparents, live-in boyfriends or girlfriends, and casual sexual partners.

As she concludes, "All this evidence gives rise to an obvious conclusion: growing up in an intact two-parent family is an important source of advantage for American children. Although far from perfect as a social institution, the intact family offers children greater security and better outcomes than its fast-growing alternatives: single-parent and stepparent families. Not only does the intact family protect the child from poverty and economic insecurity; it also provides greater non-economic investments of parental time, attention, and emotional support over the entire life course. This does not mean that all two-parent families are better for children than all single-parent families. But in the face of the evidence it becomes increasingly difficult to sustain the proposition that all family structures produce equally good outcomes for children."

Author Comment

I have no doubt that stable, loving two-parent homes—where both mother and father have a healthy emotional investment in their children—offers tremendous benefits. And I have no doubt that an unstable, unhealthy single-parent home does not offer children the emotional security they need to grow up strong.

> *But not every two-parent home is "good," and not every single-parent home is "bad." Discouraging one common family structure because some don't do it as well as others is akin to not allowing people in their 20s to marry because statistics show these are the couples most likely to divorce.*

Some parents are buried by financial problems, self-destructive behavior, and emotional instability. And these tend to be the ones who don't parent well, whether they are married or not. *[In the next chapter we will discuss in more detail the reasons children suffer under the care of some single parents.]*

A Thinking Woman who is unable to provide a secure environment —who cannot earn an income, find quality child care, maintain relationships with a healthy network of supportive people, and offer authoritative parenting *[more on these in later chapters]* is not Choice Mother material. Period. Married couples who cannot provide the same have no business becoming parents either.

Security and stability, by the way, is not the same as "lack of change." Every childhood and every life involves change. I'm not one who thinks that is preventable, whether you are married or not, wealthy or not. Nor do I think it is bad. Nor do I think it affects people in the same way, no matter how they were raised.

My brother and I grew up in the same circumstances. Our parents were always employed and never moved until we had graduated from high school. Yet we couldn't be more different when it comes to the way we live: He is raising his children in the same house in the same small town where we grew up. I fled to New York City when I was 22 and still prefer city life.

Both of my parents, on the other hand, lost a parent by the time they were 10. In sum, my mother became fearful of losing a loved one in her life. My father lost his nurturer—his widowed father was not an affectionate man.

Both of them suffered a great loss at a young age that impacted them. Yet both are caring parents and doting grandparents who had successful careers, stayed out of abusive behavior (other than smoking habits that both eventually quit), and persevered in a sometimes troubled marriage that has lasted nearly 50 years.

> *My point is, give two kids the same stable environment and they'll still grow up with different values and needs. Give two kids a less stable environment and they are still fully capable of becoming solid citizens.*

One or two variables—growing up poor, moving a lot as a kid, even losing a parent—does not take precedent over every other variable in life. We all grow up with influences and adjustments that help make us who we are. A sibling is added to the household and suddenly a first-born doesn't feel as special. A move is made to a nicer house in a different community and a child must cope with the loneliness and self-consciousness of being the new kid. A beloved grandparent dies and no one can protect a child from experiencing the pain of loss.

As we'll discuss in the next section, growing up in a single-parent home and growing up without a father will have an impact on a child. But it doesn't have to be a

Choosing Single Motherhood © Mikki Morrissette

destructive impact. There are things to be learned from every change, every loss, every difference. The trick is to help our children navigate as best as we can, so that they will grow from every experience in their own individual, healthy way.

In short, change and diversity are not negative influences when the Choice Mother gives her child the tools—required for any successful adult life—to deal with challenge and to embrace opportunity. *(We'll specifically look at how to develop those tools in Chapter 14.)*

A theme we'll return to several times in this book:
Being a good parent is more important than being a married parent.

That Was Then, This Is Now

Not since the Quayle/Murphy Brown controversy has there been so much public discussion about single motherhood. Which isn't to say that the critics have disappeared. There simply hasn't been a mobilizing event to bring the voices back to the front page.

Whitehead and Popenoe are still involved in the issue, however. They are co-directors of the National Marriage Project, which conducts research, provides commentary on the state of marriage today, and educates the public about how marital success affects child well-being. Whitehead spoke before the U.S. Senate in Spring 2004 about how marriage benefits society.[9]

On the 10-year anniversary of the Murphy Brown controversy, actress Candice Bergen spoke out about Quayle's viewpoint. "I never have said much about the whole episode, which was endless," she said. "But his speech was a perfectly intelligent speech about fathers not being dispensable and nobody agreed with that more than I did."[10]

Quayle, too, commented in 2002 to an audience at the National Press Club on the anniversary of his infamous speech.[11] "I believe it even more now," he said about the need for fathers to be directly involved with children. "I never criticized single mothers. What I was trying to do was point out the reality of their struggle, particularly a single mother who doesn't have financial wealth." He said one of his complaints with the show's premise was that the father was going to be completely uninvolved with the child.

Coincidentally, on the same night Quayle gave his anniversary speech, the unmarried character of Rachel on the popular TV show "Friends" was scheduled to give birth. "We've made some progress," Quayle said. "The father is apparently going to get involved with that child."

In 2001, Quayle published an essay in *Newsweek* entitled "Why I Think I'm Still Right,"[12] in which he wrote that "it just bothered me that the character didn't seem to care that there would be no father to help raise the child—fathers were presented as irrelevant. My concern has always been for the welfare of the child."

He wrote that the turmoil in families today is caused by many things, such as time pressure. "Time formerly spent in family activities is now spent on the computer, in front of the television, on the phone, in the car and at the mall. We are a harried

BOOK EXCERPT

THE HISTORY OF PRIVATE LIFE
BY STEVEN MINTZ[13]
reprinted by permission of author

We hear a great deal these days about traditional family values. But precisely when did traditional family values reign supreme? Certainly not in the world of the Old Testament or classical antiquity. In ancient Greece, the average woman married between the ages of 12 and 15. Men married much later, usually in their mid or late 20s—a substantial age gap, which made families very patriarchal. Newborn children were left out of doors, so that handicapped babies—and many daughters—would die. Most ancient societies permitted divorce on demand, polygamy, and the cohabitation of people who were not legally married.

In colonial America, marriages were not based on love. Ministers described romantic love as a form of madness and urged young men to choose their mates on the basis of rational consideration of property and family. In colonial Virginia, an average marriage lasted seven years. Till death do us part meant something quite different than it does today.

Families were too large to allow parents to give much attention to each child. The average woman bore between eight and ten children. Fathers, not mothers, were the primary parent. Children of six or seven were sent to work as servants or apprentices in other peoples' homes.

society. Economic pressure is another reason. Most of our 21st-century innovations are costly, so more parents are working. Our mobile society has caused more families to live far away from the support system of their extended families. Add to this the fact that pop culture focuses too much on tearing down institutions that give us a sense of stability, and it is no wonder the traditional family structure is in decline."

I applaud Quayle for putting his name to one of the more rational and well-stated formulas for raising a healthy child. As his essay said:

> *"Children must have hope. Hope comes from a good education, good values, self-respect and living in a society that values every person, expects the best from each of us and does not tolerate abhorrent behavior."*

It was not until the mid-19th century that the family patterns that we call traditional begin to emerge. For example, middle class women began to make vocations of motherhood and housekeeping. An emphasis on personal privacy emerged. Houses began to have hallways and separate bedrooms.

And yet, we must be careful about assuming that the 19th century was an era of traditional family values. Our best guess is that between 5 and 10 percent of young urban women practiced prostitution. Americans dramatically reduced birthrates, but the major method of birth control was abortion, which was legal in virtually every jurisdiction before the 1880s.

Above all, families in the 19th century were just as fragile and unstable as families today. The proportion of single-parent, female headed families was almost as high in 1900 as it is today because of the higher death rate.

Today, we tend to assume that families are weaker and more fragile than those in the past. But I think this view is wrong. From a historical perspective, however, we invest much more emotional and psychological significance in family life than did our ancestors. We regard family ties and intimacy as the key to our personal happiness. And as a result, when our family relationships are unhappy or abusive, we get divorced.

Our high divorce rate doesn't reflect a low valuation on marriage; it reflects our overly high hopes and expectations.

Quayle indicates that odds are, a two-parent household is still the best place to raise a child. But, "Since the support system of extended families in most cases does not exist today, we need to expand the idea of extended family to include neighbors, friends and community. We each need to look around our community and see who needs nurturing. Is there a child who needs a grandparent figure, a father figure, a mother figure or a doting aunt or uncle? Fill that void for them. The sense of belonging, of being a part of a greater whole, is what is sorely needed by so many."

Once upon a time, people did believe in using the village (or urban community) to raise children. As a society, we started to shift child-rearing responsibility in the 1950s solely to "nuclear" family units—and I think that's when many children started to get shortchanged. As Quayle aptly pointed out, it is connection to others that makes such a dramatic difference in the life of every child.

Choosing Single Motherhood © Mikki Morrissette

STAGE 3

Is It Fair to the Child?

Although the politics of Choice Motherhood doesn't usually inhibit single women who desire to become mothers, the psychological impact of their decision often does. Nearly half of the Thinking Women I polled in an informal survey spontaneously brought up as a major concern how a child's development, behavior and attitude toward her might be influenced by growing up without a father.

My conversations with Choice Mothers reveal that most of their kids—who tended to be under the age of ten—had no strong issues related to growing up in an "unconventional" family. Many children were curious about the absence of a father but, in general, had no particular feeling of "lack." *However*, as we will discuss in Chapters 12, 13 and 16, issues are likely to evolve when children enter adolescence, around the age of twelve.

In this section we begin to explore the myths and realities of Choice Motherhood as influences on a child's development and well-being based on what we know, rather than on what we don't know.

Two methods of single motherhood *not* by choice—divorce and young, accidental pregnancy—have largely influenced the understanding of how children can be affected growing up with one parent. In **"The Impact of a Single-Parent Home"** we examine more deeply the statistics about troubled teens to find out how family structure does and does not matter.

In **"Growing Up Without a Father"** we will honestly examine what a child can miss without a father's influence, according to child experts—and what Choice Moms can do to help.

CHAPTER 6

THE IMPACT OF A SINGLE-PARENT HOME

There are few studies that examine the impact it has on a child to grow up in a single-parent home with a Choice Mother. My ongoing interviews with mature Choice Kids—some featured in Chapter 16—are the only extended reportage of their viewpoints that I know of.

The hundreds of studies that have been done about the impact of single parenthood on children primarily have looked at how divorced or "disrupted" households compare to two-parent homes. Few have effectively looked at the impact on children of growing up in a one-parent home that was not affected by disruption. Although some critics of single parenthood like to lump Choice Mothers in the same category, with the same host of problems that can occur in divorced households, the many emotional traumas of divorce on kids is a variable too powerful to make most of these studies reliable to the Thinking Woman.

In this chapter, however, we will explore the details of two ambitious research projects—and a few others—that offer clues for Choice households.

Statistical Evidence

The most widely cited research about single-parent households are the numbers that Princeton University sociology professor Sara McLanahan published in the 1980s and 1990s.[1] She and various partners analyzed statistics from several national surveys to determine whether children who grow up with both of their biological parents are better off than those who grow up with only one.

In particular, we will explore the results published in the 1994 book by McLanahan and Gary Sandefur, *Growing Up With A Single Parent.*[2] Their pool of single mothers consisted of those who were divorced, widowed and otherwise disrupted. Although they sometimes use the term "never married" to describe parents in the study, these are not typically Choice households, but unmarried parents who were left by a former partner to take care of the children.

Choosing Single Motherhood © Mikki Morrissette

Although this makes the research not statistically reliable for Choice Mothers, we'll re-examine some of the findings here as a measure of what can happen when single women don't have the economic and community resources needed to raise a child.

The disclaimers

Critics of Choice Motherhood frequently use McLanahan's numbers as evidence that a child in a one-parent home is more likely to drop out of high school, become sexually promiscuous, or turn to crime. However, they don't usually connect the dots to explain when this tends to happen, or why. For the Thinking Women who face this criticism with some concern, first let's point out several important differences between Choice households and disrupted households, so it is apparent what is applicable and what is not.

1. Anger and resentment

McLanahan and Sandefur review existing research to point out the persistence of anger in most disrupted homes. Fathers tend to withdraw from their children in the pain following separation. Children are angry about the separation, and tend to feel betrayed and abandoned. Parents often communicate anger about the other to or through the child. Even in amicable separations, there is a great deal of stress and loss of trust felt by the children. Yet as they write:

"Children who never lived with their fathers or never knew their fathers do not feel the same kind of anger as children who experience their parents' separation directly."

2. Loss of resources

Perhaps the most important point made in the book is that family disruption often leads to a loss of economic, parental and community resources. When one household separates into two, expenses for housing, food, and utilities double. The father usually takes most of the family's income with him. Often the children end up moving to communities with fewer resources, including schools in poorer districts. The researchers found that a full 34 percent of single-parent families moved because they were evicted or could no longer afford the rent, compared to 15 percent of the moves in two-parent homes.

This change in living conditions, the book details, is the primary reason that a child's school performance, ambition and promiscuity are affected in disrupted households. As they write, "Income and residential mobility together account for all of the educational disadvantage of children living in single-parent families!"

Some of the reasons for this, according to the authors:
- downwardly mobile children are more likely to attend schools with high dropout rates;
- their schools tend to have a higher percentage of minority students and minority teachers, which on average have less money to spend per child and higher teacher/student ratios;
- mobility leads to weaker connections to friends and neighbors.

The second research study we will examine in this chapter, by Mavis Hetherington, confirmed this tendency for mobility. On average, she found, women moved four times in the first six years after a divorce, and poor women moved seven times.

A Choice household, however, generally does not suffer from this tendency for downward mobility.

I sent a brief survey to 100 Choice Mothers and Thinkers. Of the 64 women who responded, more than half had moved once since becoming mothers; three had moved twice; three had moved more than twice (one because of her law career). Sixteen had not moved at all, and had no intentions of moving, as they were happy with their child-friendly community. Most women moved into homes they purchased; 53 were home owners.

Nearly everyone who moved listed these reasons: to get into a more family-oriented neighborhood, for better schools, for more space, for a less urban setting, to be nearer to family.

Three had moved in with their mothers. One was considering relocation to get more space. One moved to be closer to doctors for her special-needs child. Another moved closer to parents and new work after being laid off. Others were not yet mothers, but were open to moving in order to get into a more child-friendly environment, or for a more diverse neighborhood for an adopted child. None of them said they moved to live in a less expensive area.

3. Mother's education
A mother's education is generally regarded as the best predictor of a child's school achievement. So the authors tested the numbers and confirmed, "Having a mother with less than a high school degree doubles the risk of dropping out of school."

It is difficult to assess the effect of single-parenthood on a child's school performance, they write. "If we want to know whether living with only one parent

Choosing Single Motherhood © Mikki Morrissette

increases the risk of dropping out of school, the answer is clearly yes. On the other hand, if we want to know whether it is the primary source of school failure, the answer is clearly no."

Many unmarried or divorced single mothers in their test samples were young and not well-educated. This not only helps explain some of the high school dropout rate, but *clearly differs from most Choice Mothers and Thinkers.* Of the women who responded to my survey, 42 had post-graduate degrees, 16 more were college graduates, four had attended some college, two had not gone beyond high school.

4. Parents' age and income
The authors noted that the average two-parent family with some college education earned $83,748 in 1992, compared to $37,745 in single-parent homes. The numbers drop significantly for those in both groups with less than a high school degree.

The surprisingly high incomes, they write, was due to the fact that in this sample they were looking at families with at least one adolescent child, "which means we are looking at families at or near the peak of parents' earning power." But most single parents are younger than married parents, they wrote. In 1992, the median income for all families with children was about $43,000, and about $13,500 for all single-parent families.

The authors' research found that lower income of young parents accounted for about half of the difference in high school dropout rates, teen birth rates, and idleness. *Choice Mothers, however, tend to be older women who earn significantly more than the poverty threshold.* Most women in my survey became single mothers in their 30s; eleven of them were in their 40s. On average, the women who were Thinkers were in their mid-30s.

None of the women who responded to my question about income earned less than $25,000. Six earned between $25 and $40K; 21 earned between $40K and $60K; 34 earned more than $60K; several voluntarily reported earning more than $100,000, including two lawyers who earned more than $200,000.

On the other hand
There are several points made in the book that could be applicable to a Choice Mother. Even controlling for education level of the parents and race, there were statistical differences between children of two-parent homes and one-parent homes that should not be ignored. Sixteen percent of white children in their study in one-parent

homes, whose parents *both* had some college education, dropped out of high school (compared to five percent in two-parent households), and five percent became pregnant as teenagers (compared to one percent).

These numbers jumped substantially for children whose parents had less than a high school degree (based on 2,700 white teenagers interviewed by the National Longitudinal Survey of Youth in the 1980s):
- 51 percent of white children with one parent dropped out of high school, compared to 24 percent with two parents;
- 44 percent of white children with one parent became pregnant as teenagers, compared to 19 percent.

Author's note: Many single-parenthood critics add these substantially different numbers together to come up with an average that is accurate, but misleading. It sounds ominous that 28 percent of white children in one-parent households drop out of high school, compared to 11 percent in two-parent homes, but most of these children have parents who were high school dropouts.

One theory offered by the authors for the lower performance standards of children in disrupted households—besides economic insecurity and greater mobility—is that a single parent is more likely to spend less time helping a child with homework, listening to them, and monitoring their leisure time.

The stress of the single-parent lifestyle, they write, can lead to higher levels of anxiety, depression and inadequate parenting, as well as reduce the likelihood that the parent is providing the affectionate and disciplined approach that is best for children.

They also point out that two parents living in the home can make sure the other is doing his or her part—reading to their child, attending school activities. "Having another parent around who cares about the child increases the likelihood that each parent will 'do the right thing' even when otherwise inclined. In short, the two-parent family structure creates a system of checks and balances that both promotes parental responsibility and protects the child from parental neglect and abuse."

Their data indicated that a child in a single-parent home is likely to have 26 fewer meals each year with Mom than a child in a two-parent home. However, "Divorced mothers appear to compensate for this deficit at mealtime by spending more time reading to their children."

Choosing Single Motherhood © Mikki Morrissette

Most mothers of all family structures had similar reports of knowing the child's whereabouts, having a curfew and having an established bedtime. But the never married mother was slightly less likely to have TV rules or chores for her child.

One interesting difference was that children reported "talking with parents" more often in single-parent families (44 percent compared to 40 percent in two-parent homes). For some reason not made clear, the authors gave this a negative connotation, attributing this to "the argument that single mothers rely on their children as confidants."

In sum

McLanahan and Sandefur concluded that children in single-mother households tend to be deprived of needed resources because of low incomes, inadequate attention and guidance, and a lack of community resources due to living in disadvantaged neighborhoods with shady peers and frequent moves.

In particular, low incomes and sudden drops in income are the most important reasons that children in single-parent families have a lower high school graduation rate than other children. A parents' time doing homework, reading, listening, and supervising activities outside of school also is vital.

THE MORAL FOR CHOICE MOTHERS:
Make sure you have the financial resources and network you need so your children have the time, security and attention they deserve.

In-depth Interviews

While the McLanahan research has been instrumental in noting statistical correlations, children and parents were not interviewed to find the deeper answers to why some kids (and parents) in single-parent homes do well and others do not. But a more comprehensive study of divorce discovered in detail what the primary influences are. The research was conducted by psychologist Mavis Hetherington with 1,400 families (and more than 2,500 children) interviewed at regular intervals during a period of 30 years. Again, divorce differs from choice in many significant ways, but her close examination of how members of single-parent families function over time offers many important observations for Thinking Women. She reported her findings in the 2002 book, *For Better or For Worse: Divorce Reconsidered.*[3]

As she writes, "The reason our current view of marital failure is so unremittingly negative is that it is based on studies that have only examined people for a year or two after their divorce, and a year or two is not enough time to distinguish between short- and long-term effects. Additionally, many divorce studies do not employ a comparison group of married couples, and thus are unable to distinguish between problems common to all families and problems unique to divorced families."

Her ambitious research sought to correct those inadequacies to give a clearer picture of how and why people in divorced families turn out the way they do. My thanks to Dr. Hetherington for allowing me to excerpt and summarize her research in the following pages.

General Findings
• Twenty percent of youth in the divorced families, compared to 10 percent in non-divorced families had serious social, emotional or psychological problems. The majority were successfully establishing careers, creating intimate relationships and building meaningful lives. Some of the young adults in her study were actually enhanced by divorce. "Uncommonly resilient, mature, and responsible, these children of divorce blossomed—not despite the things that had happened to them during divorce and after, but because of them."

• Half of the single mothers in the study had access to health care, financial resources, better schools and after-school programs—but about three-quarters of them didn't seek information about them. "They relied on information from families and friends. They chose the school or day care center that was nearest or cheapest or easiest to enroll a child in. The result? The women in the second group not only were more stressed and spent more time worrying about their child's well-being; they also missed more work time because their support systems kept breaking down."

• "An involved, supportive, firm custodial mother often is able to counter adverse effects of both the lack of a father and poverty."

Potential Pitfalls
Hetherington observed that some custodial single mothers did not put adequate limits on their children. Others were so depressed or self-involved that they neglected their children's needs and withdrew.

The most common pattern was that the stress of single parenting and divorce led to a diminishment of parental affection and time spent with the child. In its place, irritability, punitiveness, and unpredictable, erratic discipline increased.

Ineffective discipline—Instead of explaining to a child why a certain behavior is wrong, or trying to distract the child in a healthy way, the tendency is that "the tired, preoccupied woman barks out a command. If the command is ignored, the woman nags or explodes or both, and if the child still ignores her, she usually gives up or blows up. Young sons, especially, pose a problem for divorce-depleted mothers" because they escalate their misbehavior when Mom issues a command. "We actually clocked one boy performing demanding, aversive behaviors such as a cry, a hit, a whine, a nag, at the rate of one every thirty seconds."

To get relief from a child's aggression, nagging or tantrums, parents often give in or reward the child for his bad behavior—for example, by sitting them in front of the TV with cookies—which further erodes feelings of adequacy.

Lack of deflection—Parenting is often the only protective social factor in a young child's life, and the first line of defense as the child enters adolescence, when peers and mentors play a larger role. Because there is no other parent in the home to buffer the child, the quality of parenting needs to be good.

"Rejection, irritability, or neglect floods directly onto the child, with no second parent able to deflect or lessen the impact," Hetherington writes. *The bad news is that because of the many stresses in their lives, divorced women were on average less competent parents than women in non-divorced families. This is in part because authoritative parenting, which requires a great deal of energy and focus, is harder to do when there is no assistance and cooperation available from another partner."*

Mother-daughter relationships—*These can sometimes be too close in single-parent homes.* "Many divorced women described their ten-year-old daughters as being like a close friend or sister; they felt they could discuss anything with their girls, including problems or personal relationships, fears, depression, finances, dating, and loneliness. But ten-year-olds need a competent, caring parent more than a friend."

Children who are confronted with adult problems often become apprehensive or resentful. And children in the study who felt responsible for problems they could not solve began to develop a sense of helplessness, which bloomed into depression and low self-esteem by the time the girls were interviewed at 15.

Growing up too fast—If a child's responsibility and independence interferes too much with play, sports, homework and other normal childhood activities, it often leads to depression in girls and rebelliousness in boys.

The Portrait of a Successful Single Parent

One important similarity all the successful children in the study shared was the support of at least one caring and loving adult (not always a biologically related one). The qualities of a good parent are especially important as the child enters adolescence, in order to counterbalance the dangers and temptations of peers and today's evolutionary tendency for early sexual maturing. The successful single parent tends to exhibit:

Social maturity—She takes active steps to build a better life, and makes sacrifices to get there. She is able to exhibit self-control and adhere to a plan rather than make rash decisions. She is flexible and adaptable in coping with problems. She has a tendency toward social responsibility, which leads to a greater sense of community.

Autonomy—"People who are comfortable being alone and making decisions by themselves, find the intense 'singleness' of post-divorce life easier to adjust to. Although an important source of support, men and women who rely on friends and relatives to solve their problems often do not make much progress."

Internal locus of control—The person who believes problems can be solved

A WORD ABOUT STEPPARENTS

Barbara Dafoe Whitehead, who we met in Chapter 5, examined the research literature about whether childrens' lives improve in a stepfamily environment. "The research overturns this optimistic assumption," she reported ominously in her *Atlantic Monthly* article.[4] "In general the evidence suggests that remarriage neither reproduces nor restores the intact family structure, even when it brings more income and a second adult into the household. Stepfamilies disrupt established loyalties, create new uncertainties, provoke deep anxieties, and sometimes threaten a child's physical safety as well as emotional security."

- Many children feel left out or lonely in their stepfamilies, and said they wanted more time with their mothers;
- Daughters tended to have a harder time adjusting than sons;
- A large percentage of children in one study did not consider stepparents to be part of their families;
- Parents did not invest as much time in their children's lives after remarriage (again, these studies are with children of divorce);
- Many stepparents took little interest in their stepchildren.

Choosing Single Motherhood © Mikki Morrissette

through her own efforts and is more proactive after divorce. "Instead of passively reacting to events, problem solvers try to shape them. They go back to school, open new businesses, find good childcare, and build social networks." This trait can be developed. "People with an external locus of control, on the other hand, tend to feel helpless and to just endure. First, they try to outlast their problems; and if that fails, they passively try to learn to live with them."

Religiosity—Being part of a spiritual community acts as a buffer because it provides access to an unusually strong support network, which helps combat social isolation, loneliness and lack of support.

Authority—Experts agree the authoritative, loving parenting style is the best way to raise healthy children. These parents are warm, consistent, supportive, skilled communicators, and firm but responsive disciplinarians. Their discipline techniques include verbal controls, time-outs, deprivation of privileges, and explanation and reasoning, eventually enabling a child to learn self-control. Age-appropriate chores such as setting the table, mowing the lawn, and babysitting siblings are used to develop maturity, responsibility and competency.

As Whitehead wrote, researchers Andrew Cherlin and Frank Furstenburg have said, "Through divorce and remarriage, individuals are related to more and more people, to each of whom they owe less and less."

And as researcher Nicholas Zill has argued, Whitehead reported, "weaker parent-child attachments left many children more strongly exposed to influences outside the family, such as peers, boyfriends or girlfriends, and the media."

The moral for those who hope to eventually marry: It's important to be sensitive to the big and little ways the child reacts when a partner enters a Choice family, and stay responsive to the impact it might have on the child if you end up marrying after motherhood. As research later in this chapter shows, stepparents can be horrible, fantastic and everything in between. As Whitehead's survey of research indicates, there can be a lot of hurt feelings and loneliness when the family dynamic changes.

Of course, Thinking Women choose carefully. They are not likely to choose rejecting or emotionally distant stepparents for their children, any more than they would as a mate.

Successful parents have a sensitivity and responsiveness to the feelings, needs, and abilities of their children, knowing when to support and when to push.

These parents also respect their children. "Most mothers and fathers think of themselves that way; but during the study, I was surprised at how often a preoccupied, emotionally upset, distracted parent would ignore or bark at the child or interrupt her conversation, criticize the youngster in front of a friend, embarrass her in front of strangers, or unwittingly inflict some other petty humiliation."

What Hurts, What Helps

As Hetherington writes, "Parents think that children should obey and respect them because they are older, wiser, more powerful; in other words, because they are parents. But parents have to earn the respect of their children by being trustworthy and admirable."

This is especially important leading into adolescence, when parental guidance and advice won't be accepted unless there is a long history of engaged parenting. "What kind of mother or father were they when the teenager was eight, nine, and ten?

> *"A history of firm discipline, caring, and nurturing imbues parental 'no's' with the moral force that even an increasingly independent-minded, peer-influenced teen will heed."*

She cites the example of a young girl who initially tried to cope with her mother's alcoholism by helping her when she was drunk, but eventually the child became angry and scornful. As a teenager, the girl was sexually active and full of disdain for her mother. What finally turned her around was that her troubled boyfriend left town and her stepfather—a police officer—stepped in with greater limits, threatening to kick her out if she skipped school, broke curfew or otherwise ignored house rules. She found the door locked the first time she tested the limits and stayed out late. As the girl said as an adult, "Here was this guy I loved and admired saying, 'Shape up or ship out.' It shocked me and started to turn me around. It took me awhile but I made it."

Another boy at age 10 was getting bad grades, skipping school, and engaging in fistfights. But the next year, a stepfather entered his life—a concert violinist who did not bond in the typical ways of sports or "guyness." But he did know the "best way to teach a child how to get along with peers, how to control his temper, how to organize his day, how to focus on a task was to provide him with a warm, involved, adult role model." His entrance in the boy's life made the difference.

96   Choosing Single Motherhood © Mikki Morrissette

Ineffective parenting styles—*Permissive* parents usually end up with children lagging behind in emotional self-control. The rigid *authoritarian* tends to produce rebellious, defiant and confrontational children. The most harmful parent is *disengaged* and withdrawn—because of narcissism, or being overwhelmed by stress or depression. In the study, it was the children of disengaged parents who were the most troubled: wild, unhappy, and prone to problems with work, marriage, crime, drugs and alcohol.

Hetherington adds, "Parents who smoke, drink, use drugs, lie or have many sexual partners may hope that the old adage, 'Don't do as I do, do as I say' works. It doesn't. Children are more likely to imitate behavior than to heed admonitions of an irresponsible role model."

How the Children Turned Out

Two years after divorce, most boys and girls were beginning to function reasonably well again, Hetherington reports.

At the age of 10, children who had several protective traits—such as an easy temperament, an authoritative parent, an adult mentor, and/or a network of friends—generally had become exceptionally well-adjusted. They scored well academically, were popular, socially responsible, and had few behavior issues. Some of them survived by learning how to manipulate their parents, others had become caring "Mother Earth" types who were responsive to the feelings of others.

By the age of 15, another group of these competent kids excelled in many areas, but had diminished self-esteem. Even in adulthood, in spite of exceptional attainments, they had a lurking sense of failure.

> *When young they had been overburdened by the demands of needy, depressed or immature parents to provide emotional support or take over responsibilities beyond their capacities.*

Almost all of the remarkably resilient children of divorce had the support of at least one caring adult.

Another 50 percent of the kids in divorced families and 60 percent in non-divorced were categorized as "Good Enough"—in the middle on almost everything, with problems that rarely endured.

Some, by age 10, were clearly headed for trouble—10 percent from non-divorced and 20 percent from divorced households—that by age 15 had turned into either antisocial behavior or depression and anxiety. These kids were sullen, oppositional, angry and tense. In adolescence, this group commonly turned to drugs, alcohol, and delinquency. Its members had the highest pregnancy rate and highest attempted suicide rate in the study.

Importance of mentors—This is a theme we'll return to many times. Any child can begin to disengage from the family as early as 10—a likelihood especially in high-conflict homes. This can be turned into a plus if there is an adult mentor who can serve as adviser in moments of confusion. But Hetherington writes: "Being an effective mentor was no short-term thing. Contact with an involved teacher or caring adult had little effect if the relationship did not endure for at least two years."

Mentors provide a child with an alternative to the peer group, helping them avoid "the Faustian bargain so many lonely, neglected children make with Peer World today: I'll give you my future, if you give me your validation and companionship." They give a child the sense of being cared for and valued, foster skills the child might not be learning at home, and offer models and advice about what is acceptable and unacceptable.

The kids who succeed—The children most likely to be protected from the adversity of a difficult home life are intelligent, have been taught self-control, are independent, mature, had high self-esteem, and had islands of achievement in school, sports or positive peer relations. Looks, personality and gender also influenced a child's ability to attract support.

"Those who felt helpless or were impulsive, antisocial, or extremely anxious and insecure before the divorce had these characteristics magnified by the divorce," Hetherington notes. "Easy children, inherently adaptable, grow in resiliency as other people respond positively to them; while difficult youngsters, vulnerable to begin with, under the stresses of divorce often grow more vulnerable as the beleaguered parents withdraw and peers shun them."

After they enter adulthood—Youth from divorced and high-conflict non-divorced homes have more trouble controlling the roots of marital instability, "what the American psychologist John Gottman calls marriage's Four Horsemen of the Apocalypse—hostile criticism, contempt, denial, and withdrawal. The reason: a contentious home life and early disengagement often prevent young people from developing the relationship skills needed to keep the Horsemen in check," Hetherington reports.

Choosing Single Motherhood © Mikki Morrissette

"Many of our young men and women from divorced or acrimonious non-divorced families entered marriage not knowing how to negotiate and compromise, how to make their partner feel valued, how to control their emotions, or how to use humor to defuse hostility."

Children from divorced households in the study were only 10 percent more likely to divorce than children from non-divorced homes. The lessons children learn about self-respect, respecting others and the importance of self-control are protective factors in developing their own relationships—as are supportive friends with stable marriages, and picking secure, caring mates.

Long-term Perspective

In more than 45 years of studying families over time, Hetherington says she's learned a lot about what nurtures family members' well-being and what helps or hurts adults and children as they deal with the changes and stresses of life in a single-parent home. For one, she is suspicious of averages. "It is the diversity rather than the predictability or inevitability of pathways in intimate relationships over the course of life that is striking."

She also reports that most of the difficulties blamed on being in a single-parent home are often present in dysfunctional families long before a divorce occurs. "People are not passive pawns of fate, dragged down destructive or fulfilling pathways after a divorce," Hetherington says. "They play an active role in building their new life by making choices, planning for the future, developing new competencies, and seeking out and using available resources. Those who wallow in helplessness, self-pity, and inaction are left behind."

As she writes, *"The easiest family setting in which to raise happy, competent children is one in which two mature, mutually supportive adults are committed to protecting and promoting the well-being of their children in a harmonious environment. A caring partner who shares the responsibilities and joys of raising children, and who is there for advice and support when problems arise, is the most potent protective factor a parent can have. But happy, competent children can and do develop in all types of nurturing, well-functioning families, including divorced, single-parent, and remarried families, through the courageous, selfless and frequently dedicated caregiving of parents."* Focusing on the problems of a few, she indicates, is a disservice to the majority of individuals who are leading very constructive lives.

In Sum

Although 80 percent of children from divorced homes in Hetherington's study eventually became reasonably well adjusted, or better, it is the 20 percent of troubled youth in this group who make the statistical headlines.

Largely the product of neglectful, narcissistic or depressed single parents, they had the highest dropout rate and the highest divorce rate of the kids in the study, Hetherington said. They were more likely to be earning a low income. Girls in this category were more likely to have left home early and to have experienced at least one out-of-wedlock pregnancy.

She also noted that 10 percent of youth in non-divorced families had this same level of trouble. "Most of our troubled young men and women came from families where conflict was frequent and authoritative parenting rare."

Most of the troubled kids in both households had righted themselves in adulthood. One-quarter still had drinking problems, but drug abuse and lawbreaking decreased. "For every young man or woman who emerged from post-nuclear family life with problems, four others were functioning reasonably or exceptionally well."

THE MORAL FOR CHOICE MOMS:
The resilience of single parents and their children is related to how much they can depend on: 1. personal temperament (some traits can be trained, some are innate), 2. family relationships, 3. experiences and role models outside the family.

How Choice Moms Succeed

One of several child development experts I talked to for this book told me the basic needs of kids are the same in every home:
- infants need warmth, protection and sensitivity to their signals;
- children need control and limit setting;
- teens need help negotiating greater independence while remaining connected to parents.

"One person trying to provide all these things for a child, without backup of help from another involved adult, can feel overloaded and overwhelmed at times," she said. "It's harder for single than coupled parents to do all this, but it can be done."

Interestingly, small but growing research specifically with Choice households is finding that the attentiveness of Choice Mothers might actually be giving young

Choosing Single Motherhood © Mikki Morrissette

children advantages to those in some two-parent homes.

A London-based study interviewed 21 Choice Mothers and 46 married couples who had two-year-old children conceived by donor insemination. Their published report revealed that Choice Moms "showed greater pleasure in their child and lower levels of anger," along with a perception of their child as less "clingy." These young children were also exhibiting fewer emotional and behavioral difficulties than those of married couples.[5]

Another group of researchers conducted interviews in 1997 with 30 lesbian mother families, 42 single heterosexual mother families and 41 two-parent heterosexual families who had six-year-old children. Most of these same families participated in additional interviews when the children were 12, when all the mothers tended to be in their 40s.[6]

When the children were six, they reported, it was found that mothers in fatherless families showed greater warmth towards their children and interacted with them more than did mothers in father-present families. Disputes between mothers and children were found to be more serious, but no more frequent, in fatherless families, although the children did not show increased levels of emotional and behavioral problems.

At 12, there generally were not significant differences between the groups. As budding teenagers, some children from all groups were experiencing more emotional and behavioral issues, but school adjustment, peer relationships, self-esteem and gender-role orientation showed no major differences. Teachers, too, did not report more problems for children from father-absent families.

Children in fatherless homes at age 12 again perceived their mothers as interacting more with them and being more dependable. Mothers of all groups didn't show differences in their psychological state, but those in father-absent homes reported more irritability and loss of temper related to discipline. Boys raised without a father showed more feminine characteristics, although no less masculine ones.

Strengths of Single-Parent Homes

Other research helpful to the Thinking Woman was reported in *Advances in Nursing Science*[7] The premise was to identify the strengths of a single-parent family, rather than the weaknesses, in order to build upon them. The author's review of research indicated that the strengths of any family include:

- open communication
- a sense of family pride
- active coping and growth
- emotional closeness
- adaptability and flexibility
- spiritual wellness
- commitment and appreciation to each other.

One finding was that single-parent families tend to have a more cooperative and egalitarian parent-child relationship which—in contrast to the typical focus on lack of parental control—"has been linked to [a child's] higher levels of autonomy, responsibility, self-esteem and personal aspirations."

Author comment: One obvious change I have seen in my parenting style since becoming involved with Dave has been the structure of decision-making. When he and I are together, we usually decide what family activities we will pursue. When he is not around, typically Sophie and I discuss our options for the day and I often let her choose what she wants to do with our free time.

THE COST OF CHOICE PARENTHOOD

BY LESLIE TALMADGE

excerpted from a Columbia University master's project [8]

These children are cherished, concedes Anne Crittenden, author of *The Price of Motherhood,* but she worries that the trend of women having children without partners isn't great "unless we can rethink the broader sense of responsibility and communal response for kids' education and well-being. We're still a country of raw individualism. One mom is responsible for a child's entire life. What if she gets sick or loses her job? What's the safety net? That's problematic. It's too heavy a load on one parent. And it's not fair to the child."

Choosing Single Motherhood © Mikki Morrissette

Choice Moms Discuss Their Biggest Issues

I asked women to pass along advice and wisdom about what is the biggest issue for them as Choice Moms, especially in contrast to what they most worried about prior to embarking on single motherhood. I also asked them to discuss whether they felt the single-mother lifestyle was fair to their child. Here is a sampling of what I heard:

Energy—"The biggest issues now are sickness, time and energy. I had a major back injury 18 months after having my son. I had to really reach out to the village during that time. You learn that you can't do everything on your own, and definitely not when you're sick. Having a child demands lots of energy. I now go to bed at 9 p.m. Whenever I have extra time, I either take a nap, go have a massage, or go have a facial... something that's soothing and relaxing."

Time—"Five years in, time is definitely the worst issue. I started living well below my means a long time ago, so the financial issues aren't a hassle. But my well-paying job is what kills my time, especially the commute. Fairness, for me, was never an issue. It wasn't fair that I was raised by a man that was so depressed he couldn't see beyond his own nose and hampered my mother's ability to parent. It wasn't fair that I might have had a child by my first husband, who valued boys over girls. Why would one parent be less fair than these options? Other than time, I can't really think of any issues. Sure, there are days I'm emotionally drained, but I have great friends to rely on."

Said another: "My biggest issue is not having enough time with my child. What with schoolwork, her homework, meal preparation, general chores, etc., the hour or so we spend together in the morning and maybe three hours we spend together in the evening on weekdays just don't feel like enough. I find that by the time we get to Friday, I really miss her, even though neither of us has gone anywhere. This is one place my decision to eat out one night a week has made a big difference. That night I don't have to cook or clean up. We can sit and eat together, at the same time, face to face, and we talk. It's become a special time that both of us look forward to."

Money—"Finances have remained the major issue. It's tough. When he was really little there was childcare. Once full-time childcare wasn't an issue anymore, there was after-school care and after-school activities. And now that he doesn't have any after-school care, his other activities are often costly. It's no longer cool to take lunch to school so he is buying it. And then I needed to leave my stable job (something I hadn't counted on) and I took a major cut in salary. So money is definitely an issue."

Child care—"The worst time I ever had was because it was torture for me, when she was an infant, and I had to go back to fulltime work. I didn't want to leave her. I cried all the way to work. A few months later, I quit my job and used all my retirement savings to stay at home with her another seven months. Eventually I took a live-in job taking care of a younger retarded woman and deaf woman so I could stay home another year. I never would have predicted that of myself. But I never regretted it for a second, and have always cherished that time I had with her."

Fairness—"Before I got pregnant, I didn't worry as much about fairness. I was pretty sure that I'd be a good mother. I chose a known donor so that I could enable my son to know his father. In the early years, I think most of us are too busy with daily life to get hung up worrying about fairness. It stops being a question—it just is. And our kids tend to reinforce this because overwhelmingly they do really well in their single mom households. We struggled to make a decision to become a single parent, but that was never their struggle. It's just their life. But things change. Our life wasn't very different from others until my son hit middle school. Our experience was that kids were often cruel, my son wanted to fit in, and being different was like having the plague. Hormones were beginning to rise and rebellion was in the air. Sarcasm became the major form of communication.

"I think at this point in his life, my son would tell you that this lifestyle choice is not fair to children. It makes our family different, and although most of his friends don't know that I am a single mother by choice, he knows and that makes it tough on him. I honestly believe that with time this will change. I think he appreciates that our family is loving and supportive, and that if I hadn't made the decisions I made, it wouldn't exist. Maybe I'm deluding myself, but I think that he will forgive my decision with time."

Daddy issue—"My daughter is 3 years old. The Daddy issue is coming up more. She talks about her daddy all the time and almost always has a daddy in her play themes. I worry about it a little more now, from the perspective that she has to deal with being different than her peers. I don't worry that she is missing out on anything. She has a lot of male influences, including an uncle and grandfather. I read books that have different types of families, and I reassure her that our family is okay. I make sure that my child knows that not everyone is the same. I don't usually see this kind of focus from 'traditional' families. It should be there, but I don't see it."

Hindsight—"If I knew then what I know now I would have tried a little sooner. There is a significant financial cost to waiting. Using an RE and more advanced methods of conceptions starts adding up in increments of $1000 rather than $100."

Choosing Single Motherhood © Mikki Morrissette

GENDER ROLES

A concern of many single parents is how their child might be impacted by seeing only one sex operating the household. This was the focus of a study reported in *Sex Roles: A Journal of Research.*[9]

The central question of the study was whether individuals reared in one-parent families hold different gender-role beliefs than individuals reared in intact two-parent families.

Based on a review of literature, Slavkin reported, without a partnership at the top of the family hierarchy, children in one-parent families are more likely than children in two-parent families to:
- share the responsibility for running the household;
- be responsible for caring for themselves (making their own breakfasts, packing their own lunches);
- serve as confidants and provide support to their parent;
- have more autonomy and less supervision;
- have more influence in family decision-making;
- have more assigned chores.

Based on answers to survey questions, Slavkin and his associate determined that kids of both sexes raised by a single mother were more likely than those in two-parent families to describe themselves in traditionally masculine terms, such as independent, assertive, self-sufficient. In a similar vein, a small sample of kids raised in a father-headed one-parent family described themselves using traditionally feminine characteristics, such as affectionate, gentle, understanding, sensitive.

Support—"Raising a baby is very hard, especially for women used to being in control and succeeding at everything (which, in my experience, describes myself and many women who consider Choice Motherhood). You lose control of your body, your life, and suddenly become the loving slave of a tiny little being. You fail at small things like staying awake or big things like learning how to breastfeed. Worst of all, you have to learn to let other people help you. My advice is this: Don't have a baby if you don't have a support system in place. You will need parents, family, and friends to help out when you get sick, haven't slept in days, need emotional support, etc. You really can't do it all by yourself, and you shouldn't. Your baby will benefit from getting love and care from other people, and so will you. Work it out so you can pay back these people in other ways, if it makes you feel better."

Overall philosophy— "I never saw it that I had to be two parents, just one very good one. The most important thing is, don't do this unless you decide to put that child first, to give it the time and energy required. I wouldn't trade my 20-plus years of being a mother for anything. How many times I've been just so happy to be with her, to see what she does. I worked hard to do things as well as I could, letting her know she's loved, letting her know she's a great human being. Not to make light of the responsibility it is, but I was ready for it—and it was so very worth it."

BOOK EXCERPT

THE MYTHS OF MOTHERHOOD
BY SHARI THURER[10]

Good mother, history reminds us, is a cultural invention—something that is man-made, not a lawful force of nature. When mothers are able to see through the mythology, they may see that their 'failures' stem not necessarily from personal defects, but from the way society is structured. They may stop blaming themselves. When mothers understand the biases inherent in our current conception of good mothering, they may learn to select among the rules and begin to create their own philosophy of child rearing, one that works for them and their children.

Taking the non-traditional route

One relatively new Choice Mom who contacted me as I was writing this book was Carol, who discovered when she was 32 that she was showing signs of perimenipause—a genetic tendency in her family. She had been dating someone who wasn't ready to settle down, so they broke up and, after consulting with friends and getting unexpected encouragement from her conservative brother, she decided to have a child on her own through donor insemination.

"My greatest concern when I was thinking about bringing my son into the world was that I worried that I might hurt him psychologically or emotionally by not having a father in contact with him on a daily basis.," she told me. "One of my very

Choosing Single Motherhood © Mikki Morrissette

good male friends reassured me that my son would always know that his mother had so much love that she wanted to share with him. What really helped me decide though, was that I stopped thinking so much and listened to my heart. It just felt right to me.

"Now, as I look at my son beginning to reach his first levels of independence as a toddler, I realize that bringing him here was a blessing from God. The ability to show my son love, affection and hopefully guide him to become the wonderful young man I know he will be one day gives me faith that there is the divine in all of us, and in all of our actions of love and goodness."

On Being a Moral Parent

Richard Weissbourd, author of *The Vulnerable Child: What Really Hurts America's Children and What We Can Do About It,* child psychologist and lecturer at Harvard's Graduate School of Education and the Kennedy School of Government, published an essay about parenting in a 2002 issue of *The American Prospect.*[11]

In sum, he wrote that family structure matters less to a child's moral development than the quality of parenting. He says that we as a country fail to support good parenting and to cultivate important moral qualities in adults that are critical to a child's development.

My thanks to him for letting me excerpt his article here, as I think it's an excellent guide for women considering Choice Motherhood.

> These days there is once again a great deal of hand-wringing about the sorry moral state of America's children. As William Bennett puts it in *The Broken Hearth: Reversing the Moral Collapse of the American Family,* "Most of our social pathologies—crime, imprisonment rates, welfare...alcohol and drug abuse...sexually transmitted diseases—are manifestations of the crack-up of the modern American family.

> Children in single-parent families, to be sure, face obstacles to developing important moral qualities. Ethical development is rooted in emotional development. After a divorce, large numbers of children both suffer the shame of poverty and are abandoned by their fathers (10 years after a divorce, two-thirds of children haven't seen their father in a year and have effectively lost contact with their fathers). This is not the soil out of which a sense of responsibility for others can easily grow.

But the reality is that most children in
single-parent families are not morally defective.
They are growing up to be quite good people.

Moreover, the notion that single parenthood accounts for Bennett's slew of moral problems is bizarrely ahistorical. Many of these problems were prevalent before 1960, when single parenthood began to rise, and increases in these problems have not followed closely, as Bennett's argument suggests, the steady increase in single parenthood between 1960 and 1990.

Studies show that children suffer high rates of behavior troubles before their parents' divorce. Locked into decaying marriages, parents who are angry, moody, and withdrawn are less likely to provide models of fairness, respect, compassion, and other virtues for their children. They are also less likely to provide the consistent expectations and encouragement that build trust.

All of which points to the big hole in the family breakdown argument of Bennett and company. The focus on the structure of families has ignored what is most important to any child's ethical development: an ongoing, trusting relationship with at least one adult who is ethical and mature, and who listens and encourages without shying away from his or her moral authority. A mountain of research now shows that it is the content of adult/child interactions, not the structure of families, that most strongly determines the shape of children's ethical development. That's what makes parenting a profoundly moral act, and learning to parent well a profound moral achievement.

We'll explore some of Weissbourd's recommendations later in this book, but one of the important points he brings up—an echo of Hetherington's in-depth research—is that parental depression is not only a widespread problem, but has great implications for the health of our children.

As he wrote in *The American Prospect,* "As many as 25 percent of children will grow up with a depressed parent, and parental depression undermines almost every key aspect of parenting. Depressed parents are far more likely to be moody, to lash out unexpectedly, and to criticize unfairly. Children of depressed parents are more likely to struggle by almost every measures."

Choosing Single Motherhood © Mikki Morrissette

THE MORAL FOR CHOICE MOMS:

1. Single parenthood is not inherently damaging, unless the parent is too overwhelmed to provide the affectionate and disciplined style of parenting that is required.

2. A single parent needs to be the ethical, trustworthy and happy face for her child.

3. The toughest job is to maintain emotional and financial resources in order to be the authoritative parent every child needs.

CHAPTER 7

GROWING UP WITHOUT A FATHER

Paternal neglect is causing the ruin of many families.
— New England pastor, 1842

It's not a new phenomenon that observers of families have been concerned about the changing role of fathers. Once upon a time fathers were the center of moral education for their children. Throughout the 18th century, child-rearing books were directed to men, not women. Until the 1960s, according to surveyist Daniel Yankelovich, "being a real man meant being a good provider for the family."

By 2004, however, 23 percent of children were living without a father in the home, compared to 11 percent in 1970, according to a Child Trends report.[1] And authors such as David Blankenhorn were publishing books such as *Fatherless America: Confronting Our Most Urgent Social Problem* (1995).

Although an overreaching book in many respects, looking to fatherlessness as the "single most obvious factor" leading to violence and unhealthy child development—rather than a more complex set of factors such as physical abuse, availability of drugs and guns, economic inequality, and discrimination—Blankenhorn's book does cover a few important aspects of solo parenting. Including the fact that single mothers cannot provide "a father's distinctive capacity to contribute to the identity, character and competence of his children."

When I surveyed members of the Single Mothers by Choice network in 2003, almost equal to the number of women citing "can I afford it?" as their single greatest concern was the number of women who brought up an issue that purposely was not on my list: "Is it fair to the child to be raised without a father?"

The single women who wrote me, without prompting, to explain their concerns about this issue that I had not fed to them indicated to me that Thinking Women understand that fathers *do* matter. Some women reported grappling with this issue for years before deciding whether or not to go forward with Choice Motherhood.

Choosing Single Motherhood © Mikki Morrissette

As Tina told me, "My relationship with my dad is a good one for the most part. We never have been super close, but I have always known he loves me and cares about me. My memories of being young and him are that he was always tired, and came home from work usually too tired to be much involved in my life. It left me always feeling awkward around him, and that I didn't want to burden him with anything. It wasn't until he was retired and had energy, when I was an adult, that we got to know each other."

Even without a strong relationship with her father growing up, she said, "My main concern is not knowing how best to handle/navigate the effect on the child of not knowing the daddy. I know there are 'answers' to the daddy question which sound good when I read them. But I guess the answers leave me wondering how really this satisfies the child's question."

The concerns raised throughout this book are all important. But this "fairness to the child" issue I believe is most complex.

This chapter will focus on the most important differences between children raised by a Choice Mother and children raised with a father in the home. I make no claims that raising a child without a father does not have an impact on their development. Rather, we will explore what the literature says about what it can mean, hear from child experts I interviewed, and learn how best to navigate as your child grows.

First, the Skepticism

As William Pollack, author of *Real Boys: Rescuing Our Sons From the Myths of Boyhood* has said, single mothers "get the worst rap imaginable. They are blamed for everything from hangnails to violence. [Yet] women are not only very important role models for their sons, but they are often their son's heroes."[2]

Indeed, there are plenty of theories about the impact of fatherlessness that are exaggerated or based on outdated ideas. Blankenhorn, for example, has expressed dismay that the absence of a father means a child won't have someone to help them buy a car, make a down payment on a house, buy furniture for an apartment, go to college, or co-sign a bank loan.

He probably didn't realize that most Choice Mothers are highly self-sufficient, and consider that to be a positive trait that they pass along to their children.

For example, I very much grew up believing that I am responsible for making my own way. Although my parents always have been supportive, I worked my way through college and the purchase of my first home, furniture and car without expecting handouts—and got a great deal of satisfaction from that.

Blankenhorn probably also didn't realize that a substantial number of Choice Mothers have post-graduate degrees and earn more than $60,000 (as we learned from informal poll results in Chapter 6)—so are as capable as most middle-class families of supporting their kids financially if they see fit.

[Author's note: I asked to interview Blankenhorn for this book, to get his updated views on Choice Motherhood, but a representative of his Institute for American Values said he had deadlines that made him unavailable.]

Access to someone else's money is one thing. But the most serious theme in the debate is this: Boys without fathers get guns; girls without fathers get babies.

Boys and Guns

Blankenhorn has written that there is a rite of passage boys need to make from their mothers in order to grow up whole. "Both clinical studies and anthropological investigations confirm the process through which boys seek to separate from their mothers in search of the meaning of their maleness," he wrote. "In this process, the father is irreplaceable. He enables the son to separate from the mother. He is the gatekeeper, guiding his son into the community of men...Only by becoming his father's as well as his mother's son can he become a good father and husband."

Many child development experts agree with him. But Blankenhorn has his own unique perspective on what happens when a boy doesn't have his father around to teach him how to be a man.

"When this process of male identity does not succeed—when the boy cannot separate from the mother, cannot become the son of his father—one main result is rage," Blankenhorn continued. "Rage against the mother, against women, against society. It is a deeply misogynistic rage, vividly expressed, for example, in contemporary rap music with titles such as 'Beat That Bitch With a Bat.'"

A common result of growing up without a father, he wrote, is hypermasculinity— "the aggression and swagger of boys who must prove their manhood by themselves, without the help of fathers. If we want to learn the identity of the rapist, the hater of women, the occupant of jail cells...we look first to boys with no fathers."

Choosing Single Motherhood © Mikki Morrissette

Others have different theories about the roots of male violence. Pollack believes that it is disconnection from loved ones and fear of shame that leads some boys to violence. He wrote, "Violence is the most visible and disturbing end result of the process that begins when a boy is pushed into the adult world too early and without sufficient love and support. He becomes seriously disconnected, retreats behind the mask, and expresses the only 'acceptable' male emotion—anger. When a boy's anger grows too great, it may erupt as violence."

Ironically, he added, violence against others can be part of an attempt to reconnect with others and boost self-esteem, by "bonding" through violent acts in a way that other boys do through sports activities.

Some point out that aggression usually springs from deep-seated pain, and that boys who haven't been neglected or abused tend to have a greater capacity for avoiding violent behavior.

Myriam Miedzian, author of *Boys Will Be Boys*, said the problem, to a certain extent, is fathers who teach traditional masculinity—the values of toughness, dominance, repression of empathy and competitiveness.[3]

Michael Gurian, a male development specialist who consulted with me on several chapters of this book, believes basic neuroscience accounts for many differences between the sexes.[4] "Boys have dramatically different brains than girls, making it logical for them to be more impulsive, and as a result in need of more concentrated training by family, elders and other members of the community to teach them the moral codes of society," he said.

Girls And Babies
Some also believe that girls without fathers are vulnerable to turning to men to fill a void in their life. As Blankenhorn wrote, "Women who have had good relationships with their fathers are less likely to engage in an anxious quest for male approval or to seek male affection through promiscuous behavior."

He cited research by Judith Musick to indicate that girls who do not have a stable relationship with "a nonexploitative adult male who loves them" remain developmentally stuck and struggle with issues of security and trust. As Musick reported, these girls focus on one question through adolescence: "What do I need to do, and who do I need to be, to find a man who won't abandon me, as the men in my life and my mother's life have done?"[5]

Musick, however, doesn't place the blame solely on the fact of being fatherless, but as part of a more complex equation that includes the presence of many abusive men in a mother's life. (Blankenhorn mentions this in a footnote.)

Blankenhorn believes, however, that paternal disinvestment in daughters cannot be remedied. "When a girl cannot trust and love the first man in her life—her father— what she is missing cannot be replaced by money, friends, teachers, social workers, or well-designed public policies aimed at helping her. She simply loses."

In 1995, he was no more forgiving of Choice households than he was of divorced or abandoned households. "The largest consequences of Sperm Fatherhood are the decline of child well-being and the rise of male violence, particularly predatory sexual violence," he wrote.

> *"A society of Sperm Fathers is a society of fourteen-year-old girls with babies and fourteen-year-old boys with guns."*

Author comment

I mention Blankenhorn's views not simply to rile up readers of this book, but because he has been a prominent critic of single parenthood. A mission of the Institute that Blankenhorn founded in 1987 is to "change the views of U.S. policy makers on the importance to children of the two-parent home" and the "cost of unwed child-bearing." Presumably he continues to believe that even an educated and professional single woman who chooses to dedicate herself to motherhood cannot do a good job raising her child without a father—and his voice speaks for many.

In Blankenhorn's view: "As a society, we will not solve our crisis of fatherlessness with prison cells, mentoring programs, anti-violence curricula, boyfriends, anti-stalking laws, children's advocates, income transfers, self-esteem initiatives, or even mothers. We will solve it only with fathers."

Real-world experience, of course, tells us that crime and other social ills are caused by many factors that often have nothing to do with fatherlessness. In the small, white, middle-class town where I grew up, I knew several boys who ended up being attempted rapists, shoplifters, drug users, school dropouts, drunk drivers, thieves and one—who I knew in high school—was convicted of killing his wife. All of them had a decent, law-abiding father in the home. In fact, most of them had siblings who had no such issues. How do you explain that? In brief, you can't do it simply.

Children all have the potential to make bad choices with their lives—big and

Choosing Single Motherhood © Mikki Morrissette

small—and it's a combination of genetics, environment and individual emotional and mental health that plays into the end result—as well as values imparted by important role models.

Nurturing and interactive fathers can do amazing things in bringing up their children. I applaud efforts to train men to be fathers (and husbands)—and deplore policies that are designed to promote marriage as the only "right" way to live.

While there does seem to be research to support the view that women turn to skewed relationships with men to fill a "father void" in their life, when you look closely at the lives of a wide segment of women, there are persuasive arguments supporting the idea that any girl, whether from a one- or two-parent home, can grow up with relationship issues.

One of my close friends years ago grew up with a nurturing mother and a withdrawn father. Into her forties, she had never married (or had children), and tended to fall into relationships with men who did not offer enough of themselves to be committed to a future.

Another friend, with a highly accomplished father but a lonely childhood because of frequent moves, was a "daddy's girl" but very mistrustful of developing a close relationship with anyone.

Another friend emulated her strong-minded father, and grew up equally as strong-minded—making it difficult for her to sustain a loving relationship with any man.

Another friend grew up in a small town with narrow-minded parents; to this day she bristles from their example and is finding her own way in a rather rootless fashion.

An old friend who was attached to her at-home father was one of the most promiscuous girls I knew.

It does make sense that a girl who grows up with a father who leaves the family might approach commitment with a fear of abandonment or betrayal that leads to short-lived sexual relationships, inhibitions, or overboard reactions to male attention. And with the numbers of families without fathers in the home this would lead researchers to find many examples of this tendency.

But look around and listen and you'll find many women who grew up with a father in the home yet still developed their own commitment issues. Typically they turn to therapists around the age of 30 to try to confront these patterns. Ideally they work through their issues—after all, kids are responsible for moving past whatever weaknesses they grew up with.

This said, however, it does have an effect on a child to grow up without a father, as we'll explore next.

Two Loving Parents

Although many of the concerns about fatherless homes can be abated with quality parenting from one attentive mother and solid role models every child should have, there are a few things a Choice Mom cannot provide for her child no matter how great she is as a parent. The most important of these, in my view, is the absence of a second person who is actively involved and emotionally present for the child.

The bond between Choice Mom and Choice Child is intense—often more so than what children experience with parents who also have a partnership to maintain. Grandparents and attentive uncles and male role models provide invaluable love, nurturing and education. And many children in two-parent homes do not have the kind of interaction with one or both parents that we're talking about here. Yet in a different world, a loving, interactive father would be a second person the child could have a meaningful, intense relationship with.

When I married Dave in 2004, my children automatically "acquired" a stepfather. He's a loving, responsible, fun-loving man with strong values—someone my kids can grow up to love and respect. His family-oriented siblings and parents are inclusive and warm. My daughter is the right age to revel in our extended family get-togethers. But that doesn't change the fact that Dave is not a second "me."

Especially because we don't live together, Sophie thus far considers him generally to be the man married to Mom. We will not push her to call him "Dad," or train Dylan to do the same when he starts talking, unless it is the term of endearment they prefer.

If my kids had *two* of me—*two* who consider their needs first; *two* who spend lazy summer evenings enjoying simple moments at the lake on a consistent, reliable basis; *two* who help them grow day-by-day—how great that would be for them.

But I decided to be a Choice Mom, and these kids were the result. My marriage

Choosing Single Motherhood © Mikki Morrissette

doesn't change that. Having a known biological father doesn't change that. Having loving grandparents and caring family and friends doesn't change that. They have *one* bond to a deeply committed parent.

I do not consider that to be a "bad" thing. Perhaps because of our dynamic, they might be exposed to a wider network of loving relationships and diverse experiences than other kids will. Theirs will be an upbringing that I believe will bless them with unique gifts. Regardless, if they had *two* of me, what an amazing thing that would be (she said modestly).

Influence

Another benefit of having two parents in the home is the fact that there are two adults serving as active role models—two sets of good (and bad) traits and mannerisms to emulate (and reject).

From a young age, I did not like the way my parents handled disagreements. Their marriage had several rocky years, but they persevered, giving me a chance—especially after I moved out and had the distance required—to appreciate their individual strengths. For example, my mother is personal growth-oriented, returning to college when I was in junior high school, introducing me to a Holocaust survivor who was my first interview subject at age 12. She exposed me to new experiences—a gift I value highly as something I can do for my children.

My father was the one who helped me feel like I could make my own decisions. Although I often make decisions that would not be his choices, he has rarely been critical to me about the way I live my life. My hope as a parent is to give my kids the same ability to recognize that life is theirs to create in whatever way they feel they need to.

Obviously I would have grown up without either of these influences —but differently. Just as, without my friend Troy in high school I might not have gotten comfortable living outside the box (which included picking him as a friend in the first place). Without my first job at the community newspaper I might not have developed a strong identity as a journalist at an early age. Without being the victim of date rape in college, I might not have had such strong issues to work through during my 20s.

In addition to basic genetic coding that impacts the person we turn into, there are any number of pivot points and people that come into our lives and dramatically affect our direction. Having two influential people in the home allows you an alternative way of seeing how to approach life. Ultimately it gives the child yet another way of choosing their own set of values from the materials they encounter.

Balance

In his *Life Without Father* book,[6] David Popenoe made some good points about the balance that can be struck in a home with both a maternal and paternal influence. As he wrote: "In attitude and behavior, mothers tend to be responsive and fathers firm; mothers stress emotional security and relationships, and fathers stress competition and risk taking; mothers typically express more concern for the child's immediate well-being, while fathers express more concern for the child's long-run autonomy and independence. The importance of these different approaches for the growing child should not be underestimated.

"All children have the need for affiliation with others but also the drive to go off on their own, to be independent. They need both the personal security brought by strong social ties ('roots') and the push away from the group toward autonomy ('wings'). They need a parent who says 'strive, do better, challenge yourself,' along with one who comforts them when they fall short."

Although it might seem stereotypical—and a parent generally is capable of striking a balance between two extremes—it is useful to consider the ways men and women tend to differ.

Communication style

Dr. Kyle Pruett, author of *Fatherneed: Why Father Care Is as Essential as Mother Care for Your Child*,[7] talked to me about how mothers and fathers parent differently, as he discusses at great length in his book.

For one, he says, men and women not only have distinctive sounding voices, but have different verbal styles, which can provide infants with an important source of stimulation and learning. Mothers tend to simplify their words in order to help the child understand quickly. Fathers tend to talk almost as they would to an adult, which challenges the child to understand on his level and helps the child develop vocabulary and linguistic skills.[8]

An excellent handout provided by HeadFirst,[9] which I will quote from liberally in

Choosing Single Motherhood © Mikki Morrissette

this chapter, states: "Father's talk tends to be more brief, directive and to the point. It also makes greater use of facial expressions and subtle body language. Mothers tend to be more descriptive, personal, and verbally encouraging. Children who do not learn how to understand and use both styles of conversation will be at a disadvantage, because they will experience both of these styles as they enter the adult world."

[We also will talk in Chapter 14 about how women raising boys need to learn how to communicate differently when their sons enter adolescence.]

Playtime

One of the most noticeable differences between Dave and I is the way we "play." When Dylan was an infant, I was more comfortable putting him into his jumping apparatus, or taking Sophie to classes and cultural events than getting on the floor with them—Dave calls me the "intellectual one." Dave, on the other hand, will step in easily to lift my son, play "doggy" with my daughter, take his daughter swimming or to amusement parks, go hiking and camping with his son—and in general push for physical activity. This difference is largely a result of our temperaments, but there is a tendency for men to be more active as "doers" and women to be "nurturers."

Fathers tend to be louder, rougher and more competitive than mothers. Experts believe the rough-housing form of play typical of men is helpful in teaching a child self-control.

"The male play style helps develop spatial-mechanical centers of the brain, which are good for all kids," Gurian told me, "teaches a different way to handle emotion than talking, and teaches healthy competition and aggression. It is especially resonant for more male children, and for 'bridge brain girls' who are more tomboy, because the brains of these kids already format toward more gross motor activity and more spatial-mechanical-aggression stimulation."

Gurian points out that aggression is an essential and nurturing part of human nature—in contrast to violence, which is a learned behavior (sometimes genetic), and is destructive.

Risk-taking

As the HeadFirst literature says: "Go to any playground and listen to the parents there. Who is often encouraging kids to swing or climb just a little higher, ride their bike just a little faster, or throw just a little harder? Who is encouraging kids to be careful? Mothers tend toward caution while fathers often encourage kids to push the limits. Either of these parenting styles by themselves can be unhealthy. One can tend toward encouraging risk without consideration of consequences. The other tends to avoid risk, which can fail to build independence, confidence, and progress. Joined together, they keep each other in balance and help children remain safe while expanding their experiences and confidence."

This also can help a child learn tolerance for frustration, which is part of the self-control instruction. As Pruett has said, "A classic example is the child learning to ride a bike without training wheels. Although there is a huge individual variation here, dads are more likely to put the child back on the bicycle after a failed attempt than are moms. My own speculation is that the goal of such paternal behavior is to encourage the child to master the frustration inherent in learning."

Discipline

Studies tend to point out that fathers are keepers of the "justice, fairness and rule-bound duty" lessons, while mothers are the relationship-oriented ones who point out the importance of sympathy, flexibility and understanding.

As Pruett wrote, "Mothers tend to discipline by emphasizing the relational and social costs of misbehavior. A common response by a mother to a toddler who has just thrown food is, 'Do you ever think about how much work it is for me to clean up the mess when you throw your cereal?' Shame also tends to play a role when kids get a bit older: to a child who does not listen or obey, mothers express their disappointment and feelings of being personally let down.

"Fathers, on the other hand, tend to emphasize the mechanical or societal consequences of misbehavior, bringing more emotional distance to disciplining as a whole. This tends to give the impression that fathers are less able to be manipulated and more functionary when they have drawn a line. Fathers tend to make comments like, 'Don't expect to have any friends if you're that selfish with your toys.' And, later in life, 'You'll never find a job if you are going to act like such a jerk with your teachers.'"

In general, fathers help children prepare to be part of the world, and mothers tend to emphasize how behavior affects others. Pruett says both approaches are needed. "The value to children of experiencing both a maternal and a paternal approach to discipline, blended into the foundation of their conscience, can't be overestimated."

Gender Identification

As the HeadFirst brochure said: "Girls and boys who grow up with a father are more familiar and secure with the world of men.

> *"Girls with involved fathers are more likely to have healthier, more confident relationships with boys in adolescence and men in adulthood."*

"This is because girls have a greater opportunity to learn from their fathers how men should act toward women. They don't wonder how a man's facial stubble feels or what it's like to be hugged by strong arms. This knowledge builds emotional security and safety from the exploitation of predatory males.

> *"Boys who grow up with dads are less likely to be violent. They have their masculinity affirmed and can learn from their fathers how to channel that masculinity and strength in positive ways.*

Since married men *tend* to be less abusive than unmarried or separated men— propagation of the species being what it is—children who have a loving father in the home will tend to learn about respect toward women. "Girls with involved fathers are more likely to select good boyfriends and husbands because they have had a good model by which to judge candidates. Boys raised with fathers are more likely to be good husbands because they can emulate their fathers' strengths and learn from their shortcomings," the HeadFirst brochure says.

Again, most research is a comparison between children who grow up with healthy, involved fathers and children who grow up with less involved fathers. Having an emotionally distant father is the culprit in many studies. There is little research— other than the case studies of young people I talked to for Chapter 16—to reveal what happens when you have one very involved parent and no uninvolved parent. The research is clear, however, that children need strong "non-mother" influences in their lives in order to provide balance and enhance the child's autonomy. A man's warmth, masculinity and "differentness" influence a child in ways that even highly dedicated mothers cannot replace.

As Pruett puts it, "Dads offer intriguing and exciting opportunities for safe and loving interactions with a not-mother entity. Fathers offer older children an opportunity to interact with the essence of maleness and to explore male-female differences. Children seem to count on fathers to fulfill that emotional promise to get them, safe and whole, into the real world beyond their mother's arms."

Self-Control

Statistics do show a correlation between fatherlessness and juvenile delinquency. As we read earlier in this chapter, there are many theories about why this might be. And, as we learned in Chapter 6, variables including drops in income, charged emotions and withdrawn parenting are important factors. However, there are lessons in the self-control research that Choice Mothers need to pay attention to.

As Pruett wrote, "Countless single women succeed in raising wonderful sons and daughters. Still, we cannot ignore the fact that raising a boy without an involved father in the home raises the statistical probability of his becoming violent. Boys who are violent are eleven times more likely to be living without a father.

"Of course, parents do not raise their children by statistical probabilities, but this one is risky to ignore. Fatherlessness in any social class seems to catalyze a kind of obsessive hypermasculinity. Beatrice and John Whiting's classic study found that the most violent cultures had the least paternal involvement. In gang and fraternity violence, males without fathers are the most rabid disparagers of everything female— it's as though they think this is the one true path to a masculine identity.

> *"Can such probabilities be overcome by any single mother?*
> *Of course. They're overcome all the time—but not without*
> *help, thought, and a plan."*

We'll get into the plan in more detail in Chapter 14. For now, let's explore what children need in order to develop self-control.

As we alluded to earlier, some believe it is the style of play that men engage in with children—and their tendency to push children through their natural frustration level—that gives the best instruction in self-control. Fathering expert John Snarey has said that "children who rough-house with their fathers usually quickly learn that biting, kicking, and other forms of physical violence are not acceptable."[10]

A committee of the National Research Council's Board on Children and Families concluded, "Children learn critical lessons about how to recognize and deal with highly charged emotions in the context of playing with their fathers. Fathers, in effect, give children practice in regulating their own emotions and recognize others' emotional clues."[11]

Pruett suggests that children with involved fathers tend to have an inherently strong

Choosing Single Motherhood © Mikki Morrissette

internal locus of control—"the belief that one's ability to affect one's own behavior and the outside world resides more inside than outside the individual."

According to Richard Weissbourd, another helpful consultant for this chapter, who we met in Chapter 6,[12] a child whose frustration over a long period of time is not noticed or aided by a parent will begin to lose a sense of hope and fairness. "To function effectively in adulthood, all children need to believe that there is at least some justice in the world, that there is a reasonable moral order maintained by trusted adults," wrote Weissbourd. "I have spoken with many children who lose their way, who become dangerously passive or dangerously destructive, because they simply do not believe that their good intentions and hard work will be rewarded, or because they are convinced that they will never get a fair shot, that they are not playing on a level playing field because of their race, gender, ethnicity, or some other immutable characteristic."

Weissbourd reported that Harvard researcher and psychiatrist Felton Earls, in a long-term study on the individual pathways to violence, found that "aggressive impulses can be channeled by friends, families and communities in all sorts of positive and negative ways. Whether children have access to weapons, whether their older siblings are violent, and whether children learn from adults effective ways of resolving conflict may be especially important."[13]

Research also suggests, Weissbourd wrote, that "early childhood experiences of shame and humiliation as well as poor communication skills, difficulties in school, and difficulty reading social cues are factors contributing to crossing the border into violence."

Kids' Perceptions of Fathers

It's not only what fathers can provide to children that we need to consider, but what it means to children to be without a loving relationship with a male parent.

Researchers at the University of Maryland in 2000 reported the results of a study of 855 six-year-old kids who were identified as "high risk." Seventy-five percent of them identified at least one supportive male in their lives—a father or father figure—and those kids scored higher on basic learning, with a stronger sense of competence and social acceptance than those without.[14]

A dissertation we will explore in detail in Chapter 13 reported on the impressions young children of Choice Mothers had about their non-present donor fathers.[15] The reactions of children are quite individualistic, and often variable—from disinterest to embarrassment about the subject to intense curiosity and, in some cases, to expressed yearning to have a dad. For example, one young child asked if he had a father who died, and often pretended that his biological father was a superhero (Batman). A seven-year-old boy occasionally indicated he wanted a dad so his mother could stay home with him "but wants a dog more."

> *Wanting a father in order to have more time with Mom was a common reaction of young children, as was desiring a dad who would do activities that mom didn't.*

One five-year-old boy said if he had a dad, "He could be in the front driving and my mom sitting in back with me...It would be fun...we could play together and wrestle."

The dissertation included a review of a study published in 1992 that compared 35 six-year-old children born to Choice Mothers via a known donor.[16] The kids had varying degrees of contact with their biological father: some never saw their fathers and had been given little information about them ("ghost fathers"), some had sporadic contact ("visitors"), and some saw their fathers with the same frequency as a non-custodial parent ("auxiliary fathers"). They were compared to children with married parents.

More than three-fourths (77%) of the children with ghost fathers or erratic visitors felt their fathers viewed them negatively, compared to less than half (37%) of the group with married parents. Children with auxiliary fathers, or those who were close to a grandfather, were less likely to feel their fathers viewed them negatively.

We will explore this issue more deeply in future chapters *(especially Chapters 12 and 13)*, but it is statistically significant that having an important male figure in a child's life can help them feel more secure.

What Thinking Women Say

Talk to 10 different women about how growing up without a father in the home might impact their child and you'll get 10 different reactions. While many women do have concerns about this impact, and do their own reading of literature I've summarized here, the conclusions weigh differently on their minds. As one woman told me, "I wouldn't be pursuing single motherhood if I thought 'no dad' was a

Choosing Single Motherhood © Mikki Morrissette

REALITY CHECK

As we have been discussing, studies indicate that if a child has a loving relationship with Dad, the child might become:

- more confident in unfamiliar situations;
- better able to deal with frustration (because fathers don't step in as quickly as mothers to alleviate the stress);
- more patient, curious and confident as students;
- stronger in cognitive skills if their father reads to them regularly and in solving complex mathematical puzzles.

Although these studies[17] tend to be well-meaning in their attempt to point out the value of having an active father, it should not be assumed that the opposite result is true when the home has no father—which is the conclusion many people leap to.

For example, one study surveyed nearly 400 people over a 26-year period and determined that fathers who spend time alone with their kids doing routine childcare at least two times a week raised children who were the most compassionate.[18] Does this mean that a child who grows up without a nurturing father in the home will be a bully? No. It simply indicates that if you take out all the other variables, children with an engaged father tend to be more sensitive than children with an unengaged father. Makes sense.

Another point: Henry Biller, a long-time researcher in fathering, has said that the average daily amount of one-to-one father/child contact in the United States is less than 30 minutes. He found that fewer than 25 percent of young boys and girls in two-parent households experience an average of at least an hour a day of individualized contact with their fathers.[19]

In a national study of students in grades six through twelve, almost 20 percent of the children reported not having had a good conversation (lasting at least ten minutes) with their mom or dad within the last month.[20]

deal breaker. I do believe, however, that a two-parent household is 'best' for a child. Despite the studies that show it's quality of parenting that counts, rather than two parents or one, I believe there is an inherent difference for a child living with two loving adults who strive to honor their relationship. I'm counting out bad couples here, as well as bad single moms and bad single dads. That said, I think it's extremely valuable for a child to witness two parents solving their issues. I think it's the best role model for a child to see their parents experience differences and still remain bonded, to learn how women and men may think and behave in different ways, but they still can respect one another and compromise.

"I firmly believe our kids can turn out great, otherwise I would not be pursuing this," she continued. "And I do not think any of us are wrong for pursuing single motherhood. But I do believe it's a different reality. Do our kids gain from having a single Mom? Yes. Do our kids lose by not having a Dad? Yes. But if we all waited for perfection that child might never be."

Others believe that a good father figure is not necessarily a father, and that kids benefit from having a diverse set of role models—one that a Choice Mother is more likely to provide than if the child were part of a traditional family structure. Many recognize that children face tremendous stress and loss of trust and security when their family life is disrupted by divorce. They believe that losing a parent is more damaging than growing up without a second parent.

Still others believe that every child would benefit from having many things the universe doesn't always provide: paid leave for both parents for the first year of an infant's life, schools filled with quality teachers and resources for all, no discrimination or prejudice, crime-free neighborhoods, funding for arts and sports education, access to good medical care and nutrition, and on. Growing up with one parent rather than two is part of the way life sometimes works out.

In exchange for what the universe does not provide, these women point out, they are utilizing the tools available to them to help their child grow up into a responsible and happy adult.

THE MORAL FOR CHOICE MOMS:
There are unmistakable natural differences between men and women, and anyone contemplating this choice must be sure that there are strong male role models available throughout the child's life. [See Chapter 14 for details about how and when to do this.]

Final Thoughts

Most of the more than 100 women I have talked to would not hesitate to marry a loving man who will treat them as an equal partner in love and child-rearing, be a nurturing and interactive parent, and serve as a model of commitment and responsibility. The problem has been in finding him. As one woman told me, she was angry to discover at age 35 that after she had worked through her childhood issues (from a two-parent family) and was finally ready for a healthy relationship, she couldn't find any available man who had done the same and was looking for someone approaching 40 with whom to start a family.

When I started writing this chapter, my intention was to give everyone a chance to hear both sides of the issue and make their own judgment. That is still the goal of the entire book—no woman with grave concerns about any of these issues should proceed. If you think you will do your child a disservice by raising them without a father in the home you should not put *yourself* through that moral quandary.

But as I dug into the research, I recognized that the lives of people I know all have been affected from every variety of family background—divorced, abandoned, happily together, unhappily together. Every family can be dysfunctional if we let it. And every child will grow up with "issues" whether we like it or not.

Children should grow up with a value for life, responsibility and succeeding at his or her goals. When the home doesn't teach those values, kids do turn elsewhere, and might end up on a destructive path. Yes, many single parents have to work entirely too hard to feed, clothe and shelter their kids. In same cases, supervision and time and nurturing go out the window as a result. So it makes sense that a fatherless home can have serious troubles.

But a home without a father is not the same as a home without values—this is an important distinction that some forget to make.

Where Blankenhorn, Popenoe and others diverge from child experts such as Pruett, Gurian and Pollack is when they claim that only biological fathers can provide the balance in the home that mothers need to raise well-adjusted kids. The latter group believe the support of extended family and friends can—and should—play an important role in raising kids. Gurian, in fact, has written a great deal about how even two-parent homes need to actively build an extended network.

Although we were specifically talking about mothers and sons, Gurian offered me this advice useful for any Choice Mother: "I think it is human nature to try to share child-raising, and I sympathize with single parents who can't do that. If a single mother is going to raise great sons, though, she is going to have to get help—a female community to support her, male mentors for the boy once he becomes pre-pubescent, sports or the arts or something both expressive and physical. She is going to have to fight to curtail his immersion in unhealthy influences, including bad diet—which messes with hormones—and obsessive computer/video game use. She is going to have to find him some kind of religion/spiritual or identity-developing community larger than his narcissistic adolescent world. This is a lot for her to do, but to decrease the probability of having troubles with her son, or raising one who is low performing, she finds herself compelled to do a lot of these things."

BOOK EXCERPT

REVIVING OPHELIA

BY MARY PIPHER[21]

reprinted by permission of author

Americans tend to have a double standard on parenting. Mothers are seen as having great power to do harm with their mistakes. Fathers are viewed as having great power to do good with their attention. In our society when daughters are strong, credit is often given to fathers. But in my experience, strong daughters often come from families with strong mothers.

While most girls are connected to their mothers by close if often conflicting ties, with fathers they have varied relationships.

In the 1970s, I did research on father-daughter relationships. I interviewed high school girls, one-fourth of whose fathers had died, one-fourth of whose parents were divorced, and one-half of whose parents were together. I was interested in how daughters' relationships to fathers affected their self-esteem, sense of well-being, and reactions to males.

I quickly found that the physical presence of the father had little to do with the

In large part I believe the best thing we can do for our children is instill them with a sense of responsibility—for taking control of their own lives, for understanding their obligations to others—as well as giving them an open door to possibilities that gives them a love of learning and exploration and spirituality and mental health. Choice Mothers are great role models in these two regards.

quality of the relationship. Some girls whose fathers lived in the home rarely spoke to them, while other girls who never saw their fathers were sustained by memories of warmth and acceptance. Emotional availability, not physical presence, was the critical variable.

I found three kinds of relationships: supportive, distant, and abusive.

Supportive fathers had daughters with high self-esteem and a sense of well-being. These girls were more apt to like men, to feel confident in relationships with the opposite sex and to predict their own future happiness. They described fathers as fun, deeply involved and companionable.

In my study, the majority of fathers fell in the **distant relationship** category. They may have wanted relationships, but they didn't have the skills. Girls with distant fathers said they liked the income their fathers brought home, but they appreciated little else. Besides being the breadwinner, often the father had only one other role: rule enforcer. Distant fathers hadn't learned to maneuver the intricacies of relationships with empathy, flexibility, patience and negotiation. They had counted on women to do this for them.

The third category was the emotionally, physically or sexually **abusive father**. These were the fathers who called their daughters names, who ridiculed and shamed them for mistakes and who physically hurt or molested their daughters.

STAGE 4

CHOOSING THE METHOD

If you decide to become a Choice Mom, perhaps after years of debate, you face another uniquely challenging and personal question: How? Will you adopt, use an anonymous donor, or conceive with the help of someone you know?

For some women, reaching this decision can be even more difficult than choosing to become a Choice Mom.

Is adoption the "morally correct" choice—giving a loving home to a child that most likely already faces a life without a father in the home? Or is it cost prohibitive?

Should an older woman with unknown fertility, and few insurance benefits for the procedure, pursue insemination in order to experience pregnancy and birth, and to share genetics with the child? Should she select a completely anonymous donor, or would her child someday prefer an open-identity donor who is reachable at the age of 18?

Should a woman who wants the child to know the other biological half use a known donor, or are the risks of legal and emotional complications too great?

Whichever method a single woman uses, there are ethical concerns connected with each one. Some people strongly believe children should not be created with donated "material" when so many already need homes. Others strongly believe that a child has the right to know his or her genetic identity.

Entire books have been written about adoption and insemination, which I liberally refer readers to. In this section we look as closely as we can (in limited space) at the complexities of the three methods to motherhood.

Choosing Single Motherhood © Mikki Morrissette

In **"Known Donors: Pros and Cons"** we explore in depth what few resources cover: what can happen when you use someone you know to help you conceive a child (as I did). We hear the emotional story of a woman whose agreement with a former boyfriend ended up changing, against her will, as well as the wisdom of lawyers. We discuss the advantages of this method for the child. And we learn about the motivations and emotions of two donors, as well as a man who has said "no" to four women.

In **"Using Assisted Donor Insemination"** we examine the merits of the growing open-identity option. We hear from a donor-conceived woman who has mixed emotions about the fact that she is attempting to conceive with an anonymous donor, as well as two donors who have mixed feelings about the offspring they will not know. We briefly discuss the process of insemination (covered so well in other resources), and how women have chosen their donors.

In **"Choosing Adoption"** we boil down the advice of other excellent resources about factors a prospective adoptive parent needs to consider, costs of domestic and international options, sources of emotional and financial support, the home study process, and special advice about transracial adoptions.

In the next section we will look at how to address the related "daddy" and "identity" questions children naturally will have.

CHAPTER 8

KNOWN DONOR: PROS AND CONS

While in my early 30s, I wrote a short story about a woman who fantasizes about asking for sperm from three male acquaintances she approved of genetically. She would store each man's donation anonymously, so no one would know which man's sperm helped her conceive, thus alleviating everyone of pressure to play the dad role. The flash-forward twist to the story, however, was that the child as a young boy had so many familiar traits that the father's identity was no mystery. When the long-lost donor paid a visit 10 years later and excitedly saw himself in the boy, the mother sadly knew she was about to lose her place as the sole nurturer in her son's world. Her carefully constructed attempt to create an intensely reliable one-on-one family structure had failed.

Does this speak to some sort of controlling interest I sought in parenthood? Perhaps. Although I used the story as an opening to tell some people (like my mother) that I might become a single parent someday, my desire to become a mother seriously kicked in when I started dating a divorced father. Sharing visits with him and his son led me to tell him that I might like to have a child with him someday. This pronouncement apparently scared him away; he broke up with me two days after my 35th birthday. I was devastated.

After a solitary retreat on the primitive African island of Madagascar, I returned to the States, plunged energies into my executive position at a publishing company, and spent 10-hour weekend days at a coffee shop writing my dark novel, *Ocean of the Dead*. Several months later, I shared a drink with a new male friend and announced my interest in becoming a single mom someday. My genuine intention was to startle him, by letting him know how fiercely independent I was, but he surprised me instead by offering to be the donor when the time came.

It would be nearly a year before I took him up on his offer. In the meantime, I got to know him well enough to understand his story. Overall, I determined that he had fatal flaws as relationship material, but he was a good man at heart. Importantly, I had time to figure out why he would want to have a child for whom he would not have custody. His motivations were wrapped up with being the divorced father

Choosing Single Motherhood © Mikki Morrissette

of two kids he missed, longing for family due to an extremely isolated childhood, having a "live for the moment" personal life rooted in his inability to commit to any one person, and a basic lack of time because of his entrepreneurial career. In short, he loved the idea of kids, but couldn't be responsible for them: the perfect known donor.

The decision to become a Choice Mother also was made easier as my salary approached six digits. I owned an apartment large enough for two, had substantial savings, and was nearing the age of 37. It was time to act.

Getting pregnant turned out to be easy. Sophie's biological father and my parents were present for the delivery, which also was smooth in a drug-free 4-1/2 hours.

I wish I could say that everything was effortless after that, but of course—as the woman in the short story of my youth discovered—nothing is that simple. My friend was close enough to me to attend Lamaze classes and various pre-birth checkups, but he disappeared minutes after the birth. Initially, we both felt awkward about his pseudo-role in this beautiful child's life. He suggested that the child be named Sophie, in memory of his grandmother, yet I had to battle to put his name on her birth certificate. He was afraid his name on the official document would make him financially responsible in the eyes of the government, yet I didn't want Sophie to someday think he disavowed his parentage. He was disappointed that I spent the next three months living with my parents, 1,000 miles away, and that I didn't name him as Sophie's guardian in my will.

Clearly there were emotional and legal wrinkles for both of us to work through. Fortunately we were able to talk through the rough spots. But then the big whammy came. As I was preparing to return to work, my boss informed me that my position had been 'eliminated' and, unless I was prepared to take a demotion and major pay cut—which I was not—there was no job to return to. Now insecure financially, and emotionally drained by the responsibilities of single parenthood in that first year of "take care of me!" infancy, I berated my donor at length for not doing enough to help me out.

Eventually I evened out again—using my severance package to facilitate a flexible freelance lifestyle—and moved comfortably into the Choice Mother role for which I had prepared. But as he and I both learned, this route is not an easy one to take.

The ups and downs of having a "father"
The attachment Sophie and her father developed (for a time) was wonderful to

watch. This bonding didn't kick in until she was nearly three—when she was more of a person for him to relate to, and when he was less of a stranger for her to get used to. He even scheduled regular visits after Sophie and I moved to Minnesota. Seeing her rush into his arms at the airport made me extremely proud of the known donor choice I had made.

This unusually rich "father" experience came with obvious confusions. Three times in one week Sophie told people that she wanted to go to Disneyland with "her parents"—PANIC! It was the result, I know, of seeing the commercial of a happy family bouncing with joy about their upcoming trip. Did I worry that having a friendship with her father made it more difficult for her to see him as simply "the nice guy who let mom have a baby?" Yes.

On another occasion, after it had been two months since his last visit, Sophie told a friend of mine that she wished he lived with us—PANIC!

At a boat outing, fascinated with watching members of our group water ski, Sophie told a little girl that "my dad is going to teach me how to ski when I'm ten"—a partial fantasy based, I suppose, on knowing that her father is an avid snow skier. Her friend innocently replied, "I didn't think you had a dad." PANIC! I quickly stepped in with the line, "Her father lives in New York…He doesn't live with us, so he's not a dad like yours is."

> *One obvious reason I prefer the method I chose is that it allows me to give Sophie the security of knowing that two people who cared about each other as friends helped to create her, albeit in an untraditional way.*

But as Wellesley College researcher Rosanna Hertz described in a study about Choice Mothers who use donors, this arrangement places more of a "gatekeeper" burden on me.[1] I must continually figure out what I think is best for Sophie, given her needs and his personality, and then communicate those parameters to him.

Using a friend as I did clouds the issue much more than other options would have. Some women pick known donors from advertisements and lists of acquaintances and ex-boyfriends. But our friendship assured me that he would adhere to my parameters because of our ability to communicate and his respect for my role as THE parent.

Sadly, when Sophie was four, his personal distractions made him much less reliable

Choosing Single Motherhood © Mikki Morrissette

in her life. I decided to close the gate—without locking it shut—since he no longer had the time and energy (and money for airfare) to maintain the attachment she was feeling toward him. Sophie was confused by his absence for a while, but was young enough to adapt to the new arrangement of occasional phone calls. Although their contact is much more limited than it was during her first years, she will continue to benefit from knowing who her biological father is. If she wants to develop a stronger relationship with him when she is older, she will have that option.

I used the same friend to help me create Dylan. Although my son will not have the same early-year experiences with his biological father that Sophie had, I am thankful the two are full siblings. They have obvious similarities in appearance. As a family historian who has traced 16 branches, it also is important to me that Sophie and Dylan will be able to fill in some of his sketchy heritage on their family trees. I consider it a blessing that we know his family's medical history, which tends to be extremely healthy and robust. And, as my top concern, I am glad I'm able to give them the option of knowing exactly who helped to give them life.

What Can Go Wrong

Although I have no regrets about the method I chose to motherhood, my experience indicates that the known donor route requires both parties in the conception process (whether the sperm is provided for home insemination, clinic insemination, or the "old-fashioned" route) to maintain emotional stability, trust, open lines of communication, and sensitivity to the child's changing needs. It's a tall order, which is why a majority of Choice Mothers choose an unknown donor for a "cleaner" route to parenthood.

In my conversations with people for this book, I've learned of a few men who did the "donation favor" for friends, only to be sued later for child support when the women ran into financial and emotional difficulties. I've read stories of the very troubled Australian woman who lost a partial custody battle with her known donor—and killed herself and her child rather than give him visitation rights. I know of women who allowed themselves to get pregnant by unknowing donors, which raises serious ethical dilemmas.

And I've learned the story of Sarah, whose known donor ended up making her life miserable (read on).

Many states have enacted legislation that prevents donors from having any responsibility or rights to the child as long as a licensed physician is used—but these rights only extend to a donor who donates through a licensed physician, clinic or sperm bank. And no matter what paper agreement Choice Mothers might sign with known donors, they are not legally binding documents. Most courts will uphold the rights of the child, and if that means changing the parameters of a pact made between the man and woman, there is little that either party can do to stop it. "Even if there is a written agreement, if there is sexual intercourse the sperm contributor is a parent, and the courts will not unparent him," one assisted reproduction lawyer told me.

> *"You might not put his name on the birth certificate, and never ask for support, but that doesn't change the fact that he's the father. Everything is up for grabs. Every scenario in which a parent has rights can apply."*

In states with a sperm donor statute, parties who want legal protection by supplying "directed donor" sperm for insemination with a doctor must follow the exact language of the law. In California, for example, if the donor gives the sperm to the recipient to use, rather than to the doctor or sperm bank, a court may find he is the father, despite his intention to donate. *[See Chapter 15 for cases in which donors and mothers didn't get what they bargained for.]*

Andrew Vorzimer, a California-based lawyer who specializes in clients who use third-party reproduction, told me, "Although I am loathe to generalize, since every state is different, the common theme is that courts will do what they think is in the best interest of the child. Some states uphold the rights of the intended parent. Some states favor the genetic parents. Some pay attention to marital status."

In other words, if a known donor marries and wants visitation rights as part of a couple, some courts might favor that arrangement over that of the single parent. Others might protect the limitations set in the contract, or believe that the child is more secure with the mother who has been available since birth. And once the child is old enough to assert rights, Vorzimer warned, there is potential for even more complications because "that child is not governed by the contract."

Worst-case scenarios are not limited to custody issues. They could include a donor who refuses to allow a second-parent adoption in the case of the mother's marriage, or alternative guardianship in the case of the mother's death. Conversely, a donor might be sued by the mother not only for child support, but for medical costs if the child has a genetic disease not disclosed in the donor's family history.

Choosing Single Motherhood © Mikki Morrissette

Even if the mother and donor are in full agreement, if public assistance is needed—say state-sponsored health coverage—the local government will likely step in and require the father to replenish its coffers. (Sometimes this applies when the mother is seeking assistance for herself, and does not apply if the benefits are for the child.)

Although every situation is different, Jody DeSmidt, a Minneapolis-based adoption and assisted reproduction lawyer, offered these general thoughts:

• **Signing away rights** — No agreement to terminate parental rights is likely to be approved by a court unless there is a second parent waiting in the wings to adopt the child;

• **International borders** — A written agreement should be established with the donor that enables you to take the child across international borders, and carried whenever a passport is required. Because of the quirkiness of the situation, "arguing with a bureaucrat somewhere is not where you want to be;"

• **Donor rights** — If the donor has rights specified in an agreement, for contact with the child perhaps, he can take the mother to court for failure to live up to that arrangement;

• **Time** — The longer a child is raised by a particular parent, the less likely that a judge will say it is in the best interests of that child to switch to a co-parenting or shared custody arrangement;

LAWS REALLY DO VARY

One good source of information about the wide variations in state donor laws is Human Rights Campaign (www.hrc.org). As its website reported in June 2005, "In some states, if a man is known to the woman or couple to whom he provides sperm, he may be required to assume the legal responsibilities of a parent. In California, Ohio and Wisconsin, a known donor releases himself from legal responsibility if the procedure is performed with a physician's involvement. In Colorado and New York, a known donor may be able to assert parental rights; however it is unclear whether a court would impose any responsibilities on a known donor in these two states. In Pennsylvania and Utah, the law is unclear and a known donor may be assigned some parental responsibility. In the remaining states, there are no laws or cases that assign or allow a donor to assert parental responsibilities."

• **Marriage and adoption** — If the mother marries and the donor has never parented, been declared on the birth certificate, or been adjudicated to be the child's parent, in some states the new spouse can adopt without notifying the donor. Because the rules can differ even from county to county, it is highly recommended that anyone using a known donor should first consult with and then have a contract drawn up by a specialist in *assisted* or *third-party reproduction* who is familiar with local statutes. One up-to-date legal directory that offers state listings is **www.surrogacy.com**.

> **Caution:** A *family law* attorney tends to know more about adoption and divorce than assisted reproduction, and may or may not catch all of the issues. A *contract* lawyer tends to be versed in business transactions, which can be dangerous in a situation like this. "The majority of states want to see the most altruistic contract, which eliminates any commercial aspect," says Vorzimer. Even stipulating payment of $1 for sperm donation, which some might see as a distancing business mechanism, is generally regarded in the field as a no-no because "it raises the specter of baby-selling."

When the Agreement Fails

Sarah asked a friend to be her donor. After agreeing initially, he turned her down because he didn't think he could accept knowing he had a child yet not be part of the child's life. So she asked an old boyfriend, who was reluctant at first. "He finally agreed, with the stipulation that he would have no responsibilities whatsoever—financial or emotional—and that he would remain anonymous. My child was never to know, and he wanted me to tell everyone that I went to a sperm bank."

After some additional negotiations, they agreed to terms. "I swore that the only time I would contact him would be a life or death situation. He asked if the child would be able to make any claims on him or his family. I assured him that I wanted nothing from him. I went to a lawyer to draw up an agreement, but the lawyer advised me to save my money because if the father decided to become part of the child's life, the agreement would be useless as the child's rights superseded the parents. I was so confident that the donor was not going to do this that I didn't pursue it any further.

"At that point, we were still friends and he was so adamant to the point of rehearsing what I should say to people if they asked questions that I convinced myself that it would turn out okay. It was the easy way. We weren't using doctors, there would be no expenses (ah, hindsight). If he had given me any inkling that he wanted to be involved I never would have chosen him."

The donor was 35, and Sarah, 40, assumed he knew what he wanted. But shortly before her child's second birthday (who we will call Pat), having appeared casually maybe five times since the birth, he showed up to say he had made a mistake and would like to get married and be a father. "I knew I couldn't deny him the right to see Pat, but he became verbally aggressive when he wanted to visit but it wasn't a convenient time for me," she told me. "I often felt intimidated and, since we didn't have a legal agreement set up, I tended to give in to avoid making a scene around my child."

Between his aggressive nit-picking and her use of avoidance to wish the situation away, it took seven years to work out a co-parenting agreement.

She fought back harder after he enrolled Pat in religious education classes in a faith he knew Sarah disagreed with—one whose church he did not attend in the years she knew him. "In the spirit of compromise, I offered to help look for a less dogmatic religion for my child to be part of, but that wasn't good enough for him. He insisted on the religious classes he wanted. This finally got me out of my 'avoidance' mode and I got the advice from my lawyer to serve him with papers asking for full custody. In the end, I got sole legal custody. I think at that point it was more of an issue of his unwillingness to compromise that made the judge rule in my favor."

When we talked, they were still working out a financial agreement—he started to pay support after deciding he wanted to be part of the child's life, but they had yet to agree on the final details. Sarah has spent about $10,000 in legal fees so far; he has had access to legal advice from people he knows.

Were there clues in his personality?

Sarah had dated this man—we'll call him Hank—back in 1986, after five years of friendship. "He seemed like a 'normal' even-keeled type, which is what I thought I needed. There was no passion there, but he was a nice man. I never noticed much of a backbone until he wanted to become part of my child's life." Sarah has never understood why he ended up battling with her like he did, other than the fact that he says he hadn't thought everything through before he agreed.

How is the child faring?

Sarah said her child has a good relationship with Hank. "I know it is better for Pat to know the father's identity, but emotionally it will always be difficult for me to be forced into raising a child with a man I don't love."

When Pat asked why her biological father suddenly appeared in their life, "I told Pat he was a friend who helped me to have a child, but not everyone is ready to be a parent at the same time. When he was ready, he became a part of their life. Pat seemed to accept that.

"My child is wonderful, and seems as well-adjusted as any nine-year-old. Pat has a relationship with his family now, as well as mine, and seems happy about that. Hank's family has a different perspective on issues than I do, but I want Pat to be exposed to different ideas and make decisions based on reasoned and well-rounded thought," she said. "In the meantime, I try to teach Pat good values and to have a good moral compass. Right now I focus on exposing Pat to charitable giving, and we have been doing volunteer work for several years. We all do the best we can."

Regrets

"The emotional toll it took on me, particularly in the first couple of years that Hank became involved, was great. I thought about it day and night. It was an awful time for me. I understand and accept that he made a mistake and that the situation became different for him, but it is difficult for me to see him as a father since I have no emotional attachment to him.

"I love my child more than my life. Pat is the child I was meant to love, and was created because I, and I alone, wanted and desired to give the love I have to a child. If I had gone to a sperm bank instead, the time spent, and the financial and emotional turmoil could have been avoided.

> *"Obviously, in retrospect, I regret using a known donor because of the problems it created in my life. Although I have custody, I have to confer on decisions with someone I have no feelings for, and have to experience not having my child with me all the times that I had expected to."*

"I cannot picture a life without this special child in my life, but if I wanted a second child I would use a sperm bank with open-identity donors."

Choosing Single Motherhood © Mikki Morrissette

Sarah's final thoughts

"I feel as if so much of what I have said is negative. My child is the best thing that has ever happened to me. Although I spent four years planning this, it certainly didn't turn out as I expected. As time goes on I am learning to deal with it, but sometimes it is very difficult. Pat loves Hank and he loves Pat and it's great to have more people to love you in your lifetime. He and I have a civil relationship, and I never say anything negative about him to Pat, and would never deny their time together. But it's just not what I expected. Other women thinking about this should be aware of what can happen."

ANOTHER CASE

In May 2005, the Pennsylvania Supreme Court was considering a legal appeal involving a known donor and a woman who conceived twins with his sperm through in vitro fertilization when she was married to someone else. Although she named her husband as father on the birth certificate, after her divorce—and subsequent financial difficulties—she filed a case against the donor for child support.

Although the trial court and Superior Court said the woman's actions were "despicable"—and the donor since had become the married father of two—both found him liable to pay more than $1,500 a month in child support plus arrearages to the woman. The courts made their decision based on the tendency for the law to not allow biological parents to waive the interests of a child, who has the right to support from both of them.[2]

On the Other Hand

Some women know that they don't have the stomach for something as potentially complicated as what Sarah has experienced. Others feel strongly that it is important to give a child every opportunity to know their full genetic background starting from birth. For anyone undecided who lies in between, here are the main reasons some experts think—despite the legal and emotional complexities—that a known donor is the best option to give a child, and why I have no regrets about my choice.

Pro #1: Sense of Identity

As we will read more, particularly in Chapters 9 and 13, children who have been conceived with an anonymous donor or placed for adoption sometimes feel a strong sense of loss and crisis of identity.

A child's disconnection from his past can lead to periods of confusion and alienation. "I feel like a cereal box with no ingredients," said one of the adoptees quoted in *Being Adopted: The Lifelong Search for Self.* [3]

This same identity crisis has been applied by some experts to the feeling of loss experienced by children of anonymous donor insemination. Although this "half-adopted" circumstance might alleviate some of the loss, an unknown donor still leaves a child with the potential for feeling like they are only half identifiable. Said one such donor offspring, "I'd like to know about my donor's health—half of my health history is missing, and missed. I'd like to 'see' the personality traits I've inherited. I'd like to know what the donor does for a living, what conflicts he's had, how he's resolved them, what issues he struggles with." [4]

Noted Yale child psychiatrist Dr. Kyle Pruett believes that this identity issue alone is why the trend toward known donors will grow. Despite the uncertain strings attached, Pruett thinks the desire to have a "father story," and to have the ability to share the other half of one's genetic history, is beginning to outweigh the advantages of anonymity for many women who choose conception.

> *"Having useful information about the donor has a way of keeping the child's identity secure," Pruett told me. "They aren't aliens, created from Kryptonite. They have a stronger sense that they belong to a world in which kids are born of a mother and a father."*

Primarily in response to this identity issue—which affects many, although certainly not all, children—many sperm banks are now recruiting donors who agree to be reachable when any resulting child turns 18. This promise can be too tentative, however, for a mother who wants her child to know all genetic quirks and attributes. Accentuated by my understanding of the difficulties experienced by several adopted people I know, the desire I have for my children is that they not have gaps in their knowledge about who they are and where they came from. That is why I want them to know their biological father—not only as I have known him, but as they might come to know him in time.

Unless, of course, they decide they have no interest. That's what happened to Susan, a child therapist who "accidentally on purpose" conceived more than 20 years ago in a relationship with a charismatic but inappropriate man. Although the mother thought it important for the daughter to develop a relationship with him, the girl declared at age seven that she wasn't interested. When we talked, she hadn't seen her biological father for 12 years.

But her daughter does have pictures of her father, and can see how her African-American heritage came from him. "I do think it mattered to her to at least know who he was," Susan told me. And, even more importantly, it now seems, her daughter is getting acquainted with half-siblings from the man's other relationships.

Pro #2: A "Creation" Story

Having a father story to help inform her child's sense of identity and creation is the main reason Beth decided to use the sperm of an old boyfriend, even though his personal issues made it clear that he wasn't the right lifetime partner for her.

"Although I'd ordered long profiles and audio interviews for the sperm donor I'd chosen, I remembered that one of the reasons I wanted to conceive with my old boyfriend is that my child would have an origin narrative," she told me. "I think in some ways, lacking a narrative is even more problematic for DI children than lacking half a genetic history. For me, the story of how my parents met is one I tell over and over again. This way I will be able to tell my child that I met his father because we were both news correspondents who fell in love overseas. That's a good story."

For some, conceiving a child with a vial of sperm is too impersonal. Even if the woman chooses to be inseminated with the sperm of a friend, rather than procreating the old-fashioned way, creating life with someone familiar can seem less faceless, for the mother and eventually for the child. As one donor offspring who obviously was struggling with her creation story said starkly: "Some stranger masturbated into a glass vial and I'm the result."[5]

It can be easy to explain to a young child that "mommy wanted you so badly that she went to a place that gave her what she needed to create you in my tummy." The story might be less satisfying to a teenager and young adult, who wants to feel that he or she was created out of an emotional form of bonding between two people. I can understand Beth's need for a creation story for her child. And I agree with the views of Dr. Pruett, who told me:

"The mother tends to think of the conception story as hers, when in reality it is the child's."

In other words, you might write the words to the story, but ultimately it's the child's book. I know the circumstances surrounding my own birth have been more important to me than to my parents. I was born less than a year after my parents lost their first child at birth, and tended to think of myself as the "miracle" baby they created contrary to doctor's orders.

The point is, while your energies right now might be to choose what feels most comfortable to you—which is important—it is the child that will be impacted most by how he or she came to be. Make every effort to insure that the origin story you write for your child is one you are happy with.

Pro #3: Medical History

With the amazing advances in genetic testing, we are becoming increasingly able to use science and family history to warn us about our predilection for many diseases. These advances will make it more frustrating for children to grow up with large gaps of knowledge about their medical heritage.

Diane Bartel, associate director at the Center for Bioethics at the University of Minnesota, says that there will be growing pressure on adoption agencies and sperm banks to provide full medical histories over time. "There will be even more need to know family histories in the next 10 to 15 years. The lack of health information in the future will have more impact on people than in the past."

Because of my father's and grandfather's histories of heart disease, I know to regularly monitor my cholesterol. In fact, when I was having chest pain at the age of 40 (which thankfully turned out to be unrelated to my heart), doctors took it seriously enough—knowing that my father had his first heart attack at age 42—to keep me in the hospital overnight for monitoring and tests.

Unfortunately, an adopted acquaintance in her mid-50s had no such information to go on. Two doctors dismissed her complaints of chest pains as "stress-related." Because she was a woman—who are often under-diagnosed with heart disease to begin with—and had no known family history, they didn't take her concerns seriously. Until she collapsed in an emergency room with a massive heart attack a week later, suffering brain damage in the process.

Scary, but true. Especially these days, with overworked medical clinics, we are responsible for understanding and aggressively protecting our health. Any child missing such valuable information about medical history is at a disadvantage. That's the main reason, in fact, that my adoptive brother has periodically considered

Choosing Single Motherhood © Mikki Morrissette

learning more about his biological parents. He doesn't want to meet them, he has generally dealt with his resulting identity issues, but now in his 40s, with two children, the lack of genetic background is for him a significant gap.

Consideration: Cost

We don't like to be crass when it comes to discussing our child's birth, but if you are willing to have intercourse with the donor or use his sperm in home insemination, this method to motherhood is significantly cheaper than adoption and anonymous insemination. Indeed, essentially free, except for the ovulation test kits and basal thermometer to pinpoint the timing.

Banking the sperm as a "directed donor" runs about $600—for simple tests and storage—if you can claim a dedicated relationship with the donor, and about $2,000 if you can't, since clinics are legally required to quarantine the sperm for six months to test for AIDS and other diseases.

Of course, as Sarah's story reminds us, using a known donor can become an expensive option if the donor someday asserts his parental rights in court.

If You Say Yes to a Known Donor

If you want to use a known donor, the next big question is: where do you find one and what do you do if you ask someone and he says yes?

As one woman said, "It's got to be someone who is going to add more to the equation than just free sperm."

Some donors are gay acquaintances or friends who want to be partially involved with the life of a child he helps to create. Others want to see their DNA continue without getting involved. Many are ex-lovers, or even current lovers who don't have long-term potential as a mate but are willing to be involved in creating new life.

One woman I talked to was in her early 30s when an older man she knew expressed strong interest in being her donor. He had lost his family in concentration camps during World War II, had four grown children from his marriage, and felt he had a debt to pay to "repopulate" his family genes. She wrestled with moral concerns, discussed the option at length with a therapist, and worried if she might be setting a future child up "for something bad" if she chose this route. She had high regard and appreciation for the man, who wanted to be a stable and consistent presence in any life that was created. Ultimately she went ahead with it, and has two children with the donor, who is very involved in their lives.

Nancy is one woman I know who has taken the known donor option to the next level—she and a childless 50-year-old male friend have agreed, after medical and background checks, to co-parent. "We look at it that we will be friends who will have joint custody of a child," she told me. "This is emotionally and financially helpful for me, and I think it is better for the child to have a dad around. We have discussed issues like housing, schedule, child support, will, life insurance. We plan to do activities together, maybe even take vacations together. It's like a divorced couple who get along well and do things with their child. He will help me financially so I can be home for six months, and work part-time another six months."

Any known donor relationship involves collaborative parenting to some degree. This requires the Choice Mom to have several talents.

Manage the gate
The Choice Mom largely controls how the child's relationship with the donor/father develops in the pre-adolescent age. Young children tend to absorb the cues of their primary caregiver. As Wellesley researcher Hertz has written, one aspect of managing the gate is deciding what to call the donor/biological father.[6]

I remember how tentatively I introduced Sophie's biological father to her with the term of "dad" when she started talking more at the age of two. I debated whether his role in her life would be less confusing if we didn't use that term for him at all, but once the word was out I couldn't reverse it. She generally refers to him by his first name, but I'll never forget the inquisitive look she gave me when she called him "dad" for the first time. Whether she wondered if she was correct in using the word, or whether she wanted to see whether I objected, I'll never know. But it was easy in that moment to see that she was gauging my reaction. Eventually I could see that she was proud of having someone called "dad," but would adapt to the cues I gave her.

Seriously explore your ability to set limits and expectations
before you make the choice to use a known donor.

Understand what kind of relationship with the father you prefer the child to have. It will be less confusing for everyone if you can monitor this consistently over time. As one lawyer recommends, "Decide in advance whether the contributor of the sperm is a donor or a parent."

Choosing Single Motherhood © Mikki Morrissette

This was my weak spot. Although Sophie's biological father will always be more than a donor in her creation story, the consistency of their relationship changed significantly during her early years. Those long visits after we moved to Minnesota were fun for Sophie, but in hindsight temporarily created expectations that he was unable to fulfill in the long term. She adapted well to the changes, but if she had been older—or we were living closer to him with more frequent contact—it likely would have been much harder.

Know the donor better than he does

In order to manage that gate, you need to be reasonably sure that you can trust the man to respect your boundaries. You need to understand his ability to relinquish control of the child's upbringing—even if he is unable to articulate it, or understand what that lack of control might mean for him emotionally.

A friend of mine—professionally successful, attractive, intelligent —has been asked by several women to "provide seed." He has turned down every request because he knows he would not be willing to relinquish control of the child's upbringing to someone else.

If you know what you want and don't want, and understand the donor intimately enough to feel that he will abide by your wishes—and ultimately the child's—you can likely ride out the inevitable bumps and offer your child the benefits of having a known father.

You might be interested in working out a kind of co-parenting role with the donor, as I did in a limited way with Sophie's father—accepting gifts, phone conversations, visits—or not. Regardless, be sure the two of you are secure enough as human beings to be able to communicate and negotiate.

As Beth told me: "I do think my boyfriend would abide by my wishes. I would probably want him to be a not-so-involved face and name, and my guess is that he wouldn't challenge that. He has agreed to sign an agreement in which I would ask him to sign away rights. I know those agreements have no legal value, but at least the exercise would help lay out the parameters."

If you can't find a man you trust to respect your wishes about what is best for your child—one who is emotionally mature enough to negotiate fairly—then don't try to force it. This might not be the choice you can safely make.

Be accepting of change

Like any married relationship, the known donor route requires the ability to accept the ambiguities: with at least three different individuals involved (not including a donor whose future wife might not be as accepting of your arrangement, or a donor whose parents want to be grandparents), things will change over time. Realize that no matter how reasonable you are on paper, there are highly unpredictable emotions that come into play. If you are the type of person who can roll with changes and accept what comes—if you know that life never turns out exactly the way you planned it—this would be a reasonable option for you to take.

On the other hand, if you shudder at the possibility of having to negotiate rights and terms with a donor or your adolescent child, then the adoption and insemination routes might be safer. At the very least, plan to be inseminated at a clinic using your "directed donor" sperm, which might give you more protection under the law. It costs more on the front-end, but could save you *much* in the end.

WHY I'D LIKE TO BE A KNOWN DONOR

Every donor has his own thoughts and motivations. Personally, I haven't found anyone to create a family with. As the years pass by, I have started thinking, what if I die and never leave anything behind? I just want to pass my genes on to someone. I am not in a situation where I want to have any contact—I would only want to do that if I was in a relationship with someone. I know there are alot of single women out there who want to have a child but have no one to do it with. I personally think helping someone out like this is one of the greatest gifts you can give. And if it is not too much of a hassle for me personally, why not? Part of me lives on somewhere. I take comfort in this. The way I am doing it—not anonymously through a clinic—gives me a little control over it as well. I wouldn't want to contribute to create a baby to a woman that would be abusive. There are alot of loonies out there and I wouldn't want to donate blindly. Also, going to a clinic can cost a fortune. I met a girl who had spent over $8,000 trying to become pregnant with frozen sperm through a sperm bank without success. Having a baby shouldn't only be for rich women.

Questions to Ask Yourself

For her 1987 master's thesis, a Choice Mom interviewed 14 women about how they chose the method to motherhood.[7] Among other experiences, she explored the ethical decisions of women who considered "accidentally on purpose" getting pregnant with men they might not forewarn of their intentions. Many of these women agonized over "whether it was morally right" to take advantage of the men. Sometimes women chose men who were likely to "bolt when the pregnancy was announced." As she noted, "A common feeling was that men who take no responsibility for contraception had no right to oppose conscious conception."

Remember your child's right to his or her creation story. What story can you in good conscience tell your child someday? Let that guide your method to motherhood.

As you consider taking steps with someone, ask yourself these questions:

1. What are his motivations in wanting this child with you? Is it to maintain a relationship with you over time...to be a father without the commitment or responsibility...out of a desire to give you something you want?

2. Do you want him to be a semi-involved father in the child's life, or a not-so-involved face and name? When you know what you prefer, it might be easier to decide whether he's capable of sticking to the rules that you set.

3. Do you intuitively trust the man? Don't leap in the hopes that it will all work out, or let your own desire for a known donor cloud your vision.

4. How does he handle situations in which he can't get what he wants? Is he capable of compromise? Is he sensitive to the needs of others?

5. Has he thought about the legal issues involved? I wouldn't fully trust a man who hasn't thought things through.

6. How will you both feel if the child wants him to play a larger role than you envision? How will you feel if the donor wants a larger role, or says he'll be available for contact but changes his mind? What if the donor marries and his wife has a role in setting rules? What if you marry—will the donor's role change? Can both of you accept not being able to control this rather emotional area?

7. How will his family react if they are told? Will they be supportive and hands-off, or want to play a role in the child's life?

8. Even if you don't co-parent, how do his values about parenting differ from yours? Will he protest if you raise the child in a way he doesn't agree with?

WHY I'M A KNOWN DONOR

I love kids, and think everyone should have the opportunity to have them. I've helped several women have their children, and I have no regrets that I'm not playing a bigger role in those children's lives. Yes, it makes me sad sometimes—frequently—especially when I see pictures of how they're growing. But I have no regrets about doing it.

And it's not about me wanting to spread my seed everywhere. At the core, it gives me joy to know that I've given this profound blessing to a mother and her child.

There are emotions involved, but the right type of person can overcome that—to say 'that's life, there's nothing I can do about it.' It takes a realist, someone capable of being firmly grounded in logic and rational thinking to do this, I think. Men are generally able to detach from their emotions, but not all.

My advice to anyone picking a donor is to look for someone who is pretty damn logical. Maybe someone in sales or business, who is accustomed to brokering business deals without letting emotions get involved. Not someone who is a super powerful, dominant kind of guy who has to have his way all the time. Not a control freak.

I think it also would help if he has had kids already and has no interest in more. Or if he has enough to keep him occupied so he's less likely to feel lonely. Mainly he has to be capable of being detached. And ask him if he's ever initiated a lawsuit.

You should know him for at least a year, so you can have the confidence that he's capable of accepting whatever comes his way. He shouldn't have a fixed mindset about anything, but be open to change. Above all, he needs to be realistic, and able to tell himself that he can't have everything—that no matter how great the kid is, he's not going to interfere with the agreement. He understands that nothing more will happen, and is okay with it.

WHY I'M *NOT* A KNOWN DONOR

Four women have honored me by asking me to father a child. These requests mean something different now than when it first happened at age 25. Twenty years ago, I did not grasp the intense feelings about being a parent. As a young person, the responsibility and emotions played a less important role and I would have been driven mostly by the desire to replicate the pattern of my parents, siblings, peers and the community in which I was raised plus satisfy my ego—*she likes me, she really likes me!*

To contemplate becoming a father at age 45, however, one draws from richer life experience and different personal, economic and emotional circumstances. As a single gay man, in many respects I have lived autonomously my whole life. The notion of bringing another human being into the world brings a sense of duty and responsibility that I have not experienced before.

Many people have taught me raising any child (not to mention your own child) is an experience unlike any other experience in life. I imagine it's a form of intense self-actualization I would find especially rewarding. So I took the last invitation very seriously.

The reason I said no to being a donor the first three times was because I was too immature and not prepared for the demands of being a parent, even as a sperm donor. Another time it was because the woman and I were unsuccessful navigating the circles of responsibility. I wanted agreement on the principles of how we continuously balance the well-being of child, mother, siblings, grandparents, partners, friends, classmates, teachers and so forth.

In order to make this decision, I wanted to look beyond the obligations of child rearing to the emotional or spiritual connection I feel exists between parents and children. Which meant a three-part agreement (two parents and child) that gradually shifted choice from the parents to the child.

REFLECTIONS ON BEING A KNOWN DONOR
BY ANDREW BERG[8]

reprinted by permission of author

As a 25-year-old gay man, the author was asked to be the donor for a lesbian couple.

Many of my gay friends didn't quite understand what I was doing or why. My family, although supportive, was worried that I wouldn't be able to handle the emotions that might arise out of having a child who really isn't mine. I received conflicting advice from almost everyone. Even the potential mothers wondered if I had ulterior motives. Why would I want to do this knowing full and well that the child would be theirs and not mine?

The potential moms presented me with a contract that spelled out that I would have "no expectation of a relationship with the child." I would have no say in his or her name. No say in how the child would be raised. No say in his or her education or religious upbringing. For my protection, I had no financial obligations to them, ever. And finally, the child would one day come to know that I was his or her father.

The thoughts that entered my mind and the soul searching I endured over the next few months were incredibly difficult.

I wasn't invited to her birth. It was the first test of my emotional strength. I had anticipated this event for over a year—envisioning myself in the hospital waiting room, jumping up with tears in my eyes as the doctor came out to tell me if it was a boy or a girl. And now my giddy excitement had quickly turned to a quiet disappointment.

A compromise was reached and I was invited to visit them in the hospital the day after the birth. One very special moment will always remain from that day. I sat alone with this precious baby for about five minutes, telling her that I loved her and that I always would. Wiping the tears from my eyes, I got back into my car and started the three-hour drive back to my home. Leaving the hospital that day was one of the most difficult things I have ever had to do.

Two years have now passed, and the road has been fairly smooth. I visit them almost every five weeks. We talk on the phone. We exchange photos and e-mails. I've developed a very loving and warm relationship with all three of them. We have built a relationship based on trust, caring and most importantly, honesty. But there will most certainly be awkward moments on the road ahead, and times when I wish things were a little bit different.

The mothers graciously accept presents from my friends and family, even though it might sometimes make them feel uncomfortable. They've kindly allowed time for my family to get to know their daughter, even though she already has two sets of grandparents and many aunts and uncles. They have spent holidays at my parents' house, and I would imagine that seeing pictures of their daughter on the refrigerator there might make them feel a little funny.

Awkward little moments continue to arise even today. We're now at a time where we're discussing whether or not I'll be referred to as "Dad," and how to explain this relationship to a two-year-old who is quickly figuring out that not all kids have two moms.

Whether or not she calls me Dad isn't really all that important. I've slowly come to terms with and understand that there won't necessarily be a call or a card on Father's Day. I have come to terms with the fact that my parents can't treat her like their other grandchildren and that I won't always be able to see her when I want. But everything I don't get to share with her makes the time I do have that much more special.

I do my best to look at the big picture. And when I do, I see that the only thing that is important is that I continue to have a loving relationship with this special child—that I have the chance to watch her change and grow, discover and learn. That is my reward.

Postscript: Since this article was written, Andrew agreed to help the same couple, and a brother was born. "They are five and seven years old and I still continue to see them on a regular basis. They just found out that I am their biological father (it took the seven-year-old this long to ask) and they're processing the information. They still call me Andy." Andrew and his long-time partner are parents to twins. "The joke (since the twins are biologically my partner's) is that I'm the biological father of two children who aren't legally mine and the legal father of two children who aren't biologically mine."

Final Thoughts

Jenifer Firestone, director of Alternative Families Matter, addressed a conference for the lesbian and gay community in 2001 with the following (excerpted) words, applicable to anyone considering a known donor relationship.[9]

Obviously, sharing some level of parenting with a non-spouse is a life-long commitment, which we are unaccustomed to making. It can be complicated, requires genuine mutual respect, some level of shared values, trust, and the willingness and ability to solve problems creatively.

To have a child with another person and not create a comprehensive agreement that includes an explicit process for co-parenting in the event of a break-up is like abandoning children amidst the chaos and manipulations of power they might experience if you died without a will or life insurance.

What are the ingredients to any successful family arrangements? One is honoring each other's respective relationships (or lack thereof) with the child, while recognizing the possibility that at any point one of the parties could have a change of heart, mind, or circumstance that could alter the plan. In these situations the parties have to work together to find ways to accommodate the change without disregarding the original plan.

This is very dicey stuff. Even in the case of donors who don't plan to be very involved or lesbians and gay men who are close friends, attempting to conceive and, to whatever extent, be involved with children is an extremely intimate endeavor for people who have chosen not to be intimate in any other ways.

While most known donor/recipient arrangements have been successful and worthwhile, some have been disastrous and I am horrified at the cavalier approach taken by some men and women considering these arrangements. Prospective parents and their friends must acknowledge the complexity and high-risk nature of these situations, talk to others who have had children with a man or woman they know, seek out legal and interpersonal counseling, and make a pact with one another that any conflicts that may arise will be resolved by every means outside a conventional court.

We need to establish our own customs that make sense for our unique families. We can arrange ceremonies to welcome the new baby/child and publicly acknowledge and commit to her/his constellation. We can publicly assure our children that while

Choosing Single Motherhood © Mikki Morrissette

life is full of all kinds of changes, this carefully chosen family of parents, donor/dads, etc. will always be their family, and that each family member will forever honor and appreciate that child's relationship with each of them.

We could make use of "godparents" or other individuals who are mutually trusted by all of the parents to witness the recognition of these family members, to hear why they chose each other, what they felt the other(s) would bring to the child's life, and to step in and assist if problems threaten the relationships to which the child is accustomed.

Non-couples who conceive children together do so for the sake of fulfilling the child's need to know, and possibly have relationships with both biological parents, and for the richness these bonds can bring to the act of parenting. But this fulfillment can only be achieved if both parties involved accept and understand that parenting is a life-long commitment you make to the children, regardless of the parents' relationship with each other.

CHAPTER 9

USING ASSISTED DONOR INSEMINATION

Although donor sperm has been used medically since the late 1700s, the first known United States case occurred in 1884, when a couple arrived at a medical school in Philadelphia with an infertility problem. The group of doctors discussing the case chose a good-looking donor and secretly inseminated the woman with sperm. Not until after the birth was the husband told. The wife was never let in on the secret.[1]

It took another 100 years before donor eggs became an option for infertile women—and even longer for the shame and secrecy of insemination to begin to dissipate (thanks partly to the growing availability of the process to Choice Moms who had less to hide). Now insemination is a booming business. One conservative guess is that 30,000 children are born each year from donated sperm.[2] According to *Newsweek,* in 2001, single women accounted for 40 percent of the business at California Cryobank, one of the world's largest sperm banks.[3]

The process is a complex one: *Do I need fertility testing? Which donor should I pick? Which clinics are open-minded to single mothers? What do all the acronyms mean—IVF, IUI—and what do I need to be prepared to deal with? How much will everything cost?*

Entire books have been written about donor insemination. Check the Resources section for sources that go into greater detail about insemination, egg donors, sperm banks, as well as storybooks for kids about how they were conceived. Rather than cover ground available elsewhere, this chapter will focus on:

1. Why I believe women should seriously consider using an open-identity donor;

2. The views of sperm donors about why they donated and how they feel about it today;

3. The process women have used to choose a sperm donor.

Choosing Single Motherhood © Mikki Morrissette

In other chapters we discuss insemination costs (Chapter 2), how to answer a child's daddy questions (Chapter 12), and how some donor offspring feel about their conception story (Chapter 13).

Conception Methods: A Comparison

A Thinking Woman who wants to conceive has four options in choosing a donor:

1. A known donor (the topic of Chapter 8)—This option does not come with legal and emotional protections between donor and mother, as tends to be the case with an anonymous donor. As we learned in the previous chapter, it can be extremely painful and costly to deal with a known donor who changes his mind and wants to be a real father after all. However, some women have a strong desire to give a child the opportunity to know as much as possible about his or her full **genetic identity** and **medical history**. One woman I talked to stopped pursuing the ADI route and asked an old boyfriend to become her donor. She knew that using a known donor was more complicated, "but I feel better about knowing who the father is."

2. A "directed" donor—Using a known donor's sperm in a clinic insemination (also called "directed" donor) tends to give greater legal protection. A drawback is timing: In most cases (but not all, if legal release forms are accepted), the sperm needs to be quarantined for six months. This was the case with my donor, even after we had already conceived one child together. There is cost for storage, testing for HIV and the insemination process, but the donor and mother are **generally protected from custody and support issues.** However, there have been legal cases in which directed donors were granted parental rights, and a directed donor for in vitro fertilization has been sued for child support, so legal protection is not iron-clad. *[See Chapter 15 for details about legal cases.]*

3. An anonymous donor—This provides the greatest legal protection for donor and mother, although it tends to leave the child with few options for dealing with potential identity issues (subject of Chapter 13). Even with anonymous donors, exceptions have been made. In 2000, for example, one 11-year-old girl with a kidney disorder won the rights to information about her donor by a San Francisco court.

Compared to using a known donor, an anonymous one makes it **cleaner for the woman (and the child) to know that there is no partner and no father in the family.** Given the emotions involved in creating life, it can be hard to keep clear-headed when using the sperm of a known person. One author of a comprehensive book about insemination used a donor that was known to her and her husband—

and eventually divorced and married the donor. Another woman I know fell in love with a potential known donor. He got scared of what he might be getting himself into, and backed out. *[See Chapter 12 for the reactions involved when a Choice Mom introduced her young children to their anonymous donor.]*

4. An open-identity donor—I'll spend a lot of time discussing this growing option, as I strongly believe it gives *all three parties* in the conception a reasonable agreement. Children, who I think are equally entitled to choices, know that their mother tried to give them the opportunity to contact the donor after the age of 18. Sometimes the child has no interest, sometimes the donor is too nervous in 18 years to be of much help, but at least the mother has selected someone who understands and accepts responsibility for an offspring's curiosity about his or her other genetic half.

ALPHABET SOUP

ART — assisted reproductive technology, in which egg *and* sperm are handled to help a woman get pregnant.

ICSI — intracytoplasmic sperm injection, when sperm is injected directly into an egg in a laboratory.

IUI — intrauterine insemination, a clinical method that increases the number of sperm that reach the fallopian tube and thus improves the odds of an egg being fertilized. It requires "washing" the sperm to separate it from semen and is timed to occur with ovulation. It is sometimes combined with supervolution induction, which makes multiple eggs available for fertilization.

IVF — In vitro fertilization, the usual treatment for a woman with blocked or damaged fallopian tubes, or to circumvent infertility caused by endometriosis. This process was first used in England in 1978, with "test-tube baby" Louise Brown, ushering in the new age of ART. Hundreds of thousands of children have now been born this way. It involves combining egg and sperm in a culture dish and transferring the embryo into the uterus. It requires about two weeks of preparation in order to create a strong environment in the woman, including fertility drugs, ultrasounds and blood tests.

IVI/ICI — intravaginal/intracervical insemination, methods of home insemination, using a needleless syringe or cervical cap.

Choosing Single Motherhood © Mikki Morrissette

Home insemination

It can be very stressful for women to attempt to get pregnant in a clinic setting—often having to secretly fit in one or two last-minute appointments when ovulation is detected. A great deal of emotional energy can be expended waiting and wondering if any of the costly attempts will work—a fertility concern that increases with the woman's age. To avoid the clinical setting, many banks will allow frozen sperm to be shipped to the woman's home so she can use a needleless syringe or cervical cap to inseminate at home. (For tips, see www.fertilityplus.org/faq.homeinsem.html)

Home shipment generally requires a doctor's sign-off. The success rate of this low-tech option is not high—although it is common, and one bank reports that 54 percent of its clients eventually succeed at home. Some recommend that women turn to a clinic after a few unsuccessful attempts at home, to check fertility issues and to better the odds of success. (One humorous book about home insemination recommended to me is Harlan Aizley's *Buying Dad*.)

The Ethics of Donor Insemination

Perhaps the only area in which Choice Mothers have an automatic advantage over married couples is that they don't have to agonize over whether to tell the child the truth about their origins. According to a *Chicago Tribune* article, most of today's roughly 1 million donor-conceived children do *not* know the truth about their conception (one estimate is 80 percent!).[4]

Some children of married couples feel something is "off"—that perhaps their mother had an affair or was raped, for example. Some find out after the father dies, after a divorce, or during a family argument. One teenage girl was told by an angry mother: *You should be grateful. You have no idea how much we paid to have you.*

The secrecy aspect of donor insemination has given the process a bad name. Many research studies reveal that when a couple uses an egg or sperm donor and doesn't tell the child the truth, the damage of secrecy (and/or shame and distance of the infertile parent) can have a seriously negative impact on the family dynamic. Someone who learns late in life that he or she is not related biologically to a parent often experiences intense feelings of betrayal, anger, mistrust, resentment, and confusion about who they are. Many of these donor offspring turn to online support groups to vent their emotions.

It is hard to separate whether the emotions of these men and women are rooted primarily in being misled by their parents, and how much is related to being unable to get a full picture of their genetic identity. Many children who consider their donor conception to be "no big deal" typically were told at a young age and grow up more curious about their origins than angry about it.

Anonymity vs. open-identity

Secrecy is not an issue for Choice Mothers, since their children tend to know that a donor was used. But whether to use a donor who can never be identified, or one the child can make contact with after the age of 18, is an important option for the Thinking Woman.

In the United States and elsewhere, anonymity is slowly giving way to the viewpoint that a child's right to know their genetic history should take precedence. Arthur Caplan, the director of the Center for Bioethics at the University of Pennsylvania, says lessons from adoption are opening the door. Nowadays in adoption, he told me, "It doesn't matter if the records are open or not, many judges are starting to allow adopted children to appeal a sealed record. It's still case by case, but if someone says they want to screen for Huntington's disease or breast cancer, a judge is not going to deny the medical need to know more about the person's own genetic background." He predicts that someday offspring of anonymous donors are likely to be able to do the same.

ONE POLICY OF OPENNESS
This is the openness policy of one sperm bank found online.

We recognize the concerns regarding the rights to privacy and confidentiality on the part of the sperm donor, the mother, the parenting father and the child. In an attempt to balance these concerns with the real and legitimate needs on the part of the child to know about his or her biological heritage, we have developed a "Policy Of Openness," which includes the following:

1. We have never destroyed patient or donor files and plan to keep the information indefinitely.

2. If, at the age of 18 or older, the child of a recipient requests information about the genetic father we will make all reasonable efforts to supply that information either from our records or by attempting to contact the donor.

Choosing Single Motherhood © Mikki Morrissette

The Open-Identity Option

To honor the needs of parents who want their children to know more about their genetic identity, a growing number of U.S. sperm banks offer open-identity donors, who agree to be reachable after the child turns 18. In 1983, The Sperm Bank of California (TSBC) in Berkeley was the first to offer Identity-Release(sm) donors. In 2003 alone, 75 percent of the 130 children born from its program had IR donors. Other banks are adapting their policies to suit growing consumer demand. At last count on SpermCenter.com, eight of its 24 listed sperm banks offered some form of open-identity donor. Some banks are contacting anonymous donors retrospectively to see if they are willing to be reachable by offspring.

Although sperm banks might use similar terms, there is no standard program. Every bank has a different approach and should be studied closely. Sperm from open-identity donors tends to be more expensive per vial than that of anonymous donors; one website I checked reported a difference of $100. One bank doesn't charge more for the vials, but charges a fee when a child is born. *[Check Resources for sperm banks.]*

One survey of 115 single women, lesbian couples and heterosexual couples from a New Mexico clinic[5] reported that lesbian couples and single women were more likely than married couples to want a donor's identity disclosed (75 percent to 32 percent).

3. While we are NOT opposed in principal to breaking anonymity between the donor and the adult (or near adult) child, we do feel strongly it must be by mutual consent of both parties.

4. We do not believe that the semen donor or the mother should be asked today how they might feel about such a sensitive and complex issue 15-30 years from now.

5. We do believe the issues are real. Our task is to maintain our records and prepare ourselves so that we can appropriately respond to individual needs.

6. However, we are obligated by mutual agreements to maintain the anonymity and privacy of both the donor and recipient. The only exception to this would be by mutual consent of the involved individuals.

A TSBC survey, however, found both single and married people equally interested in its open-identity donors—nearly 80 percent reported it as an important criteria in choosing a donor.[6]

On the other hand, another TSBC survey reported that children of Choice Moms were slightly more likely to request information about the donor than children of married couples.[7]

Why choose open donors?

Even if a child is told openly about conception by donor sperm or egg, the child sometimes can grow up with a deep curiosity, wanting to understand the missing donors' identity as part of their own definition of self. *[See Chapter 13 for details.]* As we deepen our understanding of how influential genetics is—compared to what we once thought in the nature versus nurture balance—it also can be troubling for offspring to have an incomplete medical history. In many cases, a sperm donor's family health history is available based only on what the donor was able to divulge at the generally young age at which he donated.

Sometimes offspring might not feel a compulsion to know more until they are about to become parents themselves. Caplan told me it is common to be ambivalent until issues of heredity make the issue seem more urgent.

One adopted Choice Mother told me it was important to her that she choose open-identity. She had found her own birth family 10 years earlier. She defines family as people who raise you, not who provide sperm and egg, but "I wanted to give my son the chance to connect with his biological roots."

She felt strongly enough about the issue that she considered using a known donor, but "ultimately felt uncomfortable with all the unknown factors—would he want contact with the child against my wishes?" She ended up choosing a donor who had similarities to her in appearance and education, who wrote a great essay, and had a decent photo.

Another Choice Mom told me it was her child's right to know his full heritage someday if he desired—that it was not her right to decide what he could and could not discover. Although she ended up using a known donor, she had originally selected an anonymous donor who would allow contact in 18 years. "I don't agree that we can think of our children as only ours. My parents don't own me, and I don't own my son, even if I do call him mine," she said. "Our children will be confused teens and then mature adults one day, with questions and a need to find out who

Choosing Single Motherhood © Mikki Morrissette

they really are. There will be some kids who are content not finding the donor, but I am sure many will."

Strengthening her opinion was the knowledge of a friend of hers, conceived to a mother and father via anonymous insemination. "She cannot find her biological father and she is full of anger and resentment about it."

The trend toward openness—in adoption and donor insemination—makes it more likely that a child conceived today will expect to understand their full genetic legacy tomorrow. Using an open-identity donor will make that expectation easier to satisfy.

Why *not* choose open donors?

Although children benefit from having the opportunity to learn more about their other half if they choose to, it is not always an easy choice for the parent to make.

A primary reason Choice Moms use anonymous donors is that they are more plentiful. At last count, of the 1,400 donors listed on SpermCenter.com, only 172 were open-identity. With other characteristics important to the Thinking Woman— such as resemblance to her family and religious background—it can be tough to pick a donor from such a limited pool.

A WORLDWIDE ISSUE

The United Nations Convention on the Rights of the Child declared formally in 1989 that a child has the right to his or her genetic origins. This "open identity" right was declared law—and not optional—first in Sweden (1985), as well as Austria, Switzerland, New Zealand, Australian states, The Netherlands (June 2004) and the United Kingdom (April 2005). These countries have made it mandatory for sperm banks to use open-identity donors. All new donors must agree to be contacted at the wishes of any offspring after a certain age. Japan and Norway have considered similar legislation.

Several countries have voluntary national registries to enable adult offspring and donors to find each other.

On the other hand, France allows only anonymous donors, on the theory that the child's best interests are served by having one father. Italy does not allow donor insemination at all.

Some are reluctant to use such popular donors, whose sperm is likely to be used by 10 to 20 families before being retired, depending on bank policy. Others worry that a child who grows up with expectations of having contact with the donor will end up disappointed—either with what they discover, or what they don't.

Many don't feel comfortable accepting the agreement of a man whose life likely will change in unforeseen and substantial ways over 18 years. Rather than infringe on the privacy of the man and his family, an anonymous donation makes it a clean break.

A few women admit that, deep down, they are threatened by the idea that a relationship might someday develop between donor and child, and prefer to keep the family structure more clear. A TSBC survey reported that nearly 44 percent of its respondents who did not choose an open-identity donor did so because they preferred no contact. Comments included "not wanting to consider the donor as a person" and "not wanting the donor to assume a parental role."[8]

Author comment
There are valid reasons Thinking Women might be reluctant to use open-identity donors. But in my view, the donor and parent are affected less by this decision than the child, who typically is interested in asking identity questions, rather than finding another parent. If the child is someday interested in learning more, I believe it's better for the Choice Mother to be an ally in the search for information than to be perceived as someone who didn't think it should matter or who was trying to protect the donor or child.

On the availability front, the stronger the demand for open donors, the more effort banks will put into recruitment. The sales director of one sperm bank told me she is interested in learning more about the needs of Thinking Women. She said an informal in-house survey revealed that the 20 most popular donors at their bank were open-identity, or had an adult photo, or both.

The TSBC survey found that open-identity status was second only to physical appearance of the donor (generally matching to family) in importance during the selection process.[9]

As more people request donors who are open to revealing information to offspring, banks will work even harder to make them available. Within a year of launching its open-identity program in 2004, one-third of California Cryobank donors were open to contact.[10]

Finding siblings

Another option available to donor-conceived children is to find half-siblings through websites such as the Donor Sibling Registry (www.donorsiblingregistry.com). In its first five years, the registry grew to 4,400 members, with more than 700 matches of half-siblings.

When her son was only a few months old, Teresa was in contact with three families who had daughters using the same donor's sperm (identifiable by his number). "I wasn't sure how I would feel about this, or how much contact I would want with these families, but after hearing from two families and seeing photos of two of the girls, I was surprised at how much happiness I felt," she said. "It was both strange and wonderful to see little faces that bear a resemblance to my son's. I have no idea where this path will take us, but I'm glad I did it, and I look forward to contact with other families as well."

When open-identity children "come of age"

Another TSBC research study by Joanna E. Scheib (available in detail on the bank's website)[11] revealed that the teenagers born of its Identity-Release program, who were nearly old enough to seek information about the donor, tended to be curious—not resentful—about their donor. All 29 teens in the study said they felt loved and wanted by their family.

Nearly all of them wanted to see a photo of the donor, and most were interested in what his current life was like, what his health was, and more about family history. Most did not intend to make immediate contact, but thought they might write a letter or go through the sperm bank to get more information when the time came. [In fact, only 15 of its eligible 120 children, in 2005, had thus far requested information.][12] Most reported that contact would be helpful to learn more about what the donor was like, with two-thirds saying that it might help them learn more about themselves.

Scheib and colleagues also interviewed 27 of its donors who had the potential to be contacted by offspring soon. Most were between 35 and 45 years old, in committed relationships, and about half had their own children. Most were curious about the pending identity process, and only two regretted being an Identity-Release(sm) donor. More than half had concerns about the unknown, such as what the offspring would want from them. About a third were concerned that the offspring would be resentful about their origins, although in reality this was not the case.[13]

One story featured on "60 Minutes" in July 2003 involved an 18-year-old girl who was allowed to meet her donor (himself a child of adoption who eventually developed a relationship with his biological father). After requesting a letter from the girl to explain why she wanted to meet him, her family and his family (which then included a wife and young son) met.

Although the donor was receptive, he and his wife decided that if another child contacted them, they would provide only medical records, since the experience was emotionally draining. *[See Chapter 12 for examples of other meetings with donors that raised issues.]*

FROM: SUSAN, A DONOR-CONCEIVED THINKING WOMAN

When Susan was 27, her mother told her she had been conceived by an anonymous sperm donor. Prior to that, Susan, a single lesbian, had spent months talking to her mother about insemination options before her mother's "cognitive dissonance apparently reached a breaking point." As someone on both sides of the donor equation, with strong opinions about it, Susan offered her story for this book.

On what she'd like to know about her donor
I know nothing about the donor my parents used. There were no donor catalogs or medical histories or long profiles in 1967. The infertility doctor told my mother he would use a "dark, Eastern European" medical student to match my father. I have no idea if he did this.

Although I recognize the value of an accurate medical history, what I most want to know is "what he's like." If you gave me a choice of medical history going back four generations and a half-hour conversation with him, I would take the conversation without hesitation. Is he like me? Am I like him? What are his other children like? What kind of a person is he?

On using a donor herself
I spent a long time trying to find the right known donor among my friends because I really did not want to use a sperm bank. I thought it would be great to have one of my wonderful male friends as the donor and the child would have another person who loved them in his/her life. It was complicated and expensive — legal contracts, having people show up on very short notice for months. But in the end, there were infertility issues. I'm 36 and I really, really want to have a

The first donor meeting of a Choice Mom

Christine was 18 when she met her open-identity donor, Phillip, in 2003. Her mother Mary was a librarian and Choice Mother who used The Sperm Bank of California. As Mary told CBS's "The Early Show" at the time, pictures of the donor seen earlier didn't show much of a resemblance. But when she and her daughter met Phillip in person, "The eyes, goodness, it's like looking at her eyes in someone else's face. And they have smiles that are alike. I was amazed."

According to a *Los Angeles Times* story, donor and offspring both have gregarious personalities. "I'm completely outgoing and spontaneous," Christina said.

---

baby. So, now I am working with a sperm bank that has a large selection of open-identity donors as well as Jewish donors. It's not my first preference, but I think it strikes a decent balance. I can only hope that my child will have compassion about my choices, just as I had compassion for my mother's. And if not, that's parenting, right? May I be blessed with such problems as soon as possible.

On the ethics of donor anonymity

We know that many adoptees search for their birthparents. Not all, but many. And not only the unhappy ones — some people just feel the need to know these things. Because so many adopted people grew up and wanted to search, we have changed public policy on this issue. We have open adoptions, we have systems in place to help people with search and reunion. It is a recognized part of the adoption process — that there are feelings about the birth family. Some states, like Oregon, have opened sealed adoption records, recognizing that the child has a RIGHT to know their parentage. Why do we have to start at square one with gamete donation when we already know all of this? Giving away your sperm or eggs is not like donating blood. Blood does not become a person with feelings, and desires, and identity.

> *It's very frustrating to me when people say that biological connections should not matter. If biological connections do not matter, why are you going through this much trouble just to conceive your own child?*

There are lots of children that need homes. You are trying to have your own child because biological connections matter. Why should biological connections matter less to me than they do to you?

continued

I don't understand what people are afraid of [if I were to meet my donor]. The worst that could happen is that I don't like him or he doesn't like me. Okay. Why can't we make that decision as adults instead of being bound by a decision made 36 years ago by a doctor who is now dead?

Remember that children don't sign the contracts about anonymity. We didn't make that choice and are not bound by it. As adults, we can make our own choices. We have the right to want things. We may not get them, but don't tell us that we shouldn't want them.

My feelings about this crystallized after joining an online group of dozens of people who are donor-conceived. I became much more judgmental about anonymity than I had been before. I began to see it as a very bad practice, and a violation of the child's rights.

I am the only person in the group that I am aware of who has infertility problems, so no one else is in the same situation as their parents—wanting children and being unable to conceive. I think some of them lack compassion, seeing only their own pain. It's hard to say how much of that is tied up into the fact that almost all of us were lied to. It's hard to separate what is the anonymity and what is the lying. That's part of why I'm eager for this next generation of donor-conceived children to grow up. They will have a lot to tell us about what matters to them and I'm very interested in listening.

On the limited pool of open-identity donors
I know that many sperm banks don't carry open-identity donors. All of my lesbian friends in Washington State, where there are good laws to protect gay families, have chosen to use men they know personally as donors. But all of my friends in Ohio, where gay families are in more danger, have used anonymous sperm banks. People go to the one infertility clinic in town that is the least homophobic and that clinic happens to work with an anonymous sperm bank. Open-identity donors are not even suggested.

The entire focus of most infertility clinics is "curing" the infertility, getting you pregnant. I understand the desire for a good selection. I just think it pales in

Choosing Single Motherhood © Mikki Morrissette

comparison to the possible needs of the child. There are many high-quality sperm banks with a good selection of open-identity donors that ship all over the country. I really think it's worth the extra money in order to be able to say to your child, "I thought you might want to know."

Although it's not like open-identity donors are perfect. The bank I'm using allows up to 20 families to conceive with one donor. So, there could easily be 30 half-siblings. I think that's too many.

> *All that said, look, sometimes people can't know things they want to know. We're rarely born into the circumstances we would have chosen as adults. I try not to judge individuals for their choices.*

I am far more angry at the system than I am at individual people making individual choices in their lives.

On the emotions of donor-conceived kids

In general, it's fair to say that people with strong, loving, positive relationships with their parents seem to enact love and compassion around this issue, and those with weak, traumatized, and problematic relationships tend to enact trauma and pain. So, I'm sure that the general health of the family has some effect.

I do wonder if it's largely a question of personality. Some kids spend lots of time wondering things like "Who am I?" "What is my task in the world?" I was always that kind of kid. Other kids would rather run outside and play and not worry about that stuff. Thank God there are people like that in the world because if everyone were like me, the world would have a serious fun deficiency.

On advice to Choice Moms

You can feel bad that you don't have all the information your child might seek, you can feel bad that you could not conceive [the way] you originally wanted, but do not make apologies about using DI or the conception will be seen as something shameful. Work through whatever emotions you have so that you can convey that you wouldn't trade your child for anyone in the world.

"Definitely a wild child. He's a really positive person. Our chemistry just clicked. I think we can be really good friends."[14]

Phillip—who has bungee-jumped and fire-walked in a motivational seminar—said he had long hoped to be able to find out how any of his offspring turned out, and thought it only fair that they know him. During the meeting, he and Christina talked about their mutual love of reggae music.

Mary hoped her daughter and donor would be able to forge a type of long-term relationship. "Any kid who can get more love from wherever, I'm all for it. As long as love is healthy, it's wonderful."

Who Are the Donors?

Views about donors vary among Choice Mothers, from those who feel he is simply a provider of material to those who are appreciative of his gift and wish they had the opportunity to thank him personally. Some parents—single and married—have no interest in the donor in the beginning, but curiosity develops as their child grows and exhibits a few unrecognizable traits.

Wellesley researcher Rosanna Hertz reported that one single mom said of her donor,

---

SPEECH EXCERPT
WHAT OUR CHILDREN NEED
BY JENIFER FIRESTONE

The founder of the Boston-based Alternative Family Matters, which provides advocacy and counseling for lesbian and gay families, offered these comments at a discussion about lesbian artificial insemination. Her comments were about lesbian mothers, but what she said is applicable to any Choice Mom.[16]

Many DI offspring have very little curiosity or concern about a biological father that is a non-entity in their lives. They say that they don't miss having something they never had in the first place. The fact that lesbian moms tell their children frankly, but age-appropriately, about the nature of their conception early on in their lives eliminates negative feelings born of secrecy or misleading the child.

On the other hand, some children are almost obsessed with the daddy question

---

Choosing Single Motherhood © Mikki Morrissette

"Initially I didn't talk about him much…and I didn't really want to treat him as a person but just a sperm donor. But as time went on…I changed my attitude about the whole thing and began to see it more as [my daughter is] half adopted."[15]

So who are the donors? And what can a Choice Mother tell her child about the unknown person who helped create his or her life?

Sperm donation is much more complicated than sitting in a room with a magazine and a cup, then walking out with cash. Donors are highly probed and tested before they are allowed into a program. As Alice Ruby, executive director of The Sperm Bank of California, explained, their donors go through an extensive screening procedure. "Men hoping to donate sperm must provide blood, urine and semen samples to be tested for transmissible diseases such as HIV, hepatitis, and syphilis, and for genetic conditions such as Cystic Fibrosis and Tay Sach's," she told me.

"They complete a long questionnaire about their personal health history and health habits, and a four-generation health history detailing the health status of their relatives including their parents, grandparents, siblings, children, aunts, uncles and cousins. Potential donors also must go through a physical exam and a very detailed HIV risk assessment interview. Becoming a donor takes eight to ten weeks on average. Contrary to popular assumptions, men do not donate semen casually."

from a very early age, and experience a persistent and unabating curiosity about their donor, inherited physical traits, or other characteristics.

The issue for lesbians considering anonymous donor insemination is that one cannot know in advance which way their child will feel. In making the known vs. anonymous donor decision, I used to feel that prospective lesbian mothers could only do what they were most comfortable doing and then be prepared to explain to the child why they had them the way they did, and help their child through whatever daddy/donor-related feelings they may or may not have over the years.

The more I talk to these children, and the more research I read about children conceived through anonymous donor insemination, the more I've changed my thinking about this. Bill Cordray, a national and international advocate for children conceived through anonymous DI believes that DI should be approached like open adoptions. Ideally, he says there should be no anonymous donor insemination — that every DI offspring should have access to extensive information about their donor, and some access to the donor as well.

Will donors stop giving?

Some countries have made it mandatory to use open-identity donors. The United States is not likely to enter this debate anytime soon. One common concern of those opposed to the option is that donors are involved primarily for money, and will stop donating if they are required to take some responsibility for answering questions of offspring in later years.

The Sperm Bank of California conducted an in-house survey of donors in its Identity-Release(sm) program:[17]

- 48 percent felt the offspring had the right to know the donor's identity;
- 32 percent said they would be curious about the offspring;
- 20 percent said that if they were donor offspring they would want to have the option to know.

WHAT DONATING HAS MEANT TO ME
excerpted by permission of Donor Conception Network

The author of this story learned about donor insemination as a college student, when he saw an advertisement offering money to help infertile couples become parents. He did his own research, and learned that 1 in 10 couples had trouble conceiving, and decided to be of assistance.

I'll never forget how apprehensive and embarrassed I was walking into the clinic on my first appointment. I couldn't have become a donor if I thought that I was being paid for my "services," and I find it difficult to understand how anyone can commit themselves to a fairly de-humanizing and stressful process for a measly amount of money. I feel sure that even if most donors expect payment, the majority are primarily motivated for altruistic reasons.

I know that many find it difficult to understand how anyone can become a donor knowing that their contributions will be used to create individuals genetically related to them of whom they will have no knowledge. During my counseling I had to confront this reality, but I never let it faze me because I was clear that the reason I wanted to become a donor was to give others the opportunity to have children. In any case, donating in the impersonal and sterile setting of a clinic doesn't allow you to form any personal attachment to any new life that can be

In 2005, a United Kingdom clinic asked 32 donors (who are not paid) if they would continue to donate under the new open-identity requirement. Half said yes, one-quarter said no, and the rest were undecided.[18] The suggestion tends to be that if sperm banks invest in counseling, and recruit men with altruistic goals, donors will continue to be available.

Choosing a Donor

In the "dark ages" of insemination, even less than two decades ago, doctors decided where to get sperm for insemination, and the parent(s) had no choice in the matter. In many countries today, in fact, the woman still has no choice of donor—a laboratory specialist does the selecting.

---

created as a result.

Pleased as I am to think that my contributions may make a positive difference to some families, I still have my regrets. I will never know anything about anyone born from my donations. I often have found myself wondering whether their parents have told them of the circumstances of their conception. I wonder what any person conceived as a result of my donations thinks of me, if anything, and how their lives might develop.

The question of anonymity
The issue of donor anonymity raises all sorts of issues for me. I'm acutely aware of the distress caused to donor offspring by denying them information about their genetic parentage. Denying them such information offends their dignity and must make it all the more difficult for them to achieve a sense of completeness. Anonymity also devalues the contribution of donors and depersonalizes them. It allows them to be dismissed as men who sold their sperm for money.

Despite all this though I still remain in favor of preserving donor anonymity. The absence of information given to donors about persons conceived with their help makes me feel ill equipped to deal with the frightening prospect of being confronted by any of my offspring in the years to come. Such contact would have immense implications for me and for any future family I may have.

ABOUT BEING KNOWN

excerpted by permission of the Xytex Corp. sperm bank

This donor provided sperm to make extra cash. He had a pregnant wife, was working 50 hours a week, and learned he could make $50/week from donating. His wife agreed that he enter the program, which involved five months of screening before any money was involved. After his son was born, he remained a donor. "The money wasn't as important any more, but the realization that I was helping others to have what I had appealed to me."

Although I have been open about being a donor, I strongly believe in the right for a donor to be anonymous. I have provided a great deal of information about me and my family. I served as the purveyor of biological material. That is where my responsibility ends. But I have my concerns. I am concerned about children being born into houses with one parent, or houses with no father figure at all. I am concerned about fathers feeling detached from their children. I am concerned about children raised with a lie—never knowing how they came into the world.

Recently I was asked if I was willing to become an identifiable donor. I would talk with the parents and answer questions, but I would not be required to meet them or have any involvement with them or the child. I was emotionally ambivalent about the process. Until recently. A baby has been born. One day, he may wish to meet me. I have agreed to do that for him, and I will honor that promise. But I won't do this again.

If you are thinking about using a donor, please know that we are not mercenaries out for a quick buck. Some of us genuinely care about and are concerned about the children we help you produce. But don't hate us because we don't want to be involved with you and the child.

Choosing Single Motherhood © Mikki Morrissette

Nowadays, long profiles are available at most sperm banks, revealing extensive details about the occupations, education and personalities of the donor and several layers of relatives, to give a greater picture of a family's gene pool. Most banks provide profiles with three-generation medical histories. Many include essays from the donor about why they donated, as well as messages to offspring.

Other services offered by some include:
- photo-matching services, in which the bank selects a donor resembling the submitted photo of, say, a family member;
- online photos of the donor as an adult or baby;
- live audio interviews with donors who answer pre-submitted questions from the recipient;
- results of personality assessment tests;
- staff impressions of donors;
- videotaped interviews with the donor.

Policies vary considerably among sperm banks and clinics. As Arthur Caplan advised, "You have to shop carefully. Don't just take the one down the street."

1. Doing the research

Excellent resources for comparing and choosing doctors, sperm banks, treatment options and much more can be found at websites such as www.theafa.org (American Fertility Association), FocusonFertility.org, and FertilityPlus.com.

Sample questions for banks, for example, include: How many offspring are allowed before a donor's sperm is retired? How does the bank plan to keep records of donors and recipients in the long-term? What counseling is provided, for client and donor? Will they allow you to work with the bank of your choice?

One counselor I talked to recommended working with banks that can help you make a plan: if home insemination doesn't work after a few cycles, for example, Plan B will take effect. Otherwise many cycles can go by without success.

Another suggested considering philosophy: Do you want to work with a bank that has a "feel-good" approach to the process, or who caters to the "alternative lifestyle," compared to others that might seem more clinical? Do you want to work with a bank that will allow you to inseminate at home? Or do you simply want to register with several banks at once to find the donor that works?

2. Narrowing the field

Deciding on the "right" donor is a personal decision that varies considerably among single women. One woman I know purposely chose an older man with an existing family, to help insure his comprehension of what his donation meant. Another Choice Mom invited her closest girlfriends over to vote on her potential candidates, using her existing network to be part of the process from the start. Some women report picking donors they might have wanted as a mate.

One organized woman used a bank with donors who supplied photos, audio interviews, temperament sorters, as well as a long profile—and narrowed her selection to only those men who supplied all four. She read their free short profiles until she had only two remaining choices. After purchasing full packages of information for those two men, she made her choice based on how their essays "felt" to her.

SURVEY SAYS: BEING ABLE TO CONTACT THE DONOR

A study led by J. E. Scheib, of the University of California—Davis and research-intensive TSBC, explored the perspective of parents whose teenagers had Identity-Release(sm) donors.[19] Almost 80 percent of its clients request an IR donor, they wrote, reflecting the desire of parents and children to "avoid a possible sense of futility in having incomplete knowledge about the child's origins and the child becoming preoccupied with this lack of information."

Emotions about meeting donors—Most of the Choice Mothers represented in the survey felt that open-identity was the right option for their child to have. About half reported some concern and anxiety as their child neared the age of 18, although none indicated they regretted giving the child the option to receive information about the donor. Concerns included:
  • whether the donor would live up to the child's expectations,
  • the child's reaction if the donor had died,
  • whether the donor would respond if many other offspring had already tried to contact him.

The older child's views—With the child now a teenager (only those with DI children aged 12 to 17 were included in the survey), most parents reported that their child still had no negative feelings about their origins. A common reason for this was thought to be because the parent was honest with the child, and that DI

Choosing Single Motherhood © Mikki Morrissette

Recommendations to consider:

- **If open-identity** is important to you, start with that limited pool.

- If you believe **genetics** plays an important role in a person's personality, make sure you are working with a bank that offers many profiling options. Are you particularly interested in physical characteristics, personality traits, creative talents, athletic skill?

- Do you prefer a donor who believes in a certain set of **values**? If so, use a bank that provides essays for you to assess.

- Do you hope the child looks like you and your family? Many women attempt to increase the odds by finding **similar appearance** factors in a donor, or **shared ethnicity**. One sperm bank counselor said height seems to be an important criteria for many women.

---

was not a major focus—"they had a life outside DI," and "homework [was] more of an issue at this point." Others reported that the child understood that DI was simply part of his or her life, and "did not know any differently."

Other facts that came out of the study:

- Most birth mothers (which included married, lesbian and single women) had told their child of the circumstances of their birth by the age of 6, with the average age being 4.8.
- Almost all parents (nearly 91 percent) said they expected or knew their child was curious about the donor, with almost two-thirds reporting that the child looked forward to meeting the donor.
- About half (nearly 49 percent) thought their child would want genealogical information, with 42 percent expected to want health information. Parents from six households thought their child would do nothing with the information other than read it and keep it as family history.
- Parents from nearly 83 percent of families thought their child would contact the donor to "learn more about himself or herself/increase sense of identity," and 20.5 percent thought it would help create an ethnic connection.
- Parents from about 47 percent of the households thought their child might want a relationship, generally depending on what the initial contact was like.
- The three top questions listed by the children were: "What is the donor like?" "Is he like me?" "Can I meet him?" All but one wanted a picture of him.

- Check **medical history** for special concerns you might have.

- Most banks **retire a donor's sperm** to reduce the potential for too many children coming from the same donor. Some women purchase multiple vials to assure availability for many attempts. Others pay to store these for future use in creating siblings.

Some women consider choosing the donor to be the uncomfortable equivalent of genetic pre-selection, or are suspicious of the honesty of the profiles, and don't put much thought into the selection process. Others believe the way the child is raised is more significant than genetics. Still others look but do not find a "perfect" donor, and end up choosing from a list of options. As one woman said, for her the donor choice ultimately was a minor part of the motherhood process.

Of course, any child's inheritance is imprecise. Picking donor traits may seem logical or fun to some, but should never be considered true science. Your child will be the one you were meant to have.

The Process

Many women are optimistic that the first insemination attempt will work, and then supremely disappointed when they find that they are not pregnant. Many women report this crushing news doesn't get easier, no matter how many times it happens.

The process, described well in other sources and online, can be intensely emotional, requiring you to wait patiently for the right day, fit in a doctor appointment with little notice, look for signs—*I'm feeling bloated, is that good or bad?* Some women need a demanding series of drugs, which makes the process even more difficult. Several women have told me that in retrospect they wouldn't have told as many people as they did about their attempts to conceive, to avoid the repetitive "Are you pregnant yet?" questions. But do find a select few who can offer you moral support, especially those who have been through the insemination process. One woman recommended the online source Fertility Friend (*www.fertilityfriend.com*) for its upbeat circle of single women.

One sperm bank reports that 1 in 12 of its clients who used IVI (the home insemination technique) succeeded in conceiving, compared to 1 in 6 for IUI. Depending on mother's age, cycle regularity, and fertility issues, the American Society for Reproductive Medicine indicates that getting pregnant using frozen

Choosing Single Motherhood © Mikki Morrissette

sperm has a success rate of eight to 15 percent. In general, industry trends indicate it takes four to eight attempts to conceive.

A 2002 research report revealed that, per cycle, IUI had a success rate of 18.5 percent for women under 35, 11.9 percent for women 35 to 40, and 5.4 percent for women over the age of 40. In comparison, timed intercourse succeeds at a rate of roughly 20 percent.[20]

FROM: JEANNE, AN EXPERIENCED SINGLE MOM

As someone who did 13 inseminations, one tubal transfer and seven invitros, I have alot of knowledge I wish someone had imparted before I started the process. For the insemination process, if you haven't gotten pregnant within four cycles (twice for each tube) you need to get more proactive. Your doctor should be monitoring your follicle growth and if you aren't producing eggs you'll need fertility drugs. If after two or three more cycles you haven't gotten pregnant, insems probably aren't going to do it. There may be tubal factors and in vitro may be the best option. It is expensive. This is the point where you want to consider adoption.

If you go the IVF route, check doctors' and clinics' success rates for live birth. My first four attempts were at two hospitals that I later found out had only 20 percent success rates for "chemical pregnancy." I got pregnant with twins at one of them but the fetuses never developed heartbeats and I miscarried. This was recorded as a "successful pregnancy" with this group. Another doctor transferred all 11 embryos at once while I was under general anesthesia, "for a better shot of success." Needless to say, I switched doctors, and clinics. The doctor I eventually used for my first child, and then my twins, had a success rate of 38 percent.

The first two clinics I used were "in-network providers." While for me that didn't cover much, every dollar helps and I didn't know better. But after that, I figured there was only so much my body could handle and I decided I'd rather pay myself and get results.

My first try I had an ectopic pregnancy that ruptured my tube. The silver lining here is that we then knew I had "tubal factor infertility" so I could finally get covered with insurance. The second attempt gave me the first of my three wonderful miracles.

Final Thoughts

Being conceived from donor sperm is not inherently problematic to a child. One study examined the behavior of donor-conceived children, who averaged seven years old. The children who were having behavioral or socialization issues were not significantly affected by biological connection, sexual orientation or relationship status of their parents. Rather, the predominant factor was related to the stress a parent reported simply being a parent.[21]

Donor children, however, can be affected by the realization that they were not created from a physical union between a man and a woman. Research indicates that it is important to convey that the donor is a real person who cares about the child and the mother, even if they've never met. *(We'll learn more about this in Chapter 13.)*

Consider the conversation you will someday have with your child about how and why you chose the donor that you did. If you end up with a donor whose information is sketchy, consider compiling information about donors, such as the essays featured in this chapter. Help create a general profile about the average donor. For example: someone comfortable doing things in a different way, proactive, interested in helping others, confident, open-minded.

I'd also recommend that you actively participate in any available counseling. In a wonderful letter that Emily, a Choice Mom who gave me permission to reprint, wrote to members of the Donor Conception Network, she said in hindsight she might have approached counseling differently.

"My own fears of being judged led me to see it as a hurdle rather than an opportunity," she said. "Now I think it would have been good to talk through some things to which I wasn't giving much thought. I was oblivious to some significant issues. Don't fear raising vague thoughts, fears and questions with the clinic counselor. If they're worth their salt, they shouldn't be telling you anything, only helping you find your own answers. It's important not to ignore the things that are most difficult: at some later stage, you may well have to answer to your child about the same issues."[22]

Chapter 10

Choosing Adoption

Adoption is about finding families for children,
not finding children for families.
— Lee Varon, author of *Adopting On Your Own*

My parents never sat my brother and I down when we were kids to talk about the facts of his adoption—it was simply part of who he was, something we knew at the earliest age. Just as we knew the three boys down the street were adopted, and two of our cousins were adopted. It was not a big deal—no deal at all, really. He never expressed much sentiment about being adopted when we were growing up.

Eventually, though, as adults my brother and I started to have conversations that helped me recognize that adoption was an issue for him—sometimes. His red hair and hunting interests were not the only traits that made him feel like he stood out in our family. He's an outdoorsy, traditional family man who—although quite intelligent—never enjoyed school. Our parents and I are city folk who earned college degrees. We are vocal Democrats; he is an Independent who likes to tease us about his propensity for voting Republican.

From my perspective, over the years he tended to seem disengaged and disinterested in the family. In hindsight, from his perspective he likely felt that the connection between my parents and I excluded him. He occasionally expressed frustration at being "the last to know" family business.

Some of this has likely been the consequence of the tendency for boys and girls to differ in family attachment. But as I researched this chapter—thinking I knew a lot about adoption and discovering I knew nothing—I recognized how much of my brothers' feelings might be attributable to the "genealogical bewilderment" phenomena social scientists had named.

In short, my brother periodically struggled with "how do I fit into this family?" questions that were never spoken out loud, and not debilitating, but there nonetheless. Likely there were things we could have done as a family to soothe any

Choosing Single Motherhood © Mikki Morrissette

identity struggles he was having. But none of us, my brother included, recognized that there was anything to talk about. It took decades—and fatherhood and other events—to realize there was an adoption nerve that sometimes hurt.

The complexities of adoption have been discussed in great detail by excellent resources listed in the back of this book and on the website. For this chapter I have largely used advice from:

1. Lee Varon's book *Adopting On Your Own: The Complete Guide to Adopting as a Single Parent* (which she graciously allowed me to liberally excerpt),[1]
2. Lois Gilman, author of *The Adoption Resource Book*,[2]
3. National Adoption Information Clearinghouse website,
4. Archives of *Adoptive Families* magazine.

In the limited number of pages we have here, the conversation will offer an overview of the adoption process, the costs, and bring up the potential identity issues of adoptive children, including those of transracial adoptions.

The Adoption Debate

After Tara decided to pursue Choice Motherhood, she debated whether to adopt or conceive. As she told me, she wondered whether she should have a child of her own when the world was overpopulated and there were so many children living in orphanages. Yet she also worried what effect it would have on the child to be removed from country, culture and family environment.

Bridget, however, went straight to adoption. She wasn't quite 35 when she made her decision, and others counseled her to wait for the right man and conceive, but fertility statistics about women over the age of 35 scared her.

She didn't want to spend her savings on insemination, not conceive, and then have no money left for adoption.

Many women are clear that bearing a child with the sperm of someone they do not know is of no interest to them, nor do they want the complications of a known donor. Adoption is the clear preference for many. But for others, the choice is not as clear. Some are intimidated by the long waiting lists and grueling selection process involved in adoption. Others worry that the time-consuming scrutiny of home studies, as well as single-parent quotas and agency-controlled referrals, leaves too much arbitrary power in other hands. Still others fear that a birth mother might change her mind.

In my case, I briefly considered adoption for my second child, but ultimately decided that the unknown factor of genetics bothered me. For one, I'm a strong believer in the influence of nature, partly because of adopted children I know who veered considerably from the nurturing they were given. Two (the primary reason), as an avid genealogist I was uncomfortable not knowing the full history of my children. Three, my interest in giving my children the opportunity to see shared characteristics in each other—something I didn't grow up with—led me to use the same known donor.

Yet another woman I know loved the fact that there were unknown genetics at work with her daughter—she was curious to see how the nature/nurture blend was working out, and joked that she was happy to see some of her own inherited traits stop with her.

A note about grieving

Many women turn to adoption after trying to conceive, and need time to grieve the change in plans. A good article on the American Fertility Association (www.theafa. org) website[3] suggests that trying to adopt while continuing infertility treatment can be emotionally draining, and recommends that most women need a point of closure on one before fully engaging with the other.

There are other issues to be considered as well. Adoption book author Dr. Lee Varon is the Choice Mother of two. She was excited about the idea of adoption when she was 14, and as a professional woman years later eagerly adopted a Latino son. It wasn't until she adopted her fair-haired daughter, and started hearing comments such as "she looks just like you," that she felt an unexpected pang. "I realized that I would never experience the feeling of being biologically related to my children. My sadness took me by surprise."

As co-founder of the Adoption Network, she counsels women to explore any deep-seated feelings about not conceiving. As she wrote:

> *"Resolving feelings about not having a child by birth is a process, just as coming to terms with parenting without a partner is a process."*

On the other hand

Although many single women who choose to conceive report being criticized for creating new life rather than adopt an already existing child who needs a parent, there are—as with any choice in life—those who oppose adoption. A few Thinking Women report that family and friends question their decision to adopt rather than conceive, believing it to be better to know more about a child's history, or that a child from an orphanage might have life-long emotional issues, or that the trauma of being "given up" for adoption might be too weighty for the child in later years.

At least one website is devoted to minimizing the incidence of adoption. Believing that the multi-million dollar industry of adoption is leading to black-market trafficking of children, and leads to identity issues that result in a higher rate of imprisonment, this group works to keep kids with their birth families and encourage others to use infertility options.

No matter what method is chosen, there will be pro and con arguments. The important factor for a Choice Mom is to consciously decide that adoption is the right step for her to take—whether it was the first move or not—and prepare for it with eyes wide open.

Phase 1: Deep Thinking

1. About the age of the child

The typical couple or individual is looking to adopt a newborn, so competition is strongest for that age group. Of the more than 21,000 international adoptions in 2003, less than half involved children under the age of one, according to immigration statistics. Of the 119,000 children in U.S. foster care who were waiting to be adopted in 2003, the largest percentage of them (32 percent) were between the ages of 1 and 5. Private, independent U.S. adoptions more commonly involve newborns, but it is sometimes more challenging—although not impossible—for a single parent to get a placement.

2. About race

If you are white, will you feel comfortable raising a non-white child? Are you willing to handle persistent questions, from your child and others if you become the mother to a son or daughter who clearly does not look like you? Would you consider moving to a more diverse neighborhood? Is a Russian child a stronger match for you than a Chinese child?

Jolene, whose daughter is from Guatemala, told me, "I'm clearly of the mindset that there's no shame in being honest about one's abilities. I personally had no problems adopting a child of another race and ethnic background with one big exception — I felt in no way equipped to handle the societal issues of a child with African/African American heritage.

> *"As far as I'm concerned, the child could be green and*
> *I'd have no problems nor would most of my family.*
> *However, I recognize that in this country there are huge*
> *issues around discrimination that as a very WASPY-looking woman I*
> *don't have the understanding or energy to tackle."*

She also recognized that her first assumption—that she would adopt a girl from China—was not the right fit for her. "As shallow as this might sound, I don't like Asian art and culture enough to be excited about it—and I felt this alone would be a huge liability for my child." *(See the end of this chapter for more on this topic.)*

3. About special needs of the child
Are you open to exploring the idea of adopting from the foster care system? Would you be willing to adopt siblings? Is a child with special developmental, behavioral or physical needs someone you would be comfortable with? *(Read the essay about the adoptive mother of two special needs children in Chapter 1 if you haven't already.)*

There are so many children waiting for adoption from U.S. public agencies and the foster care system that single parents tend to be welcome. In fact, singles are sometimes considered an advantage for a child who needs the attentive nurturing, strength of character and less crowded environment of a Choice Mother home.

Numbers: According to a Children's Bureau report, the average age of the more than 500,000 children in foster care is 10. In 2003, 119,000 were looking to be adopted—and had been waiting more than three years for placement. Roughly 35 percent were black and 39 percent were white. Of the 50,000 children who were adopted from the system in 2003, nearly 13,000 were placed with single women.[4]

4. About contact with the birth family
Like any method to motherhood—using a known donor, an open-identity or directed donor, or an anonymous donor—the adoptive parent is single only in lifestyle. No child is the sole "property" of any one parent. Even with married couples, the child has a triangular relationship with the birth family, even if they never meet. Today there are a wide range of relationships adoptive families have with birth

Choosing Single Motherhood © Mikki Morrissette

parents. Some are interviewed and selected by birth mothers in person, some work through attorneys and agencies with no face-to-face contact, some arrange for sporadic contact with the child over the years, others have no contact whatsoever. The relationship you feel most comfortable with has a big impact on the type of adoption you should pursue.

It also makes a difference whether you can tolerate waiting for a birth mother to deliver, with plenty of pre-birth assistance and information-swapping, or whether you prefer to get a referral and wait by the phone or mailbox.

Will you want to share information and photos about the birth family with your child? Will you want to meet the birth mother so you can talk about her later? Are you afraid that a birth mother might change her mind about placement and derail your plans? Are you comfortable "competing" for a child with other candidates?

As Varon warns, "In making a decision regarding the degree of openness of your adoption, try to think of your child and his welfare, but also be aware of yourself and what arrangement you would feel most comfortable with. Nothing is harder than the situation of an adoptive parent who feels pressured to take on a degree of openness he or she is not really at ease with in order to be chosen by a particular birth mother. By the same token, it can be devastating for a birth mother if she has been assured an open relationship and this relationship fails to materialize after the adoption has taken place."

5. About adoption itself

As you explore these fundamental questions, talk to other adoptive parents, parents of multicultural families, and adoption counselors. Read the text that follows to understand identity questions your child might have someday, as well as some of the books listed in the Resources section to help you examine these important issues.

Genealogical Bewilderment

As British researcher H.J. Sant explained in 1964, adopted children can sometimes feel a sense of loss and crisis of identity, generally starting in their teenage years and reappearing at critical junctures during adulthood. This phenomenon, labeled by a predecessor in 1952, is referred to as 'genealogical bewilderment.'[5]

Adoption therapist Dr. Joyce Maguire Pavao has said, "Every young person is trying to figure out who they are not, and who they are. For most children, the people around them are mirrors on which they measure themselves, until the adolescent years. At that point they look in the mirror and see themselves. They become more aware of how different they are. I think it is a complicated process for adoptees during the teen years. They begin to realize that they do not know another person in the world genetically related to them."[6]

Some adoptive children feel a sense of incompletion and disconnection, resulting in sadness, confusion and anger. They might feel a lack of control, that they were never consulted about important matters in their life.

A paper presented at an adoption conference in 2001 reported that one adoptee summed up the feeling like this: *Where did I get my red hair? What nationality am I? What kind of body am I growing into? What talents or special skills are in my family line? What hidden illness might show up in my life? All these questions follow me as I move into adulthood and no one has an answer. I feel like I am walking around with gaps and holes in my life that I cannot fill.*[7]

Lois Melina wrote in *Raising Adopted Children* that 90 percent of adopted children are well-adjusted, according to studies. But every adopted child will need to make sense of what it means to be adopted and will need to understand the influences on her identity twice—in relation to her adoptive family as well as her biological family.[8]

About curiosity

I know many people who were adopted—including a housemate who is deciding whether to contact her possible birth mother, and a cousin who has met hers. Some have been frustrated at not knowing enough about their birth stories. Others aren't interested at all. Many are ambivalent about finding their biological heritage.

When my brother was the 30-year-old father of two young kids, he talked to me for the first time about trying to locate his birth history. Eventually he registered on an adoption site, but never fully followed through on a search. Shortly before his 40th birthday, he received a phone call from a 38-year-old woman who believed she might be his half-sister. She told him that her father, since deceased, had as a teenager impregnated his 15-year-old girlfriend. A boy was born in a particular city on a particular day and placed for adoption through the Catholic agency that my parents used to adopt a boy born on that same day in that same city.

Although my brother is interested in his medical history for the sake of his kids, even now, many months after receiving that phone call, he remains skeptical and

Choosing Single Motherhood © Mikki Morrissette

ambivalent enough that he has done no DNA testing to see if the woman is related to him biologically. Some adoptees want to know more, others do not. Curiosity is healthy, but does not always get acted upon.

According to the American Academy of Pediatrics, a child's interest in biological roots is a sign of healthy emotional growth in the search for identity. One report published in 2002 indicated that feelings of loss might be "more rooted in societal expectations of genetically based attachments rather than in any inherent biological loss." Another study, reported in 2004, found "no evidence that desire to search is the result of poor adoptive family relationships or adolescent maladjustment."[9]

The child's point of view
In the book *Being Adopted: The Lifelong Search for Self*, which we will explore in more depth in Chapter 13, the authors quote children who experience the emotions of adoption in many different ways.[10]

Some express anger at their birth parents, such as a 10-year-old girl who said, "I hate them for what they did. They didn't care enough to keep me. They just gave me away, like I was ugly or something."

A seven-year-old boy said he would punch or drown his birth parents if he could because "they didn't want me and I don't care 'cause they just stink."

Another seven-year-old boy thought his birth parents lost him and might be looking for him. He was mad that adoption people gave him to his adoptive parents because they didn't have a baby.

A nine-year-old girl said, "It isn't fair that they could buy me just because they have more money. Kids should be with their real parents. I'm not a toy or something you just decide to buy."

Others worry that they ate or cried too much, which is why they were placed into an adoptive home.

And still others express no such emotions.

In *Chapter 13: Confronting Identity Issues*, we look at specific and practical ways you can help meet an adoptive child's emotional needs in regards to feelings of belonging and identity. At the end of this chapter we have a special section about transracial adoption issues.

Phase 2: Explore the Expense

There are wide variations in the cost of adoption, depending on the agency and type of adoption you pursue. Consider whether you are receptive to a less expensive adoption from a public agency. If you are open to a "special needs" child—which is defined as someone from a minority group or an older child; someone with physical, developmental or behavioral issues; or paired siblings—you will likely qualify for reimbursements, subsidies, counseling, medical coverage, child care aid and more.

Costs below generally include the cost of a home study (about $1,000 to $3,000), document preparation ($500 to $2,000) and attorney fees ($2,500 to $12,000). Variables are listed. The detailed, up-to-date estimates about costs are available from the National Adoption Information Clearinghouse (*http://naic.acf.hhs.gov/pubs/ s_cost.cfm*) and Adoptive Families (*www.adoptivefamilies.com*), which indicate these **average** typical expenses:

U.S. Foster Care
Domestic public agency fees are minimal (generally under $2,500), or waived. In recent years there has been a greater effort to help the more than 100,000 children who are looking for an adoptive family each year, with roughly half finding placement. Many of these are considered "special needs" children. Hundreds of dollars in subsidy payments are often provided each month, as well as Medicaid coverage. A written agreement will specify financial and medical aid, social services and reimbursements. Asking for a deferred adoption assistance agreement gives the option of seeking funding assistance if the child develops needs that were not noticeable at the time of adoption.

Private Domestic
The National Council for Adoption estimates that more than 20,000 U.S.-born infants are placed for adoption each year. The typical domestic adoption requires post-placement supervision, parent physical, attorney fees, and extensive expenses for the birth parent. Some agencies require psychiatric evaluation of the adoptive parent. Requirements vary according to state law.

Domestic private agency — $5,000 to $40,000-plus (average $12,000). This typically pays for birth-parent counseling, birth expenses, and other agency costs for overhead and temporary post-placement supervision. Some agencies use sliding fee scales based on the adoptive parents' income. If a birth parent is located by the adoptive parent, an agency will often provide these services at a lower cost. Fees can generally be predicted in advance, but vary considerably from agency to agency.

Choosing Single Motherhood © Mikki Morrissette

Domestic independent — $7,000 to $40,000-plus (average $15,000). Some states allow advertising to locate birth parents; others don't allow independent adoptions at all. Check state laws early in the process. The often unpredictable costs are for legal representation of birth and adoptive parents, as well as birth expenses (roughly $7,500, which tend not to be reimbursed for birth parents who change their mind). An experienced lawyer is needed who can help screen and minimize the risks.

DEFINITION OF TERMS

Closed or confidential adoption—The agency makes a match between birth mother, who presumes the agency will find a good home, and adoptive parent; there is little or no contact. This is becoming more rare among private agencies.

Semi-open adoption—Similar to open adoption (described below), although less identifying information is exchanged between birth parent and adoptive parent, and less contact is made between birth parents and child.

Open or cooperative adoption—The birth mother chooses the adoptive parent, with mediation from an agency. Generally there is a pool of prospective applicants to choose from. An agreement can be made for any degree of ongoing contact between child and birth parent—regular, sporadic holidays and birthdays, none. According to one study, however, the type, frequency and individuals involved in the contact typically varies considerably over time.[11]

The open method of adoption is increasingly popular with birth parents. Some estimates are that half of today's roughly 15,000 domestic agency adoptions are open. One study reported that between 1989 and 1999, agencies that offered fully disclosed adoptions had grown from 36 percent to 80 percent.[12]

Note that birth parents are entitled to change their mind about placing the child for adoption. Some speculate that 1 in 10 do, generally before the birth. As of 2005, 18 states have laws that make open agreements legally enforceable. An experienced adoption attorney is essential.

Noted adoption therapist Dr. Joyce Maguire Pavao has written, "The success of open adoption depends on clear boundaries, the participants' respect of each other's roles and responsibilities, and the ability of the adults involved to put their egos aside in order to do what is best for the child."

International

Intercountry private agency and independent — $10,000 to $30,000-plus. The typical international adoption varies considerably according to local law and whether the placement is from a government agency, orphanage, charitable organization, or independent attorney. It costs less to adopt from some countries than others. Expenses include fees for immigration processing. Foreign attorneys, medical professionals, and court fees are usually required. Other variable expenses can include fees for psychological evaluations, translation services, escorts to accompany the child, and a "donation" to the orphanage or foreign agency.

Usually expenses involve travel (and meals, lodging, long-distance phone calls) to process the adoption abroad. Requirements for length of stay and number of trips vary by country. A child's medical care and foster care can be an additional expense. U.S. doctors with familiarity in international adoption can be found at the website for the American Academy of Pediatrics, at aap.org/sections/adoption.

THE NUMBERS

Since 1992, there have been roughly 125,000 adoptions to U.S. families each year. In 2001, about 40 percent of these were adopted from public agencies (up from 18 percent in 1992). More than 15 percent were international adoptions (up from 5 percent in 1992). The remainder were private or tribal adoptions, or children adopted by relatives. The state with the highest number of adoptive parents each year tends to be New York.[13]

Intercountry adoptions have increased significantly over the years. According to the U.S. Department of State, there were 6,536 adopted children brought to the U.S in 1992. By 2004, there were 22,884. China, for the fifth year in a row, was the leading country of origin, with 7,044; Russia continued to be second with 5,865; Guatemala continued to be third with 3,264.

All three countries are open to singles. As of this writing, China and Guatemala require signed statements that the adoptive parent is heterosexual. Adopted Russian children tend to be aged 1-4 when they come to the U.S. Most adopted children from Guatemala are newborns.

Choosing Single Motherhood © Mikki Morrissette

Phase 3: Find Assistance

6. Financial aid

Before despairing about the expense of adoption, check the options available in your state and at your company. There are many incentives designed to help people afford adoption.

Current tax law allows a healthy federal adoption tax credit, which can give you a nice "cash back" option at tax time. For 2005 returns, eligible adoptive parents can qualify for up to $10,630 (receipts often will be checked). The Internal Revenue Service website (www.irs.ustreas.gov/) has up-to-date details. Some states allow tax credits for children adopted from the public child welfare system. And as we've mentioned, many expenses for special-needs children can be reimbursed.

Many large companies offer extra benefits for adoptive families. Human resource departments have details about leave policies, referral services and reimbursements. The National Adoption Center estimates the average expense reimbursement is $3,750—eand can be as much as $10,000 at some places.

Loans, home equity programs and grants are available from many places, including the National Adoption Foundation. Check online resources such as:
- The National Adoptive Information Clearinghouse
- National Endowment for Financial Education website (www.nefe.org/adoption), which offers a booklet of information
- www.adoptionfriendlyworkplace.org
- www.benefitsguides.com
- www.adoptivefamilies.com/adoption-cost.php

7. Seek out adoptive parent groups

Networking with other adoptive parents, online and in local communities, is invaluable. From beginning to end, these experienced peer advisers will offer information about local agencies, social workers, attorneys, pediatricians, therapists, financial aid, post-placement issues, and much more.

Online sources to check, with special support for singles, include:
- AdoptiveFamilies.com
- AdoptionInformation.com
(*www.adoptioninformation.com/directory/singlessupport.htm*)
- Single Parents Adopting Children Everywhere (508-655-5426)
- National Council for Single Adoptive Parents (*www.adopting.org/ncsap.html*)

• National Adoption Information Clearinghouse
(*http://naic.acf.hhs.gov*, or 1-888-251-0075)
• Single Mothers by Choice (SMC-adopt@yahoogroups.com) email list
• SingleMom.com (*www.singlemom.com/RESOURCES)*

"When I was looking for an agency and attorney for international adoption, the best advice I got was to get on email discussion lists," Jolene told me. "There's at least one for every major country and these are, hands-down, the best way to locate an agency that is experienced, reputable and embraces singles."

Phase 4: Start to Focus

8. Narrow the type of adoption you prefer

After you have explored the level of openness you prefer, your capacity for building a multiracial family or raising a special needs child, and the expense you are prepared to absorb, you will be ready to pursue the type of adoption that seems right for you. In general, an **intercountry adoption** will require international travel and extensive paperwork, and will likely involve minimal contact with the birth family.

A few countries do not permit adoption by single parents. Government policy changes frequently. At the moment, China, Russia and Guatemala tend to be flexible

---

ONE CHOICE MOTHER'S STORY: THE DAY I MET MY CHILD

When I was 37, the relationship I was in ended and I cried all day about how I would never have a baby. But I read a story about women who were having children on their own, and realized "why not me too?"

I tried donor insemination first, but after a series of infertility issues I realized that adoption was my obvious next step. I became obsessed with having a baby. One day, a friend called me about a malnourished child at the hospital (no longer an infant) whose birth mother was unable to take care of her. After a frenzied process of paperwork, I was cleared to pursue adoption.

The first time I met this child, she was screaming at the top of her lungs, trying to break ropes the hospital personnel had used to restrain her. I could see in her eyes

---

Choosing Single Motherhood © Mikki Morrissette

about age of the parent and open to singles—although officials in the latter two countries were considering policy changes in 2005. One good place to start research is www.internationaladoptions.org.

A **domestic agency** can be welcoming to single applicants, especially depending on the type of placement preferred. Some are less accepting, but might not come right out and say that. But it is definitely easier than it used to be for singles (and lesbians) to adopt, partly because studies are finding that children raised by singles are as well-adjusted as those in two-parent homes, and that special-needs children were experiencing fewer problems in single-parent homes.[14] You will need to do your homework, be determined about what works for you, and ask an agency how many placements it has made with single parents.

If **public agency** adoption is an option for you, books with biographies of waiting children will jump-start the process. Check your library, or online at the Adoption Resource Exchange for Single People (*www.aresp.net*), National Resource Center for Special Needs Adoption (*www.spaulding.org/adoption/NRC-adoption*) and AdoptUS Kids (*www.adoptuskids.org*).

An **independent** adoption tends to be less restrictive and bogged down with bureaucracy. I know several parents who received a child placement by letting everyone they knew—including gynecologists, social workers and church

---

that she was trying to figure out a way to get out. I picked her up and she stroked my cheek. I was hooked.

It was a struggle for many years. She had trouble sleeping, tended to be hyperactive, and even crawled into the bathtub with me fully clothed because of her need for connection. For me it was a long path of coping, without collapsing, so that I could allow this child to get on with her life. Sometimes I wondered how suburban me got to this point: What am I doing here? But with age, therapy, love and nurturing, she outgrew it all.

I never doubted my decision to become her mother. At times I wondered how we would get through everything together. But I have enormous respect for her, from that moment I saw her trying to break through the ropes. She wanted life, and I became totally absorbed in enabling her to experience it in her unique way.

personnel—become aware of their interest in adopting. If the birth parent and adoptive parent find each other through word of mouth or advertising, an agency might be involved little or not at all. It is imperative to find an experienced attorney, to minimize your risks. It is rare, but possible, for a birth parent to change their mind, within a limited time frame after the birth (many change their mind before the birth). Contact with the birth parents can be extensive; sometimes the adoptive parent is even present for delivery. Check online (*www.adoptivefamilies.com/adoptionlaws*) for up-to-date states rules.

9. Research agencies

The agency you end up selecting will have a huge impact on how much you spend, how smoothly you will get through the home-study phase as a single parent, and what kind of information you will have about your child. You should check out the agency as carefully as they will research you. This is where the experience and referrals of adoptive parents groups play a vital role. As you narrow your list, attend informational meetings by the agency to get a feel for their personnel and services.

Varon recommends that you ask any prospective agency:
   • What kind of family history will they try to secure? (Some adoptions don't include much.)
   • Will they help to get medical and developmental information about the child? (This should be done whether the agency handles it or not.)
   • How many children have they placed with single parents?
   • Where do the children waiting for adoption come from, and how do they assess the placement services of other countries?
   • What services are included in the overall fee, and what are not?
   • How long will you have to decide whether to accept a child?
   • What happens if you change your mind after acceptance?
   • What counseling services are available, for you and the child?
   • Get an itemized estimate, including hidden charges, and wait time.

10. Understand an agency's criteria

Most agencies, domestic and international, have a set of criteria they are looking for in applicants. Many have a small quota of single parents they will place children with each year. One U.S. agency that specializes in the placement of Chinese girls, for example, accepts first-come, first-served applicants who meet this criteria: aged 30-50, with one or no children in the home, minimum of $30,000 income, in excellent physical and mental health, with documentation stating their sexual orientation is heterosexual.

Choosing Single Motherhood © Mikki Morrissette

Although it is legal in all U.S. states for single people to adopt, and generally for gays and lesbians to adopt *(see Chapter 15 for exceptions),* that does not mean that an agency will consider the loving and stable home of a Choice Mom to be suitable, even if they cannot say so. Some will go through many intensive steps with you—including home study—only to drop the ball when it comes time to find a referral. Ask upfront how many children the agency has placed in single-parent homes.

In general, most domestic agencies are looking for candidates who are at least 25 years old and show stability, maturity and flexibility. With single parents they'll want to see a solid plan for child care, support and role models. A large income and home ownership are not required.

TIP: DON'T PAY UPFRONT

The bulk of payment is usually required after an actual assignment to a child has been made and accepted. Be suspicious of anyone who might be preying on the vulnerabilities of a single woman eager to be a mother.

---

11. Find an attorney

It is advisable to consult with your own attorney—you want a lawyer who is protecting your interests, not the agency's. A good source is the American Academy of Adoption Attorneys (*adoptionattorneys.org*).

Phase 5: Prepare Yourself

12. The home study

Beyond the underlying requirements of an agency, there are certain things every adoption process will examine closely in a home study, which takes from three to six months to complete. Independent private adoptions are usually less extensive, and every state varies in its requirements. Some private adoptions require only a post-placement home study. The process involves extensive written comments and face-to-face interviews with one person or a group.

Many people worry that this part of the process is a close scrutiny of flaws, but it is also an opportunity for any reputable agency or social worker to help prepare prospective parents for the adoption experience. The home study will look into your full family, religious, educational and professional background. It will examine your neighborhood, home and community ties, as well as your health, support network, and financial situation. According to Varon, the social worker may ask for honest answers to questions such as:

- your experience with children (it's not required)
- how you plan to balance work and family life
- what male role models might be available
- why you are adopting
- your relationship history and sexual orientation
- how you will discuss adoption with your child
- your discipline and parenting philosophies
- what you will do in the event of disability
- whether you will have a will and guardian in place
- childcare and emergency plans
- job flexibility and availability of parental leave

In the end, the home study agents want to see that you are resolving issues, confronting fears, committed to adoption and realistic about parenthood. Review your home study report afterward to weed out any errors. This report often can be used with other sources if your original agency is unable to place a child with you. If you are rejected after a home study, get a reason in writing if possible. Other agencies you may try will want to know why you were rejected. If you believe your sexual orientation or your marital status might become part of an unstated reason, Varon recommends that you talk to the agency director about withdrawing your application before it is officially turned down.

Be open to advice from your social worker, who might help you uncover emotions you have not yet allowed yourself to explore, such as whether you are "grieving the childhood dream" of a two-parent family, or are unhappy about being unable to conceive, or are concerned about adopting a child from a culture that is not your own. In many cases, it might simply take time to work through these issues and does not mean the door is permanently closed.

13. Paperwork
The paperwork is intense, particularly for intercountry adoptions, since there are two countries to satisfy. You will likely need the record of your home study, your birth certificate, medical clearance, divorce decree if applicable, letters of reference, employer financial information, tax returns, bank statements, photos of your home, criminal record clearance, copies of passports.

Choosing Single Motherhood © Mikki Morrissette

BOOK EXCERPT

IF YOU ARE A LESBIAN
by Lee Varon, Adopting on Your Own

You need to decide whether to disclose your sexual orientation to your agency. If you adopt internationally, it is imperative that if you are open with your agency, your agency is willing to word your home study obliquely so it will be acceptable to the officials in the other country. Although it is legal to omit information (don't ask/don't tell), it is illegal to lie if you are asked a direct question. To do so can be grounds for denying the adoption.

Whether you decide to come out in your home study is an entirely individual choice. You'll need to consider several factors. First, you will need to determine the laws in your particular state. Even if there is no law in your state that precludes lesbians and gay men from adopting, some agencies and social workers may still be discriminatory; therefore you will need to get a sense of the political and social climate of an agency before you make your decision about how open you want to be.

As Felicia reflects: "Finally I decided that for me it was important to be myself and be able to discuss the issues that relate to sexual orientation and how that would affect my parenting and my child's life. I did a lot of homework before I picked an agency and a social worker with whom I could be myself. But in the long run it paid off. The home study was a breeze, and my adoption went smoothly." *See Varon's book (listed in Resources) for more details about this issue.*

14. The waiting game
Many Choice Mothers recommend waiting before you tell many people your plans, or you will have months of tedious "have you heard yet?" questions. The process of getting from home study to placement generally takes from six months to two years whether adopting domestically or independently. It can take that long to find a birth mother in independent adoptions as well. In some cases, the referral might come faster, but the paperwork doesn't.

15. After referral
With an international referral, Varon recommends that you try to get a videotape with sound of the child. "Is the child talking? Responding to speech? How does the child interact with other people in her environment? If the child is in an orphanage,

do your best to find out what her preplacement history was. It is a good idea to show the videotape and whatever medical records you are able to obtain to a pediatrician who specializes in adoption." She also details psychosocial history questions you should get answered, including: *How many moves has the child experienced, why did the moves happen, and how did the child react? What methods of discipline has the child experienced? Does the child have siblings, and if so, where are they? How does the child interact with peers?*

Especially if you are adopting an older child, get a full history, including any issues related to abuse, neglect or drug and alcohol use. Whatever the age, you'll want a pediatrician familiar with adoption to check developmental and medical issues. Check the website *www.fwcc.org/doclist.htm* for experienced medical professionals.

She also writes: "You should never be pressured to take a child whom you feel uncomfortable parenting. In one study, one of the strongest positive predictors was the adoptive parent's feeling that the placement was 'a good match.' Although I was ambivalent about adopting, once I received an assignment I would have gone to the ends of the earth (and almost did) to bring both of my children home. Trust your gut feeling about this, and try not to react to the pressure of being told that if you don't accept a particular assignment, you may not get another one for a long time."

BOOK EXCERPT

THE SERENDIPITY OF ADOPTION
BY LEE VARON, ADOPTING ON YOUR OWN

Adoption is a miracle just as birth is. I believe there is a reason we are led to adopt a particular child at a particular time and in a particular place. Once you have made the decision to adopt, hold fast to the belief that somewhere in the world there is a child waiting for you and that eventually you will meet. I have heard countless stories of people who lost assignments and were devastated. Eventually they did adopt, and all of them have come to feel there was a reason for their previous disappointments, and that they ended up adopting the child they were meant to parent. Although the road might seem bumpy at times and you might even hit some dead ends, have faith that the child for you is out there, and in time you will be together.

Choosing Single Motherhood © Mikki Morrissette

Bonus Section

Transracial Adoption

The transracial family has two separate issues to address: loss of birth culture, and absence of genetic identity. As with everything in this book, challenges are not meant to be ignored or denied, but to be acknowledged and tackled with honesty.

Adoption experts agree that ignoring the differences between a parent's race and a child's race is not helpful. A multicultural family needs to have a multicultural approach to life. There will be issues and there will be conflicts. The Choice Mom who builds a transracial family needs to be prepared to embrace this inevitability in order to deal with it in a healthy way.

There is bias and prejudice in every community, and the adoptive parent of a non-Caucasian child will need to help her child confront it. It is a very hurtful and often demeaning place to be, and it can be difficult to find the words to explain it or resolve it with a child. The balancing act of helping a child prepare, while not overburdening them with self-consciousness about skin color, is difficult.

"Most people believe they are aware of racial issues, but a large majority don't have as clear an understanding as they are going to need," Amanda Baden, a New York City psychologist, told me. For some people, their "differentness" from others—sexual orientation, for example—can be hidden. But a child growing up in a community, and extended family, in which no one else looks like them can be extremely difficult.

Cheri Register, author of *Beyond Good Intentions: A Mother Reflects on Raising Internationally Adopted Children,* said in an online conversation with members of the "As Simple as That" community,[15] "What I have come to feel most sorely is what one daughter calls her 'perpetual foreigner' status. It comes clear in the stupid questions people ask, like 'Where are you from?' or 'How did you learn to speak English so well?' The notion that they don't really belong here turns Asian Americans invisible—in public life and in popular culture. It still hurts to think how excited my daughter was about buying her first *Teen* magazine and how she thumbed through it looking in vain for the Asian faces. I encouraged her to write to the editor, which she did. I truly believed she'd get a response, which she didn't."

Baden was adopted from Hong Kong and has extensive experience with members of transracial families as a therapist and adoption researcher. She suggests that the goal is not for the parent to simply decide she will cope with issues as they arise. "I don't encourage prospective parents to get past this," she told me. "Some people turn to international adoption because they think it gives them more options to become a parent, but convenience, or altruistic goals, are not enough to sustain that relationship over time. If someone is questioning their ability to confront issues of race before an adoption takes place, that's a good thing to know. It might be a good idea to parent a child who is not so different from you. Often, my advice is to look somewhere else."

Register offered these tips:
- If you would never consider living for a time in a certain country and can't imagine marrying a person of that ethnicity, then don't adopt a child from that country either.
- Read, listen, learn. Be humble about your aspirations as a parent and be ready to hear what adult adoptees and older parents have to tell you.
- Stay in touch with other adoptive families.
- Especially when your child is a teen, listen to them and be grateful whenever they confide in you, even if what they say makes you uncomfortable. They may scream at you and dump on you, especially if they trust you not to run away.

In the end, Register said, "What do we parents want most of all for our children? Is it happiness? Security? Success? A kind heart? Their achievement of these goals requires confidence about who they are and a place of comfort and safety in a world where many people ignore, stereotype, misperceive, fear, or even hate them because of the way they look. How will we help them mature if the mention of race makes *us* uncomfortable or defensive? To raise children of a race different from ours, we need to come to terms with ourselves as racial beings."

Choosing Single Motherhood © Mikki Morrissette

How We Are Creating Our Multicultural Family
From: Leslie

I adopted my two girls from China. I have had people make comments to me that I 'rescued' my daughters and brought them to a 'better life.' This doesn't take into account what they left behind: family, language, culture. I try to drop pebbles along the way to encourage them to share their feelings. And there are many ways that we have incorporated Chinese heritage into our lives, even in our modest Midwestern community, such as:

1. We have artwork and other mementos from China on display in our home. I have been careful to intermix these with other pieces from my travels as well as multigenerational family photos etc. I don't want my house to look like a Chinese museum, but I do want it to reflect the girls' cultural heritage. I want it to just be a natural part of who we are as a family.

2. Both girls attend Chinese language and dance classes.

3. We celebrate Chinese New Year by decorating our home as traditionally as possible and going out for a special dinner. We also participate in the Chinese New Year event sponsored by our local chapter of Families with Children from China.

4. I have at least a dozen books, both fiction and nonfiction, about China, its folklore, and adoption from China that are readily available for the girls to look at and ask me about.

5. Each year on the anniversary of their adoption, we go out for a Chinese dinner at which the girls receive one of 18 small gifts I purchased for each of them when I was in China adopting them.

In addition, I plan to return to China with the girls in the next five to seven years. I want them to have a foundational knowledge of where they came from before they hit adolescence.

THE VELVETEEN MOTHER

BY KATHRYN B. CREEDY

excerpted by permission of the author
originally published in The Washington Post, May 10, 1998

"Now this is real," I thought, flexing my stiff hand as I finished stitching the numerous patches onto my daughter's Brownie sash. My mind had drifted back to an encounter on the train that morning, when a seat mate noticed I was reading *Adoptive Families* magazine. She had all the usual questions of someone unfamiliar with adoption: Where were my two daughters from? How old were they when they arrived? How old are they now?

Then the conversation took another typical turn. "I don't know how anyone can give up a child," the woman offered. "I just can't imagine. Do you know why their real mothers gave them up?"

I've always met that question with a lighthearted response. "I feel pretty real," I said, leaving the next move to her.

Usually, when faced with that question, I try to discuss what it means to be a parent — not an adoptive parent or a stepparent, but what it really means to parent a child. As families have changed in the past few decades, society also is struggling for a definition.

"I mean the birth mothers," she said. "Why would they give them up?"

I decided to answer her question by educating her on the etiquette of adoption, a speech I'd repeated many times. "I'm so glad they made adoption plans," I said. "It was the answer to all my dreams. All I know is their birth mothers were very great women to do what they did, and I thank God for them every day."

I went on to gently explain that the girls' adoption stories were theirs to share, not mine. I also said that if my daughters were with us, I was sure they would tell those stories. Because we are all proud of our family history, unusual though it is.

I've been a mother since 1991, when I brought my oldest daughter home from Romania at the age of 14 months. Like many other women in this decade, I became a mother on my own. At 39, with no marriage on the horizon and my career firmly in place, I wanted children. But unlike some "Murphy Browns," I wanted parenthood without pregnancy.

Adoption was my first choice for many reasons, the most important of which was that pregnancy didn't look fun. Delivery looked even less fun. Second, I had no special investment in my own genetics. I knew genes provided no guarantees, because there are none in life or with children.

I knew how deeply I could love a child the moment I met my 2-week-old nephew, Matthew. He showed me what I was missing. I knew that any child I adopted would be my own regardless of how she joined the family.

As one of four children, I also knew I wanted to adopt more than one. And so, in 1993, my other daughter arrived. She was 5 months old — three years younger than her sister — and came from the Bolivian plains. She has the golden glow and almond eyes of the Quechua Indians, descendants of the Inca.

During these seven years, the feeling I've always had is not exactly a feeling of being real. It's more like utter amazement. Even to this day, I walk away shaking my head in wonderment, thinking, "Do people who birth their children have this much thankfulness for the gift they've been given?"

Others have described real to me in terms of chores — as if quelling fights, toiling over homework, changing diapers, nursing sick children and coaching innumerable soccer games somehow grants us an entitlement to be called Mom or Dad. All that, like the Brownie patches and birthday parties at Chuck E. Cheese's, represent our patches in this troop called parenthood, to be sure.

But what few realize is that our paths are not so different. While they grew a life within them, we grew a mountain of paperwork and researched the way we would build our families. We, too, went through endless medical checkups, but also had extensive home studies. We rearranged the rooms in middle-of-the-night nesting rituals. Our emotions rose and fell wildly as we waited. Waited the long months for our assignments, then months more before a precious picture or shaky video turned into someone who could fill our aching, empty arms and hug us back.

Even so, it is not persevering through similar stages of pregnancy or adoption that make us real. There is so much more to it.

Real is a tiny hand in mine as we cross the street. Real is the whisper of breathing as my daughter naps in my arms. Real is as light as a baby's touch. Real is lying in bed reading stories with small bodies on either side interrupting with so many questions you think the story will never end.

It's planting flowers and jumping in puddles. It's tickling. It's catching a running youngster as she jumps into your arms when you pick her up in the evening. It's mastering rollerblading and ice skating. It's secretly watching a 2-year-old sing lullabies as she lovingly lines up her baby dolls and covers them for a nap. It's listening to kids pound down the stairs on Christmas morning, their feety pajamas swishing along the bare floor toward the prizes ahead. And it's passing on the family traditions, as your child takes your place at your father's side to become the official Thanksgiving turkey taster — her small hand reaching up to remind him she's ready for her job.

Real is, quite simply, the thrills all parents get from just being a parent and loving their children.

Finally, around midnight, the once-bare Brownie sash was festooned with patches: the Troop 1351 patch, the theater, dancing and sleepover patches. As I turned it over and pictured it on Alexis, it didn't surprise me to discover that my rare and feeble attempt at sewing had resulted in all the patches being affixed to the back of the sash. "Typical," I thought, shaking my head. "Well, it will just have to do."

As I readied myself for bed, I thought again of my favorite passage from "The Velveteen Rabbit."

"What is REAL?" asked the Rabbit one day -- .

"Real isn't how you are made," said the Skin Horse. "It's a thing that happens to you. When a child loves you for a long time, not just to play with, but REALLY loves you, then you become Real."

Real is also when you get lucky enough to have a child to love.

And, yes, it's also taking all the patches off and sewing them back on the right way.

STAGE 5

DAY-TO-DAY PARENTING

We've discussed the various psychological issues related to the "should I or shouldn't I?" debate single women face. Now let's get down to the bald truth that everyone wants to understand better: How DO Choice Moms cope with the stress and the questions that inevitably come when potential child turns into actual baby, toddler, child and teen? If you want to understand what you might need to deal with someday—or are a Choice Mom looking for advice—this is the section for you.

First fact is this: After a single woman becomes a mother, the issues she thought were important as she made her decision ultimately become faded memories of doubts and fears. For example, the typical Choice Mother cares much more about earaches and how to pick a preschool than on how to deal with disapproval in the community.

Second fact: There are far too many questions that a typical mom has on any given day for us to deal with in this book. We won't, for example, discuss real concerns such as: "What happens if I get seriously sick?" "Do you leave your baby inside the house alone while you're shoveling snow?" "How do you deal with the *boredom* of taking care of an infant all day?" "Should I take steps to help my child find donor siblings?"

What we will discuss in this section is the foundation of what Choice Moms can do right, for themselves and their child, as they are:

"Dealing With Stress," including a special section on having two kids;
"Answering the Daddy Question" at each age and stage;
"Confronting Identity Issues" for adopted and donor-conceived children;
"Raising a Well-Balanced Child," including a specific plan of execution for raising happy and healthy children without the help of a father.

CHAPTER 11

DEALING WITH THE STRESS

"I discovered that being a parent was the most difficult, frustrating job in the world. I wanted to be an accepting, nurturing parent—the great Earth mother—but I was totally unprepared for the reality of coping with two active, imperfect children. I found that I had a terrible temper and amazingly little self-control. I wanted to be empathic, but I was critical. I wanted the boys to get along well, but they were always quarreling. I wanted them to treat me with respect, but they talked back to me. I wanted them to listen, but they tuned me out."
— Nancy Samalin, author of *Loving Your Child Is Not Enough: Positive Discipline That Works*

You have to have multiple game plans for dealing with the stress of Choice Motherhood. Yes, there will be many beautiful moments when your child says the funniest thing, or you are watching your angel sleep peacefully, or you are giddy singing loudly together to a favorite song.

But that doesn't help when you are dropping your infant off at daycare, rushing to meet with a client, and she spits up on your red silk shirt. It doesn't help when your tired child is in a heap on the floor of a dirty airport bathroom, screaming as if you are trying to abduct him, when all you want to do is get to the gate with carry-on luggage before your flight takes off. It doesn't help when your seventh grader is embarrassed that she has no "father" side to the family tree for her social science project, and instead of telling you about it she's become unusually hostile and resentful about ever being born.

My daughter has always been a rather easy-going, self-sufficient child. But when she was four, she entered a phase in which whining and crying over little things increased. Undoubtedly this had something to do with me suddenly having a boyfriend, adding her new brother to the house, and having a future stepsister who liked to pull her hair.

I could rationalize the reasons for it, but to be honest, that didn't help me when she was sitting on icy steps in below-zero temperature wearing a thin skirt and insisting that her pregnant mom carry her to the car. Or when she and my beau locked horns

Choosing Single Motherhood © Mikki Morrissette

for ten minutes about her saying "please" before he would pass the ketchup. Or when I was trying to rest after a long night with infant son and she demanded that I pick out her clothes for the day—knowing that she would reject whatever I picked. After any contentious behavior had worn me down I would yell, or want to yell: *"Can't you see that I have my hands full? You should be old enough to help, instead of simply adding to the problem!"*

Most of the stages of parenting are predictable, as you'll read in recommended books like Mary Sheedy Kurcinka's *Kids, Parents and Power Struggles.* But even if it's not your *fault*, and you've read the theoretical tips about how to correct behavior over time, it's still difficult to cope with the dark side of motherhood in that moment. There are a few things you can do, however, to help yourself deal with the inevitable stress of motherhood, especially when you don't have a partner to unload on. We won't re-invent the wheel here. Good advice is available every day in magazines and bookstores and websites. But here, in a nutshell, is what most of the advice books end up saying.

How to Reduce the Impact of Stress

1. Take care of yourself
We know we're supposed to eat, sleep, exercise and be merry.

And, by the way, don't forget to shower, get dressed, brush teeth and hair, cook, clean, work, pay bills, nurture and humor the little one, turn the TV off, help with homework, keep up with friends and family, chauffeur, shop, do laundry, take time to pamper, open the mail, read the paper, organize family entertainment, read to your child everyday, mend, repair, garden, do home improvement, attend functions and school meetings, record your child's history in albums and journals, read about how to be a good parent, play, plan, save for college and retirement, get involved in the community, show your child the value of volunteering, keep up with e-mails, drink water.

I didn't even take care of myself well when I was without child.

The best any of us can do is make a priority list for each day and week, and then see how much we can cross off before we make the next list. Just don't forget that if you eat well, exercise and get enough sleep, it will be easier to deal with. Nearly any time that I've snapped excessively at Sophie, it's because at least one of us hasn't had enough good food or sleep that day. And it's usually me.

2. Embrace community

This is non-negotiable. When I lived in New York, I had a wonderful babysitter who handled much of the cooking and cleaning as well as taking excellent care of Sophie. I had an easier life as a Choice Mom with her, ironically, than when I was simply a single woman. Yet it wasn't enough. And it wasn't until I moved to Minnesota that I discovered why.

Without realizing it, my New York life had become too isolated. I was upset that my single friends didn't seem to have time anymore. The few that I did see regularly didn't seem to offer enough. I felt like a machine—eventually getting more uninspired, hating work, stressing about my small apartment, wishing I had more money for travel.

I considered this a byproduct of new motherhood—until I moved and discovered a better life. One in which I made the effort to talk to people at the playground instead of sitting on the bench reading. One in which I discovered the joy of being able to drop off my child with another mom simply so I could go to the dentist without using up valuable child care time. Of course, I could have discovered this in New York. But until I moved, I didn't make an effort to widen the circle I had before I became a mom.

> *I assumed the friends I had would carry me through—*
> *but you need more when you become someone else's caretaker.*
> *You need to be part of a larger network.*

After I moved, I was closer to my brother's family and my parents—which was huge—but I also started to, slowly, become more connected to people I didn't already have a relationship with.

It does take a village to raise a child well. It's not simply a matter of having your work hours covered, or being able to go out one night a week, or being able to run errands unencumbered. It's also being able to have someone take over for a few hours when you have the stomach flu. It's having someone teach your child how to make a beaded bracelet that you don't have the ability to do yourself. It's having someone stronger than you help your child swing from bar to bar at the playground. It's giving your child the experience of boating and fishing and camping if you're a city girl. It's having someone in addition to you teach concepts about religion, world culture, sportsmanship, family, patriotism. Your child needs many teachers.

To be a good Choice Mom, you need to cultivate your network. Find the secure base

Choosing Single Motherhood © Mikki Morrissette

of family and friends your child will grow up with while getting acquainted with neighbors, community groups, recreation instructors.

Find the people you can turn to for emergency child care at the same time that you're finding people who will introduce your child to new things, like how to tell the difference between a sparrow and robin.

If you're like me—and maybe half of you are—widening the circle is *not* something that comes naturally. As I got older, I found my network getting smaller. I knew who I liked, why, and didn't "waste" my time and energy adding anyone to the mix. But you can't be a good mother that way, whether you like it or not. And you won't be able to maintain your own mental health either. Talk to people, open up your world—one person at a time. Most of them won't become close, long-term friends. But being engaged with others is a very necessary step to keeping your own balance, as well as your child's.

How to Reduce Stress

3. Learn to be adaptable

My daughter was never a napper, which meant that when she was younger I had little time to myself without paying a babysitter. That could have been tough, but thankfully by three months she easily slept 10 hours every night, so I learned to work with her schedule.

My son, on the other hand, is a light sleeper who woke up several times a night until his first birthday, and was usually persistent enough to cry himself awake rather than back to sleep. By the time he was seven months I had already tested three strategies—until I threw in the towel and gave him a watered down bottle of formula to get him to relax enough to stop crying and fall easily back to sleep. It was against the rules, but it worked.

Being a mother does mean that you compromise much more than you'd like in order to get what you need done. You discipline and instruct and give timeouts when they misbehave, but if your child is exhausted, there is no amount of rational conversation that will get them from Point A to Point B. It is always you who needs to think on your feet, find a creative solution, revise plans if needed.

This also includes picking your battles. I can be embarrassed when Sophie wants to go out with five pigtails in her hair, or sparkle "make-up" on her lips and eyes, but ultimately her appearance isn't worth fighting about unless we're getting a portrait done. I let her choose her methods of self-expression and save my "absolutely nots" for matters of safety, health and behavior.

The happiest Choice Moms I know are the ones who can "go with the flow," rather than feel the need to stick to an agenda their children aren't capable of meeting. Flexibility, ability to compromise, and a calm demeanor are definite strengths.

One woman who was contemplating this decision talked to single mothers.[1] She found that the ones who said the lifestyle was tough tended to be "women who might find very easy things to be difficult, or were women who refused to modify activities that would lessen their load."

Ultimately the woman ended up having two children. "This isn't brave or courageous," she said. "It is simply that I gave in to a great need and desire to nurture a family. It would take courage to try to live a life without this experience."

4. Understand your child

Children don't usually misbehave because they want to make our lives miserable. Yes, they test us, and the limits we set for them, to see what happens, but most of that is the result of going through predictable phases of development when they are learning to assert their own independence—a necessary ingredient to maturing into a non-dependent adult. Child expert Michael Gurian calls these "little bursts of behavior" a natural part of the child's process of discovering how to be his or her own boss. This usually starts with about a year of willful behavior in the toddler stage—which Gurian says can be a foreshadowing of the teenage years—then again around age five, in prepuberty, in puberty and in adolescence.

It is normal for a toddler to become aggressive when frustrated, emotionally manipulative, easily distracted, and wound up. Starting at about 18 months, your child is ready to be trained with discipline designed to regulate natural urges in a way that builds character, tests self-esteem and teaches social skills. Being able to remain calm in the face of adversity is another personality strength—although it will frequently fail even with the most serene parent. (Now that I am a parent, I have a much shorter fuse than I thought possible.) Advice from Choice Moms is to remind yourself that this too shall pass.

RAISING YOUR SPIRITED CHILD
BY MARY SHEEDY KURCINKA[2]

The good days couldn't be better. Profound statements roll from his mouth, much too mature and intellectual for a child of his age. He remembers experiences you've long since forgotten and drags you to the window to watch the raindrops, falling like diamonds from the sky. On the good days, being the parent of a spirited child is astounding, dumbfounding, wonderful, funny, interesting, and interspersed with moments of brilliance.

The dreadful days are another story. On those days you're not sure you can face another twenty-four hours with him. It's hard to feel good as a parent when you can't even get his socks on, when every word you've said to him has been a reprimand, when the innocent act of serving tuna casserole instead of the expected tacos incites a riot, when you realize you've left more public places in a huff with your child in five years than most parents do in a lifetime.

You feel weary, drained, and much too old for this. It's hard to love a kid who keeps you up at night and embarrasses you in shopping centers. You may wonder if you are the only parent with a kid like this, scared of what is to come in the teen years if you don't figure out what to do now, in the early years.

5. Help them express themselves
The stubborn and irrational resistance of a child is one of the most common triggers of stress in a parent's life. To be able to break through the wall requires communication skills even more so than discipline—because often the behavior isn't prompted by willful disobedience as much as the inability to navigate frustration. Understanding that simple bit of psychology can help a parent a lot.

I was referred to Ross Greene's excellent book *The Explosive Child* [3] by a Choice Mom's mother, who was a specialist in child aggression. Because my new husband has an adolescent daughter whose special needs issues includes difficulty controlling aggressive impulses, I read his book to understand her meltdowns. I realized his wisdom about dealing with verbally and physically aggressive children had some useful advice for any parent dealing with the inevitable tantrums of a child.

In his view, a toddler starts to freak out over little things—putting on pull-ups, getting shoes on, exiting the playground—because he or she doesn't yet have the ability to understand why something is bothersome and then articulate it in a mature manner. As he wrote:

> *"Instead of asking yourself, 'What's it going to take to motivate this kid to behave differently?' you need to ask yourself 'Why is this so hard for my child? What's getting in his way? How can I help?'"*

One example Greene used was of a girl who carefully saved the last popsicle so she could eat it the next day, and then became incomprehensively unglued when her brother took it. If she'd had the capacity to say "I wanted to eat that tomorrow, so perhaps we can ask mom to buy more before then," the crisis could have been averted. (When an adult's reactions get triggered in a seemingly irrational way, we call it "pushing our buttons.")

Usually as a child matures they develop—with the help of their parent—the ability to express themselves and find a workable solution. Thankfully this capacity generally begins to kick in around the age of five for normally developing children whose parents don't end up needing the advice of experts like Greene. But it's not a seamless process, and takes effort on the part of the parents to see signs of wearing down that are particular to the child.

When that child is recognizably moving toward the edge—perhaps exhibiting restlessness, irritability, intense reaction to routine tasks. Greene recommends using empathy to help the child put the frustration into words and come up with logical solutions (offering choices, compromise), as well as use humor as a distraction. Once the meltdown occurs, it's too late, so the key is to recognize the warning signs. Communication skills are a personality strength.

6. Take your own timeout

Yes, this is a good technique to give you and your kids the space to cool down. But here I'm talking about something even broader. Actually take the time to come up with a creative strategy for coping with patterned behavior—yours and theirs—rather than simply repeating the same tired "kid acts out, mom gets mad" syndrome. Melissa is one Choice Mom I admire for her ability to find imaginative solutions.

"The six months between 4.5 and 5 were the closest I came to committing homicide in my entire life," she admitted about living with her daughter. "The constant

Choosing Single Motherhood © Mikki Morrissette

talking, the constant need for attention, the oppositional attitude and behavior." She came up with several effective coping mechanisms to address any new hot button. Such as:

• When they spend entire days together, for at least one hour they have to be in separate spaces with closed doors between them.
• They agreed on a code word that Mom uses to indicate it's time to stop talking. "For some reason, it works!"
• "There's nothing to get her out of a black mood, and us out of a power struggle, faster than something silly. It is hard to do, since I'm usually madder than a wet hen myself, but it really makes a difference. When I get the 'I'm too tired to get into my pajamas' whine, I turn into the mommy monster who chases a shrieking, laughing child around the apartment. Within a minute she is dressed."

Other helpful strategies moms (and child experts) devise involve giving the child a sense of control at early points of combat: *Do you want to wear the green pants or the purple pants? Do you want to eat carrots or tomatoes? Which shoe goes on first?*

One of the most common struggles for Choice Moms is getting kids out the door in the morning, and/or into bed at night. This is where rituals play a great role in keeping things on track. Some families put together schedules, using kids' drawings of a toothbrush, hair comb, etc. Others combat distractions by turning it into a "beat the clock" game, using timers to keep focused on each task. A good imagination—of mother and child—will help.

How Do We Handle It Alone?

Trick question. As I'll repeat a few more times, no one *can* handle parenting alone. Many Thinkers feel that if they embark on motherhood without a partner, they'll be worn out from providing for, supervising and carrying the emotional and physical load single-handedly. And they're right.

What can be easy to forget is that even married mothers need outside help. You need many people around you—not simply one amazingly helpful, attentive, sensitive partner—to raise your child. You're still the one who needs to have the stamina to get through 365 days a year of diapering, feeding, cleaning, consoling, transporting. It can be a pain in the back, monotonous, and irritating to be on call so much. So how do we do it?

7. Don't feel sorry for yourself

It's easy to think that all of the troubles of our world have something to do with being single. It's also too simple to point out that married women usually have partner stress in addition to basic mom stress. Life is about dealing with stress, everyday. The sooner you get over thinking your situation would be better "if only," the sooner you will do something about it.

Even if you had the most loving spouse imaginable, your adoring infant who simply needed you to feed, clothe, comfort and love will still turn into the preschooler who drives you crazy, bouncing from fiercely independent (*"I can button this myself,"* even though the buttons are in the back), to whiner (*"I can't walk anyyyy morrrre.... carrrrry meeee"*), to "smarty pants devil" who tirelessly rebuts everything you say.

When I lived in New York, feeling sorry for myself that I didn't have anyone to carry the folded stroller into the bus while I carried my daughter and a shopping bag, I would get angry that no one offered to help—instead of swallowing my pride, and my pity, and simply asking a stranger to give me a hand. When you stop focusing on the negativity, it's easier to find a solution.

8. Embrace the challenge

Most of us have experienced the scary thrill of going off to college, or travel, away from our parents for the first time. Before my kids were born, I found travel to far-flung places like Russia and Hungary and Madagascar exciting. I glowed during a three-week solo trip through Ireland, proud of being able to handle every detail myself. In my first years after divorce, I proved to myself that I could handle any mishap, hardship and change that the adventures of travel threw at me.

In my late 30s and early 40s, I became a Choice Mom twice. It has been like living the challenge of travel or college all over again. It's difficult... lonely... exciting... empowering... satisfying.

When we were younger, maybe we gained the freshman weight, or missed our train connection, or got a D in that early-morning history class, or suffered from Montezuma's revenge. But we learned and adjusted and did what it took to get by—with as much fun along the way as we could. That's the same determined, self-fulfilling mindset the Choice Mom needs. Maybe we'd rather stay in beach resorts than cheap youth hostels now, but we still have the same capability to find our rhythm and survive everything.

Choosing Single Motherhood © Mikki Morrissette

MY FAVORITE "STRESS" STORY
FROM: MARLENE

My daughter was not quite two and I had been working non-stop, 50 hours a week, for *months* without time off. It was Memorial Day weekend and I was desperate for that extra day off. Well, wouldn't you know, she got up at 5 a.m. Single mom, no one around to help, I put on cartoons, gave her a juice box and some toast and went back to bed for an hour thinking that I would hear her if anything went wrong. I dozed for a while, no sounds from the other room, then finally figured I wasn't going back to sleep anyway, so got up.

In less than one hour, my daughter had:
- gotten up on the kitchen counter into the candy jar, there were about 20 candy wrappers on the floor;
- gotten into the magic markers and colored on my beige carpet;
- gotten into a box of bandaids and put them all over the long haired cat (I had to cut them out of his fur);
- gotten a pair of scissors and cut two fist sized holes in her brand new pajamas.

She was calmly watching cartoons when I got up. Did I cry? Did I punish her? No, I realized that this is my lot in life and I knew when I took on single parenthood that the responsibility was ALL MINE. I took a deep breath, cleaned it all up and never left her unsupervised for more than 5 minutes again, no matter how sick or tired I was.

9. The most obvious advice

Besides reminding yourself that your child is going through a rite of passage that will change over time—one that you didn't cause and that you can't prevent—commiserate with other moms, single and married. And if you are feeling overwhelmed, hopeless or depressed, see a therapist. An unhappy parent can be as detrimental as smoking or drinking while pregnant.

The Difference a Partner Makes

When a partner essentially fell into my lap—after nearly five years of Choice parenting and another five months of pregnancy—the primary advantage was to give me more "me" time: date nights without kids, back rubs, snuggling. Sure, on paper I could have accomplished the same things by going out once a week with friends, paying a massage therapist, been satisfied with my daughter's embraces. But truthfully—even for someone like myself who didn't feel the need for a man in my life—it's not the same. Plus, his experience at parenting, including his four years as a single dad, has made him a solid role model for my kids to look up to.

Yet in the pre-Dave days, I functioned quite well with the logistics of running a Choice household. With Sophie, I got used to the mindless diapering and feeding duties. I had my priceless parents to help with the first months and vacations. My babysitter was a godsend. My unexpected return to the self-employed lifestyle was a blessing because of the flexibility. In short, I found solutions to get through the day-to-day without much fuss. Otherwise I wouldn't have decided to have two.

There were obviously times when it would have been easier to handle situations with a second pair of hands around—such as carrying my sleeping daughter out of the car when I was suffering from intense lower back pain during my second pregnancy. But when I met Dave, I was not longing for a partner to "save me" from the demands of Choice Mothering. Even now, as the primary caregiver for Sophie and Dylan—with a partner who works, volunteers and has two children and a house of his own—I handle the job largely alone, with my community of helpers. I consider Dave one of my parenting partners, just as my parents, friends, babysitter and sister-in-law are.

From: Anne, a Married Mom

Honestly, we went through about a year (maybe it was only months—felt like a year) where Clare had a fit about the car seat if it made her shirt, skirt, or whatever stick up or out in any way that she deemed "puffy." Much screaming ensued along the lines of "No, no, no, it's too puffy—it's toooooo puuuuuffffyyyy!!!" All delivered as if being brutally murdered with an ice pick. And forget about coats. Coats can only be worn in the car seat EXTREMELY RARELY. Coats, you see, are definitely 'too puffy,' not just in the car seat, but sometimes in general.

I have resorted to an "it's okay to take your coat off to ride in the car and then put it back on again" policy on coats in the car seat. This sometimes leads my husband—who is not 100 percent behind my "no coats in the car seat" policy since he doesn't ride in the car with her so often—to screaming fits of his own. In general, I've adopted an "it's okay not to wear your coat, but we'll bring it along just in case" policy. Believe it or not, Clare originally had a problem even with

Choosing Single Motherhood © Mikki Morrissette

As I write this, Dave is in the second week of a hiking trip in New Mexico with his son. There have been no phone calls, no e-mails, no contact at all since he entered the wilderness. Sophie is on summer vacation, my son is still not sleeping through the night, I have only two days of child care per week, I'm planning a wedding, writing this book. Yet I have generally felt on top of the world parenting-wise.

I'm delighting in my son's smiles, his boundless enthusiasm for new taste sensations, his fascination with every sound and movement. I'm doing morning yoga with my daughter and teaching her about other countries as we watch the Summer Olympics together. She's helping me prepare the wedding invitations, pick out the bridal accessories, choose music for the reception. The three of us are enjoying bike rides around the lake, with stops at the beach and the playground. We had a wonderful day at an Irish Festival, watching sheep-herding, learning step-dancing, bouncing to live bands. We're looking forward to the Renaissance Festival and State Fair. This, for me, is what being a mother is all about. Not the baths and the laundry and the relentless need to get food ready. And none of these activities are less in the absence of my partner. In fact, now that our family is extending, I appreciate this threesome time even more.

Not unlike most two-parent households, Dave and I have different approaches to parenting—as man and woman—enhanced by the fact that we're both independent and strong-minded people who, in our 40s, have developed our own child-rearing

the idea of bringing it along (this is me carrying it, not her), but has now come to love saying, as if it's her own idea. "I don't think I want to wear my coat, but how about if you bring one along, Mom, just in case?"

Humor sometimes works and usually at least helps (if Mom can manage to keep it together to find some humor, which I must say, I can't always).

Personally, I've come to believe all children are relatively nuts—or at least the really brilliant, creative and interesting (and they are!) kids we seem to know. I mainly keep plugging away on helping Clare learn to identify and find positive ways to express, or release, her emotions.

Sometimes I feel as if I'm making no progress at all, and then one day she'll suddenly say to me (as she did, one day), "Mama, did you notice when you said no to me, I didn't cry or scream or get angry; I just said, 'Okay, Mom.' Wasn't that good?"

systems. I'm not surprised that a typical point of stress between couples is how to raise the children. As a married friend told me, when her husband is traveling on business, being a mom tends to be less stressful. "Sometimes I don't like what he says to the kids, or how he says it. Or I don't like what he does. When there's no other adult around to chime in, it can be easier in many ways."

SURVIVING WITH AN INFANT

FROM: TERESA

1. Be shameless about asking for help. At the baby showers I passed around two sign-up sheets. One was for meals. A friend coordinated this by contacting people on the list after the baby came. This was great! I think I had meals delivered to my house 3-4 times/week for about six weeks. The second sign-up sheet was for other help. People indicated how they wished to help (run errands, babysit, etc.). I personally contacted people on this list throughout my maternity leave. It allowed me to go out without the baby for about an hour or two twice/week. It also gave me a reason to call people, and that contact was very important during the first few months. I still call people on this list.

2. Take walks (inside malls or out). I should have done this regularly, but it seemed I usually didn't do this until I was losing my patience. It always calmed him down and was good for me to get some exercise and fresh air.

3. Pay for services. I hired out lawn work and had my groceries delivered. These were unplanned expenses, but there's no way I could have kept up without them. I could have used cleaning services as well, but let it go. Laundry and dishes were all I did.

4. Day care. I was pretty close to losing my mind from sleep deprivation. Once I did go back to work and he started daycare, life got easier. It was such a relief to have a few hours a day where I wasn't consumed with his needs. There are drop-off centers that will take infants (six weeks or older) on an hourly basis.

Accept that Stress Doesn't End

When I was talking with Wendy Kramer for the chapter about anonymous donors,

Choosing Single Motherhood © Mikki Morrissette

I presumed that for her the stress was over in her life as a single mother. Her son Ryan is a remarkably well-balanced, happy and poised young man—able to make numerous TV appearances to talk about the Donor Sibling Registry website the two of them launched to national acclaim, as well as to enter college at age 14 because of his status as a gifted student. But I presumed wrong.

"This past fall was one of the most difficult times I'd ever been through, and pushed me beyond where I thought I could go stress-wise," she told me.

Ryan had started his first semester at college, and she had closed a restaurant of eight years and was laid off from a job of 10 years. "We both had complete meltdowns. Ryan was struggling at school, emotionally, mentally and academically. I thought I was a bad parent. 'How could I have put him in such a situation?' It was brutal. I thought I'd set him up for failure. 'What have I done?' For about two months it was almost unbearable. We were walking around here like zombies."

Because of the strong relationship Wendy had developed with her son, however, even at that rebellious age of 14 he wasn't acting out against her. The way she had handled stress and anger with him in past years paid off *(read more in Chapter 16)*. "We kept in touch with each other about what we were going through," she said. "We were on each other's teams, even if it felt like our teams were losing. He saw me panic, but we did the best we could do and we both came through it. We relied on each other."

Everyone—single or married, parent or not—needs to accept that life always will be visited by stress, sometimes big (*boiler broke down and will cost thousands to fix*), sometimes small (*I've got to be somewhere in 15 minutes and he just pooped all the way up the back of himself*).

> *Being a mom adds to the stress list on a daily basis. Be prepared to accept this, develop your skills of creativity and empathy to minimize it, and don't let yourself be a martyr about it.*

Tips for the Caregiver's Soul

A lovely book by James E. Miller titled *The Caregiver's Book: Caring for Another, Caring for Yourself,*[4] has several good recommendations for anyone who is taking care of another human being, including:

1. List things you can do to restore yourself. Such as "order Chinese food" or "read a mystery." Put this long list in a place you'll see everyday and make a check mark next to each one when you do it. Be sure that you are making several check marks each day.

2. Schedule time off. You should always have short breaks and long breaks planned in advance so you have down time to look forward to.

3. Talk to someone honestly. Every caregiver needs someone to open up to without judgment in order to unplug, get perspective, and listen to their own emotions while explaining them to someone else.

4. Create a "time out" sign. As Melissa has done, when your child is old enough, each of you should have a sign—wearing a certain hat or pin, for example—to signal that you simply want time to yourself without talking, interruptions or demands.

5. Keep a notebook of the gifts you receive from caregiving. Write about how your child inspires, educates, touches you.

6. Accept caregiving from others. As a single woman who consciously chose motherhood, it might be tempting to pretend to be superwoman, especially around people who warned how hard it would be. Don't let that happen. Graciously allow them to help you. People gain a lot from helping others.

7. Make emergency plans. Don't wait for illness to strike to devise options and strategies. Make sure anyone involved is willing to help when asked.

8. Start a co-op. Share shopping, driving, cooking with other caregivers. Exchange a skill you have for one they have.

9. Create a sacred space. Especially for homes that are overrun with plastic toys and baby equipment, set up a quiet place filled with items of special significance to you. Perhaps photos, art, candles, incense, travel mementos.

As Miller wrote, "It's not easy being a caregiver. There are days when your vitality runs low, when your spirit sags, when your anxiety peaks. There are times when the hours are too long, when the demands seem too many, when the rewards feel too few…Yet through the discipline of your caregiving, you will experience marvelous new awareness.

"In being a blessing for another, you are blessed. In being a vehicle for growth, you grow. You will realize that you are cared for on the grandest scale possible. And the most fitting response you can make is a prayer that contains only four words: Thank you. Thank you."

Final Thoughts

No one can truly "conquer" the stress of parenting. But the most relaxed moments of parenting can come after you master three requirements. These three strategies, boiled down from this chapter and explored in Chapter 14, were neatly summarized by parenting expert Mary Sheedy Kurcinka when I asked her what the Choice Mother in particular needs to do to alleviate stress.

1. Establish daily rituals that calm and connect, such as eating breakfast, cooking and washing dishes together.

2. Schedule predictable breaks from your child.

3. Find support. "Whether you are single or part of a couple," Kurcinka told me, "finding adult support is vital. There are many married women who are actually parenting alone. The key is finding friends and other adults who will back you up."

Bonus Section

Having Two

Once upon a time pioneering single women decided to have one child on their own. Some of them have told me they regretted not having two kids. Today, a growing number of Choice Mothers are having two (or three) kids.

For some women (including me) the decision to have a second child is harder to make than the first decision to become a Choice Mom. Others, especially with enhanced fertility, accidentally conceive multiples and have to get used to the idea. Still others—more than a few I've talked to—are elated to have two at once.

Morgan was "totally delighted" when she learned that two of three embryos had survived in vitro fertilization. "At that stage, I was only ever really, really happy and grateful and desperate for both babies to be okay."

On the other hand, Patty initially had no intention of becoming a Choice Mother even to one child, knowing how hard it had been for her mother after her father left. But when she was 33, with no partner on the horizon, she decided it was time to act.

> *Enhanced by fertility drugs for her fourth cycle, she conceived. "When I saw two embryos on the ultrasound screen I was SHOCKED! How was I going to raise two babies on a single income? How was I going to raise two babies with one set of hands! I started to cry."*

Others have every intention of having more than one from the start. Dina, for example, has two boys three years apart and would have a third if she was younger. She doesn't feel she is under any more stress than a married mother. "Of course, I am only one mom, and I can't be in two places at the same time, but that is true of any mom. We are all experiencing similar difficulties and stresses. Mine are not different or worse because of my marital status."

Choice Moms who want two generally hesitate *not* because of stress and logistical issues, but because of financial issues. It's simply harder to save up for another round of insemination or adoption costs when you're paying for child care. As Leslie said, "The financial piece was very scary. I had to consider the cost of the actual adoption as well as other child-related expenses. I have stretched the equity in my house pretty far, both through refinancing and a home equity loan. However, I believe if people waited until all their finances were completely the way they want them to be, no one would ever have kids."

For those who are debating the choice of having two—or struggling simply with the decision to have one—here is what some Choice Mothers of two have told me.

Support is always important, but especially when there are two kids. Before she proceeded with her second adoption, Leslie talked with her mother and other close friends and family members to make sure she had their support.

House-wise, cooking and shopping needs are about the same, laundry is slightly more frequent, tidying up takes longer. As Marlene put it, "The majority of the extra effort is for refereeing fights and trying to give equal time to each child.

Health is doubly affected with two kids. The school-aged one brings new viruses

Choosing Single Motherhood © Mikki Morrissette

home, and it's impossible to keep siblings from sharing germs, even if they won't share toys.

"Being the single parent to twins who pass bugs back and forth—and to me too—is impossible to deal with, but you just do," said Morgan. "I vividly remember crawling around my home at 3 a.m., with one baby tucked under my arm and the other crying upstairs and me having a temperature of 104 degrees, with mastitis, thrush and still recovering from my C-section…barely making it to the bathroom to throw up and knowing there was no end to this in the near future."

Personality dynamics can become more complicated when the simpler one-on-one relationship changes between parent and child. That was the one thing I worried about most with Sophie—she and I had such a wonderful bond and I hesitated to affect it. But the unanticipated plus is that she and I sometimes feel like partners in affection as we watch Dylan grow up.

Dina found that "not only did my heart expand to encompass my love for my second son, it expanded in a third direction to encompass my love for them as brothers. I love my older son, I love my younger son, and I love their relationship with each other—that relationship is like a third dynamic in our family."

Patty got over her initial shock about having twins and ended up embracing the idea. "I've been raised to believe that you are given what you can handle, and I ran with it. I loved being pregnant, and kept a diary of the experience to remind myself—and later, them—how wonderful it is to be pregnant with twins."

Her daughter was born easily a few hours after the water broke, but her son was breech and Patty had to be put under for an emergency C-section. She cried because "I wasn't going to see my little man until the next day."

Age Difference
The dynamic is not always perfect, of course. Timing seems to be a crucial variable: How many years apart is best? Can Mom handle diapering and feeding two young ones at the same time? Or can Mom handle the diverse emotions and activities of two kids who are several years apart? For this, there is no easy answer, since every situation depends on unique temperaments.

For me, having nearly five years between the two has thus far been great. Sophie enjoys Dylan's cuteness, sometimes getting tearful at how "adorable he is." It really does feel like a shared adventure we are having together. Plus, she is old enough to take care of many of her own basic needs while I tend to "the little guy." She generally enjoys entertaining him, and gets him to giggle like no one else. Another benefit of the five-year split was that Sophie was in free public school before I needed child care for Dylan, so I never had to pay for two at once.

Marlene, on the other hand, has a similar age difference between her two girls, but her circumstances haven't been ideal. Her youngest was adopted at 20 months, when her oldest was six. "In my experience, this is a bad split. Perhaps if I had brought an infant home to my five-year-old, things would have been okay. I have dealt with horrible jealousy and tormenting from the older one, who had much more trouble adjusting than the little one, has reverted to three-year-old tantrums, and picks fights constantly. There is a huge territory war about what is 'my stuff' and what has to be shared. If I had it to do again, I would try to adopt a four-year-old or would have done this a few years earlier. I think bringing a toddler home who touches everything and breaks small toys was probably a form of torture for my oldest."

Age difference also can have a big impact, in the early years, with varying nap and bed routines. As the kids get older, the more years between the two the tougher it will be to find mutually satisfying activities. A benefit of having them close in age is that they can eventually take recreational classes together.

With twins you don't have the age difference issues—and sometimes wish you did. "It's definitely been harder than I expected," Morgan said. "But maybe not any different to the huge shock that hits all new parents at how hard it all is. The worst part was sleep deprivation. Total deprivation. My babies were almost six weeks premature and put onto a three-hour feeding schedule. As I was determined to breastfeed (with bottle feeding augmentation) this meant every three hours I spent all but maybe 15 minutes feeding, sterilizing equipment, pumping milk, changing babies—then the cycle would start all over again.

> *"I was hallucinating with lack of sleep, often going days and nights without any sleep at all, and this went on for six to eight months at least. But I managed to breastfeed until they were 28 months old."*

Morgan has no family nearby, or experienced friends who can help, so she fully takes care of her twin boys with paid help. "Initially I hired an expensive mother's help for a few hours a day. I wish now I'd paid out even more just to get some sleep in that first year. After that, once I returned to work when the babies were six months old, I had nannies and home day care providers, then part-time school."

Choosing Single Motherhood © Mikki Morrissette

Patty's mother helped her for the first two months. "I'm really not sure how I would have handled being alone after the birth. I hemorrhaged ten days later and was bedridden for 24 hours." Her breastfeeding and pumping demands also were exhausting. She had her "one and only breakdown" at the end of the first month.

About Stress

The old adage is that having two more than doubles the energy required. But other than the difficulty of keeping track of two, this did not seem to be the complaint of most women I talked to.

Dina says, "I have absolutely not found two twice as difficult as one. In many ways, having two is easier than having one. They entertain each other and are more self-sufficient than my older son was until his brother came along. In other words, mommy is not the sole source of entertainment. In fact, as they grow older, in some ways life is becoming a little easier — if one of them wants me to get something, it is possible that the other one will actually do it, so I get to keep sitting on the couch (ha). Don't get me wrong, life with a three-year-old and newborn was hard, and I still don't get enough sleep, but again, my married friends don't have it much better."

What can be lost when a young one enters the picture, however, are private moments that were savored when the older child was beginning to be away from home for longer periods of time with babysitters, teachers and drop-off playdates. One woman told me, with two kids she had less money to spend, and found herself limited to chauffeuring the oldest to activities while still maintaining a nap schedule for the other.

"Going shopping with two kids is like trying to herd cats," Marlene said. "One you can hang onto, but two are impossible unless both fit in the shopping cart. I do almost all my shopping on my lunch hour now."

Morgan said she has her nearly four-year-old twins strapped in to strollers or toddler reins instead of letting them run free as she'd prefer. "Having twins on my own has meant their lives have been more restricted. We can't easily do family activities, like swimming and going to cafes, as there's only me to supervise. They still tend to run off in opposite directions, to different dangers, and I'm forever having to assess the potential dangers in a split second and leap towards the greater need. It keeps me very fit, physically."

Patty says she's happy she doesn't have the added stress of validating her parenting decisions with someone else. "I truly believe that life would be much more difficult with a spouse," she said. "In my world, I make the decisions and I live with the results. There is no one else to blame or hand off to or hug. Just mommy."

Regrets are few, no matter what the path has been. In the big picture, the stress of motherhood tends to be minimized.

"Do I sound sorry for going for two?," Marlene said. "I'm not. Just stressed and frazzled, like having an infant with colic all the time. I figure that if they survive childhood without killing each other, they will be great friends and finally appreciate each other. Of course, when the youngest turns 18, I'm packing up and moving to the tropics with no forwarding address."

Morgan's only regret is that she rarely gets time alone with each twin. "They're so completely different from each other, with different needs, that I wish I could give each more unique Mommy time."

Leslie says, "Bottom line, having a second child has added a wonderful new dimension to our family. I love watching the girls be sisters and hope they will always share a special bond. I want them to have someone to share hopes, fears and memories with, now and in the future. Even on the toughest days, I cannot imagine a world without either one of them. I never thought I could love someone as much as I love my first daughter. Then along came my second daughter. She adds such a wonderful new dimension to our family. I have no regrets about my decision to adopt again."

Coping mechanisms

Patty says she "didn't know a THING about raising a baby, let alone two at the same time. It has all been flying by the seat of my pants. I didn't have patience to start with, but have gained an ounce a day since my cubs came to me. Laughter is a must. And the reminder to myself that I chose them, they didn't choose me."

Morgan says her planning and thinking about Choice Motherhood in advance of pregnancy—"being very sure I wanted children so much"—has helped her cope with twins in a way she might not have if she'd had children in a traditional relationship without as much thought about becoming a mother.

"My children have a mommy who can at least laugh at herself for her crazy moments, apologize to them for her mistakes, and beyond everything, feel deeplygrateful to have such beautiful little beings in my life," she said.

Choosing Single Motherhood © Mikki Morrissette

"It's really the first time in my life that I've experienced something so incredibly and impossibly hard that, at the same time, is so incredibly and unbelievably wonderful. A unique paradox!"

THE AUTHOR'S JOURNEY TO TWO

After 9/11, and after a beautiful trip to Hawaii for my 40th birthday that reminded me of quality of life elsewhere, the piece of the puzzle I had never considered before dropped into my lap: I would move out of my beloved city of 18 years. After leaving New York City, I realized that what I wanted to accomplish more than anything was to add a sibling to Sophie's life.

Oddly, the love for my daughter really did impel me to think of a second child as a gift for her, rather than for me. Even throughout the pregnancy, I wasn't as excited about the new arrival as I thought I would be. I worried, as many mothers do, whether I would be able to love the new one as much as my first. Being nearly five years older than I was the first time, I was unexpectedly more concerned about the pain of childbirth. I felt more back pain, more hemorrhoids, more exhaustion. I still loved the sensations of having a child in the womb, but I was much more nervous about whether I was up to the challenge. I had gotten used to having a well-behaved daughter and knew this time I was having a son—whose kicks were more intense!

When Dylan made his arrival, my daughter was there to witness the miracle. She squealed with delight when she saw his head emerge, and was mesmerized for the rest of the day, barely letting anyone else (including me!) hold him.

That night, however, when the hospital room was quiet and it was just Dylan and I, the bonding began. It amazes me the capacity for the human heart to open wider, when you thought it was already as wide as it could get.

I have enjoyed motherhood even more the second time around—although he didn't let me sleep through the night the first year. Since I know what I'm doing this time, I'm finding it much easier to relax and enjoy our simple moments.

CHAPTER 12

ANSWERING THE DADDY QUESTION

Sooner or later every Choice Mom will be answering the "where is my daddy?" question. It likely will come up many times over the years. And it often will appear out of the blue—while you're watching a TV show about dogs, or standing in line at the grocery store, or driving to church.

So it pays to be prepared ahead of time. But many women I've talked to who are worried about how they will answer this question generally are focused on the complex background the mother might feel guilty or emotional about herself: *Why did you bring me into this home without also giving me a father? Why don't you know anything about my donor, or my birth mother? Why did my father reject us when you were pregnant? If that man helped you create me, why don't you let him live with us?*

Look at any single parent website and you'll find some of the agony women can put themselves through about answering the daddy question. Wrote one woman on Single Parent Central: "My boyfriend left me when I was six months pregnant, moved to another state, and was never heard from again. My daughter is almost three and has been asking who her daddy is. She is very intelligent and I don't want to lie to her. She asks me everyday, and even the daycare teachers have said that she tells them almost daily that she doesn't have a father. I feel worthless and don't want to say the wrong thing, something that will mentally harm her!"

A Choice Mom I know who used a known donor didn't struggle with the daddy question when her son's donor was living in another country, but after the man unexpectedly returned to live in their state she was not sure how to answer her inquisitive boy's questions. Should she tell him his father lived nearby, or stick to the 'other country' story even though it was no longer true? How would her boy react if he knew that the man had no real interest in meeting him? Wouldn't it be simpler to lie about his whereabouts?

A woman who used an anonymous donor confided in another who had done the same about the pain she was going through watching her daughter struggle with identity issues as she entered her teens. The first mother had long worried about this day, when her daughter might resent not knowing her other half. The second mother

Choosing Single Motherhood © Mikki Morrissette

wondered if, deep down, that's why the struggle was happening—years of unspoken apology for the way the daughter was born being passed down.

No matter what your situation, it is natural to feel like *this* is the answer that will determine whether your child will be happy—and how you will be perceived by him or her going forward—which is why so many women are fearful of screwing up when they answer their child's daddy questions. Yet a mother's emotions about why there is no father has little to do with the child's natural curiosity about family.

It's important to support their interest and emotions—to empower them to ask questions and find answers. Your job is to make sure they know they are blessings, not victims.

What Kids Really Want to Know

Jamie told me of an experience she had with her 5-year-old adopted son. He asked why he doesn't have a father. "I started to give him the 'all different kinds of families' response, and he stopped me. He said he knows that, but why doesn't he have a father? So I decided to give it to him straight. I said because I hadn't found a man I wanted to spend the rest of my life with, but I was ready to become a mom. His response, 'well, I'll marry you.' When I said that moms and sons can't marry, he said he'd marry me when he was an adult. I said no, moms and sons can't marry then either. But when he found someone he wanted to spend the rest of his life with, he could get married. He said, 'I want to spend the rest of my life with you.'"

As we'll discuss further in this chapter, a child's daddy questions spring out of their own predictable concerns. For a young child, that includes feeling secure that a parent will never abandon them—that family is permanent. At first, they want to understand not how babies are made, but how exciting *their* arrival was. As they get a little older, they want to be reassured that they are the same as other kids, created in the same way.

Understanding the basic development phases of each age—and really listening to what your child is asking—can take pressure off the mother who worries that she won't give the "right" answer.

In the early years, the idea is simply to lay groundwork for more complex discussions that can come later.

Keeping It Simple

It took me awhile to understand what my daughter really was asking in some of our "deep" conversations. It wasn't as instinctive for me as deciphering when she was hungry or tired. Our early talks ended up not feeling satisfying because I was thinking about what I wanted my smart little girl to grow up understanding, rather than understanding what she was needing to hear.

When Sophie was three I explained—since she had a known donor—that he is her father, but not the kind of daddy who lives with us. But she didn't understand yet that some dads are integral to family life, so for her the distinction wasn't important. The only thing she wanted to know, I realized later, was that she had a dad, like other kids.

When she was four, I explained that many people are married when they have kids, but I was one of those women, like others we'd met, who had a baby but hadn't yet found someone I wanted to marry—that her dad helped me to create her, but wasn't the right person for me to marry. The explanation was too complicated. The only thing she needed to know was that there was a mom and dad who created her.

When she was almost five and Dave had entered our lives, I explained, when she asked what she should call him, that she could call him Dave, and that someday (it was apparent by then) he would be like a daddy to her. "Then I have two dads!" she said gleefully. Initially she decided to call him her "pretend daddy," and her biological father became known as her "real daddy." Now, with Dave and I married, I have tried to explain the "stepfather" term to her—but all she cares about is that her family is getting bigger, and that's good enough for her.

The code phrase here, as I've been told several times but have a hard time managing, is: "Keep it simple." As I'm learning, when a child first starts asking about dad, often what the child wants to know is simply whether he has what his friend on the playground has. Any answer that doesn't respond to that simple question won't really be what the child is looking for.

Our kids have their own agenda when they ask questions,
and generally it's MUCH less complicated than what
we feel we need to impart to them. When the questions
get more complicated, the answers can.

One approach to telling a child's story, proposed in an article about donor

Choosing Single Motherhood © Mikki Morrissette

insemination, but applicable to any origins story, suggested that a child's beginnings initially do not need to be told in biological terms (seed and egg coming together) or as the parent's story (child created to make Mom happy). Rather, it can be told as an important step toward building family. "In this approach, the emphasis is on 'us' as a family rather than 'you' as a child," the authors wrote. "It means parents are sharing information concerning how they, as a family, were formed/built/created. It is 'our family' story that is being told to the child rather than the child's story."[1]

Basic Do's and Don'ts

My conversations with child experts and Choice Moms reveal simple rules:

1. Work through your own issues about why there is no daddy for your child. Children who are conflicted about their origins often have parents who are conflicted about it. As psychotherapist Patricia Mendell said in a good article published on the American Fertility Association website (www.theafa.org), there is a growing consensus that "a child's understanding and adjustment is profoundly influenced by how the parent(s) feel about forming that family in the first place."[2]

2. Start early. One strategy used by many Choice Moms is to tell the story out loud from babyhood, so that the words get comfortable before the child is old enough to comprehend them. Lay the groundwork early, so the term "dad" or "donor" is never considered a taboo word or dismissed as unimportant. The goal is to make the child feel secure and loved, to tell the story simply and honestly.

3. Shrugging off the "dad" concept is never a good strategy. Even if you are happy not having a dad in the home, don't expect your child to feel the same. And if you used a known donor, never disparage him in front of the child, even if he hasn't played by the rules you expected of him.

4. Emphasize the normality of being different. Every young child wants to be perceived as normal. They will notice earlier than you think that having a father is normal. Be sure they know by then that there are many ways to create a family. There are several storybooks in the Resources section that tell the stories of different normal families.

5. Always remember that the birth story is theirs. As Dr. Kyle Pruett reminded us in Chapter 8, it is easy to forget that ultimately the way a child came to be is more important to him or her than to the parent. If your child is sensitive about the way he or she was created, don't push it in the hopes of making her embrace it.

6. Keep in mind that privacy can be very important to children. Many Choice Moms report that their school-aged children aren't comfortable sharing their story with friends. Sometimes they don't want to appear to be different. Sometimes they understandably don't want to explain the concepts they've learned about conception, donors who help people have babies, and how biology doesn't always relate to who your family is.

7. Realize that every child processes differently. My daughter, for example, is the type to ponder before finally asking a question, and even then it isn't always directed at me. She asked my housemate, for example, why her real daddy doesn't live with us. She mentioned to my mother that "all the other kids had daddies there," but never gave me a clue that this was a distinction she had noticed. I need to be ready when she is—and make sure she knows the door is open when she's ready to ask.

Expert Opinion

Anne C. Bernstein, author of *Flight of the Stork: How Children Think (and When) about Sex and Family Building*,[3] has given parents excellent information about what adopted or donor children need to know and when. My thanks to her for allowing me to excerpt her findings in this book.

In her 30 years as a family psychologist who studied how children understand sex and birth, she found that children question their own birth story in parallel to their growing comprehension of how other things in their world come to be. It starts with the young child's interest in where babies come from. "Young children are egocentric and concrete. Of course they want to hear their own story." As their understanding evolves, so too will the questioning about their birth.

As she wrote in *Flight of the Stork,* questions about a "missing" parent generally come when a child has "the experience and the ability to recognize that people come in two sexes and that many families include both male and female adults." This usually occurs when a child is about three.

Toddlers: "Do I Have a Daddy?"
Bernstein suggests three goals for the earliest conversations.

- **Understand what they are asking** before you jump in with an answer.

Choosing Single Motherhood © Mikki Morrissette

• **Reaffirm that you will be in their life forever.** "Younger children need to know that a parent's commitment to them is unshakeable, whether or not they are linked genetically."

• **Create an atmosphere of trust and openness.** Early discussions should be considered a first installment on what will be a continuing discussion. "It is not necessary to include every detail. Children will understand and misunderstand, but it is the feelings that leave a lasting impression."

DADS, TRUCKS AND BABIES
BY WENDY, MOTHER OF A DONOR-CONCEIVED BOY

I wasn't prepared when my 2-1/2-year-old son asked, "So did my dad die or what?" I thought the question would come up later than that. I walked him down the driveway, explained about women having eggs and men having sperm, and that I used some donated by a nice man. A passing truck caught his attention, and that was the end of that conversation.

After that, I would always take his cues when he brought it up. Everytime he asked a question we'd go a little deeper into it. It usually happened every six months or so. Eventually he was mostly curious about how people have babies. He wasn't so much missing the dad thing as overall curiosity about the process. By the time he was six, he'd introduce himself by shaking hands and saying, "Hi, I'm Ryan and I'm a donor baby." It wasn't intended to shock people. For him it was simply part of who he was. It was how he identified himself.

Preschoolers: "Why Don't We Have a Daddy?"
Preschoolers see people as related to each other because they want to be.

• **Relate to their need to understand relationships.** Such as: "I wanted very much to be a mommy, but I didn't know anybody I loved enough to live with."

• **Talk about what makes a parent real, as well as the many ways to be a parent.** Ask the child to list what childrens' daddies do, "so that they can realize for themselves that daddies are clearly the fathers who take care of children."

• **Give the foundation for their birth story.** Point out that they are a family with one mommy. "It's important to add that they have a birth mother or a biological father, so that they know how to respond when other children tell them that it is impossible to have a baby if you don't have both a mother and a father."

Although children this age don't automatically connect a father with pregnancy and birth, "discussions of this topic occur much sooner than most parents expect, so some mention of the other biological parent needs to be part of the story of a child's origins early on."

As Ellen told me, after kids in her son's preschool asked about his dad, he replied that he didn't have one. They told him that was impossible. He asked Mom, and she told him about the role of his birth father and the doctor in helping her to conceive. The next day, his preschool teacher reported that he excitedly told everyone, "I do have a dad! My mom just doesn't know who he is or where he lives!"

When the conversations get more complex

• **Confront your own conflicts, on an ongoing basis.** "Children will understand the feelings associated with the discussion of a subject long before they can clearly understand the details. Children will pick up on mixed messages, so parents will do well to try to resolve their own conflicts. Sometimes I have had parents suggest to me that, since they have ambiguous feelings, perhaps it would be better not to talk about the subject. These parents run the risk of not being viewed as resources that the child can depend on in time of need."

• **Acknowledge, if it's the case, that the subject is difficult for you to talk about.** Be sure to mention that you are glad the child asked and that you will try your best to answer.

• **Don't assume your child comprehends certain concepts.** "In my research, the single biggest mistake parents made was assuming that their children understood something accurately simply because they used the 'right' words. Children take information and draw vastly different conclusions than adults. Nor do all children of the same age or developmental stage think alike."

An example from Bernstein's book describes how two children believed that the food a pregnant mother eats goes directly to the baby in her stomach. But they drew different conclusions about what this meant. "One little boy concluded that

Choosing Single Motherhood © Mikki Morrissette

this was the way the mommy was feeding the baby. He was delighted to think that the baby got to eat some wonderful confection whenever mom did. A little girl, with the same assumption, stopped eating for fear that she would harm her future baby, which she thought of as already in her belly. She was worried about putting food on her baby, who might get hurt or dirty or somehow not be okay."

Basic concepts of child development

Bernstein supports Piaget's theories about the ages and stages of a child's thinking process, and describes them at length in her book. It's important to understand what stage of development your child is in.

A *preschooler* uses words without having much of an idea about what they mean. "Yet they do understand the feelings underlying the story, and that's really all that will be retained."

As Mendell has said, young children don't usually push for more information, and are likely to create their own imaginative twist to anything you say, so choose your language carefully, but don't be surprised at how it is digested. For example, "If you talk about eggs, kids often picture a carton in the supermarket," she noted.

Bernstein explains that, "Children *between ages four and eight* exhibit a great deal of curiosity and will be interested in understanding details of all sorts. Typical are elaborate scenarios that include magical thinking."

Starting *around the age of six*, they will start to understand basic concepts of reproduction—such as the role of sperm and egg—and that a man and woman need to love each other to be in a relationship.

After the age of eight, they become more concerned with accuracy. "They are capable of a more accurate understanding of social relationships at this age, so this is a time when sadness and questions regarding permanence may arise in children," Bernstein wrote.

By the age of 12, a child is able to combine all the information they have been given into a complete story. They might be angry that they were not conceived to a man and woman like their friends were. Their questions might be more uncomfortable to answer. But the groundwork you've laid together over the years will help.

THE QUESTION
From: Dina, Choice Mom to two boys

"Where is my daddy?" was my elder son's first question about his father, spoken when he was about 3-1/2. I thought I was prepared for it. My son knew the story of his creation from infancy. From birth I had told him a bedtime story about a lady named mommy who wanted a baby, couldn't have one by herself, and met a very, very, very nice man who helped her make a baby. I tried to make the fact of how much he was wanted be the focus of the story, not the failed relationship between the man and the woman. As he got older, I would ask if he knew who the lady named mommy was, and he'd point at me and yell "MOMMY." The answer to who the baby was came even more quickly: "ME," he'd yell with delight.

My son asked The Question after seeing his friends with daddies. Although I thought I was prepared, The Question drove a stake through my heart.

I immediately felt guilty—guilty that I had not managed to make a successful relationship with an alcoholic, guilty that I did not mind that the man did not want to be part of his son's life, guilty that I had accidentally gotten pregnant in the first place, guilty that I hadn't waited until Mr. Right or Mr. Almost Right came along. There was a little silence after my son asked The Question. I took a deep breath and was about to launch into some kind of explanation about grownups, responsibility, alcoholism and assorted other adult issues. But my son looked so innocent, so unaware of how loaded his question was, that I paused.

"What do you mean?" I asked.

"Where does he live?" he clarified. "Florida," I said truthfully. "We don't have a daddy in our family, but we have a mommy and grandma and…."

My son seemed satisfied, and that was the end of the conversation. A few months later, we were at a playdate. The other little boy (then about 4) asked my son where his dad was. My son said, matter-of-factly, "Florida but," he said, pointing at me, "my mommy is right over there and she loves me a lot!"

For myself, I learned an important lesson. The Question, when spoken by a small child, is not laden with all the questions and nuances imbued into it and implied

Choosing Single Motherhood © Mikki Morrissette

by it when spoken by an adult. For virtually all questions now, I pause and think about what could be their simplest, most concrete meaning. I ask for clarification about exactly what he is asking, and I try to answer only that question.

Sometimes, I ask an additional question or two to make sure I've completely answered the question to my son's satisfaction.

My elder son is now 6, happy and well-adjusted. He seems content with the fact that our family has no daddy and that his father lives in another state. He knows now that his father can't be a daddy because he's sick from drinking wine.

I was a little chagrined recently to discover that he told a friend that he has met his father (he hasn't), but realized that he was confused after meeting his paternal uncle when his paternal grandmother (Nana) was in town. Once I cleared up the confusion, my son was fine.

Daddy questions haven't come up much recently, especially after I showed him a picture of his father and offered to call his Nana if he had any questions. He didn't, and hasn't brought up his father in about six months, but when he does I'll answer honestly, in an age-appropriate manner.

My younger son (now 3) was conceived via ADI. His bedtime story is a continuation of my older son's. The lady named mommy wants another baby, can't have one by herself, so the doctor gives her the seeds to make a baby. (In addition, through an internet donor registry, I discovered a woman on the east coast who used the same donor to conceive her daughter. So, the bedtime story ends with the discovery of another lady named mommy who used the same seeds to make her baby.) My younger son has not yet brought up The Question, but when he does, my answer will be honest: "We don't have a daddy in our family."

I believe each person has his/her own "baggage." For my sons, not having a father may be theirs, but who knows? The most important thing, I think, is that I am at peace with my decision to have my children.

I tell them that I'm the luckiest mommy in the world, and I mean it. They may wonder about their fathers, but they will never wonder about whether they were wanted and loved.

Bernstein's advice in a nutshell

• **Don't worry about giving the perfect story.** "You will get many opportunities to go over this material. If you don't like how you handled something the first time, you will get a chance to do it again."

• **The most important thing your child will retain is what it was like talking with you.** "Statements like 'I can see how you might have thought that,' are always helpful.

• **Ask questions first, answer them later.** "Don't feel compelled to tell the whole story, but do answer what they actually asked. You can then inquire if they want to know anything else. Often children only want one bit of information at a time, so that they can chew on it before coming back for more. You can also ask them what they remember from the last time you talked about the same subject, to hear what conclusions they have drawn."

• **This is a lifetime conversation.** "One that you and your child will remember with love and laughter. This is the breeding ground for healthy intimacy and comfort with our own feelings, both happy and sad."

BONUS SECTION

BLURRING LINES:
WHEN KIDS MEET DONOR "DADS"

As reported in a *Chicago Tribune* article by Judith Graham,[4] a donor named Bobby was plagued with questions after coming into contact with 21-year-old Katie, one of his offspring. "I'm still trying to figure it out," he told the reporter. Coming into contact with Katie had "shaken everything up."

Katie, who was raised by married parents, learned during an argument with her mother as a teenager that she was conceived by donor insemination. She told Graham that she wasn't hurt or angry, but confused. She contacted the sperm bank, and someone there made a phone call to the donor. "This wasn't supposed to happen," the donor reacted. Over several weeks, he discussed with his wife the reality of an offspring attempting to find him. He accepted a letter from Katie, who

Choosing Single Motherhood © Mikki Morrissette

wrote, "No matter what contact we have, half of my chromosomes are yours."

He agreed to meet with her not so much because of what she said, but because of: 1) his own experience as an adopted child who searched for his birth parents, and 2) a photo of the girl. "I looked at that picture and I saw myself and I knew, this was the real deal," the donor said.

As Graham reported: "Things progressed quickly. [The donor] wrote back, [the girl] called, they spoke on the phone for almost three hours, she and her family drove to [his city] for a visit. More visits followed, and in 2003 [the girl's divorced mother] decided to move with her daughter to [the same city] so the relationship could be something more than long-distance."

The donor and his family, which includes two sons, "opened their home and their hearts" to the girl. "They've taken me to barbecues and trips to the zoo, and they've taken me being a pain-in-the-butt teenager and hitting bottom," the girl said.

Graham reported that the girl's mother and the donor's wife had become friends. The girl occasionally babysat her half-brothers. All of them have spent Father's Day and Mother's Day together.

But the donor said he was "reeling" from the intense emotional impact of the encounters with the girl. "There's no book you can go to and learn what is the etiquette," he told Graham. He wondered what he was supposed to do when the girl wasn't doing well in school, or wore low-cut shirts. Act like a dad and say something? Or not?

As his wife told Graham, "To think about all the interactions and make sure they're appropriate and healthy and don't hurt people, it's taken a tremendous amount of energy. People don't want to comprehend the power of a biological connection. These kids, they're going to find their donors, they're going to look for their half-siblings—it's going to happen because there's a fundamental drive to do it, and these sperm banks need to start counseling families that this is what could come."

Two Young Kids Meet "Daddy"

In a similar story involving a Choice Mom, reported in a *Washington Post* magazine article by Michael Leahy,[5] 44-year-old Raechel flew with her two young children to stay in the home of their "anonymous" donor, Mike.

In their case, both parties found each other because of the Donor Sibling Registry, where Mike had made himself available for contact by anyone who was conceived from his sperm. He is a 45-year-old divorced, childless artist. The Choice Mom is a psychotherapist. When they met, Aaron was nearly 7, eager to meet someone he could call "dad," and Leah was more shy, at 3.

According to the article, other Choice Moms who used anonymous donor insemination told Raechel she was crazy for agreeing to stay a week in his house. Although both had made contingency plans, they did end up spending the full week together. Leahy painted a picture of very comfortable moments, especially between the donor and Aaron.

Raechel told Leahy that, "Some women in my position wanted nothing to do with a man. That was never me. After I had Aaron, I thought it would be important for a child to develop an important relationship with a male. More than ever, I wanted to meet [the donor]. I'd become so grateful for everything I had, particularly my family, and I wanted to express my gratitude to the man who'd helped me to do it."

She made a point of conveying tidbits about the donor to her kids from an early age, wanting them always to think of him as the real person he is. For example, she would hold up a drawing and point out that red was one of the donor's favorite colors, or encourage them to send hugs and kisses to the donor on Father's Day.

After Raechel became acquainted with Mike in email and phone conversations, Leahy reported, the kids started mailing him cards and drawings, and he sent gifts. Eventually the visit was planned. As the article said, "Not wanting the emotional stakes of the visit to become too high for her children, she subtly downplayed their get-together. She told the kids that their trip would be 'a wonderful vacation,' careful to make [the donor] sound like just one more part of the itinerary."

Raechel herself was excited, Leahy wrote, "especially about the possibilities for her son, who had not had a chance to bond closely with a man. Her own father had died many years earlier, and she had no brother or brother-in-law. A T-ball coach had been kind to Aaron, as well as a hockey coach and a playmate's father, but none of the men could possibly be more than a pale substitute for a committed and unencumbered man," she thought.

For his part, the donor placed pictures of the kids in his home, referring to them as his "children" with friends. He told Raechel that if the kids felt comfortable, he hoped during the visit that they would call him Dad. He was clear in his own mind

Choosing Single Motherhood © Mikki Morrissette

that he did not see himself as a family man in the conventional, day-to-day sense. The donor told Raechel that he saw a lot of his own tendencies in Aaron. Particularly a need for time alone. The mother had wondered about her son's less outgoing nature. As Leahy wrote, "Listening to the man who accounts for one-half of her son's genetic makeup, she believes she is hearing the reasons for Aaron's personality." She felt that explanation alone was worth the price of a plane ticket.

Bystanders comment

Aspects of the week-long visit make apparent, however, the tricky aspects of having a "donor dad."

One of the issues with any known donor is: *What do you call him?* Raechel and Mike encouraged the kids to call him "daddy," which Aaron became comfortable with. *After a man becomes known as "Dad," especially with younger children, how do you steer them through longings for a home-based father that will naturally come up?* As Aaron blurted out to his mother, "Can we just stay here? With Mike? We could live here."

In the weeks after the meeting, Leahy reported, Mike got back to his work, realizing that he needs a lot of solitude to be an artist, still cherishing connections with the children. Raechel, in the weeks after the trip, began making plans to move her therapy practice and children closer to the donor, perhaps in a year's time, so the relationship between the kids and donor could grow. With Mike's approval, she took steps to redo her will to give custody of the children to him, and she changed their names to include his last name as well as hers.

> *As comments about the story from Choice Moms and others reveal, there are many views about the unconventionality of this particular family—the most intense opinions focused on the use of the term "daddy," as well as the decision to relocate.*

In an online chat with Leahy, one reader voiced suspicion that Raechel was trying to form a relationship with Mike by moving closer. But Leahy responded, "Raechel stressed at several points that she wouldn't let any silly romantic fantasy harm her children's well-being or their possible connection with [the donor]."

Another bluntly wrote to Leahy, "How in God's name does Raechel think she's not going to be confusing her kids by introducing them to a man she doesn't know and calling him Daddy? You have better things to do than dip into such fanciful nonsense as a woman chasing a man to the other side of the country and making her children hostage to her fantasy. What the heck are the kids going to do when Daddy says he can't see them for a month because he's painting and needs his solitude? Or has a beautiful model posing?"

A less strident reader commented, "I am 100 percent in favor of unconventional families, and totally support whatever path an individual or couple decides to take in order to fulfill their dreams bringing children into their lives and hearts. But every time she referred to [the donor] as 'your Daddy' to the children, I grit my teeth. No, this is NOT their Daddy, this is the DONOR. A daddy has a loving, permanent, committed relationship with a child — whether he is the biological father or not. As a psychotherapist, she should know that Daddy is a loaded word, and should not be thrown about lightly, especially when there are vulnerable children involved. Your article states that [Racheal] didn't want the emotional stakes of the visit to become too high for her children—was calling him Daddy all the time wise?"

Therapists respond

I contacted two women who have special insight into donor-conceived children, and asked them to comment on the story about Raechel and her kids. One of them was Anne Bernstein, whose advice about answering the daddy question we've discussed in this chapter. The other was Ellen Sarasohn Glazer, a clinical social worker with 20 years of experience focusing on infertility, adoption and related issues.

Bernstein told me she is a strong supporter of the view that all donors should be knowable, even if they are not 'known donors,' and that she would support a move toward allowing only open-identity donors (a distant but potential policy, which was discussed in Chapter 9). She indicated that the story seemed to capture a "so far so good" moment in Raechel's children's history with the donor, but—although not knowing the people or dynamic—it seemed to her that the decision to relocate was made quickly, "given that the father's commitment to parenting is more sustainable when contact is for a week or two at a time, at most a few times a year, than when proximity offers the promise (and the challenge) of more day-to-day involvement."

> *Glazer, too, said that it is difficult to comment from a distance, but that she would caution anyone from assuming that a donor becomes a father. "A relationship can still be there without being a parenting one," she told me.*

"On the positive side," Glazer said, "I feel strongly that children need to know where they came from and that these children are better off knowing who their donor is."

It also can be helpful for children to have influences from two prominent individuals

Choosing Single Motherhood © Mikki Morrissette

in their life, to help balance out the influence of one (as was discussed in Chapter 7). But Glazer, too, was concerned by the possible impulsiveness of the decision to more fully incorporate Mike into the existing family structure. She felt that contact could have been made with the donor without involving an at-home visit, using the "daddy" term, and making plans to move.

As Bernstein pointed out, it also could potentially be a difficult position for Mike, given that he might have dozens of offspring. "Developing ongoing consistent relationships with more than a few would be an unsustainable responsibility leading to inevitable disappointment should other mothers seek similar relationships."

In short, both women [as do I] agree that it can be emotionally difficult for young children to navigate relationships with donors.

Of course, it also can be difficult for children to navigate emotions about not having a father to form a relationship with—even those conceived to a married couple with a distant parent. The challenge is to make whatever bonds form be as enriching as possible.

Key to all of it—one theme of this book—is that the Choice Mom must truly have the best interest of her child at heart, and the judgment to make sound, loving decisions. No one knows yet how Aaron and Leah, and how Katie of the previous story, will be influenced by knowing their donor. In large part it depends on how receptive and open the donors remain, which requires a great deal of navigation of their own emotions in this unregulated network of biological connections.

As we discussed in Chapter 8, about using known donors, expectations of all parties need to be clearly communicated and negotiated, on a continuing basis, which can be difficult for people who tend to be independent—but highly rewarding, when done well.

CHAPTER 13

CONFRONTING IDENTITY ISSUES

"Every young person is trying to play different roles, experiment with different looks and figure out who they are. I think for [some], there is an awareness that they don't have the genetic information to do that kind of sorting out of their identity. They are basing it on their family of intimacy, but that's not necessarily where their abilities, interests and traits have come from."
— Dr. Joyce Maguire Pavao, adoption therapist[1]

General industry estimates are that each year there are roughly 125,000 adoptions involving U.S. families, and 30,000 conceptions using an unknown donor. If that's true, and a reliable average, in a typical year more than 150,000 children become part of a family that doesn't include both biological parents.

Of the donor-conceived children who are told the truth of their origins (many are not), and the adopted children who have no contact with their birth families, many will be curious about the missing pieces of their history. Some will feel loss, anger or resentment. Others will have little or no interest.

No one knows why some kids feel compelled to learn about their donor or birth family while others don't. In the case of donor offspring, a child whose conception has been an open book since birth is less likely to consider it a big deal compared to someone who learned later in life. Many kids who report insemination as a non-issue in their lives attribute it to the parents' upfront and casual attitude. But even those who are told early can grow up with identity-related issues.

Some speculate that a parent who feels guilty might unwittingly prompt the child to feel deprived of something. A glance at the varied stories of children, however, reveals that there is no fixed pattern. At best, it's the unpredictable and uncontrollable temperament of a child that determines how deeply they look at questions of identity. As one donor-conceived adult told me, "How much of who I am can be traced to the DNA of a man I've never met?"

Choosing Single Motherhood © Mikki Morrissette

In the case of adoption, children naturally will wonder why their birth parents couldn't raise them, if they were to blame for the adoption, if their adoptive parents might give them up, if their adoptive parents will be hurt by questions about birth parents, and much more. Some kids will openly ask these questions, and some will not. But all will wonder. And in some cases, these questions will have an impact on who they become.

As the excellent book *Being Adopted: The Lifelong Search for Self*[2] points out, "The search for self is not restricted to adolescents going through the much-touted 'identity crisis.' It begins at birth and continues through old age, with many ups and downs along the way to resolution. Indeed, just when the issue seems resolved, something usually happens to churn everything up again.

> *"Adoptees go through the search for self in some unique and characteristic ways, and many of the differences can be explained by the fact that adoption cuts off people from a part of themselves."*

They also report that every child searches for their birth parents, whether it becomes a full blown attempt to make contact or not. They write, "It begins when the child first asks, 'Why did it happen?' 'Who are they?' 'Where are they now?' These questions may be asked out loud, or they may constitute a more private form of searching—questions that are examined only in the solitude of self-reflection."

Sometimes the internal search can eke out in unusual ways, they report, such as a seven-year-old boy who seemed to stop blinking. Eventually it was discovered that he was afraid to blink in case he lost sight of his birth mother passing by on the street or TV screen.

There are important differences between adopted children and donor-conceived offspring. In adoption there is no biological connection between parent and child, there is no pregnancy process for the adoptive parent, and it is a live baby—rather than donor "material"—that is offered. Yet there are important similarities as well, which is why donor offspring are sometimes referred to as "half-adopted."

As we look in this chapter at the typical issues children face at stages of their life, and what Choice Mothers can do to help, the wisdom of the authors of *Being Adopted* (referred to throughout as Brodzinsky et al.) will be quoted extensively (my thanks to Dr. Brodzinsky for permission rights). Although they write about adoption, much of what they say is applicable to the donor-conceived child.

What Is the Identity Issue?

"We have an infertility industry that is built on the desire for biological connections and then these same people turn around and tell the kids that biological connections do not matter."
— Susan, a donor-conceived adult who is using a donor to conceive

A child's right to know their genetic legacy can arouse intense emotions, on both sides of the debate. Many of the most vocal are those who learned late in life that their genetic inheritance is not from the parents who raised them—and parents who are afraid of losing the opportunity to build a family.

After an "Oprah" segment aired in 2003 about donor offspring, viewers commented at great length on a website message board. Wrote one woman, "the sperm donor is just like the parent who adopts out a child. They deserve their privacy."

Another concurred, saying, "I think it's dangerous to say the donor's privacy is less important than the right of the child to know his or her parentage. Saying that sperm and egg donors must be willing to meet the children later is forcing an issue that would cause many people to refuse to become part of the donor programs. As someone who doesn't have the ability to have a child with my husband, I prefer having as many options as possible."

Although many agree that giving a donor the right to agree or not to give up anonymity is fair, some feel that a child's right to know should outweigh that choice. Others fear that children who cannot get access to their donor will resent the fact that others can.

As one woman wrote, "The only person who didn't agree to anything at the time of anonymous DI is the child, and that child should be the one who decides whether or not to contact the biological father. I have a child from anonymous DI and he has a very loving dad, but that doesn't negate the fact that he still wants to know who his biological father is and what he's like."

Wrote another, "Medical info taken at the time of [donation] is sometimes useless. As an adoptee who adores my family, I must say that it is time that society quit denying us birth rights of our identity, in all of its complexity."

And another, "I am adopted. I love my family. The only thing I can advise someone who is considering sperm donation is: please think about what the needs of your

Choosing Single Motherhood © Mikki Morrissette

child might later become. I am 35 and still stuck with answers I will never have."

Why it matters to the kids

An adoptee I know of who successfully searched for her heritage said that looking for her biological connections was not to replace her parents, but to complete the picture of identity, and "get the answers every other kid has."

As she said, "What's one of the first things said when you see a new baby with her parents? 'She looks just like her daddy/mommy.' This continues throughout life in many ways. Some of the comparisons will be to the adoptive parents, which are valid. I have definite ways about me that I picked up from my dad and my mom. When I found my birth family, I got many of the missing pieces. My birth family had many parts to my identity that I needed in order to move on and feel confident about who I was, where I came from," she said.

When Christine, the 18-year-old daughter of a Choice Mom, was allowed by the sperm bank contract to get in touch with her donor, one of the first things she asked him was whether he had big feet. "I knew it," she exclaimed excitedly into the phone when he said yes. Her next question was whether his sense of humor sometimes got him into trouble, as hers did.[3]

Not pressing questions, perhaps, but for this enthusiastic young woman the need to attribute certain unexplained traits to her mysterious donor had been strong since the age of 10.

Others have written that children who do not know both biological parents sometimes grow up struggling with "a sense of unreality, of not being born properly, not being real."[4]

To better understand this tendency—sometimes known as "genealogical bewilderment," two British researchers, A.J. Turner and A. Coyle, solicited the perspectives of adult donor offspring who were members of support networks, as they reported in *Human Reproduction* in 2000.[5] Said one child-turned-adult they talked to, "I needed to know whose face I was looking at in the mirror. I needed to know who I was and how I came to be. It was a very primal and unrelenting force which propelled the search, and it was inescapable and undeniable."

Others expressed feelings of being part of a science experiment. One woman bluntly stated that "some stranger masturbated into a glass vial and I'm the result."

Susan, the donor-conceived adult we met in Chapter 9 who learned of her origins at the age of 27, told me that none of the roughly 50 donor-conceived people she knows of in an online community are happy about donor anonymity. "It is pretty powerful to me that absolutely no one in the group feels that it's 'okay' that they cannot find out who their biological fathers are. No one feels that this is right or fair. All of us feel that something has been taken from us."

Of course, people who seek out support networks tend to have something they are trying to confront and heal. Many kids don't grow up feeling the issues as intensely. For example, according to the U.S. Census Bureau, 5 million people listed in the 2000 census were adopted (1.5 million of them under the age of 18). Despite such high numbers, relatively few seem to be reporting major identity issues.

But as Brodzinsky et al. point out, whether they seek answers and resolutions actively or not, all children start to ponder who they are by bouncing off the images of the people who helped create them. A 2005 report from the American Academy of Pediatrics indicates that interest in biological heritage is healthy.[6]

Understanding normal developmental stages will help the Choice Mother understand what questions her child is trying to resolve—especially helpful when the answers are harder to come by.

Typical Ages and Stages

No matter how a child is conceived or whether he or she is adopted, every child ponders similar questions at certain ages, as we saw in the previous chapter about answering the "daddy" question.

Noted psychoanalyst Erik Erikson believed that each stage of life involves a conflict between two directions. When the struggle is resolved, its inherent issues recede in importance—although never completely disappear—and the individual moves on to the next stage. Not all conflicts are resolved satisfactorily, and they can be particularly difficult for adoptees (and half-adoptees). Brodzinsky et al. created a set of developmental steps based on these seven stages.

1. **Infancy**—trust vs. mistrust, developing secure attachments.
2. **Toddlerhood/preschool**—autonomy vs. doubt, learning about birth, recognizing differences in physical appearance.
3. **Middle childhood**—ability vs. inability, contemplating rejection by a

Choosing Single Motherhood © Mikki Morrissette

biological parent and physical differences from family, coping with peer reactions, stigma, loss.

4. Adolescence—ego vs. confusion, connecting origins to sense of identity (including racial identity), resolving an internal family romance, coping with loss, considering a search.

5. Young adulthood—intimacy vs. isolation, facing unknown genetic history especially related to having children of one's own.

6. Middle adulthood—creating vs. stagnating, reconciling an unknown past.

7. Late adulthood—integrity vs. despair, resolution in a life review.

Most Choice Mothers start telling the birth story to their child at a very young age, before the words are even comprehensible. As Brodzinsky et al. point out, no matter how many times the story is told, the meaning of it doesn't usually start to sink in until the age of four or five. One child, for example, presumed 'adopted' meant the same as 'born.' Another assumed everyone was adopted.

Preschoolers do start to recognize racial differences, even if they don't understand how it came to be. Brodzinsky et al. report that transracial children start to react early to differences in skin color and hair type between parent and child. One four-year-old adopted girl asked if she could paint her skin color the same as Mom's.

Many young donor-conceived children, interviewed in a study we'll learn more about later in this chapter, believe their donors were unable to marry and have children of their own, so gave up part of themselves. Children don't have the context to understand what their origin story means to their life until about the age of six or seven. In early childhood, they define family as whomever lives in the house. They don't see biological connection as a factor, and don't realize that blood relationships are a common part of the family definition. One study co-authored by Brodzinsky, for example, found that children initially might feel special about being "chosen" by their parents, but often will feel less positive over time when the process is more fully understood, sometimes via peers.[7]

After they are old enough to understand basic biology (seed and egg), it will be easier to help them understand the distinction between "birth father" and "life father." This is when it becomes more useful to have conversations that let them know the donor father is a real person who wanted or helped to bring them into the world.[8]

When context starts to set in

After the age of six, children start to feel odd or confused about being different from peers. They begin to understand that blood connections exist with people not living in their family. Some donor-conceived children become more reticent about discussing their origins. In the case of adoption, Brodzinsky et al. note, "this is when the child, because of his growing capacity for logical thought, begins to realize that there's a flip side to his beloved [origins] story—that in order to be 'chosen,' he first had to be given away."

Roughly starting around the age of eight, children become more aware of the characteristics of others and use them as a way to measure and evaluate themselves, the authors wrote. A lack of similarity with parents—especially in interracial families—can give pause to a child's self-concept. "Looking in the mirror each day and seeing one set of features, and looking at other family members and seeing a different set of features, can be disconcerting, especially for the child under eight, who tends to define himself in concrete terms."

They tell the story of a six-year-old black child who was adopted by a white couple. He noticed that other black children in his kindergarten class had black parents, and the white children had white parents. "Am I black or white?" he asked. After he was reminded of his adoption story, he replied, "I know that, but I still don't know if I'm supposed to be black or white."

> *A ten-year-old boy who was adopted from Korea said, "It's weird being part of something you don't know about. When we had to do a family tree in school, I didn't know what to do. I wondered whether I should have included my Korean parents. I certainly look more like them than my parents now."*

Some children embrace the emerging awareness of their origins as part of their self-identity. At the age of six, one donor-conceived son of a Choice Mother started introducing himself to others enthusiastically as a "donor baby." As his mother explained to me, it was simply part of how he identified himself. At the age of 14, he continued to see his origins positively as a unique part of who he was.

Brodzinsky et al. explain that at this stage of life, children begin to understand not only the 'family building' concepts their parents have explained to them, but they also independently recognize the correlating factor of 'family loss.' This awareness is what sets the stage for adjustment problems that can be seen in later years.

Grieving is a natural part of the process. Some grieve quietly and for a brief time. Some deny and avoid their feelings. Some welcome opportunities to talk about them. Some become infused with a mask of bravado and oppositional behavior.

Choosing Single Motherhood © Mikki Morrissette

Some will concoct fantasies, such as the boy we will hear from later in this chapter who said his sperm was put in his mother's stomach from an alien space ship, and the girl who thought a Hollywood star she resembled was her birth mother.

Donor-conceived children go through the same processing steps as adopted children, although the comprehension of their story will vary at this age. A preteen is not likely to put the picture together of how their conception differs from that of others.

The young child who shows little interest is not guaranteed to feel the same ambivalence at 14. The job of the parent is to keep in step with the child—not push for interest that is not there, and not ignore questions that are. Setting the stage for openness is the goal.

Many children naturally begin to feel envious and jealous of others, and this is especially true of those who feel their origin story makes them "different." They might struggle with feeling unconnected from their "normal" friends, or that something important has been denied them. Their self-esteem can suffer as they feel shame or are teased, unwittingly or purposefully, by peers.

One piece of advice for developing healthy self-esteem comes from the pages of Erikson. He said the middle childhood years (between six and twelve) need to offer a sense of mastery.[9] How children cope with the natural sense of grief and loss about their origins can be influenced at this age by how well they feel they are able to have an impact on their surroundings.

EMPOWERING YOUR CHILD
From: Wendy, co-founder of Donor Sibling Registry

When my son was seven and curious about his donor, I encouraged him to write the sperm bank so he wouldn't feel powerless. He wrote a cute letter to "Dear Hospital," saying he would appreciate hearing from them if they had any information, even if he had to wait until he was 18 to get it. We slowly started putting a profile together, like pieces of a puzzle. (I didn't even know the ethnic background of the donor.) He knows he probably will not learn much more about his anonymous donor, but he'll always be curious, and together we've found ways to help him feel proactive.

Brodzinsky et al. wrote that difficult as it is for parents to watch their children try to deal with emotions related to their origin story, "They can do nothing to spare them. They can, however, help ease the process by providing a supportive, nurturing environment in which the emotional storms of grieving can be weathered. When parents ask us what they can do to make this period easier, we tell them to be available to their children, listen to them, help them clarify their emotions, and accept whatever feelings they are expressing. By their nonjudgmental responses, parents can show their children that these ups and downs are normal, real, acceptable—and temporary."

Inevitable questions of independence

In late adolescence, no longer is right and wrong a matter of what gets punished, as it is with young children. And no longer is it defined by behavior that wins approval from others, as it is in preteen years. Starting around the age of 12 or 13, young people feel they can set standards in their own unique way, Brodzinsky et al. report. They begin to pull away from authority, especially parents, in making discoveries about who they are in relation to other people. Friendships become intense, and conformity to peers is more important than ever. At the same time, the teen is trying to make sense of how ethnic and genetic identity is part of his or her unique self.

The impact of being adopted or donor-conceived can take an added significance during these inner-focused years, when the child is searching for clues about who they are, who they will be, who they relate to, who is important to them. Some teens will consider their missing pieces to be intriguing, while others will find it unsettling. Some will consider themselves special in a positive or pioneering way, while the self-esteem of others will be affected negatively. Some will build fantasies, while others will distance themselves from the idea.

Brodzinsky et al. tell the story of a teenage girl, raised in a well-to-do home, who stopped hanging out with the bright girls of her childhood in favor of kids on the verge of flunking out of junior high school. She started running away from home. She told her mother she felt more comfortable with her new friends, because "I think they're more like me."

It turns out, the authors wrote, that the girl was increasingly bewildered about whether she was more like her birth family or her adoptive family. As some children do when confronted with unknowns in their history, she believed that her "good" side came from one family and her "bad" side from another. She was subconsciously trying to decide which was her "real" self.

Choosing Single Motherhood © Mikki Morrissette

The girl had been told from an early age that her unmarried mother was too poor to take care of her. From that, the conflicted girl reasoned that she must be poor too. At the age of 16, she married a high school dropout from a blue-collar family.

What can you do to help?

Sometimes a confused teenager might act out in disruptive ways as a way to test out what the unknown inheritance might be. Brodzinsky et al. recommend that discovering more information about the missing players of their lives can help simplify the usual task at this age of separating from family by giving a more well-rounded image of what to separate from.

One family recognized their daughter's need to know more about her origins, but couldn't open sealed records. So they took a trip to her birthplace, visiting the hospital where she was born and the agency that facilitated her placement. Although she didn't get most of her questions answered, the girl felt better about knowing more about the neighborhood of her birth.

The authors also recommend two-way correspondence between child and missing parent, written entirely by the child. It gives the child an opportunity to express emotions, fantasies, frustrations about the unknowns—as well as imagine the perspective of the other party. Sometimes this helps foster acceptance and understanding.

Adult comprehension

The sense of loss can be even more intense when the child is a young adult, especially when considering having their own children, or getting involved in intimate relationships. They feel that part of themself is missing, that there is an unfilled void. Some recognize this as being part of the nature of having unanswered questions about their history—others don't know what to attribute it to.

Brodzinsky et al. reported the stories of new parents who suffered unexpected emotional pain with the birth of a child, many of them confronting for the first time the absence of their own genetic links.

As a pregnant mother, I worried about what hereditary surprises would occur. I resented not knowing what color eyes the child would have.

I realized that [my daughter] carried my genes and would begin to resemble part of me, both physically and behaviorally. When I realized this, I was surprised by my sense of jealousy.

I had terrible postpartum depression. I think it was because I was grieving all over again for the fact that I didn't have what my baby had—a mother who wanted him and kept him.

Despite the committed support of family throughout childhood, sometimes a child can still grow up with an irrational and inarticulated view of being abandoned or rejected. Brodzinsky et al. wrote of a 22-year-old woman who was unable to be involved in a relationship for more than a few months. She was afraid of making an emotional commitment. Having been placed for adoption as an infant, she grew up feeling she wasn't worthy of being committed to. "I want to leave them before they leave me," she said. "That way I'm the one in control."

Some donor-conceived children have reported feeling a loss about being created in a sterile environment from a commodity that was bought and sold. This stark view was offered by an unhappy woman conceived by donor sperm, as excerpted from literature available from the Infertility Network: "My biological father was paid for his 'services.' I feel like a product. I was sold, bought, frozen and defrosted. I feel illegitimate and manufactured. My mother paid for the little vial containing 50 percent of my genetic material. Most people enter this world freely; my conception was contractual, a mere transaction between two strangers. I regard it as putting a price on the value of my creation, my existence. It's dehumanizing and degrading."

What Does It All Mean?
The conflicts brought up here are not intended to dissuade anyone from adopting or using a donor. Rather, it is hoped that the Choice Mother who consciously wants to understand and assist her child through the stages of development can learn from the experience of those who have had strong identity issues.

In the next pages, we will focus separately on the donor-conceived child and the adopted child for perspectives and advice particular to their origins, including a section on building a transracial family.

The Donor-Conceived Child

For her doctorate in psychology from Yeshiva University, Elizabeth Groisser did in-depth interviews with 22 children, aged 5 to 10, who were conceived by Choice Mothers using donor insemination. All of the children had mothers who were open with them about their conception at an early age. My thanks to her for allowing me to excerpt her findings from the dissertation she completed in 2003.[10]

Choosing Single Motherhood © Mikki Morrissette

Imagined Characteristics—Many children considered donors to be adult versions of themselves. One 7-year-old boy believed his donor worked at a company that made Nintendo and Gameboy "cause I like electronics and if you have people in your family, or that helped, you kind of like the same things." Others attribute traits they cannot find in the mother to the donor. One 10-year-old said she must have inherited her swimming ability from the donor because her mother "hates cold water" and doesn't like to swim.

Imagined Relationships—An 8-year-old boy said his donor would allow him to have a pet snake or lizard, that he would have a beard and be very cool, and he would do anything with him except girly stuff. A 6-year-old girl imagined her donor to have red hair and red overalls. She wished she knew his name since then "it would feel like he was here." Another 6-year-old girl called her donor her "fake dad," and described him in great (and largely made up) detail. She then said he was like a man she saw on the news with dark glasses, hat and a microphone, "and I would say, oh brother, that guy looks like my dad, and one day I would find out he was my dad."

Ambivalence—Others are much less attached emotionally to the idea of their donor, and prefer to avoid the topic. One 7-year-old corrected the interviewer who referred to his donor as "dad." Some said they were too busy to think about the donor. One 6-year-old girl had a detailed image of her donor as a photographer (which was a known detail from the sperm bank). But she was clear that she didn't want to meet him because he was "not part of my family and not part of my life," and said that the letter F reminded her of him—because it was part of the word father but not the whole thing.

Another 6-year-old girl alternated using distancing mechanisms in the conversation—saying she believed he ran in marathons like she would like to; that he had curly hair like hers, although she had just straightened her hair; and that he was "a million years old," but she would like to meet him. One boy said his donor was like the middle of a ball you couldn't get to, but said he didn't want to know more about him because he wasn't going to meet him or "be what he is."

Understanding insemination—Most of the children described their donors as nice men who gave their mother sperm or seed so they could be born. Some attributed this to the desire of the man to help other people, others thought it was because he couldn't find anyone to marry and so had to give up his sperm. One 7-year-old boy believed his donor to be brave because he had to have surgery to give up pieces of his body. Several children were unclear about the process, and believed it to be an invasive procedure. Some believed that after the donor gave his sperm he could never get married and have his own children. One imaginative boy believed he once lived in a different mom, died, his spirit rose up and collided with an alien ship, then came back to earth as a spirit in sperm that went into his mother.

Factors influencing a child's reaction

Most of the single mothers interviewed as part of this research project had a **permissive attitude** about allowing their child to meet the donor (even though most of the sperm banks did not offer that option), which likely contributed to their child feeling free to understand the donor as a real person. Many of the Choice Moms provided the child with known details about the donor's appearance, occupation, education, hobbies and ethnicity. One mother of 10-year-old twin boys worked with her sons on projects tracing the ethnic background of the donor.

In a literature review, Groisser included the story of a 7-year-old boy conceived to a couple with donor sperm. His parents did not talk about what they knew about the donor. Perhaps as a result, the boy believed that the unknown donor could steal him away, which is why he needed to remain hidden until he was 18. Eventually this family was convinced that it was healthy to encourage their son's imagination about the donor in order to build a "family romance" together.[11]

OP-ED EXCERPT

KIDS NEED A REAL PAST
By Elizabeth Marquardt[12]

The author, an affiliate scholar at the Institute for American Values, talked with a woman who co-founded Family Evolutions, a company that produces products designed to be silly and fun in empowering donor-conceived children—such as a T-shirt and bib saying "My daddy's name is Donor."

For donor-conceived kids, [the company co-founder] said, "There is no daddy." She went on: "Kids who are empowered will grow up well-adjusted."

Her philosophy holds up well so long as donor-conceived kids grow up conforming to the view that they don't care about where they came from. But what if they do care? If the adults around them dismiss their donor origins as no big deal, will they feel empowered to express the deep sense of loss that they might have? Or will they be left silently to assume that if they feel any loss they have only themselves to blame?

Choosing Single Motherhood © Mikki Morrissette

Another factor thought to be important in the child's feelings about their donor was having **male role models** to help them understand men on a real level, rather than as fantasy or negative influence.

One researcher speculated that some mothers deny the existence of the donor, thinking of him as nothing more than a vial of sperm, perhaps to avoid acknowledging feelings of "shame, loss, and disappointment." Other women might construct the donor as a glorified member of the family who completes a picture, often resulting in an unhealthy fantasy for the child that this wonderful man might someday show up. In either case, the children might end up with negative feelings about insemination, as one 10-year-old boy who said, "Nice man, yeah, right. I bet you he just did it for the money."[13]

Groisser also quotes Wellesley College researcher Rosanna Hertz, who we met earlier in this book. Hertz discovered in interviews with 56 Choice Mothers that women who used donors—both anonymous and known—tend to create a picture of the father as the child grows to give them a broader sense of genetic kinship. She wrote that this "ghost father" image is important to validate the child's sense of self.[14]

Hertz concluded that the mother needs to **acknowledge and embrace elements of her child that derive from the donor**. In so doing, the child can avoid feeling rejected by a genetic father, and can feel he or she was produced from a human being rather than a "deconstructed part of a man."

Be a role model in telling the story

Someday the donor-conceived child will be telling other people about her origins, and answering questions from others. The way the parent tells the story—to loved ones as well as strangers—will be the model for how the child responds someday.

Elizabeth Carr, who was the first U.S. baby conceived through in vitro fertilization, was seven when she finally understood how much effort her parents went through in order to conceive her, according to an excellent American Fertility Association online fact sheet.[15] She says that every parent who uses unusual means to have a child must be prepared to handle the child's eventual reaction to it. For her, it hasn't been a negative experience, she says, because her parents never communicated her origins as something different or abnormal. "If the parents are comfortable and can talk to the child openly, then I don't think the child will have any problems," she said.

Most Choice Moms find themselves telling the conception story to their child by the age of three. Some start the story earlier, so that the words become comfortable by the time the child is more aware of them. Many kids want to hear the story again and again. A few children ask practical questions about the donor, such as *"Does he have a family?" "Why can't I know his name?"* Other parents report their children give no real response or reaction to the story. Both reactions are common.

Seven-year-old Helen would like to meet her donor someday, and doesn't mind not having a father since she likes getting all of Mom's attention. But as her Choice Mom told me, the difficulty for Helen is "when other children ask questions that she finds hard to answer. She tried to explain donor insemination to them, but said they didn't understand because they didn't know what sperm was."

When kids get teased, some parents report that it doesn't seem to bother their children as much as being kidded about their hairstyles or sports prowess.[16]

A 14-year-old girl reported that a friend once threatened during an argument to tell everyone in school about her donor-conceived status and that it meant that she didn't have a father. Although her friend's threat (not carried out) was upsetting, the girl said she was able to withstand it without feeling self-conscious "because of the way I have been raised to believe in myself."

FROM: SUSANNAH, AGE 14
excerpted with permission from Donor Conception Network

I can't remember my parents telling me I was a donor baby — it is something I just seem to have always known. At school one day when I was about eight I remember us having a biology lesson and everyone saying things like, 'I look like my dad or I have my mom's nose.' Right from then, whenever the subject was raised I would always say I was born through DI and they would ask what it was. I loved telling them because it made me feel special. I am not at all ashamed about it.

As much as I get all the love and support I need at home, it upsets me when people say things like 'I have my father's nose and my mother's mouth' without realizing how special it is just to say that. When you know which bits of you came from your mom and your dad then you can focus on who you are. Knowing could establish what is what and help me feel relaxed and secure. It really is about knowing tiny details: what my donor likes and dislikes, his hobbies, favorite TV shows, his views on life, what his values are. I believe these things are the key to understanding myself.

Choosing Single Motherhood © Mikki Morrissette

What can you do to help?

1. Whether you choose an open-identity donor or not (this question is explored in Chapter 9), my advice is that you have a **method for determining which donor you choose** to someday help your child respect the fact that there was, indeed, a process you went through to create his or her unique self.

2. If you've used an open-identity donor, be sure the child recognizes that there is no guarantee that he will be reachable, and that they probably won't have a relationship, but that she is **entitled to know as much about this person as the two of you can find together**.

3. Especially if you don't have much information about the donor himself, consider **gathering articles and videotapes** of shows about donor insemination, for your own special library collection you can offer to your child. Acknowledge that it might be difficult to have unanswered questions—just as it's sometimes difficult to not have a father—and that together you are creating a family with a loving network of friends and relatives.

4. Create a **life book and/or family book**, described in the next section.

General Tip: Don't be overly concerned about the depressing stories of angry donor children often featured on TV talk shows. Happy, adjusted children are in the majority, but don't bring in the ratings.

The Adopted Child

As we've already discussed, adopted children might be ashamed of their origins, or angry about not having a simpler, more "normal" story to share with others. These emotions will often appear periodically over the child's lifetime, and can hit hardest anytime after about the age of ten.

Particularly in the middle childhood years, these growing problem solvers might begin to ponder other choices that might have been made. Brodzinsky et al. quote children of this age who suggest:

> *"If she didn't know how to be a mommy, then someone should have taught her. She should have gone to school to learn, then it wouldn't have happened."*

> *"If she didn't have enough money to keep me, why didn't she get a job?"*

"I often wonder why she and my first dad didn't get married. Together they probably would have been able to keep me. That gets me angry, that my first dad probably just left and didn't care enough to try."

Some might act out as they cope with the emotions of a story they're not yet ready to accept. A Korean-born child had an uncharacteristic meltdown in a Chinese restaurant when she was eight. Brodzinsky et al. quote the girl as saying, "All the Orientals in there kept looking at us as if I was a freak. I looked more like them than I looked like Mom and Dad. And then I started to wonder: could they maybe even know my [birth] family?"

One Choice Mom told me her seven-year-old daughter tends to ask questions such as: *Do you think my birth mother is all right? Does she miss me?* She rarely asked about simple biographical details, such as favorite color or food. "The sophistication of her questions is amazing to me when you realize she is seven and thinking about these things already. I wonder about the questions she *isn't* asking me."

Although every adopted child wonders about the birth parents, few take the step—even as adults—to mount an actual search for information or contact. On the other hand, one man gave this reason for his search: "I want to stop running from life, to feel complete, to stop looking at every stranger wondering if I'm related, to settle my self-image anxiety."

Brodzinsky et al. report that the typical person who searches for birth parents has an average age of 29, and that the majority of them are female. The typical searcher tends to be married and the search has been triggered by a life event, such as a marriage, birth of a child, or death of an adoptive parent.

The authors point out that whether or not the adopted child feels compelled to search, it has little to do with satisfaction with the adoptive family.

What can you do to help?

Even if the questions and confusions cannot be avoided, there are proactive steps that parents can take to help an adopted child embrace the knowns and unknowns of his or her past. Suggestions from a variety of adoption experts, particulary Lee Varon (author of *Adopting on Your Own,* which we discussed in Chapter 10) include:

1. Provide the child with as much **information** as possible about the birth family and culture, the circumstances of the adoption, and other available details (without making them up).

Choosing Single Motherhood © Mikki Morrissette

2. Through your example, **help your child learn how to answer prying questions** such as: *What happened to her parents? Why did they 'give up' the child?* One Choice Mom was rudely asked, in front of her daughter, how much she had to pay for her. Varon stresses the importance of being matter-of-fact, non-defensive and, if possible, humorous when dealing with questions that are no one else's business. One good resource to teach children how to handle comments and questions is the *W.I.S.E. Up Powerbook* and parent guide, written by Marilyn Shoettle *(see Resources)*.

3. Make a Life Book

Varon recommends that parents start a life book, which can be added to over time, to tell the story of where the child was before placement, as well as the story of his adoption. For her children, she collected photo albums and souvenirs from the birth country. The goal of a life book is to tell the story of a life, answer future questions, and enhance self-esteem. It includes:
- child's birth information, family history, religion history
- letters and mementos from birth parents and others
- important milestones, special events, interests, stories
- memories by the child and other important people

4. Make a Family Book

Guidelines from Holly van Gulden and Lisa Bartels-Rabb about creating a family storybook[17] include:
- recording thoughts and feelings as well as events
- being simple for a child's understanding
- photos, illustrations, mementos
- brief description of your own birth, family, childhood, education, career, process of becoming an adoptive parent
- your emotions waiting and meeting the child for the first time
- information about the birth parents, as available, including first names and why they might have chosen adoption
- child's vital statistics and first-day stories
- information about where the child was living before adoption

5. Update your vocabulary. Varon includes a list of positive and negative terms in her book. In reading over the list, I realized that my "old" vocabulary was tied to the language used in the 1960s, when my brother was adopted, and is quite out of date. For example, it is a **birth** parent, not a "real" parent, who decides to **terminate parental rights** or **make an adoption plan,** rather than "give up" a child. The birth parent does not decide whether to "keep" the child, but whether to **parent.** If the **child in need of a family** (not an "available" child) decides **to locate** or **to contact**

the birth parents someday, this is not referred to as "tracking down" the ***biological relatives*** (not "natural" or "blood" relatives).[18]

The Multiethnic Family

According to 2000 U.S. census information, 17 percent of the 1.5 million adopted children under the age of 18 were a different race than that of the head of their household.[19] That makes for a lot of multicultural families.

It should never be the goal in a multiethnic family to leave the child's cultural references in the past, and effectively force the child to think of himself or herself as "white." That is a supreme disservice to the child, akin to asking him or her to pretend to be of the opposite sex.

As Brodzinsky et al. wrote about transracial adoptions, "The healthiest adjustments are made among children whose families have managed to redefine the very meaning of family. When people adopt children across racial or cultural lines, they no longer are just a white or black family. They become a multiethnic family. The culture from which the adopted child originates must be brought into the family in meaningful ways, through holiday celebrations, trips to the country of origin, and frequent

---

ARTICLE EXCERPT

RAISING A CHILD OF ANOTHER RACE
By Jana Wolff
excerpted from Adoptive Families[20]

Ultimately, we have had to come to terms with an inescapable reality: we cannot master transracial parenting. No matter how exemplary we ourselves might be as role models, no matter how much we love our sons and daughters, we cannot be our child's color and part of his or her cultural heritage. Once we acknowledged the challenges facing us, we could reduce the tasks into manageable pieces. Then we did what all parents do: try hard, stay in the game, and hope for the best.

At times, we've found ourselves forcing our experiences and relationships. I remember sitting through a Sunday morning service in an all-black Baptist church. Sure, Ari got to see lots of lovely and friendly black families, but since we are Jewish we could never truly belong to a different religious community. We have since learned to customize our family traditions so they fit our particular

---

Choosing Single Motherhood © Mikki Morrissette

interaction with other children of similar background."

They also write, however, that two adopted children in the same family will resolve their search in different ways. One family with teenaged boys took a family vacation to their home country; one son felt reassured from the trip, the other was withdrawn and anxious.

A white couple reported that the older son was conflicted about his racial identity—calling himself an Oreo, "black on the outside, white on the inside"—whereas the younger sister had no trouble feeling herself to be black.

Some kids feel reassured by dressing and talking like their peers, regardless of a different in cultural identity. Others feel stunned to realize that they wouldn't be able to speak the same language as their birth parents if they met.

Transracial families can encounter unusual challenges. Tips for dealing with them, from a variety of experts, include:

1. **Do not ignore the fact of racism** and discrimination, but attempt to define and explain it in ways your child might understand.

combination of cultures. One December, when Kwanzaa and Hanukkah overlapped, we hosted a Kwanzukah party, which has since become a tradition bringing together our African American and Jewish friends.

The range of transracial parenting experiences has forced us out of our comfort zone, and developed an extra measure of courage in us all. Being part of a mixed race family has not only challenged and enlightened us, but also altered our individual personalities. We've had to become more boldly public as a transracial family. We look to proud and successful men of color for clues on how to raise our son. Asking strangers to help in this way can be scary, but we've been amazed at their generosity, and at the value of these discussions. The more we have reached out to people unlike ourselves, the easier building a rapid rapport with strangers has become. Our hope is that Ari one day will make this quest to know his heritage. Parents can nourish young kids with healthy foods, but young adults pick their own menus. We hope that when that time of searching for himself comes, Ari's early experiences will resonate with a deep meaning. We also want Ari to know how much we care about who he is, as a unique individual.

2. **Work out possible responses** to prejudice with your child, which emphasize the protection of his or her rights. Methods should include both confrontation and avoidance, as well as occasional intervention and advocacy by Mom as a model.

3. Actively seek out role models from the child's community, and **proactively embrace diversity** yourself. Consider relocating to a more diverse neighborhood or school. (And note that living in a multiethnic neighborhood is not the same as having members of the child's particular culture available—such as a sports coach, or manager of a favorite store or restaurant.)

4. Together seek out greater understanding of your **child's cultural history**. See Chapter 9 for the ways a Choice Mother of two has incorporated her daughters' Chinese heritage into their daily life.

5. Make sure your child grows up **feeling proud** of her culture, but also independent of it. The goal is to identify with members of the community, and not be ashamed about being part or apart from the culture.

6. Be sensitive to the **religious background** of your child, and be willing to observe services or find a mentor who will accompany your child.

Many Choice Mothers of multicultural families have been careful to move to a more diverse community. This is a good step—although it doesn't resolve every issue. One such mother I talked to discovered years after moving that her tough-minded daughter had not been telling her that other girls were taunting her because she was middle class and they were not.

More than anything, this mother told me, it was the race difference between parent and child that became a focus of attention for her daughter over time. Of little or no consequence was being raised by a single parent, the basic fact of being adopted, or missing the presence of a father in the home. "She was fascinated by our different skin color, our different hair texture, our different religious backgrounds."

Through it all, Mom followed her daughter's lead, allowing her to become attuned to issues of ethnicity in her own way. "I didn't make a big deal of it, I just exposed her to it in whatever ways I could." Today, cultural differences are a big part of her daughter's life. She has lived in and traveled to a variety of countries and is interested in cultural anthropology and identity. Although she struggled greatly with some issues growing up, she is a highly dynamic and active young woman.

Choosing Single Motherhood © Mikki Morrissette

Final Thoughts

As we know from our own childhoods, every child will grow up with issues. The Choice Mom should be prepared to be yelled at by her child someday for the way he or she was added to the family. If you are confident in your decision, however, it will be easier to accept the tirade and not feel threatened by it. Providing the child with as much truthful information as you can about inherited traits and characteristics can alleviate a child's sense of disconnectedness. And respecting the need to know can go a long way to helping a child cope with any identity crises.

As Anne Bernstein (who we met in the previous chapter) has written: "The most important factor in children's psychological adjustment to the circumstances of his origins is how parents feel about how they formed a family. A parent who can discuss these issues matter-of-factly and without defensiveness, who is open to a child's questions about key figures in her conception and birth, will foster the child's positive self-regard."[20]

Santa Monica-based clinical psychologist Elaine Gordon[21] also told me about the importance of welcoming open discussion of a child's biological origins. Speaking about donor insemination, she said, "Hopefully the acknowledgement of there being a father is answered and discussed both from the genetic and social perspective. One of the most destructive things I see in my practice is that single women, both lesbian and straight, will sometimes try to deny the existence of a father, which is not in the best interest of the child. Children want to be like everyone else, and were born like everyone else, albeit into different circumstances."

Whether you are the parent to an adopted or donor-conceived child, there are several steps you can take to help your child.

1. Build **strong family connections and rituals**, especially if the child indicates a sense of being abandoned or rejected.

2. Use **family consultations** as part of the decision-making process, especially if the child expresses a need for a better sense of control.

3. Ensure the child feels able to **talk easily and openly** in the home about identity issues or his or her origins.

4. **Form friendships with other families with similar histories** so that the kids grow up knowing others with non-standard origins.

5. Embrace the origin story in a matter-of-fact way, rather than treat it as unimportant. Discuss it casually—but openly—with friends and teachers as needed until the child is ready to handle it in his or her own way.

6. Be an advocate. Varon wrote about a woman whose adopted son came home in tears after his class starting doing a family-tree assignment. The woman said that she realized that she needed to be proactive on behalf of her child. "Part of this involved sharing information about adoption and single-parent families rather than blaming other people for not having taken the time to do this work," the woman told Varon.[22]

7. Respect the child's privacy. Tread softly on advocacy, however, based on your child's comfort zone. Some children are reluctant to disclose their story to others by the age of six. Ask before sharing a life book or initiating public discussions. By the age of 10, many children are deciding whether or how to disclose the story.

8. Other kids might not retell your child's origin story the way you or your child prefer. Be prepared to **help your child with self-consciousness** about loss of privacy if curiosity compels peers to ask personal questions. Often the most awkward stage (about anything) is between the ages of 10 and 14. It's best to arm them—with your example of poise, confidence and words—before the age of 10. After that, they will likely want you to butt out.

ARTICLE EXCERPT

INTERNATIONAL ADOPTEES WELL-ADJUSTED
reported by Reuters news agency[23]

A study in the Netherlands compared kids who were adopted internationally in the U.S. and Europe, children who were adopted domestically, and similar children who were not adopted. "Contrary to common opinion, international adoptees present fewer behavior problems than domestic adoptees, and they have lower rates of mental health referral" regardless of age, the study said.

The study was published in *Journal of the American Medical Association*.[24]

Choosing Single Motherhood © Mikki Morrissette

Chapter 14

How to Raise a Well-Balanced Child

The ambitious cultural shift I am hoping for is this: that adults come to view appreciating and being generous to others, acting with fairness and integrity, and formulating mature and resilient ideals as evolving and subtle capacities. This shift is especially important for adults who are becoming parents. For parenting is clearly a prime instance when adults are faced with hugely complex challenges to their core moral qualities: their capacity for empathy and fairness, their ability to disentangle their own interests from those of others, their generosity.
— Richard Weissbourd, essay in *The American Prospect*

It is a daunting task for any couple to raise a healthy, well-balanced child. It can be even more challenging for a single parent, since there is no solid partner available to help alleviate stress, play "good cop, bad cop" in matters of discipline and enforcement, and provide a child with two different sets of skills, perspectives, and networks of family and friends.

As we read in Chapters 6 and 7, growing up in a single-parent home, without a biological father, can affect a child. But as we also read, good parenting requires skills and supplements that are not exclusive to married couples.

The challenge of any parent is to find the time to create and implement a vision—a strategy for molding a confident, hopeful and happy moral character out of the little personality you have been given. After that baby enters the house, parenting can easily dissolve into a daily struggle to earn, nurture, enjoy, discipline and stress.

On the front end, we are consumed asking ourselves if we're prepared to be Choice Mothers. The middle years of parenthood involve an even longer list of questions. *Is this the right child care provider? Why won't he sleep? Shouldn't she be talking more by now? Why won't he eat? Am I letting her watch too much TV? Is he becoming resentful about not having a dad? Is she doing well enough at school? How do I get him to talk*

A mother loves her child like no one else, yet in the end, after the child is grown and we breathe a heavy sigh as the door closes and they eagerly depart for college and family and friends of their own making, what will our years of questions and hard work have added up to? How will our child turn out? Will we have raised a well-balanced person?

One of the basic needs of any individual is to feel connected to a larger universe. Our well-being depends on it. And our children will increasingly look to this wider universe for their lifetime of meaningful experiences and relationships. How will they do, when they are navigating on their own? How will we have prepared them? Will they embrace their future with hope and optimism? Will they be able to commit to intimate relationships? Will they achieve goals, respect others, act responsibly?

This, after all, ends up being what the stuff of successful parenting is. More than whether they were breastfed or bottle-fed, cared for in a daycare center or a home, out the door on time with hair combed and teeth brushed, it is the quality of the connections they will make—how they fit into the larger community—that will determine if they are the happy and healthy individuals we want them to be.

Developing a child's inner core is the most important thing a parent can do, yet it is often lost when the juggling act begins. Michael Gurian, one of the experts we talk with in this chapter, has said, "Most of us are too busy to think of our children as being anything other than 'boys' or 'girls.' This, like thinking of them as 'kids,' is worthy and important, but how little we think of them as souls."

In this chapter, we will hear from nationally respected child development experts I consulted for this book. Each of them offer different specializations and insight helpful to Choice Moms. We will boil down their theories, and other things we have learned throughout this book, into a definition of what children need in order to become well-balanced individuals. Then we will turn these concepts into a game plan that any Choice Mother can use as a guide until her guiding days are done.

In a nutshell, I propose that the plan we develop in this ambitious chapter is the minimum requirement for any parent. Any Thinking Woman must be prepared not only to consider the expense and logistics of raising a child alone, but to contemplate how she will single-handedly cultivate that child's connection to the world.

The Experts

There are countless experts across the country who offer good insight about what makes "good kids" and what makes "bad kids." The Parenting shelves at bookstores and libraries are filled with their wisdom. Sometimes the advice focuses on dealing with an overwhelming list of things that can go wrong with the kids we love so much: violence, drug use, depression, eating disorders, learning disabilities, promiscuity, delinquency.

Although there is wisdom from many quarters for this chapter, I have singled out four experts for advice specific to a Choice Mother. These four have written excellent books about their philosophies. They are:

Mary Sheedy Kurcinka
Parent educator; author of books and workbooks, including "Raising Your Spirited Child" and "Kids, Parents and Power Struggles" [1]

Kurcinka's advice about how to understand a child's temperament and emotions—as well as the parents' own—is helpful for the busy Choice Mother who needs to communicate effectively with her child in order to establish mutual respect and the essential authoritative style of parenting. The stress of being the sole disciplinarian and conflict-mender is great, making it vital for the Choice Mom to have keys to unlock power struggles.

Her highly regarded books have enabled parents to see the temperament behind their children, how the child's personality matches and clashes with their own, and how to create a better "fit" together. The idea is not to rewire parent or child, but to better understand and enjoy each other so parenting doesn't dissolve into a depressing and never-ending tug-of-war.

For example, as she speculates in *Raising a Spirited Child*, the inventor Thomas Edison was likely a frustrating child. "I wondered how many meals had gone cold when he forgot to come home for dinner or how many times his dad had yelled at him to stop taking apart everything in the house. Today we celebrate his persistence, single-mindedness, perceptiveness and drive."

"You don't get to choose your child's temperament nor does your child, but you do make a big difference," she writes. "It is you who helps your child understand his temperament, emphasizes his strengths, and provides him with the guidance he needs to express himself appropriately."

Kyle Pruett

Child psychiatrist, Yale Child Study Center and Medical School; president of Zero to Three: National Center for Infants, Toddlers and Their Families; author of "Fatherneed: Why Father Care Is as Essential as Mother Care for Your Child" [2]

As we discussed with Pruett and others at length in Chapter 7, children need men in their life. Men and women naturally offer different skills and temperaments that help a child grow up in a balanced way. It is difficult, and not advisable, for any one person to attempt to handle the yin and yang of every situation. As he points out, "Men are the single greatest untapped resource in the lives of American children. Natural, renewable, and by and large nontoxic, they couldn't be healthier for the country's children. We can't afford to let another one get away."

Among other things, his book offers suggestions to help ease a child's need for a father at different stages of development.

Michael Gurian

Therapist, educator, and long-time specialist in male development; author of many books, including "The Good Son," and "The Wonder of Children." [3]

Anyone who has ever been in a relationship or watched toddlers of different sexes knows that "Men Are From Mars, Women Are From Venus," as John Gray put it. But neuroscience, enhanced by new imaging technologies, gives us evidence about why, as Gurian details in his books. For example, the differences between the brains help explain why males tend to try to problem-solve quickly, compared to females who tend to delve into emotional issues.

Gurian also writes at length about the importance of community and ritual in a child's life. What kids need besides a primary caregiver, he says, are elders to help them understand how everything they experience is helping to form them into adults. Not unlike the useful aspects of a kibbutz, he wrote, "With many voices teaching the child, the child hears echoes of values, wisdom, self-worth. Parents have back-up systems, babysitters, respected partners in child-raising. When children make their inevitable moves toward independence, there are other community members with whom they've bonded and to whom they can turn for advice, help, or embrace."

Richard Weissbourd

Harvard-based lecturer, child psychologist, and author, "The Vulnerable Child: What Really Hurts America's Children and What We Can Do About It" [4]

Choosing Single Motherhood © Mikki Morrissette

Weissbourd, who we heard from in Chapter 6, says important things about the "big picture" aspect of quality parenting. Namely, that national debates about family structure and income level tend to overlook a vital aspect of quality parenting: the emotional stability of the caregiver. It is common, he has written, for social workers to find children whose needs are not being met because a primary caregiver is depressed and feels helpless and hopeless.

Concept #1: The Basics

Children do not need perfect lives in order to grow up whole. They learn from mistakes (yes, even mom's) and can develop strength from bad times. What they *do* need are a few essentials designed to make them feel secure, connected, accepted and hopeful.

Weissbourd suggests in *The Vulnerable Child* that a well-balanced child needs:
- order and consistency;
- a continuous relationship with a caring adult who sees the child as special;
- interaction with an adult who stimulates, engages, challenges and provides a compass for meeting social and moral expectations;
- strong friendships and community ties;
- protection from exploitation and discrimination, as well as a sense of justice and opportunity for achievement;
- attention to any special health, social and educational needs.

"When children have these ingredients," he writes, "they are likely to have trust in themselves and in the world, inner vitality and resourcefulness, and the capacity in adulthood for zestful play and for gratifying work and love, even if they suffer hardships and abrasions. Children who grow up without these ingredients are clearly not African-American children or underclass children or children in single-parent families only. Looking at children in this way forces policy makers and the public to see the many vulnerable children in this country who are not poor."

Concept #2: Understanding the Child

Gurian, Kurcinka and others talk a great deal about 'nature-based parenting.' Rather than attempt to mold children to a parents' vision of who they should be, the attentive parent reaches in to understand a child's strengths and weaknesses, and teaches that child how to recognize and handle their own feelings.

The more "emotional intelligence" a child develops in this way, the more able he or she is to make connections, tackle challenges with confidence, negotiate differences, maintain self-esteem, cope with ups and downs—and cooperate with Mom.

As Kurcinka explains, if a parent realizes her child is introverted, for example, she will understand that he needs time alone in order to feel energized after a long day at school. When he starts to get surly, she will help him recognize that he needs alone-time, and enable him to get it until he's recharged—rather than push him to talk about his day and get upset when he grunts.

Extraverted children provide a special challenge to the single parent. They are at their best when they can be engaged in activities and need regular feedback. "There is no way one parent, especially an introverted parent, can keep up with the interaction needs of an extraverted spirited child," Kurcinka says. This kind of child needs to be taught to ask for attention and encouragement from grandparents, mentors, friends and neighbors, rather than simply have mom yell "Give me a break!"

It is easy for a Thinking Woman to agree with this philosophy. It is more difficult to implement. But understanding how the brains of boys and girls are wired differently helps (see Gurian's books). Understanding the innate temperamental styles of children—which you can't yell out of them—helps (see Kurcinka's books). And letting the child know that mom is attempting to understand helps tremendously.

Concept #3: Community, Community

There are so many reasons community is vital to a child that it has appeared in many chapters of this book already—and every child development expert I talked to specifically for Choice Mothers brought it up as an essential component of successful parenting.

As we discussed in Chapters 6 and 7, research indicates that children grow up best when they have a balance of influences that single parents will struggle with alone. One of the (stereotypical perhaps) benefits of having a father in the home, for example, is generally to serve as the rule-driven parent of authority, compared to mom's flexible stature as nurturer.

This is one reason why Pruett and others recommend that a team of secondary caregivers—at least one of them male—be in place at the earliest age to help Mom:

Choosing Single Motherhood © Mikki Morrissette

- encourage both connection to others *and* independence;
- instill a sense of personal safety *as well as* assertiveness;
- offer predictability *and* flexibility;
- have respect for relationships *and* rules;
- be duty-bound *as well as* empathetic;
- provide an environment that is demanding *and* responsive.

Gurian talks about the importance of community to help form character in an even larger sense. "Mentors and intimate role models rarely exist to show in any long-term and consistent way how both to serve a group and flourish as an independent self," he wrote in *The Wonder of Boys*. With busy parents and little emphasis today on cultivating the soul, celebrities too often become the heroes, peers the role models.

The typical Thinking Woman is considering what family and friends can help her get through the first few years as a Choice Mom—but community is so much more than that. And the sooner she develops a creative list of outlets, the better able she will head off the often predictable stages of loneliness and isolation that can occur in single parenthood.

Kurcinka advises that community organizations and individuals be found early to give parents predictable breaks from their child. "That way you know your child is with other good, healthy adults and you can have time to pursue some of your own interests and needs," she told me. "The more you can set up a predictable routine that includes time together, time with others as family, and time apart, the smoother things will go. When you're feeling tired, for example, you'll know that Tuesday night is YOURS while your child is with his 'big sister' or at Scouts."

This benefits more than Mom's sanity. As Weissbourd points out, "Children of all ages should have a variety of opportunities for exploring their environment and talking with adults."

That means communities, not just parents, need to offer meaningful activities for children that build trust, self-confidence and a sense of hopefulness and excitement about the future. "Decent environments not only provide clear discipline and encourage children to absorb basic social expectations and norms," he says, "they also give children the knowledge and skills, the practical strokes—such as how to ask for directions or for change—that will enable them to swim in the mainstream."

This emphasis on community means you need to identify adults in your neighborhood whom children respect, who look out for their safety as if they were their own. You need to generate or find informal networks and events that support kids. You need to help build communities that believe that all adults are responsible for all children—not just their own. And it means, even as a busy single parent, you eventually need to get out of the house and the workplace and *participate* in that community. A dedicated Choice Mother will volunteer to coach or teach a skill at the community center or church where her child grows.

Concept #4: Establish Mutual Respect

Some believe a child without two loving parents in the home miss out on the lessons of seeing adults work out conflicts in a healthy way and relate to each other with love, trust, and respect. However, many of the children I talked to for *Chapter 16: How Are the Kids Turning Out?* didn't agree with this concern, indicating that the strong relationship they have with Mom (for those who did) was example enough.

[On the other hand, none of the children I have interviewed so far—who range in age from 10 to 30—had truly fallen in love yet, so it is hard to assess how well they will do when the opportunity comes.]

What I did see, with those kids who had loving connections with their Choice Moms, was a great deal of mutual respect. And this, I believe, is the key ingredient to building healthy relationships with anyone. It also ties directly to the other concepts we've discussed.

When a child has a mother who attempts to understand the innate personality within, and helps him or her find words to express frustration as well as appropriate outlets for energy and emotion, that child grows up not only with self-respect, but with respect for the authority and the nurturer that is mom. And when that child *and* mother have several others in the community to turn to for support and encouragement, the parent-child relationship doesn't get overburdened and overwhelmed.

Wendy and her teenage son are one of several parent-child teams I interviewed who I greatly admire for their strength in this area. Wendy is not a traditional Choice Mother—she was married when she conceived using a donor, but divorced soon after. She was relieved that her son wouldn't grow up in an atmosphere of hostility, but was intimidated by the awesome responsibility of nurturing "this little human being alone. Any mistakes that are made, it's all me. I would get the glory, but also all the blame."

Choosing Single Motherhood © Mikki Morrissette

Like most women who actively choose to raise a child without a partner, Wendy embraced her role as Choice Mother as "the most important job I would ever have in my life. I worked on my own issues so they wouldn't be passed along. I knew I couldn't be a perfect mother, but I would ask for forgiveness when I made mistakes. I would keep the playing ground equal so we would both be very accepting of each other—and then hopefully he would be with himself too."

More than a decade later, Wendy's strategy has paid off noticeably. Even in private, under guarantee of confidentiality, her teenage son had terrific things to say about the way she raised him. "I have a great, involved mom," he told me. "From handling almost every aspect of my education to instilling in me a sense of right and wrong, she's done it all. And to be perfectly honest, I feel that she has done most everything right. She gives me all the freedom a teen needs without ever having to worry about me trying pot or a cigarette or anything like that."

Concept #5: Authoritative Parenting

Wendy brought up another important aspect of quality parenting: maintaining the division between parent and child by establishing the mother's authority. In fact, mutual respect enhanced her ability to be The Enforcer. She has never needed to yell or threaten her son, she told me. All she needed to do was give him "the look."

"Even now, he towers over me, is 50 pounds heavier, and I can almost bring him to tears with 'the look,'" she said. "It comes from having respect for each other, I think. At this age, he sees friends yelling at their moms, and families where the teenager becomes the boss. But he would never say anything disrespectful to me.

"It's challenging—you need to have a friendship, when it's mom and one kid together so much of the time you need to like each other. But having clearly defined boundaries between parent and child is very important."

Diana, whose college-aged daughter also expresses great respect for Mom, said establishing authority was difficult at first. "I didn't know how to say no," she told me. She adopted her daughter at 13 months from a family that had provided little nurturing. "I just wanted to hold her. For a long time when she was a child, all she wanted to do was sit on my lap. It was hard for me to learn how to discipline her." But slowly she managed to put rules in place that helped establish her authority. *When I'm eating you can't interrupt me. There is no time it is appropriate for you to hit someone.*

It helped Diana to realize that setting limits didn't have to involve anger, but developing her daughter's sense of empathy. *It hurts my feelings when you do that. When you wake me up at night it makes me tired and more likely to get colds.*

Diana's daughter is now a highly disciplined, moral young adult. As Diana told me, "I recently asked her whether I was a successful authority figure. She said, 'Absolutely not. You were never any kind of authority figure. What you always had was an ethic that what you communicated was inviolable.'"

Establishing rules is naturally harder for a single parent—even a strong one. Speaking from experience, with the wisdom of many other Choice Moms I have talked with, it is difficult to always be the "heavy" with your child. And it is tough to avoid caving into demands without the support of another adult. Especially since, as Pruett says, any parent working alone gets "old," with a natural lessening of authority over time.

Research by gender-identity specialist Barbara Risman[5] revealed that even in single-father households there tend to be weaker controls and fewer demands, suggesting that it is the logistical factor of solo parenthood, rather than the sex of the parent, that makes the difference in establishing the important authoritative approach to parenting. Kids in single-parent households tend to seem more mature, which leads the parent to be more permissive and take less of a supervisory role.

But not only is it easier to avert trouble with kids if the parent consistently establishes her authority, but as Wendy and her son are a good example of, it helps to create respect.

As child expert and Temple University psychology professor Laurence Steinberg wrote with co-author Ann Levine in the highly regarded *You and Your Adolescent: A Parent's Guide for Ages 10-20,*[6] the authoritative parent:
- solicits the child's opinion,
- allows the child to voice disagreements,
- can be persuaded to reconsider a decision,
- values curiosity and self-direction
- wants their child to understand the reasons for their demands and restrictions, so explains why behavior is inappropriate,
- does not hesitate to assert their authority if reasoning fails,
- does not demand unquestioning obedience,
- sets limits based on love.

"This is in contrast to 'permissive' or 'indulgent' parents, who love their children dearly but have difficulty setting limits or imposing rules, and 'authoritarian' or 'autocratic' parents, who are controlling and in charge, but who discipline their children harshly and without sufficient affection or discussion," they wrote.

They echo the concerns raised in Chapter 6, and Risman's research, pointing out that the biggest issue for single parents with adolescents is maintaining control, because they grant more independence, don't have the time or energy for authoritative parenting, and have only one set of eyes and ears for monitoring a teen's activities. They also point out, "If a single parent maintains an authoritative relationship, however, any problems that might develop can be averted."

The Four-Point Game Plan

So we've learned a lot of mumbo-jumbo psychology and philosophy. How is a typical, busy Choice Mom to make sense of it and turn it into action?
Here are the basics of a suggested game plan. Make these steps part of your planning process *before* you jump into Choice Motherhood—just as you would assess and improve on your financial health.

Step #1: Develop a strong child care plan
Research suggests that the importance of the quality of early childcare is not a myth. The first few months in particular, and the first two years in general, are crucial for helping a child develop the attachment and security that will serve him or her in later years. This is why programs like Head Start have been, in strong economic times, a priority for funding initiatives. Most researchers agree that getting adequate childcare is more important than family structure. And this requires not only money, but identifying the most loving caregivers for your child before you need them.

As we discussed in Chapter 2, there are many caregiver questions to consider. No matter what you end up choosing, make the effort to develop a rapport with the caregiver, since this person is your back-up parent. And check out the staff-child ratio; suggested standards are no less than one adult for every four infants, every five toddlers, or every ten preschoolers. Are employees well-paid and educated? Is the turnover low? How well is the place managed?

Ideally, your child will be taken care of by a secondary caregiver who is consistently present when mom is not—available to snuggle, talk and play like a second mom (or a dad). Without this level of attachment, research tells us, he or she will grow up spending more time trying to be safe and loved than growing emotionally healthy and strong. And, as Gurian points out, a mother who feels guilty about the care situation her child is in will ultimately damage her authority—by overcompensating, avoiding discipline—and the child, picking up on signals that "mom wants me to punish her," will do just that by pushing her away.

Most Choice Moms *do* feel guilty for not being available full-time to their child. Make sure you are capable of devising a loving community of caregivers.

Step #2: Pick your mentors and male role models

Based on Weissbourd's checklist of requirements for a successful childhood earlier in this chapter, and the balance/counterbalance needs we've discussed in Chapters 6 and 7, identify your weak spots and take steps to correct them. That includes actively bringing people into your life—family, friends, community members—who not only support your needs, but can provide the yin to your yang. If you happen to be strong at setting rules and limits, identify someone who provides a model of flexibility. If you are an accountant and strong in mathematical abilities and problem-solving, find someone to nurture the creative side of your child.

Don't hesitate to start adding to your tribe. You will need them as soon as you become a Choice Mother, and will need different ones as your child matures. Look to godparents, the parents of your childs' friends, Boy Scouts and Girl Scouts, Big Brothers, religious organizations, extracurricular school activities, youth groups, coaches and teachers. These are not simply sources to keep your child busy. They should be actively explored as places to find good people. (Interestingly, I met my husband because I was looking for male role models for my kids.)

There is no shame in not being able to offer everything to your child. As Pruett says, "Children need you to be who you're best at being, not who you think you should be." Pruett's recommended secondary caregiving, as detailed in his book, includes:

Infancy — Invite close male friends and relatives to hold, walk, rock, play, and babysit (before stranger awareness takes hold around seven to nine months) so your child gets a sense of the body, face, smell, voice, and comforting styles of others.

Toddlerhood — Have close male friends and relatives engage in rough-and-tumble exploration with your boy or girl; they should also read and comfort, as the different behavioral styles of "not-the-mother" time are stimulating and fascinating.

Preschool years — Find someone in your closest circle to offer toilet-training boys a demonstration of stand-up peeing; encourage reading by men, since this is an

Choosing Single Motherhood © Mikki Morrissette

important activity that men and children can *do* together; gender identification begins, so boys will want to practice "being a guy" with male role models and girls will want to explore the "power of their femininity."

Early and Middle School years — Look for men engaged in religious education, recreational sports, Scouts, Big Brothers and other community activities that typically begin at this age. My daughter's *capoeira* instructor is an excellent role model for her of strength, discipline and respect.

Adolescence — At this age, kids make their own choices about adults they want to be with, are more private, and pay attention to your dating behavior as a model; make sure they have an open line of communication to other adults, including a masculine one; look for a close male family member who loves your children to help affirm and clarify expectations and limits.

Step #3: Establish rituals
An essential tool for busy parents is to create rituals that provide connection between parent and child, and with community.

Kurcinka advises Choice Mothers to create daily rituals designed to help calm and soothe: eating breakfast together, cooking together, washing dishes together instead of tossing them into the dishwasher, sitting next to the bath tub while the child relaxes and plays, dimming lights and putting on soft music in the evening, making time for walks and exercise.

Gurian stresses the importance of developing rituals at an early age—for bedtime, reading, family meals, drives, family get-togethers, family story telling. The connection that comes from rituals is even more important as the child gets older— and nearly impossible to implement if they haven't already been put in place.

In Gurian's family, for example, Thursdays are Extended Clan Gathering time. Several families with kids, elders and godparents get together for talk, Ping-Pong and food. "This kind of ritual is a complete celebration of child, family and community. As the children leave infancy and grow older, they have people to turn to, they have a night to look forward to, and they have a big family close to home," he says.

The less involved that children are with their parents and extended clan, the more susceptible they are to bad influences among peers and in the media. The strongest relationships, Gurian indicates, are forged by mothers who "keep communicating, keep talking, keep family rituals strong, keep having dinner together, family time together, reading time together."

Respected family therapist William Doherty has written a book about the importance of ritual, *The Intentional Family: How to Build Family Ties in Our Modern World.*[7] As he wrote, "Entropy—the loss of energy, connection, and focus— is the wolf at the door of all families, but especially threatens overburdened, full-time single-parent families and part-time nonresidential families. Single parenting is one of the most difficult tasks in contemporary society. But it also offers the opportunity to start family life anew, to be creative about family rituals, and to involve the children in shaping the family's values and its future.

"Some of the most highly intentional families I know are single-parent families, as are some of the most overwhelmed and entropic. The key differences appear

---

BOOK EXCERPT

POSITIVE DISCIPLINE
BY NANCY SAMALIN[8]

• Acknowledge the child's right to feel the way he or she does. Often we try to fix emotional hurts fast and unwittingly minimize their feelings with *"there's nothing to be afraid of"* or *"it can't be that bad,"* or by pointing out the sunny side, or trying to talk them out of emotions with logic. That response convinces them that they aren't being heard.

• Invite the child to be a problem solver ('can you think of a way...')

• To get your child to listen, talk less. As your child matures, learn to use one word, *"Boots,"* instead of a long, automatic response, *"How many times have I told you to take your boots off on the porch? Look at this mess you've made. You think I have all the time in the world to spend mopping up floors? You're inconsiderate. Why can't you remember something as simple as taking off your boots outside?"*

• Avoid arguments by playing with fantasy. *"If I had a million dollars a year I'd... [do what the child wants]"* Or use drama to defuse demands. *"I guess you've mixed me up with the Wicked Witch of the West,"* or, *"let's hit rewind and start over."*

• Rephrase their statements to let them know we understand without sitting in judgment. When children are in the throes of strong emotions, our empathy lets them see us as their allies.

Choosing Single Motherhood © Mikki Morrissette

to be the ability of the single parent to focus on what is most important about family rituals of connection and celebration, and on the degree of support from the extended family and community."

It's easy to lapse in connection time when you're too stressed and overworked to take a breath. Don't let yourself get isolated, overwhelmed or depressed enough to lose conscious daily moments with your child. Find your rituals, tribe and relaxation techniques before you need them.

Step #4: Be happy as a non-mother

As Steinberg and Levine wrote: "The best of us have bad days. When parents are under stress, tired, or preoccupied, they often slip into domination ('Just do it because I say so') or permissiveness ("Do whatever you want'). A bad day or a pressured decision will not have a profound effect on a child. What matters is the general pattern, over time."

To be a loving, authoritative and successful Choice Mother, you need to pay attention to your own mental and physical balance. As they advise on airplanes, put the oxygen mask over your own mouth before assisting your child—you cannot help anyone if you're passed out.

Weissbourd reports that even the child in a low-income household who has one loving and attentive parent is generally much better off than the child in a middle-class household with a parent who is depressed, withdrawn or self-involved.

Narcissistic and cold the Choice Mother generally is not. But the single parent who finds herself disconnected from others can become depressed, overwhelmed, unfocused and burdensome on her child. Who will you turn to, what non-mother activities will you be involved with, as you help your child mature?

Gurian writes that the greatest gift a single mother can give her child is *her* stability. In the beginning, she is the only anchor. As the child begins to reach out to others, she must roll up the anchor, notch by notch. It is a disservice to children to make them feel that they are your life, he points out. When they start feeling secure enough to pull away, it is the emotionally healthy moms who are able to let them go—who can see them as emotionally powerful and as competent as she is.

He writes in *The Wonder of Boys* about a man he counseled who said, "My mother and I were always so close. I remember one time when I was about fourteen she started to cry and said, 'How am I ever going to live without you?' I felt so sorry for her, so sad." The man grew up to have several loving relationships with women, but eventually he would resent the woman, get distant, and the relationship would end. "To this day," the man said, "I still don't have the heart to tell [mother] I had become her little man but never became my own."

As Gurian puts it, the message mothers need to give their children—male and female—as they go through adolescence, is this: "Every day you need me less and less, both physically and emotionally, and I need you less and less. And that's okay."

A mother needs her own emotional health in order to maintain her separateness—and allow her child to do the same. Again, in order to maintain authority and success as a parent, the Choice Mom needs a community of people and rituals to support her.

Final Thoughts

The strategy behind most of this game plan—and indeed much of the advice in this book—boils down to two words: **Community** and **Authority.**

The reality is—as it has been throughout centuries of child-rearing—that it takes a village to raise a child well. If community ties are weak or resources are not sufficient, it is the kids who suffer, and ultimately society.

At the same time, since there is one face of parenting for a child, that face had better be the reasonable, affectionate, responsive, respectful and authoritative parent that every child needs.

If your day-to-day life consists primarily of working and caretaking, it might seem like you are being responsible to your child, but you are not doing enough. We are self-sufficient women, capable of doing incredible things, but none of us can raise a child alone—or even with one partner. Offering children the authoritative voice that raises them up in a well-balanced way over time demands poise, which requires keeping the stress level down.

Your responsibility, as someone who wants to raise a child in the best way that you can, is to be involved in your community…help build your community into a stronger one…find members of your community who have something to give—for your child *and* you.

In the end, the secret to raising a well-balanced child is not necessarily to think of

Choosing Single Motherhood © Mikki Morrissette

yourself as a single parent. Rather, you are the one who navigates you and your child through a variety of important people, activities and experiences—encouraging his or her development of self-control and self-esteem—until the one you have been chosen to guide is old enough to hold the compass alone.

Bonus Section

If You Are Raising a Boy

As male development expert Michael Gurian told me: "Males raised in homes of single mothers are definitely at more risk for social and personal problems than males raised in two-parent homes. I don't believe there is any credible research that denies this. However, I don't condemn a single parent, nor do I argue she/he can't raise great kids."

There are many reasons why it is more challenging for single mothers to raise boys—and knowing those reasons can help a Choice Mother do it better.

Brain Science
Because male brains are wired differently than female brains—coupled with different levels of hormones and social expectations—boys are in some ways more challenging to teach, Gurian says. They are naturally more impulsive, for example, because their prefrontal cortex is less active than girls and develops at a later age, and because they have less serotonin in their bloodstream and brain.

Girls and women have 15 percent more blood flow in the brain, are able to process more things simultaneously, and have stronger neural connectors enabling them to retain more from the senses and detect tones of voice more easily. Girls use more parts of their brain for verbal and emotional functioning, whereas boys use more areas for spatial and mechanical functioning.

Since a girl's brain "lights up" in more areas of her brain than a boy's, Gurian says, "She is often more flexible and adaptable and full-brained in her responses to the world around her. He is often more narrowly focused, and may end up with a narrower emotional, behavioral and therefore moral range of response."

So what does this mean? Do we throw up our hands and let innate behavior take its course?

Gurian says the science tells us that boys generally need more love, discipline and modeling behavior than they are getting today in order to learn how to respond to situations in a less simplistic way. As he told me, "no one is saying girls are more moral than boys. What we are saying is that boys need *a greater concerted effort* on the part of the mom, the family, the elders, the community, and the social institutions in order to inculcate all the moral coding of a social group."

Girls need the same training, of course. But not only do girls absorb these relational skills more easily, a girl's mother is more likely to understand the way she behaves and processes experience.

Boys and Emotions

In the early years, it's easy for moms to recognize when something is bothering her son: he cries, he hits, he yells. But as the brain grows from toddler to child, around the age of five or six, boys start processing their emotions differently. Some of this is because boys are taught to hide pain more than girls. But a lot of it is natural to a male brain.

"Unlike many of my colleagues, I don't worry about boys masking their feelings," Gurian told me. "Most boys are going to naturally grow into males who cry less than girls and talk about feelings less than women. It begins in childhood and continues when puberty hits and testosterone becomes a very big influence. I disagree with some colleagues who feel that the salvation for males is to learn how to feel through the use of talking and crying.

"I prefer that each child be provided profound attachment by primary and secondary caregivers—attachment so useful to the child that he will develop his own personal system for handling emotion. That system will include masculinity, masking, femininity, physical exercise, problem-solving, repression, free-expression through art or sport. The list is endless."

Gurian told me that the best thing Choice Mothers can do to help their sons be emotionally healthy is not necessarily to get him to talk more, but to make sure he is attached to at least four other caregivers: grandparent, godparent, male mentor, teacher. An unconnected boy is more worrisome than a quiet one.

Choosing Single Motherhood © Mikki Morrissette

Communication Strategy

Male development experts tend to agree that one way single mothers raising sons are at a disadvantage is that they have very different styles of communication. As Gurian explains, girls have a much greater need to connect and attach than boys do. He refers to this as the "intimacy imperative." Females will bond by chatting before playing together, for example, whereas males will bond simply by the process of playing.

A Choice Mother needs to learn new strategies of conversation. As Gurian told me:

"A mom with a father involved in the boy's life typically does not have to do too much to extend out beyond who she already is. If she is alone in raising her son, however, then she has to hold onto her own identity as a woman and try to extend toward the masculine."

"She finds herself trying to learn how to play basketball with her son. She finds herself trying to learn other ways of processing emotion than feeling-talk or eye-to-eye conversation."

There are things a mother can do to encourage his connection with her, as Gurian and others have detailed. Boys do much better bonding while doing, rather than simply sitting and talking. William Pollack calls this "action talk." For example, start a conversation after engaging him in physical play, or while driving or biking together.

A discussion starter: "You look like you feel angry," or "What do you think about that thing that happened?" Less effective: "How do you feel?"

STAGE 6

THE LEGACY OF CHOICE

"Think for yourselves
and let others enjoy the privilege to do so too."
— Voltaire, Essays on Tolerance

I have never considered myself to be a strongly political person. But I am a huge believer in protecting the principle of Choice, in its myriad forms. I believe that any healthy person who desires to be a parent, or marry, or whatever, should be allowed to do so.

In most U.S. states, single women are not prohibited from becoming mothers. But that does not mean that they are given the same access as married women. Clinics, insurance companies and adoption agencies are free to develop their own policies—and they do, resulting in variance from place to place, state to state.

In the chapter that follows, ***Of Politics and Policy,*** we will look at ways family life is being decided in legislative and judicial halls, as well as clinic and agency board rooms. Although the news is largely good for single heterosexual women, the chapter will look at obstacles designed to discourage "non-traditional" families. I think it is important for us to be aware of the ways in which decisions are being made about how families can be created.

In ***How Are the Kids Turning Out?*** we will hear directly from the older children of pioneering Choice Moms about how they have been influenced by the way they were raised, and what they think about the lifestyle as a family model. I hope to collect more of these stories into the future— positive and negative—so that we can continue to honestly understand the legacy of Choice parenthood.

CHAPTER 15

OF POLITICS AND POLICY

After often painful self-scrutiny and debate, intense scrimping and saving, and time-consuming research, a Thinking Woman who is resolved and ready to take the next step toward becoming a Choice Mom sometimes meets with powerful opposition: Laws, Regulations, Politics and Policy.

The new reproductive technologies and loosened adoption criteria have made it much more possible than it used to be for single women to become mothers, gay couples to become parents, and infertile couples to raise children using sperm and/or egg donors. But the yellow caution flag is being raised by some who believe the parenting field is being confused by too many biological and non-biological players. And some who set policy throw up their own red flag, believing that a single mother (or homosexual parent) is not "fit" to have a child, and thus should not be aided in the effort to do so. In Florida, for example, gays and lesbians are forbidden to adopt, even through the foster care system—a policy reinforced in a 2005 decision.

Some policy-makers believe strongly that every child should have a mother and a father, which is why they enact rules to discourage single parents or lesbian couples from adopting or conceiving—even though research indicates children do quite well in these "non-traditional" environments.

Many countries today are establishing laws that affect adoption, open-identity donors, and access to reproductive services. Several are supportive of single parenthood. A few are not. For now, the United States is less proactive in regulating the adoption and insemination industries than Australia, Canada, the United Kingdom and other European nations.[1]

By and large, single women are finding little resistance from doctors and clinics. But tell that to Carol, who was turned away by two clinics because she wanted to use the sperm of a gay friend. Tell that to a Minnesota woman I know whose long-time female gynecologist wouldn't help her get pregnant because she was not married—and Gretchen, who was dismissed by five doctors for the same reason. Tell that to all the lesbian women in Florida who have to withhold truth—or move to another state—in order to have children.

In this chapter we will look at how some women face obstacles to motherhood because of their marital status or sexual orientation. We also will look at the general state of insurance coverage, open-identity donors and adoption law today, as well as court cases that have attempted to address the complicated ethical issues that arise with the new reproductive technologies.

Who Gets to Try?

Some believe that any healthy person has the right to use medical technology in order to conceive a child, and that the role of the provider is to offer it, without judgment. Others believe that those who need medical assistance to conceive should not be offered services unless the provider has verified that the resulting child will be brought up in a proper home. In between these two views, of course, is a lot of gray area. When is someone "too old" to be a parent? Will a single woman, or a lesbian couple, provide a "fit" environment for a child? Is it ethical for a child to have many unknown half-siblings? And, importantly, who is entitled to make this judgment— and on what basis?

There are many players involved in insemination: donors, sperm banks, doctors. All of them are subject to scrutiny by outside forces, such as reproductive medicine society guidelines, FDA regulations, judicial review, state and federal legislation, and insurance company policies that decide what is covered and what is not. Yet the industry is relatively unregulated in terms of broader, ethical issues—which is why individuals find very different policies from place to place.

For example, in the case of assisted reproduction technology (ART), which involves advanced fertility treatment (such as in vitro fertilization, but not including the more common IUI procedure), a study sponsored by the Center for Bioethics at the University of Pennsylvania School of Medicine indicated, "There is no guarantee of access to ART in the law."[2]

Study results were based on responses to questionnaires by 210 program directors (out of 369 contacted). Many respondents indicated a belief that it is wrong to help bring a child into the world to be cared for by a parent who would be unfit, and that the program has a responsibility to consider a parent's fitness.

Ironically, however, a substantial number of programs reported being likely to turn away candidates on the basis of characteristics that they did not actually collect information about, such as sexual orientation. And on average, programs offering

Choosing Single Motherhood © Mikki Morrissette

these expensive services report turning away only 4 percent of their candidates each year (3 percent for medical reasons, 1 percent for emotional/psychological reasons). Responses revealed that:

• Only 28 percent of ART programs have a formal policy that describes on what grounds they might turn away a given candidate.

• All programs collect information about physical health and age. Nearly all check marital status (95%). Other information gathered can include sexual orientation (66%), reasons for wanting a child (53%), financial stability (52%).

• At only 18 percent of the programs do candidates meet with a social worker or psychologist (80% meet with a financial coordinator).

• Overall, 59% of ART program directors agree that everyone has a right to have a child, and 43% feel they do not have the right to stop anyone from attempting to conceive.

• On the other hand, 64% believe it is their responsibility to consider a parent's fitness before helping them conceive. But judgment about who is fit and who is not varies considerably. Given a series of hypothetical situations, respondents indicated they would be most likely to turn away a couple in which the man has been physically abusive to his existing child (81% very or extremely likely to turn away, compared to 5% not likely or slightly unlikely to turn away).

• A couple on welfare is *not likely to be turned away* by 46% of programs, yet is *very likely to be turned away* by 38%.

• A single man looking for surrogacy services is likely to be helped by 37%, but likely to be turned away by 53%.

• A single woman is likely to be helped by 77%, but turned away by 20%.

• A lesbian couple is likely to be helped by 82%, but turned away by 17%.

• A couple in which both partners are at least 43 years old is likely to be helped by 77%, but likely to be turned away by 18%.

Researchers involved in the study recommend that the U.S. begin to formalize guidelines to ensure equality among the programs. However, one of the authors of the study, Arthur Caplan, told me that regulations aren't likely to happen anytime soon. Unlike countries including Canada and the United Kingdom, the United States has no federal regulatory agency in place to oversee assisted reproduction issues. It is a largely self-regulated industry that most politicians are reluctant to get involved with.

Caplan believes that single women and the gay/lesbian community would benefit from regulations, since they'd likely be approved as "fit" parent material, and thus clinics would not be allowed to turn them down.

A question of age
Some people are critical of older women who are allowed to use donated eggs and

---

I WAS TURNED AWAY FIVE TIMES
FROM: GRETCHEN, TRYING, AT 40

As a straight women with decent finances and a terrific doctor, I naively thought the two years I spent thinking and soul-searching about this choice would be the hard part. After getting a thumb's up from my doctor about my ability to conceive, he told me his practice did not help single women get pregnant. I was surprised—could people who didn't know me decide I can't do this? My doctor apologized and referred me to someone who worked with a different practice. Seven weeks into a 10-week waiting period for first-time appointments, after I had returned some standard paperwork, that clinic called to verify that I was single. When I said yes, I was told that the referral doctor wouldn't work with a single woman either.

I was referred to another doctor, who had no trouble with me being single, but didn't work with insurance company paperwork. Okay, this was important to me—I would pay out of pocket and file claims myself. We started a cycle on my first appointment, after he laid out the facts based on my age, weight, medical history, etc. After it was determined that I was not developing enough follicles on a low dose of Clomid, on our second appointment he said I wasn't going to be able to get pregnant. It felt like I didn't fit his success parameters so he cut me loose.

Back to my original doctor, whose office referred me to the first doctor again. I pointed out their mistake, and was given a new referral, to a woman. Turns out

---

Choosing Single Motherhood © Mikki Morrissette

bear children who will have an aged parent earlier than peers. When a 66-year-old Romanian woman gave birth to a 3.2-pound baby in 2004, it raised questions about whether there should be stronger guidelines to determine who should be eligible to have a child. Later that year, a 56-year-old New York woman gave birth to twins.

According to the *Boston Globe*,[3] in 2002 alone, there were 286 births to U.S. women in their early 50s, and more than 5,000 in their late 40s. The age at which a clinic will not work with a woman varies considerably. At 18 percent of clinics in the Center for Bioethics study, there was a formal or informal cutoff of age 43.

Most American adoption agencies will not work with women over the age of 45, although that, too, varies considerably.

---

she, too, wouldn't see me because I was single—although if I'd been part of a lesbian couple it would have been okay.

I called for yet another referral, and was told that my original doctor would help me after all. I was confused, but didn't protest. We started a cycle of Clomid. The day of the ultrasound, a different doctor was there who told me, as I was sitting there with follicles ready to go, that they did not do this at their clinic and this cycle would be wasted.

I was crushed and had no idea what to do. Didn't they understand how important this was to me? That I am a sane, intelligent woman who would also like to be a mother? My own doctor called to apologize for the confusion. He referred me to doctor #4. It took six weeks to get in, and when I met with him he said I would need genetic counseling, a psychological evaluation and fertility testing. After that, he would meet with his partners and they'd decide whether to move forward. He said not to take it personally. *How was that possible?* If I had shown up with an abusive husband, none of these steps would be required because I'd be married. But, as irritated as I was, I realized if I didn't take the steps, the process would end.

Which brings me to today. I passed all my 'tests' and am waiting to see if I am pregnant from a third attempt at donor insemination.

The process has been much more emotionally draining than I expected. But without a doubt, I would truly regret not trying.

Who Can Be a Donor?

In New York State, where gay rights tend to be strong, two clinics rejected a woman's gay donor because of their (erroneous) interpretation of state regulations. Although donor sperm in New York, like everywhere, is tested and quarantined for six months before being retested and used by a recipient, Carol was surprised to find that her donor's frozen sperm could not be used. Her donor agreed to offer fresh samples for clinic inseminations, but was told state regulations wouldn't allow that either, since she did not have an intimate relationship with him.

"I feel caught in the corner between regulations that exist purely to absolve institutions and practitioners of liability," she told me at the time. "Neither my known donor nor I have a problem with a single lie ("no, he is not gay") but a lot of insemination clinics want a session with a psychologist, a long verbal interview, access to the donor's medical records, etc.—all of which would reveal that he is gay or require extensive lying and concealment, which we're not okay with."

She considered pursuing insemination in nearby New Jersey, where regulations are more lenient. The early morning commutes would be exhausting and challenging, but doable. "However, it's depressing to have to select an RE based on whether they practice over the state line rather than who is the best doctor for me to work with."

Her story had a simpler solution, however. The truth is that it is *not* generally prohibited to use a known (or "directed") donor who is gay. The first two places she went to simply followed unusual policies. On her third attempt, she consulted with an RE in private practice who "did not care at all about my donor being gay, and in fact said it was irrelevant to what he was doing for me medically. I loved that he was so sane about it."

The doctor agreed that a donor who does not have HIV posed no risk to her health. "I was incredibly relieved to hear his position at my initial consult. I just wanted the best medical care I could get from someone I trusted and respected, and that is what I feel I am getting." She and her donor did need to sign paperwork that acknowledged the man as the biological father. "This type of document would not be acceptable to everyone, but it was for us."

FDA controversy
In May 2005, Food and Drug Administration guidelines (12 years in the making) were poised for release that recommended that any man who had had sex with

Choosing Single Motherhood © Mikki Morrissette

another man during the previous five years be disallowed as an anonymous sperm donor. The reason given was that gay men as a group were at a higher risk of carrying the AIDS virus.

Sperm from a healthy gay man is no different than sperm from a healthy heterosexual man. Since all sperm is tested, quarantined and retested after six months before being used, there is no scientific reason to believe that anyone will contract HIV from unaffected sperm. There have been no known cases of AIDS passed on through donation since testing procedures were enacted in the 1980s.

One person who was incensed by the proposed guidelines was Leland Traiman, director of the California-based Rainbow Flag sperm bank, which offers gay sperm donors. The only people categorized as "criminals" by the FDA in this way, he pointed out, were IV drug users, prostitutes and male homosexuals. "A heterosexual man who has had sex with an HIV prostitute could donate after one year," he told me, "but a gay man in a long-term relationship could not. It's clearly not based on science, but on bigotry."

And it gave a false sense of security to think that if gay men are removed as donors there is no HIV threat, he indicated. Some opponents of the guidelines suggested that anyone who has had sex with an individual of unknown HIV status should be rejected as a prospective donor. The point should be the *sexual behavior* of the candidate, not the sexual orientation.

As Aubrey Noelle Stimola, the assistant director of public health at the American Council on Science and Health, wrote: "I would hope that even a genetic masterpiece who attended Harvard and who has never been ill a day in his life, would be tested for HIV, regardless of claims that he had never used intravenous drugs, had sex with a man, or received a blood transfusion before HIV testing became routine. What is accomplished by barring homosexuals from donating sperm? Does it save money? I don't see how. Will it save lives? Nope. Is it mere bias? It seems so, given the fact that while homosexual men do have a higher risk of HIV—tests for which are now extremely accurate—heterosexual men are by no means without risk."[4]

When this book went to press, the guidelines had not been officially released by the FDA—the oppositional outcry had been effective. Sperm banks continue to be allowed to use gay donors. And FDA rules currently do not prohibit gay men from being a known or directed donor.

FDA GUIDELINES MISS THE BOAT

By Dave Plotz

reprinted by permission of author, originally appeared in The New York Times[5]

Consumer choice is an incredibly powerful force for improving practices. Customers insist on safety and health, and [sperm] banks compete vigorously to satisfy them. Banks have replaced fresh sperm with frozen, in order to have time to quarantine the sperm and retest the donor for HIV. They screen not only for HIV, but also for gonorrhea, syphilis, hepatitis and sexually transmitted diseases that most of us have never heard of. Sperm banks force donors to pass a panel of genetic tests for cystic fibrosis, Tay-Sachs disease, Fanconi anemia and other awful abnormalities. Banks take exhaustive medical histories, perform elaborate personality tests and require high standards of personal behavior.

At California Cryobank, America's leading sperm collector, less than 5 percent of donor applicants make the cut. I would bet that the pool of American sperm donors—which includes gay donors who have passed all of these screens—is smarter, healthier, cleaner-living and freer of dread genetic defects than perhaps any group of men on earth.

With its late and largely unnecessary obsession with sperm safety, the government

Taking It to Court

While most women who meet with resistance find a more receptive doctor, clinic or agency, some women attempt to change the system by doing battle in court.

As Womens E-News reported,[6] a Florida woman named Melinda helped deliver thousands of babies in her 20 years as a nurse. When she was 39 and unmarried, she looked to her hospital for help getting artificially inseminated, and was shocked when they refused, indicating donor sperm was used only for married heterosexual couples. She argued with doctors that she had a stable job and a strong support network. She argued that 50 percent of marriages end in divorce. But six clinics turned her down.

After six years of battling her employer, the Shands HealthCare and Faculty Group

Choosing Single Motherhood © Mikki Morrissette

is missing the real issue in the sperm bank world: donor anonymity. Thousands of Americans are born every year without the right to know who their father is.

Until a few years ago, it was assumed that children conceived by donor insemination would live with a father, and that father would—following the advice of the time—pretend he was the child's biological father. But today the psychological advice has changed: many parents now tell children who are the result of donor sperm where they came from. And a growing number of sperm bank customers are single women and lesbian couples. In these families, there is no paternal secret to protect. In an age of genetic determinism, many of the children are haunted by the fact that they can't know half of their genetic heritage, and thus half of themselves.

The move to end donor anonymity is still small in the United States—it lags far behind the similar effort to open adoption records—but it will grow as the huge current generation of donor-insemination children reaches adulthood. So far, the federal government has shown not even a vague interest in the issue, which is a shame, because government is the only force that can really help. It will take federal government action to establish a national registry and to reduce the barriers such children face when seeking their fathers. I don't know whether they all should have the right to know their donor fathers, but I do know it's a public policy question that lawmakers should be considering. And it certainly deserves more thought than a pointless ban on gay donors.

Practice in Gainesville, Fla., in federal court, the woman, then 45, lost both her legal case and her hopes of having a biological child, since her eggs were no longer viable. "If I had just brought a man with me to the clinic six years ago, I would have received treatment," Melinda said. "But I didn't want to have to lie to get health care and I don't think millions of other single women should either."

In Ontario, a 39-year-old lesbian also challenged laws governing sperm donors. After the woman was unsuccessful at self-insemination, she turned to a doctor. Since she was attempting to use a known donor who was over the age of 40—and gay—he was automatically disqualified on two counts as a donor for assisted conception.

For a fee of more than $600—and a great deal of time—the federal government would have granted her special permission to use him as her donor. But she hired an attorney to (unsuccessfully thus far) attempt to change the law instead. Her attorney argued that it was unfair for fertile women to conceive with men who are over the age of 40, or who have a history of genetic defects, but not allow those seeking assistance from a doctor the same right.

The woman eventually gave birth to a son because of a successful home insemination, so the judge dismissed her case thinking it to be moot, but she and her lawyer continued trying to get her case heard. A second woman with a similar story joined the case in April 2005.[7]

Four Cases, Four Judgments

One needs only to look to California for examples of the many ways insemination in particular can find itself in the courtroom. Here are four examples. (Reminder that state laws, and judges, can vary considerably.)

1. KNOWN DONOR IS *NOT* DAD (MARCH 2005)[8]

Steven and Deborah were sometimes intimate friends. He provided semen to a doctor to inseminate her. After one miscarriage, they had sexual intercourse for a few months, which did not result in a pregnancy. Deborah ended the sexual relationship and went back to the doctor, using the sperm Steven had originally provided. She became pregnant and gave birth to Trevor.

In the initial judgment, Steven—who had petitioned to establish a parental relationship in 2003 with Trevor, who was three years old—was granted that right in a trial court. However, Deborah won on appeal.

Citing the language of California law, the Superior Court opinion indicated there can be "no paternity claim from a sperm donor who is not married to the woman who becomes pregnant with the donated semen, **so long as it was provided to a licensed physician.** The statute does not make an exception for known sperm donors, who will be denied a paternity claim so long as the semen was provided to a licensed physician for insemination of an unmarried woman." *(See Chapter 8 for details of a Pennsylvania case involving a known donor who was forced to pay child support for a single mom.)*

2. KNOWN DONOR *IS* DAD (MARCH 1986)[9]

Mary and Victoria chose Jhordan as their known donor. He provided semen to Mary several times over a six-month period. She performed home insemination herself until she became pregnant and gave birth to Devin. After the birth, Jhordan pursued rights as a parent—they disagreed in court about whether this had been verbally agreed upon prior to insemination, and there was no written document. In a related

Choosing Single Motherhood © Mikki Morrissette

issue, Victoria sought joint legal custody of the child as co-parent with Mary and requested parenting rights.

As the court opinion stated, in cases of artificial insemination in which a licensed physician is *not* used, there is *no protection from a paternity claim* by (or for) the sperm donor. The trial court determined Jhordan was Devin's legal father, but awarded sole legal and physical custody to Mary and denied Jhordan input into decisions about Devin's schooling, medical care, and day-to-day life. He did, however, receive substantial visitation rights as recommended by a court-appointed psychologist. Victoria was determined not to be a parent, but was also awarded visitation rights. The judgment held up in appeal.

In this case, it was determined that California law gave married and unmarried women equal rights to protect themselves from paternity claims of donors, but **using a licensed physician is a requirement for this protection.**

In an important detail, however, the opinion stated that the physician is not required to perform the insemination. In cases when a woman prefers the atmosphere of a home insemination, the opinion stated, California's legal protection is allowed if the sperm is simply provided to a licensed physician.

Author's note: One woman told me that a friend who was a licensed physician accepted a donor's sperm at her front door, then handed it off for use in home insemination.

3. When an Anonymous Donor is *Not* Anonymous (May 2000)[10]
A married couple filed a lawsuit against a sperm bank claiming that it failed to disclose that the sperm they used came from a donor with family history of a serious genetic kidney disease. Their daughter was conceived with this sperm. The family requested that the donor's identity be divulged as part of a court disposition.

A trial court denied the motion, ruling that the donor's anonymity and privacy interests should be maintained as part of the confidentiality agreement he signed with the sperm bank. The court found that the family had access to other relevant medical information, and that the donor would not provide new insight into the medical condition.

On appeal, however, the superior court determined that the agreement between the sperm bank and the donor went too far in providing for anonymity "and thus conflicts with public policy." The opinion stated that the sperm bank agreement includes a provision that "good cause" by court order could preclude privacy. As the opinion stated, "a contract that completely forecloses the opportunity of a child conceived by artificial insemination to discover the relevant and needed medical history of his or her genetic father is inconsistent with the best interests of the child."

It also stated that since the donor deposited more than 320 specimens of his semen, for more than $11,000, the substantial commercial transaction involved makes it "unreasonable for donor No. 276 to expect that his genetic and medical history, and possibly even his identity, would never be disclosed."

The court determined that the state's interest, and the petitioner's, outweighed the donor's interests. It required him to appear at a deposition, answer all questions, and produce documents needed. But it also ruled that full identity might not be required, and that all efforts to retain some anonymity should be attempted.

4. AN "OOPS" ERROR (JUNE 2003)[11]
Susan, a single woman, went to a fertility clinic for help conceiving with an embryo created from anonymously donated ova and sperm. She used anonymous donors to avoid any paternity issues. Robert and Denise went to the same clinic to fertilize a donated ovum with Robert's sperm, and signed a contract stating they would be the parents of any children produced from the resulting embryos.

Robert and Denise produced about 13 embryos. Because of a clinic error, three of those embryos were implanted in Susan. Both women got pregnant around the same time and gave birth to full genetic siblings ten days apart.

After the families were made aware of the error, Robert and Denise sought parenting rights of Daniel, the boy Susan had given birth to from the embryo created with Robert's sperm. A trial court determined that Susan is Daniel's mother, Robert is his father and Denise had no standing as a parent.

Susan appealed, stating that California law should protect her from any paternity claim, since she contracted for anonymous sperm that a licensed doctor used to inseminate her. Superior court, however, denied her appeal, stating that Robert did not provide his semen for the purpose of inseminating anyone other than his wife, thus **the anonymous donor regulation was not applicable in her case.** Robert has visitation rights.

A Surrogacy Case
A 2005 case in Pennsylvania involving a well-off couple and a surrogate mother indicated an interesting twist on questions of biological parenthood and what is best

Choosing Single Motherhood © Mikki Morrissette

for children.[12] A woman gave birth to triplets on behalf of an older couple—using donated eggs and the man's sperm—but grew uneasy after leaving the hospital because the adoptive parents had not been an active presence in the hospital during the first week of the children's lives. With the hospital preparing to put the children into foster care, the woman named the triplets and brought them home with her.

The intended father was a 63-year-old math professor who said complicated paperwork had kept him away from the hospital, that he could provide a better life for the children, and that he "wanted to leave something behind when I die." His girlfriend was a 60-year-old woman with two grown kids. The couple did not marry because they relied on the pension she received as a policeman's widow.

He testified that the younger couple lived in a small and dirty home, in a depressed city with a poor school system. In contrast, he said his salary of $136,000 would allow him to raise the children in an affluent community, and that he and his girlfriend had more time to spend with them.

Hospital personnel testified that the older couple's primary concerns in that first week seemed to be about insurance coverage and equipment, but not about the newborns.

Fourteen months after the triplets were born, a court decided the 30-year-old surrogate and her husband, who lived well below the poverty line already with three other children, could have permanent custody of the triplets. **The judge declared the mother, who had filed for bankruptcy a few months before the birth, was "the better caretaker by far."**

The judge indicated that the math professor alternated between complaining about his legal costs and boasting about his affluent community. He questioned why the man didn't take any days off from work when the triplets were with him for 12 days during the summer. He ordered the man to pay $1,750 a month for child support, and gave him weekend visitation rights. The three children were given his last name.

He planned to appeal. Like most states, Pennsylvania has no surrogacy laws in place.

Rights Around the World

Many countries are ahead of the United States on establishing formal regulations for the insemination industry. Here are some of them, current when this book went to press. (My thanks to Diane Allen for her invaluable work with Infertility Network.)

New Zealand — In April 2005, a report was given to Parliament to examine the legal definition of parenthood and recommend several changes to existing laws to reflect changing family structures and developments in reproductive technologies. The emphasis in the proposals is on principles of the child's best interests, from an early age; access to genetic information; desirability of collaborative parenting; and the equality of children regardless of the circumstances of their creation or family form. One of the suggested reforms is to give donors of egg and sperm legal parenthood status, which could mean that a child would have more than two parents.

Sweden — Approves IVF for lesbian couples, and declares that both women should be regarded as the child's mother. (Although gay marriages remain illegal in Sweden, they do allow civil unions and adoption by gay couples.) Only open-identity or known donors are legal; anonymous donors were disallowed in 1985.

Denmark, the Netherlands, Finland, Great Britain, Russia, and Spain also allow IVF for lesbian couples.

Australia — A commission in the state of Victoria in May 2005 recommended legislation to reform IVF law so that lesbian couples and single women would also receive medical assistance to have children. As chairwoman of the commission said, "There is no evidence that marital status affects the wellbeing of children. Removing the marital status requirement means more women will access the clinic system to have semen screened. This will ensure the identity of sperm donors is recorded for any future children to access and will provide greater protection from transmissible diseases for women and children." The committee also recommended that a dead male's sperm may only be used to father children if he gave prior written permission.

Ireland — The Irish Commission on Assisted Human Reproduction issued a report in May 2005 that, among other things, recommended that fertility treatments be available to unmarried parents, including lesbians. A highly controversial recommendation in the report proposes that children born through a surrogate mother should be presumed to be that of the commissioning parents. Typically, the surrogate is regarded as the legal mother until an event such as formal adoption takes place (In the U.S., Illinois and California are exceptions.)

Italy — Passed legislation in February 2004 forbidding anyone to use donated eggs or sperm. Only heterosexual couples are allowed to use in vitro fertilization. Many

Choosing Single Motherhood © Mikki Morrissette

infertile Italians reportedly are traveling elsewhere for services. A special referendum to consider loosening the rules was scheduled in June 2005, but not enough voters were available.

Croatia — The Catholic church condemned IVF as a "crime against human life," believing that to bear children from any method other than intercourse between a man and a woman transforms the child "into an object." A bill has been in the wings for many years that would allow infertility treatments for single women, but has not been turned into law, many believe because of strong church opposition.

Wales — Guidelines that were being considered in 2005 include prohibiting IVF treatment for a couple if one of them has a child from a previous relationship, and requiring participation in a smoking cessation program for smokers seeking IVF services.

India — In 2005, was in the process of setting up an accreditation group for review and mandatory licensing of clinics. Recommended guidelines under consideration include allowing single women access to services, use of only anonymous donors, and prohibition of known donor sperm.

Anonymous donors are not allowed in Sweden, Switzerland, Austria, The Netherlands, New Zealand, the United Kingdom (as of 2005) and the states of Victoria and Western Australia.

Open identity issues in the United Kingdom

A British regulatory agency decided, after consultation with many experts, that it is in the best interests of children to know about their conception. Although it might lead to fewer men being willing to donate at the beginning, the agency determined that the rights of children are paramount—leading to a sweeping change in the law, effective in 2005, which reversed a 1990 decision to authorize anonymity.

The director of the London Fertility Centre co-authored a column after the law was enacted, emphasizing the need for additional monies to be spent on donor recruitment.[13] According to its survey of egg donors, of the nearly 200 past donors who responded, 52.1 percent said they would donate again even if they were not anonymous, and 36.4 percent said they would not. A survey sent to past recipients indicated that 53.5 percent would not use fertility services again if the donor was not anonymous. One concern raised by the authors was that its clients would go elsewhere for treatment.

The United Kingdom regulatory agency also was considering a requirement to change the birth certificates of DI children. Instead of listing the non-biological parents' name, a proposed change would be to say "Donor," making it impossible for married couples to hide the truth from children.

A U.K. court case in 2002 fought to establish a voluntary register of sperm and egg donors, in order to make it easier for donor offspring to trace their genetic parents.[14] The suit was based on the argument that everyone has the right to form a personal identity, and that without full knowledge of genetic inheritance, people can never truly know who they are. The suit invoked an anti-discrimination provision to argue that donor offspring should have the same rights as adopted children to trace their biological parents. And it sought to force a regulatory agency to collect and store a greater range of information about donors, including a requirement that donors report any medical conditions that develop after donating their sperm or eggs.

A similar voluntary donor registry was established in the Australian state of Victoria in 1978. Although donors are free not to register, Victoria clinics report that nearly all do.

A movement for open identity is building slowly in the United States. **One reason anonymity will remain a choice in this country for some time, Caplan told me, is that it is a political hot potato that many legislators don't want to touch.** In the United States, a donor-conceived young man and his mother have privately set up www.donorsiblingregistry.com to help donors and half-siblings find each other. *(We covered the open-identity topic in detail in Chapter 9.)*

Changes in Adoption

As of 2005, adult adoptees in New Hampshire, Alabama, Alaska, Kansas, Tennessee, Delaware and Oregon have access to their original birth certificates. In Ontario, Canada, a similar law was being considered. Britain allows any birth relative of an adoptee to use public records and legal documents.[15]

Some believe strongly that this is a violation of the rights to privacy of past birth parents. Others believe that every individual has the right to know who they are, where they come from, and what their ethnicity is—and that there should not be "haves" and "have nots" in adoption information access. Some point out that confidentiality was not necessarily a guaranteed part of the adoption process.

Choosing Single Motherhood © Mikki Morrissette

Another interesting development in U.S. adoption policy is related to the rights of gays and lesbians. In New Jersey, for example, a judge in May 2005 granted full co-parenting rights to the lesbian partner of a woman who bore the child they intended to raise together, without requiring the usual lengthy adoption proceedings.[16] Both the American Medical Association and the American Psychological Association support partner co-adoptions.

About 60 percent of U.S. adoption agencies accept applications from gays and lesbians, according to a 2003 survey from the Evan B. Donaldson Adoption Institute.[17] As the Institute's executive director, Adam Pertman has said, agencies are evidently concurring with research that gays and lesbians make good parents. The survey included 307 adoption agencies and found that 40 percent of the agencies had placed children with gay and lesbian parents.

"The child who is older, who is of color, who has special needs—those are the children who are more likely to be adopted by gays and lesbians," Pertman said. He said agencies that deal with children in foster care, with adoptions from abroad, and Jewish- and Lutheran-affiliated agencies were most likely to work with gays and lesbians.

However, birth parents who choose to have a say don't always accept these placements. As the survey said: "Although stereotypes and misconceptions still perpetuate policy and practice...the willingness of adoption agencies to accept gay and lesbian adults as parents means more and more waiting children are moving into permanent, loving families."

Note: Pertman told me that the Institute has not explored how many agencies accept applications—and make placements with—single parents, but he suggested that it is safe to assume that there are more agencies that accept single applicants (including a growing number of men) than gay and lesbian ones.

Where Gays and Lesbians Need Not Apply

The American Psychological Association released a 1995 review of research, *Lesbian and Gay Parenting: A Resource for Psychologists,* that reported that "not a single study has found children of gay or lesbian parents to be disadvantaged in any significant respect relative to children of heterosexual parents," and concluded that "home environments provided by gay and lesbian parents are as likely as those provided by heterosexual parents to support and enable children's psychosocial growth."[18]

Yet Florida—which had more than 8,000 children awaiting adoption in 2002—prohibits gays from adopting children, either as couples or single parents. Four gay men there—foster parents attempting to adopt children in their care—challenged the law at the U.S. Supreme Court level. Although the Child Welfare League of America urged the Court to review the restriction, and defended the parenting abilities of gays, in January 2005 the Court refused to hear the case. A majority of the judges in the 11th U.S. Circuit Court of Appeals was required to grant a rehearing, but the ban was upheld by a 6-6 decision. *(The court's opinion can be read at www.ca11.uscourts.gov/opinions/ops/200116723.pdf)*

According to an Associated Press story, the state's attorney wrote in his filing to the court, "It is rational to believe that children need male and female influences to develop optimally, particularly in the areas of sexual and gender identity, and heterosexual role modeling."[19]

And the president of a conservative Florida law group, Liberty Counsel, said the Court's refusal to hear the case sends a message to other states that "you can follow Florida's lead with policies that encourage kids to be placed with moms and dads." In fact, anti-gay adoption bills were subsequently introduced (but rejected) in Tennessee, Virginia and Arkansas. As of 2005, a similar bill was active in Alabama.

The law prohibiting adoption by gays in Florida was passed in 1977, at the height of Anita Bryant's anti-homosexual campaign. Florida Gov. Jeb Bush maintains that adoptive children, who often come from unstable backgrounds, should have a mother and father. Florida does, however, allow divorcees, singles and people with disabilities to adopt—and reportedly does not specifically ban people convicted of abuse or molestation from adopting.

As of 2005, six states specifically allow adoptions by gays: California, Connecticut, Massachusetts, New York, Pennsylvania and Vermont, as well as the District of Columbia. Two states restrict gay adoptions: Mississippi prohibits gay couples, but not gay individuals, from adopting; Utah bars unmarried cohabiting couples (gay or heterosexual) from adopting. The other states have no formal law.[20]

Family structure research redux
As social scientist Louise Silverstein reported,[21] a qualitative study of 200 men of different subcultures who were actively involved with their children—including Haitian, gay, Latino, divorced, Greek and Orthodox Jew—revealed that "a wide variety of family structures can support positive child outcomes. We have concluded that children need at least one responsible, caretaking adult who has a positive

emotional connection to them, and with whom they have a consistent relationship.

"Because of the emotional and practical stress involved in childrearing," the report went on to say, "a family structure that includes more than one such adult is more likely to contribute to positive child outcomes. Neither the sex of the adult(s), nor the biological relationship to the child has emerged as a significant variable in predicting positive development."

Insurance News

Some advocacy groups, such as RESOLVE: the National Infertility Association, are pushing for stronger, all-inclusive polices governing coverage for infertility treatments, believing the option to pursue treatment should be available to all. (They also lobby on behalf of increasing benefits to adoptive families.) But whether a fertile single woman is entitled to help paying for treatments is a wider philosophical question not likely to be mandated anytime soon, especially with health insurance already as costly as it is.

In most cases, single women who find supportive sperm banks and doctors have to pay for insemination services themselves, since only one-fourth of health plans offered at companies with more than 10 employees cover infertility treatment, according to RESOLVE. And usually, women are eligible for coverage only if they are unable to conceive after a year or more of unprotected sexual intercourse.

Insemination can be cost-prohibitive for many women. Each insemination attempt also includes fees for donor sperm, consultations, physical exams, and the preparation, storage and shipping of sperm. And since the chances of conceiving using frozen sperm is about 8 to 15 percent per monthly cycle, insemination without insurance can be quite expensive—especially for those who require fertility treatment.

According to a 2003 *Women's News* article,[22] artificial insemination can cost $500 to $5,000, in vitro fertilization (when a woman's eggs are harvested from her body, fertilized with sperm, then implanted back in her uterus) $25,000 to $75,000, and gestational surrogacy (when the embryo from in vitro fertilization is implanted in the womb of a surrogate carrier) costs $50,000 to $100,000. (Prices tend to be coming down over time.)

Some states allow women to self-inseminate using an anonymous donor from a sperm bank—but not all.

A danger to single women who can't afford to be inseminated at a clinic is that they sometimes use the sperm of a donor who hasn't been tested for sexually transmitted diseases. As we discussed in Chapter 8, this leaves both parties open to the risk of paternity or child support lawsuits, which is not the case when a clinic is used.

According to reporter Felicia R. Lee, the average cost of one in vitro attempt in the United States is $12,400. She wrote an article for *The New York Times* in January 2005 about American fertility clients who go overseas in pursuit of less expensive options. In Israel, for example, in vitro is free for citizens, and about $6,500 per cycle for others.[23]

One woman she talked to had priced Thailand at $3,000 (dismissed as too primitive), and London at $7,000. Germany was discounted because of low success rates. The quote at her local California clinic was $18,000. The married woman ended up getting two in vitro efforts in Naples, Italy, for less than $8,500.

At last count, 15 states had laws requiring insurance policies to cover some level of infertility, but that coverage is dependent on medical necessity—and having children is not considered a medical necessity.[24]

How Marriage Policy Pertains

The political debate about gay marriage, which became part of the platform during the 2004 President election, has ties to Choice Motherhood.

In decrying the idea of gay marriage, for example, prominent conservative James C. Dobson, founder of Focus on the Family, dusted off 1990s arguments against single motherhood. As he wrote in the May 2004 issue of the Freedom Club Report: "Same-sex marriage advocates want us to believe that gender does not matter, and that the biblically defined roles of husband and wife and mother and father are merely optional. In the face of this radical ideological shift, we must ask: How will an intentionally motherless or fatherless family affect the children involved?"

He quotes David Popenoe, who we heard from in Chapter 6, as saying: "We should disavow the notion that mommies can make good daddies, just as we should disavow the popular notion of radical feminists that daddies can make good mommies. The two sexes are different to the core, and each is necessary — culturally and biologically — for the optimal development of a human being."

Choosing Single Motherhood © Mikki Morrissette

In a less headline-grabbing way, marriage continues to be considered by some to be a solution to poverty. In his infamous speech of 1992, Vice President Dan Quayle said, "For those concerned about children growing up in poverty, we should know this: marriage is probably the best anti-poverty program of all."

Social policy advocates who agree with this position tend to resurrect arguments about how single parenthood is detrimental to kids. Many believe that single parents should not receive the same benefits as married parents.

Long-time family values commentator Barbara Dafoe Whitehead testified to the U.S. Senate subcommittee on children and families in 2004 about the importance of marriage to children, adults and society—eleven years after she authored her *Atlantic Monthly* article titled "Dan Quayle Was Right."[25]

Using more recent research than Dobson, she indicated that "researchers now agree that, except in cases of high and unremitting parental conflict, children who grow up in households with their married mother and father do better on a wide range of economic, social, educational, and emotional measures than do children in other kinds of family arrangements."

This is one reason policy-makers in the George W. Bush Administration have created government-subsidized programs that give aid to married couples, and men who live with their families, in the form of specialized housing, economic assistance and job training. It has especially invested in marriage promotion programs, to help couples avoid divorce. In 2002 and 2003, the U.S. Department of Health and Human Services committed at least $90 million for marriage-related grants, research and assistance.[26]

According to the Center for Law and Social Policy,[27] 19 states offer state-funded welfare programs that make it easier for married couples to receive financial assistance. Florida requires four hours of relationship and marriage education for high school graduation. West Virginia gives a $100 monthly "bonus" to married welfare recipients. Tennessee and Vermont forgive child support debts to the state if the parents marry or reunite. In Louisiana, about $1.4 million has been spent since September 2002 to, among many other things, develop products for unmarried parents emphasizing the value of marriage.

While there is nothing wrong with attempts to strengthen marriage, those who promote marriage policies often disparage single parenthood in the process, without acknowledging that Choice Moms tend to be self-sufficient, well-educated, and highly attentive to their children's needs. *(See Chapter 6 for more on this topic.)*

Final Thoughts

Does an agency, clinic or doctor have an obligation to provide their service to single women, or not? In the U.S., this has been a generally unregulated area of the law. It is easier to avoid the subject rather than open up another issue largely based on an individualistic sense of morality, as gay marriage and abortion have proven.

As more women turn to the Choice option, questions that affect them increasingly are being raised and addressed in clinic and agency board rooms, and in legislative and judicial chambers—and will continue to do so.

For that reason, as well as for the sake of women who face opposition from agencies and clinics in their communities, I think it's important that readers of this book and visitors to the website (www.ChoosingSingleMotherhood.com) be aware not only of rules that might affect them, but of the policies that could be if the collective successes of Choice Moms are not reported.

Just as the success of Choice pioneers made it easier for single women today to make this decision, I hope the legacy of today's Choice Mothers will be to collectively help others see that our families should not be feared or prohibited. We need help to raise our children, just as every parent does. And ours is not a model that will work for everyone. But as responsible, thinking women we can raise wonderful, loving children—despite the absence of a father.

When policy-makers need to hear about our family model, I want the stories of Choice Moms and Choice Kids to be heard. The chapter that follows, and a special online resource I have launched on the website, is a start in that direction.

Choosing Single Motherhood © Mikki Morrissette

EXCERPT

HELPING ALL PARENTS AND CHILDREN IS BEST
By Stephanie Coontz[28]

The more I listen to debates over whether we should promote marriage, the more I am reminded of one of my father's favorite sayings: "If wishes were horses, then beggars would ride." Yes, kids raised by married parents do better, on average, than kids raised in divorced- or single-parent homes. Yes, the long-term commitment of marriage confers economic, emotional, and even health benefits on adults as well. Certainly, we should remove marriage disincentives from government programs. We should expand health coverage to include couples counseling for all who wish it. With better support systems, we may be able to save more potentially healthy marriages and further reduce rates of unwed childbearing among teenagers.

But there is no way to re-establish marriage as the main site of child rearing, dependent care, income pooling, or interpersonal commitments in the modern world. Any movement that sets this as a goal misunderstands how irreversibly family life and marriage have changed, and it will inevitably be dominated by powerful allies who are not interested in supporting the full range of families that exist today and are likely to in the future.

For more than 1,000 years, marriage was the main way that society transferred property, forged political alliances, raised capital, organized children's rights, redistributed resources to dependents, and coordinated the division of labor by age and gender. Precisely because marriage served so many political, social, and economic functions, not everyone had access to it. Those who did almost never had free choice regarding partners and rarely could afford to hold high expectations of their relationships.

During the last 200 years, the growth of bureaucracies, banks, schools, hospitals, unemployment insurance, Social Security, and pension plans slowly but surely eroded the political and economic roles that marriage traditionally had played. It increasingly became an individual decision that could be made independently of family and community pressures. By the early 1900s, love and companionship had become not just the wistful hope of a husband or wife but the legitimate goal of marriage in the eyes of society. But this meant that people began expecting more of married life than ever before in history—at the exact time that older methods of organizing and stabilizing marriages were ceasing to work. The very things that made marriage more satisfying, and more fair to women, are the same things that have made marriage less stable.

The outlines of the problem were clear by the early twentieth century. The more that people saw marriage as their main source of intimacy and commitment, the less they were prepared to enter or stay in a marriage they found unsatisfying. Divorce rates shot up so quickly that by the 1920s many observers feared that marriage was headed for extinction.

The divorce rate peaked in the late 1970s and early 1980s, and has fallen by 26 percent since then. But the marriage rate has dropped at the same time, while the incidence of unmarried couples cohabiting, singles living alone, delayed marriage, and same-sex partnerships continued to increase throughout the 1990s.

Although welfare-state policies diverge, these trends are occurring in every industrial country in the world. Where divorce remains hard to get and out-of-wedlock birth is stigmatized, as in Italy and Japan, rates of marriage have plunged.

I don't believe that marriage is on the verge of extinction — nor that it should become extinct. Gay men and lesbians are now demanding access to marriage — a demand that many marriage advocates perversely interpret as an attack on the institution. And marriage continues to be an effective foundation for interpersonal commitments and economic stability. Of course we must find ways to make marriage more possible for couples who want it and to strengthen the marriages they contract. But there's a big difference between supporting measures to help marriages succeed and supporting an organized marriage movement.

Choosing Single Motherhood © Mikki Morrissette

Despite the benefits associated with marriage for most couples, unhappily married individuals are more distressed than people who are not married. Women in bad marriages lose their self-confidence, become depressed, develop lowered immune functions, and are more likely to abuse alcohol than women who get out of such marriages.

For children, living with two cooperating parents is better than living with a single parent. But high conflict in a marriage, or even silent withdrawal coupled with contempt, is often more damaging to children than divorce or growing up in a single-parent family. According to the National Center on Addiction and Substance Abuse at Columbia University, teens who live in two-parent households are less likely, on average, to abuse drugs and alcohol than teens in one-parent families; but teens in two-parent families who have a fair to poor relationship with their father are more likely to do so than teens who live with a single mother.

The most constructive way to support modern marriages is to improve work-life policies so that couples can spend more time with each other and their kids, to increase social-support systems for children, and to provide counseling for all couples who seek it. But many in the center-right marriage movement resist such reforms, complaining that single parents and unmarried couples—whether heterosexual or of the same sex—could "take advantage" of them. If we grant other relationships the same benefits as marriage, they argue, we weaken people's incentives to get married.

But that is a bullet we simply have to bite. I am in favor of making it easier for couples to marry and to sustain that commitment. But that cannot substitute for a more far-reaching, inclusive program to support the full range of relationships in which our children are raised and our dependents cared for.

CHAPTER 16

HOW ARE THE KIDS TURNING OUT?

"I want to do it myself," used to be the phrase that made me swell up with pride that Sophie was turning out to be like her mom. But then I realized that she was in the first stage of independence, and the phrase was not uncommon for kids her age.

She's the little girl who felt overwhelmed on her first day of kindergarten, sitting in a lunchroom with 60 other first-timers who were experiencing a range of comfort levels. She tends to be shy in unfamiliar situations and prefers to observe before putting herself out there—like Mom. Not like her classmate Dante, who was chatting it up with every adult he saw that first day, finding it hard to stay in his seat. But not either like the little boy who quietly cried because his older sister had left him with his class and gone off to her own.

When that first day of school started, Sophie was proud of her ability to write her name, do basic addition, and read several words. As the year progressed, she made friends easily—boys and girls—and showed a surprising zeal for competition. Most people who worked with her commented on how quickly she learned, and how attentive she was in class. She especially stood out, as the lone white and female participant, in the Brazilian martial art *capoeira*, where she was at least two years younger than her cohorts. She always had an energy for learning, but I had never seen her so determined physically. In a matter of weeks she was proudly doing unaided handstands, and had noticeably improved in cartwheels and push-ups. Clearly the lack of a father in the home had not affected her in stereotypical ways.

Now that she is six, my primary concern for her is whether she will have the mental toughness required to deal with kids who might not be as sweet/soft or fair-minded as she tends to be. The worry is largely my own nervousness about letting her go—being in situations without Mom. My little girl is becoming a big girl who will need to protect herself from things I won't always be there to help her with.

From the looks of it, her brother will be the social one. He smiles easily, likes attention more than Sophie ever did, gives flirtatious and charming grins to anyone who fusses over him. Like his sister, at 18 months he already shows an ability to focus for good lengths of time at independent play, is extremely attentive to sights and sounds, and learns quickly. He isn't much of a talker, preferring instead to figure out how to get things open so he can explore—such as the front door, refrigerator, dishwasher. Surely he, too, will end up being a happy child.

> *I find that my fears no longer have anything to do with single parenthood. I know I can handle things on a day-to-day basis. But there are those nagging questions that can't be answered until they grow up.*

Will they resent having half of their genetic identity such a detached part of their history? Will my snappishness when I am exhausted from juggling do long-term damage to our relationship? Will they reject me someday because I didn't play with them enough? Stay tuned...

In this chapter we consider some of the stereotypical weaknesses of the Choice lifestyle: lack of time for parenting, lack of a model of trust and intimacy for developing adult relationships, intense attachment that might hinder separation, absence of a father's influence on development.

And we consider some of the strengths of Choice Mothers: genuine love and desire to nurture a child, independence, self-sufficiency, ability to set and achieve goals for personal fulfillment.

I boiled these stereotypes down into a standard set of questions asked for the first time of Choice Kids—young people raised by a single mother who consciously decided to raise them on her own. For this chapter, my interviews with seven Choice Kids are included to help answer the big question: How are they turning out?

The young people featured here, who range in age from 11 to 30, were discovered in a random fashion. The kids chosen for this chapter were not selected because of the answers they gave, but because they represent different age groups and methods to motherhood.

Everyone I talked to spoke to me confidentially, away from mothers. All of them were advised that they could ask for greater anonymity if they didn't want to be recognized in the book. I asked them how they felt growing up without a father, the strengths and weaknesses of the Choice lifestyle in their view, and how they feel their personality and life goals were impacted by their family structure.

I found that most of them were not shy about their opinions. However, several that I wanted to interview were not interested in participating—and likely would have offered interesting perspectives.

With such a small sample included here—the conversations are a book unto themselves—there are no grand generalizations that can be made, especially since I am talking only to kids willing to be interviewed. But as I continue these conversations (Choice Kids are encouraged to contact me through the book's website), and as the large generation of today's young children mature, I hope to publish another book specifically about this topic in a few years.

Before getting to the perspectives of the Choice Kids, I will briefly summarize what my conversations with them have helped me discover so far. And I will include the perspectives of pioneering Choice Mothers who talked to me about their kids.

Overall Findings (so far)

Social development
Some sociologists have suggested that boys raised by single mothers sometimes make better partners, who listen and show greater compassion and respect than boys from other backgrounds, and that girls grow up with a can-do attitude of open possibilities that serves them well professionally.

Others, who primarily have talked to children of divorce, report that a sudden drop into an impoverished environment, feelings of rejection, and the inability to trust can have a great impact on a child's self-esteem and life choices.

Considering how randomly the kids I talked to were found, one thing that stood out for me was how accomplished most of them were. Many of them were unusually intelligent and precocious—even gifted. One boy entered college at the age of 14, and most were top students.

Was this genetic? Several had anonymous donors who were bright. Many Choice Moms, as we reported in Chapter 6, have master's degrees, and obviously are strong-minded individuals.

In general, the kids I have talked to so far are confident and secure, likely because of the commitment and attention to parenting offered by their mothers.

Choosing Single Motherhood © Mikki Morrissette

Socially, a few of them seemed withdrawn, but most had close friendships with friends and family. And yes, most of them—not all—seemed to have very close relationships with their mothers.

The effect of stigma

When my daughter was three, Sophie seemed obsessed with prince-and-princess stories of romance. This fact concerned me—*might she feel she's missing something?*—until I realized that most young girls had the same fascination, regardless of family structure.

Yet the desire to fit in is a natural part of childhood. And the model of "mommy, daddy and me" is valued in general society. As one therapist told me, especially in early adolescence, the emphasis is on being "just like" one's peers, so if a teen differs from his/her friends it may be a source of personal friction and stress. Of course, kids can feel bad or be teased about lots of issues (e.g., too fat, too thin, too tall, too short, etc). As she said, "The best remedy is a supportive home environment in which adolescents can learn to love and care for themselves, and maybe get some coaching about how to cope with teasing and other experiences of being made to feel different."

Gender identity researcher Barbara Risman[1] discovered that children raised in untraditional households tend to grow up with more egalitarian attitudes about male and female roles and responsibilities. But because the child's identity is still developed largely from the influence of peers, they can struggle as they attempt to reconcile contradictions between how society sees things and life at home.
Do the children of Choice pioneers feel stigmatized or odd by not growing up in a "traditional" household?

In general, the ones I have talked to so far do not. A 30-year-old women clearly had some issues—she articulated how she felt unusual growing up—but in hindsight, she said it had more to do with her mother's evasion of the topic than from a desire to fit in with other kids.

The young people I have talked to so far tend to be highly independent, with little shame about not coming from a "normal" family. One young man, for example, expressed disdain for the notion of conformity—not an uncommon response for his age. He said that although he appreciated regular contact with a male role model, and although he was sure it did have an impact on him to grow up without a father, it didn't bother him to come from a Choice household when he was growing up, especially since so many kids came from divorced families.

However, a lack of shame or embarrassment doesn't equate with being an open book. Many kids don't want others to know the full, private details of their lives, which doesn't seem unusual.

The "daddy" story

Even if it wasn't a matter of stigma in their community, a basic question I asked every Choice Kid was whether they grew up wishing they had a father.

One girl was seven when she told her mother, after a few visits with her biological father, that she didn't want a relationship with him, even though the mother thought it would be a healthy option for her to pursue. Now an adult, the girl still has little interest in her father, but is developing a close relationship with her half-siblings.

One of the younger boys wished that he had a father to play with him when his mom was busy—playtime was clearly a priority in his young life.

On the other hand, a boy who did not want to talk to me was 13 when he started expressing hostility to his mother for denying him a father. Research indicates this is a natural age for this type of resentment to show. Which is one reason I was surprised to find less reluctance or ambivalence from a few other teenage boys I talked to. A 14-year-old boy expressed open affection for his mother, in fact, proudly declaring that she had done nearly everything right in raising him.

Several children I know who were conceived by an anonymous donor were in their early teens when the "unknowns" started to bother them—but others had no interest.

Will Choice Kids marry?

In 2004, David Popenoe and Barbara Dafoe Whitehead, who we met in Chapters 6 and 7, released a report titled "The Marrying Kind," which examined men ages 25 to 34 to determine who marries and who doesn't.[2] In short, they determined that young men whose parents were married were more likely to "express readiness" to be married than men from other backgrounds. They reported as well that young men from married households had more positive attitudes toward women, children and family life.

One teenaged girl I know of thought her mother's single status was working out so well for them that she didn't see any negatives to the lifestyle. Another teenager didn't feel comfortable in solo dating situations—and preferred group dating. Another extroverted girl dates, but hadn't yet met anyone she thought was worth investing time with, and seemed wise to the "use them and lose them" tendencies of some of the men on her college campus.

One girl I was not able to talk to was timid around men, which her mother attributed to the mother's conflicted feelings after a difficult breakup. But others were strong-minded and open in developing relationships with the opposite sex. One young man reported having good friendships with women as well as normal "hanging out" time with men. He was not opposed to the idea of marriage, and although he dated infrequently in college, he was embarking on more serious relationships in later years.

The older the child, the more introspection they are able to give to what, really, their upbringing meant to them. That's why I intend to continue conversations with young adults who have had more time to reflect. I do not expect there will be big surprises in store about what they have to tell us, but there are more complex insights to be gained as Choice Kids make their own lifelong commitments as partners and parents.

The Mothers' Perspective

I had several conversations with experienced Choice Moms—many of them in the psychology profession, and all of them with kids who were at least 14—who had interesting perspectives about how their children were turning out and why.

Relationships

One woman said her daughter didn't seem to miss having a father, but did tend to have boyfriends who served as a buffer between mother and child in the teenage years. The relationships weren't serious, but seemed to satisfy her hunger for cuddling.

The girl had reserves of inner strength, however. The mother reported that "she's more radicalized than I—a professional reformer." She seemed able to handle anything, as a top student, with passionate interests and a thirst for knowledge. How she handled the men in her life "blows me away," the mother reported. For example, one of the "players" at her school pursued the young woman for a long time before she told him that she didn't want to be friends because she didn't respect him.

Respect and integrity were important values to several young women. One young girl told her mother she no longer wanted to visit with her known donor because she didn't respect him. Another teenager tended to be suspicious of the intentions of boys who crossed her path. When she started dating, she did not feel comfortable in one-on-one situations and preferred group dating. "I have worried about her not having a model of a good relationship," said her mother. "But in my work, I see kids who get terrible models of relationships. Ideally kids would see perfectly communicating men and women, but many do not. And when divorce happens, that's torture on children. The experts tend to compare parenting to an image of perfection, but life doesn't work out that way."

Another mother, whose child was still too young for serious dating, also worried about whether the lack of a relationship model would be a problem for her child. "My concerns might be totally unfounded, but that does concern me," she said. "I know that he respects women, and has self-respect. He's got a good core, and maybe that's what it takes. Maybe his relationships will be modeled after him and I—mutual respect and kindness."

Identity

A mother told me her daughter started to confront identity issues around the age of 14. "No one else in the family has a mole on the side of their face," the girl remarked one day. She became ultra-aware of how her conception story differed from others, and declared that she didn't want to have to explain everything to friends and teachers.

"My advice to other single mothers," the woman shared, "is that you should bring it up. You open the door. They might be nervous talking about it. But they'll be much less likely to [be nervous] if you help them discuss it openly. Even though my daughter is an extroverted child, she still wouldn't bring it up."

A biracial girl didn't have many questions about her father growing up, but issues of race concerned her more. After she entered college, she embraced the African American community for the first time. She also confronted head-on her loneliness as a teenager growing up without siblings. As a young adult, she started connecting with her many half-siblings, and formed a particularly good relationship with a half-brother close to her in age.

One woman said the only men she was involved with socially were gay men, so her daughter didn't have many male role models. "I think my father has been a father substitute for her," she said. "They're very close, more so than he and I ever were."

Choosing Single Motherhood © Mikki Morrissette

Strengths

In terms of what children gain by growing up in a one-parent family, one mother said the relationship with her child was so deeply complex—"a wonderful model for creating intimacy"—that her child, even in the turbulent teenage years, seemed able to talk to her about everything.

Another said that her daughter's former boyfriend had once said, "She knows how to do everything. She doesn't need a man around for the things men do—and that's true," the mother said. "I'm not complaining. I'm glad she is self-sufficient. She definitely learned that from me. I think I'm a little obnoxious about not asking for help. She's much more independent than a lot of kids grow up to be."

One woman talked about how lucky she and her son were to be able to spend so much time together, "so much more than most families I know. We've had it very special." She said she had raised him to understand that his opinions do matter. "When we bought a new car, I asked for his opinion. He knows I want him to speak his mind. Some days that makes me want to pull my hair out, but the good far outweighs any negatives." When he became an Eagle Scout, he asked to pin both the "mom" and "dad" recognitions on her.

One young adult I read about, who was adopted from El Salvador and raised by a Jewish Choice Mom, said in an article that appeared in *Hadassah Magazine*,[3] "I always felt like an outsider in the synagogue and in Hebrew school. I was the only person of color, with a white mom. I'm comfortable culturally. I celebrate Passover and Hanukka, but I don't have much of a Jewish identity."

It wasn't until college that the young woman found a racially mixed community she felt comfortable with. She majored in African-American studies and spent a semester in Namibia. Despite the racial disparities of her youth, the young woman was highly positive about her upbringing. "There's nothing more empowering than being raised by a single, amazing, independent woman," she said. "[Her mother] led this alternative lifestyle by choice—one most people would not have chosen."

Weaknesses

One woman admitted that her child was spoiled—"materially, no, but attention-wise, yes. I definitely think that's the product of growing up with one parent." Another said her teenager seemed a little selfish and self-centered—"but aren't they all at this age? I'm sure I'm not as disciplined about asking for help and support around the house as I should be."

Another reported that her child was easy from the beginning—good at following rules—but that it might have had something to do with not having anyone else to compete with. "I remember when she was five, we went to the zoo with her friends. My daughter wanted to get popsicles, they wanted ice cream cones, and there was a big hassle over which one to get. It was the first time she acted like a brat—she'd never had to deal with others like that."

One woman said she and her son had some regret about not having a larger family. She tried to adopt when she was in her 40s, but it didn't happen.

FROM MY EXPERIENCE...

BY DIANA, PIONEERING CHOICE MOM (AND THERAPIST)

My daughter has clearly learned much from our relationship over the years about how to maintain a trusting, committed connection. But there are some vulnerabilities of Choice Motherhood that I do think we need to be mindful of:
• The intense attachment between mother and child might hinder separation; the mother must be conscious of supporting age-appropriate separation;
• There is no other influence to buffer or moderate the parent's world views and emotional reactions;
• The demands could be overwhelming without another primary caregiver;
• No matter how many other supportive figures there are in the child's life, there is only one primary caregiver for that child to turn to—as my daughter has said, 'If my mom isn't there, it is up to me.'

Conversations With the Kids

Kyla, adult
Her mother was one of the earliest Choice Moms—using an anonymous donor in 1975—and perhaps as a result missed the benefit of wisdom about how to communicate about the Choice Child's origins that today's single mothers now have access to.

I felt some resentment about not having a traditional dad, mostly when I was a school-aged kid. It wasn't so much missing a dad as feeling weary about being an oddity, weary of explaining something I really didn't understand myself.

I think it is selfish in a sense—although my mom was not aware of it at the time—to

Choosing Single Motherhood © Mikki Morrissette

have a child in such a way that the father is anonymous and remains anonymous. I think a person has a right to know the identities of both parents. I do not think it is selfish to single-parent. Is it selfish to carelessly happen upon parenthood as a couple that has no inspiration for long-term commitment?

Selfishness seems unrelated to the form of conception. We all act upon our desires. Whether or not we are willing to take responsibility for the consequences of our desires is what ultimately measures our 'selfishness.'

My mother did so many things right. She was devoted to me. She was on my side—irrationally so at times, which I believe is absolutely necessary for normal development. She was more interested in discovering who I was than in molding me into any preconceived image. Her parenting style was relatively hands-off, trusting me to make choices that would aid me in my own process of knowing myself. So even when she didn't approve of the choice, she was more likely to let it run its course than to interfere.

The tragedy of my childhood was that my mom failed to stay in communication with me around some essential features of my existence. First, she didn't stay current with me about my understanding of how I was conceived. She told me about it when I was too young to understand, and then dropped it, such that I really didn't know what 'artificial insemination' was, but only remembered that clinical term. I made up stories about a dead dad to avoid what seemed a humiliating and incomprehensible truth.

Second, and more important, when I was seven we moved in with my mom's (female) partner, who ignored me to such an extent that I'd guess we exchanged less than a dozen words in the last eight of the nine years we lived together. My mom acted as though this was not happening.

I think part of her confusion/motivation here was the financial and emotional security the partner provided. It allowed her to give me material things I wanted, and also to work half-time in order to be more available to me. These were certainly not conscious choices, but they were part of the fear that kept her from changing what became an ugly and painful home.

My mom also never communicated with me about being a lesbian, but rather, called her partner our 'housemate.' So this was another thing I knew but didn't really know in an articulate way, and so lied about.

What I do see in myself now is a lack of attachment for men. I have chosen female partners (in spite of every wish not to become what I saw modeled by my mom and her partner), and although I have had male lovers, I have not ever felt attached to them. I do not have a clear sense of whether this is directly related to the lack of a man in my life who I was close to when I was a child. It may just be my nature, or it may just be circumstantial. It seems possible that tomorrow I might feel attached to a man—or not. Either way, this is not intrinsic to single-momhood. It's rather specific to my story that in addition to not having a dad, I did not have a brother, or uncle, or grandpa, or friend, who was close and present.

Q: Some feel that a child who grows up in a Choice home won't see what it's like to be in a loving relationship with a partner, and might consider marriage unnecessary to happiness. Your thoughts?
Again, this seems unrelated to a Choice home. Choice conception does not preclude a loving relationship between adult role models. I do consider marriage unnecessary to happiness—I consider just about any external circumstance to be irrelevant to happiness. If my upbringing helped me to see this, I credit it for that.

I felt a lot of stigma about our family structure when I was young—but I believe this was due to lack of communication rather than the family structure itself.

If a proud and open approach to our 'difference' was modeled for me, I'm sure I'd have spoken with pride and openness. As it was, I lied, felt enormous shame, and evaded all inquiries.

About my donor—I just want to know who he is. I want to sit across from him, see him, hear him speak, experience him. I'm not looking for someone to fill the role of father. I do think the identity of a donor should belong to the child.

And I do feel there is a hole in my knowledge of myself. Before I made a concerted effort to find him, it was a conceptual idea—a curiosity more than an emotionally-driven need. It's hard to feel much of anything about an absence. In the course of my looking, however, I was surprised by how raw, how tender, I felt every time I thought I might have found him.

Greg, young adult
His biological father left when his mother was pregnant.

I don't think I had many "daddy" questions, but I did grow up with a strong disregard for fitting in. I wasn't a wild child, but I was extremely independent. I tend

Choosing Single Motherhood © Mikki Morrissette

to make my own conclusions, set my own values, rather than feel bound by social expectations. I definitely would like to get married, have kids, although I was shy about dating for a long time, because of some self-confidence issues. I have resolved most of my issues through lots of introspection, and have dated a few women since graduating from college. I am currently seeing someone.

I wasn't ostracized for our different family structure. It wasn't like I was seen as some kind of freak. Maybe more so by the parents of kids than anything.

> *I used to be asked if I missed having a dad, and my standard answer was that you can't miss what you don't have. In hindsight, I think by being raised by a single parent, I wasn't exposed to the same levels and varieties of social interaction, so when I was a kid I probably developed socially more slowly than others.*

As far as fears some have that a guy like me will grow up overly aggressive, or less analytical, because of the lack of a father in the home—it doesn't make sense. I was excellent as a math and science student in high school. (I was only average in subjects like history and English.) I went to a competitive prep school, and graduated Phi Beta Kappa from college as a computer science major. There are a lot of stereotypes about single parenting, and it seems as if we're all clumped into the same category.

On the role model front though, since the mother is the one and only parent, it is clearly important that they be excellent role models, but to be careful not to appear infallible. With no one to dispute them or argue with, it may be easy for the child to think of them as such when they are too young to know any better.

An advantage to the way I grew up, I think, is that I never witnessed my parents fighting. My mother is a very independent woman, and I think I got that personality trait specifically from her—not the fact of single parenthood itself. I definitely learned from her example that you don't always have to do things the way everyone else does. Especially through my college years, I tended to question everything—I wasn't so eager to fit in. In the years since, though, I've seen the benefits of "fitting in" and, although I am still pretty independent, I don't have as strong a need to be different and I don't always mind if I'm doing things the way everyone else does. I'm still not trendy, but I think that's mostly because I know trends don't last.

Money and material things aren't so important to me. I don't mind living alone. I don't really relate to the stereotypical jocks, or get into macho competition. I consider it a waste of time. People tell me I'm easy to talk to, maybe a little more sensitive than some.

In college I had several one-to-one relationships with girls. At this point in my life, though, I definitely prefer having drinks with a group of guys than having intense one-on-one conversations with girls.

The weak points of the family structure are just common sense: you don't have a dad around to teach you to do the guy things. It's more the missing of someone who could be a good role model. The husband of my mom's good college friend was my godfather, and good role model. From about the age of 7 to 13, I saw him maybe once a week, and we are still very close—as I am with my godmother. After that I was in the Big Brother program for a few years. I was against it at first, but it turned out to be fantastic. He was about 30, married, with no kids then. He lives in Texas now, with three kids, so we don't talk as much.

When you try to determine the source of a child's personality, it's difficult to tell what came from the lack of a father and what came from the mother's own personality. These days I tend to think that any personality traits one can attribute to the lack of a father are probably just social handicaps due to less exposure to social interactions at home. I have a hunch that having a sibling probably would have made up for some of that.

As far as inherited personality traits from the mother, I think it's important to expose the kid to many different role-models, because with only one parent, the kid may end up inheriting an unusual amount of that parent's personality.

I think every kid of a single mom will have a different experience, but the effects of a missing father might be visible among most of them. I am pretty interested whether or not that's true.

Laurabeth, young adult
Adopted at 13 months, she had some rough periods in her earliest years, but now in the middle of her college years at an Ivy League school, she is thriving—socially, academically, emotionally.

The way I grew up—with a mother and no father—was never an issue at all. In fact, it took me a long time to realize that there were fathers who played a role in their kids' lives. And I never felt like an oddball growing up. Several of my friends thought it was kind of neat that I didn't have a dad. I certainly never felt resentment about it.

Choosing Single Motherhood © Mikki Morrissette

I don't really agree with the idea that men do some things better than women, and vice versa—the idea that you need a man and a woman to balance the parenting. People are complex. One person can do so many things, in many different ways. And as far as needing to see a man and a woman as a couple in order to learn how to relate to others—you don't need two parents for that.

I also don't agree with the theory that the absence of a father might make them seem like inferior beings. I think men are great. I've had a number of serious relationships. One great thing about living with a single parent is that it teaches you a lot about compromise.

My mother and I have always been extremely close. Although we have really intense arguments. When there's no other parent to run to, no third opinion on anything, it can be frustrating.

I think the strengths I got from the way I was raised are that I work well with people, I'm honest—the relationship I had with my mom was a good thing for me to learn from. It also made me stronger, needing to fend for myself when mom wasn't around.

What I especially learned from my mom was to do what you feel really strongly about, and have integrity in doing it. Those are major character traits I got from her. She's very intelligent and knows what she's doing.

Ryan, teenager

He is a minor celebrity in the donor insemination industry, because he launched a donor sibling registry with his mother. He is an exceptionally mature young man, who entered college at the age of 14.

For the most part, I don't feel resentful about not having a father, because I have had such a great, involved mom. Most of the time not having a traditional dad never crosses my mind. There are occasions though—like wondering if college would be easier, if I would be in Calculus 5 by now, if I had a mathematics-oriented father who could help me. Other than occasional thoughts like that, I am more than okay that it's just my mother and I.

I don't understand why some people would consider it selfish for a single woman to want a child. Perhaps the thought is that it's not fair to the child to subject him/her to a life without a father figure? But as long as the woman is committed to raising the child herself in a responsible way, then I believe it to be preposterous to think that would be a "selfish act."

What has my mother done that was "right" in raising me? I'm not sure how to answer this question without sounding like I'm bragging. To be be perfectly honest, I feel that she has done most everything right. She gives me all the freedom a teen needs without ever having to worry about me trying pot or a cigarette or anything like that. Going to college early as I did is a big challenge for anyone, and she has been there 100 percent of the time. From handling almost every aspect of my education to instilling in me a sense of right and wrong, I would say she's done it. In fact, that's probably the primary reason that I'd be scared to have a child of my own. I'd know that I could never do as good a job raising him/her as she has with me.

Q: Some child experts feel that a boy who grows up without a father will lack a sense of discipline, be overly aggressive, lack analytical skills and/or have trouble understanding what it is to be a man. Do you see any of that in yourself?
Oh no, I'm all man baby. Seriously though, I have friends who have grown up in a traditional family. As far as analytical skills, discipline, aggressiveness and "manliness," I see very little difference. Consciously or not, I have learned to acquire those qualities elsewhere. Sure, my mother probably isn't the best at teaching me to be a man, but I think father or no, much of that comes from within. The day any dude is born, they have some element of this already established, and I think that it's going to show through no matter how you're raised. All my life, I've been dragged through clothing stores and jewelry stores and I still hate it. Just because I was raised with it doesn't mean that I'm gonna like it. Father figure or not, I'm always gonna like hurting myself on my bike, gadgets, welding, building and all that stuff that comes naturally with being a man. I really feel that alot more of who a person is comes from instinct, rather than their upbringing.

I have found male role models in many forms over the years. The earliest I can think of was a mentor named Sean. He taught me alot about math and science and mechanics and engineering. I looked up to him perhaps because he was so smart. Over the years I found role models in teachers and friends and mountain biking coaches, and sometimes even television. The person I probably most admire is late night talk show host Conan O'Brien. He's basically what I want to be when I grow up. Smart, hilarious, witty, Harvard-educated, tall, and fun loving. I think that's basically the definition of a role model—someone I aspire to be.

Q: Have you felt stigma from others about your family structure?
Only once that I can recall. It was from a high school physics teacher whom I loathed, and she loathed me. She would openly attack me in front of classmates

Choosing Single Motherhood © Mikki Morrissette

about what I've done to establish the donor sibling registry. It was a horrid situation, but I no longer attend that school. Other than that, people seem to really embrace what I've done, and where I came from.

I think that one great thing about being raised by only my mother is that it has given us an unusually strong bond. My mother means the world to me, and me to her. I think that had I been raised by two parents, that bond would logically be decreased by half. But it's hard to say how my life would have been different with a father.

I am extremely curious about my donor. I feel it is a curiosity that can only be understood if you grow up with half of your family missing. Imagine looking in the mirror and not knowing a damned thing about half of yourself. Half of your physical characteristics, half of your interests, half of everything.

What would I like to know? EVERYTHING. Why do I like engineering? How did I end up with OCD? Where did you go to college? What are my other grandparents like? What Scottish clan am I? How many uncles/aunts do I have? How many half-siblings do I have? Are you married? Where do you live? What do you do for a living? The list goes on. I could ask him questions for years before I caught up with all of the things that I would have known by now.

Do I think donors should remain anonymous? Absolutely not. The ones that have already donated signed up for complete anonymity, and I believe that we should respect that, but in the future, they should have a total openness policy. Because sooner or later, if the child isn't lied to about their origins (and even in some cases if they are) the child is going to be curious about where they came from. And the donor has to be prepared to satisfy that curiosity.

Personally, it would be a dream come true if I could meet my donor. At the same time, however, I know that he signed up for complete anonymity, and I want to respect that, but in the future, there absolutely needs to be a major policy change.

Hunter, teenager

His mother forged uncommon ground in their community by choosing not to marry but to raise her child on her own after she accidentally got pregnant. Because we had a less fluid conversation via email, rather than a direct interview, I am summarizing his comments here rather than quoting him directly.

Careful to point out that his perspective doesn't speak for everyone, and that he believes many of life's answers can be found in the Bible, he finds it troublesome that many adults "don't have open minds and do not listen to anyone else." He believes that anyone who wants to have a child but hasn't found a partner should simply "go for it" if she is prepared. In some families, a father is "a plus," he said, but being without a father can sometimes "have no effect."

He told me that he has felt some resentment about not having a father "because a male influence can be important." He also thinks it would be helpful to have another person around to parent. Since most of his close friends are guys, he presumes having a parent of the same sex would be helpful to "experience things and learn from."

He didn't grow up with male role models. His mother was there for him, he said, and he had friends he could turn to. He does wonder how life could have been better if he'd grown up with a father—what different experiences he could have had.

On the other hand, he doesn't understand why anyone would consider it selfish for a woman to have a child without providing a father. "That's simply how it is."

He understands that his mother did all she could in supporting him. His advice for future single mothers is to "not only see your child as your kid, but as a human being. Remember how it was with you, going through childhood. Have an open mind. There's no reason not to get help or advice. Ask your child what they think."

Since every family dynamic is different, he says, it's impossible to generalize about why kids in one single-parent family turn out differently from others. From his view, "not every mother or father is ready to be a parent, just because they are an adult."

He doesn't think the absence of two parents in a loving relationship will impact his ability to find happiness in his own relationship someday. "Loving relationships are everywhere. Anyone will learn about them when they are ready and old enough."

Zac, pre-teen

This precocious boy acquired a stepfather when he was six. Together the threesome went to China to adopt his sister. Zac has the unique benefit of having a donor who wrote a letter to be given to any offspring.

My donor wrote a letter telling me about his family, and about his ups and downs through college. He talked about growing up in a multiethnic neighborhood— basically, he's not racist. He was very good at sports, like tennis and running. He always wanted to go to medical school, since he was in seventh grade.

Choosing Single Motherhood © Mikki Morrissette

He wrote this message: "I wish the very best to your parents. I hope they give you the love that I got from mine. And to you, I wish you all the best in life. I hope you can become whomever you want to be, and I will always have a place for you in my heart."

I think I was seven when I decided I wanted to meet him. I thought about it, but didn't really mention it. That's the youngest I remember being interested. I've asked my mom a lot about meeting him. I'm very curious about him. Even though he sent me an entire four-page letter, there are still some questions unanswered. One of them was: Why did he donate his sperm to create kids?

Mom answers my questions, but I do have one she can't. What does he think, truly, about me, myself? Not just any kid that he donated sperm to create. (Not that he really knows I exist, but if he did.)

When I was younger, I was sad about not having a dad. Whenever my mom was doing things, I had nothing to do and no one to play with. All my friends would have dads and they would be playing with them all the time and saying what a good time they had with them. I wasn't angry, but just plain sad and sometimes distressed. When my mom would play with me, though, I didn't think much about having a father then. She would show me pictures of my donor and also tell me what he wrote to me, so I felt a bit better about that.

Now, because of having a stepdad, I also have brothers and sisters. I liked it when my mom started dating my dad, because he was really nice. He played with me a lot. But there was a bad side to it. His son was the meanest person ever to me. That cleared up by now, four years later, but there are still some rough spots with him.

Q: Some people consider it selfish for a woman to decide to have a child on her own. What is your opinion on that?
Why would she only care about herself when she was giving birth to me and helping me to grow up to be a great man?

Q: What has your mom done that is "right" in the way she raised you?
She would play with me a lot. She buys me ice cream and lets me have sleepovers whenever I want. She takes me around the world. She played with me when I was a baby and takes pictures of me. She says I was a cute baby. She is very fond of me.

Q: What would you suggest for future single moms about ways they could avoid making

mistakes in raising their child?
First of all, don't keep anything from your kids. My mom told me absolutely every secret. For example, she told me as soon as I was six that Santa Claus wasn't real. She tells me everything. My mom also told me everything about my donor. She showed me pictures of him and the note that he wrote.

Q: What strengths and weaknesses do you have that you feel are related to being raised only by your mom when you were little?
I'm not jerky like my brother is. I got lots of privileges that normally a father wouldn't let me do. For instance, sleepovers, trips to the ice cream shop, playing with friends a lot.

Sage, pre-teen
Although younger than most of the Choice Kids I interviewed, this precocious young woman was motivated to share her views. Her mother was the divorced parent of one when she used anonymous donor insemination at the age of 34. I am summarizing her comments here, rather than quoting her directly.

When she was younger, Sage tended to be emotional at bedtime about not having a father—although the emotions would sometimes come out indirectly. As her mother told me, she would say she felt like she wanted to go home, even though she knew she already was home. "I interpreted this as some kind of soul loneliness," her mother said.

But Sage told me she does not think it is selfish of a single woman to have a child. "Just because a woman wants a child and isn't with a man doesn't mean she should be denied a child."

She said that what her mother did right was "not treat me differently than any other kid" and "love me like any other mother." Sage's advice for future single mothers is to "tell your kids the truth, and make time to be with them every day."

When she was three, Sage asked her mother "Is my dad dead?" In reply, her mother "told me the truth in a format I would understand" and "told me more complicated versions as I got older."

As male role models, Sage says she turns to her brother—six years older than her—and the man who has been her mother's boyfriend during the past year. "I also turn to my family's close friends that are male"—two in particular have had warm, loving relationships with her over the years.

Choosing Single Motherhood © Mikki Morrissette

Sometimes she feels a little stigma from other kids (she attends a private school), but Sage says it's not purposeful.

Although Sage herself doesn't know how she would be different if she had been raised with a father, her mother indicated that "one quality which I think is definitely related to our family status is that we are very close and spend a great deal of time together."

She is interested in knowing more about her donor. "I would like to know what he looks like, and what his personality is like. I don't really care to meet him. I think a child should be allowed to know the donor at 18, but they should be told that the donor doesn't want to take a fatherly role."

Final Thoughts

Most of the young people I have talked to so far have healthy and nurturing relationships with their mothers—which is perhaps why they talked to me in the first place. And, reluctant commentators or not, most of the Choice Kids I know seem to be well-balanced, highly individualized young men and women.

There is perhaps a streak of self-absorption, which might have something to do with the age, something to do with the self-sufficiency of their mothers, and/or something to do with the tendency for the earlier generation of Choice Kids to have no siblings. Another tendency I expect to explore over time is whether a subset of Choice Kids have grown up more socially isolated than others—and what impact this has.

Although support networks and role models are highly recommended in this book, not all kids have grown up with them, and I'm curious about the effect of growing up in such a one-on-one household.

Perhaps the most logical issue in Choice Households is separation difficulty. "Letting go feels harder when you're a single parent," said one woman. "We share things and are close in a way unique to a one-on-one parent-child relationship."

We will learn much from this new generation of Choice Kids, and I welcome any of them to contact me at www.choosingsinglemotherhood.com.

CONCLUSION

CONNECTING THE DOTS

As I was finishing this book, preparing to write my final words, several interesting points from my life came together over a period of two weeks that offered me a "wrinkle in time" glimpse at the journey I have taken thus far.

I attended my 25-year class reunion, where we celebrated balding heads, the first grandparents among us, and a heartening number of classmates in their second decade of marriage. I watched an old friend—always the ambitious, studious one among us—let loose on the dance floor, having remade herself from a Pentagon consultant into a California vineyard owner. I admired the self-possessed Texas sheriff who strode into our small Minnesota conclave with cowboy hat and twang. And I marveled at the ability of so many in our class of 200 to remain connected to the community we grew up in, living the classic American dream of family, work and simple pleasures.

I was reminded that there are many different lifestyles, and that I am very content with the rather non-conformist path I have taken.

A few days later, I was in northern Minnesota with an old college friend and her large family of siblings, watching their second generations bond during the summer ritual of a week together with little else but boating, swimming, fishing and food. I have long enjoyed being an "adopted" member of the family, and admired the matriarch for raising such a close family of seven kids largely on her own. Over the years I have seen all four of my friend's brothers turn into active, hands-on fathers, now spread out around the continent but faithful to the semi-annual family get-together. I was eager to retain connection to these excellent role models so that my kids could see good, "traditional" family living up close.

I was reminded that many kids have great fathers who offer them something special, and that even those who had less-than-ideal upbringings can turn into good people—and was confident that my kids always would have solid role models and experiences to draw from over time.

A few days after that, Sophie and I returned to New York City for the first time since selling our home there, to show off Dylan and reconnect with old friends and favorite places. Our first stop was the apartment I had shared with my ex-husband before we separated in 1993. Creative, generous and genuine as he and his second wife are, they opened up their home to us for three days, and it was wonderful to see my children bond with the man who had once been such a large part of my life.

I was reminded that once upon a time I did not foresee having children on my own, and that in my 20s I was focused on goals rather than listening to instinct, emotions and needs. I was thankful that I have since then learned to be more vulnerable and open-hearted, and that conflict is not to be avoided but dealt with.

As the New York trip unfolded, I proudly talked with a documentary filmmaker about Choice Motherhood, met with a mother and college-aged daughter featured in this book, and relaxed with my former therapist as we watched my children play.

Then, it happened. After we had relocated from the spacious digs of my ex-husband to the darker, smaller, typical NYC apartment of a friend, an old, familiar depression started to creep in. The sense of isolation I had felt in my early days of Mom-hood was coming back to me—the feeling of being someone I didn't quite recognize in a place that no longer seemed to fit. With kids in tow, I noticed the garbage, congestion, noise, unsavory characters and disparity between economic classes much more than I had when I was single and carefree. I felt out of place and adrift.

At our first playground of the day, I had found my daughter in tears, telling two girls they had hurt her feelings by saying they didn't want to play with her. I brought us back to my friend's apartment to recharge and hide from the hot, midday sun. While I was in one room—trying to keep Dylan from rearranging my friend's shoes, jewelry and clothes—and Sophie was watching TV in the other, she suddenly, uncharacteristically, said, "I'm lonely." I panicked. Had she picked up on my own plummeting mood? Was she, too, feeling exhausted from the disparity of being in a city that no longer felt like home?

Although we were only 20 feet apart, Sophie asked me to come closer. I picked up Dylan and the three of us huddled together on the living room futon, propped up against sequined pillows, watching cartoons. It felt better, but still not great. So I got us outside again, to yet another playground. Almost instantly, a two-year-old girl attached herself to Sophie. The two of them jumped and splashed and slid, and

I knew "big sister" Sophie was no longer feeling lonely. Dylan, too, was gleeful (as usual) in the fresh air.

I knew I should be happier, but still I felt alone. Surrounded by honking, rushing, busy people, I felt like an insignificant bystander sitting uncomfortably on the edge of a sandbox in Central Park. I was lonely too, I could have told Sophie—being Mom in a space where I had once been something else. I wondered if I could shorten our one-week visit to the city that had been mine for 18 years.

But then an interesting thing happened. I struck up a conversation with the mother of the two-year-old. We sat together, with our feet in the sandbox, and she mentioned that she and her daughter would be moving to Pennsylvania soon. Something about the way she phrased it reminded me of myself. "Are you a single mother?" I asked. "Yes, I adopted from Russia," she said.

And just like that, we made a connection. We talked about how we became Choice Moms, how we unexpectedly transformed our lives because of our children (she had lived in New York 15 years and quit a lucrative but time intensive profession), the difficulties and the joys. My fog lifted. I had found the sense of community I had been missing. Being with my kids wasn't enough. Seeing old friends wasn't enough. Introducing Sophie and Dylan to the Statue of Liberty and favorite stretches of real estate wasn't enough. Talking proudly about Choice Motherhood wasn't enough.

What I rediscovered, in my moments talking with this Choice Mom, was a kindred spirit. The conversation was relatively brief, and we barely exchanged names, but she had become, in that fleeting period of time, a much-needed member of my support network—perhaps vice versa.

Our daughters, too, seemed to feed off of the energy of each other. They held hands and, when it was finally time to go separate ways, sweetly hugged goodbye. Many days later, after returning to Minnesota, when people asked Sophie about favorite moments of the trip, she mentioned meeting that little girl.

The moral of this extended story I am telling is this:
Connections to people become even more important after we
become Choice Mothers, because we need more energy and support
than we did before, when we were able to fill our days with work,
or solitude, or shopping, or travel, or boyfriends.

Choosing Single Motherhood © Mikki Morrissette

Our connections don't have to be simply with other Choice Moms—although they help, and I hope the women you've met in this book help you over a few humps. But if you decide to transform your life, the Old You will be invigorated by meeting people who understand the transforming nature of shaking out life and becoming something altogether New. Your old friends help, but might not intersect with you in the same way. Your beloved child(ren) will bring you great joy, but cannot fill the spaces when you feel disconnected from the world beyond diapers and playgrounds and moody adolescence.

Parenting is not always light and sunshine. There are dark clouds and claustrophobic spaces as well. Especially absent a partner to share the highs and the lows, the Choice Mother needs to make sure solo parenting will not become an isolating experience.

The Real and Remarkable Journey

Personally, I think Choice Motherhood is one of the most remarkable journeys a single woman can take. There are many unremarkable moments of parenthood (in my case, for example, Dylan peeing through his saturated diaper onto my lap after we barely made our connecting flight back to Minnesota). And many of us consider our lives—married or not, childfree or not—relatively unremarkable. Sometimes that fills us with angst, sometimes not.

But when you stop and listen to the moments of our lives, interesting stories emerge. In the last few weeks I've heard a classmate talk about how his family of six keep communication lines open by sharing family time in the hot tub, and another classmate talk about moving his family further into the country so they could continue to see the stars. I've seen three generations enthusiastically toss squishy balls around a living room while bopping for more than an hour to the "I Like to Move It" song from the Madagascar soundtrack. I've watched a non-kid-oriented friend bond with my six-year-old fashion queen daughter by trying on "New York chic" shoes together. I've watched my son squeal with delight at every bubble that seemed to magically appear from the wave of a wand—and the 50-year-old bubble-maker giggle along with him because of the contagious joy.

These scenes might not seem remarkable enough to qualify for a reality TV show. But they are part of the wonderfully simple, connect-the-dot moments of our lives that end up meaning so much.

When you are a single woman facing 24/7 responsibility for the well-being of a malleable child, it is easy to sometimes feel despair. When you are a teenager growing up with one parent or in a transracial family, it is easy to sometimes feel lost confronting questions of identity. When you are a young child with a mother stressed from juggling work, family and a minimal social life, it is easy to sometimes feel afraid and powerless.

The simple moments when we connect with other human beings in a warm, relaxed, open-hearted way are fleeting, but the memories of being part of a larger universe are what sustain us—and help lift us out of low points when we are detached, isolated, lonely. That is why anyone embarking on Choice Motherhood must be capable of building community consciously, serendipitously, and everything in between. She must actively seek out role models and rituals that will help her and her child connect to the larger world.

The Choice Mother must surround herself with positive, nurturing, enlightened people so that she and her child will grow up together in an environment that cultivates strengths and balances out weaknesses.

Hippy-dippy as this might sound, I unabashedly maintain that the most essential tool of any successful parent is a strong, extended support network made up of men and women, young and old, single and married—family, friends, teachers, spiritual guides, people down the street...even pets. (An adult man raised by a Choice Mom told me one of the smart things his mother did was bring a dog into their home so that he would have more than one place to share attention and affection.)

In short, developing a village for a child is how you become a responsible parent, and no one should build a family without it.

In the words of my daughter
After we returned from New York, Sophie took a Rhythm and Rhyme class at a local writing center. Over the course of a week, while learning some drumming patterns as accompaniment, she was encouraged to write a poem that answered questions about who she was and where she comes from. Her teacher sent her home with questions to consider. I purposely let others help spell out her answers so that I wouldn't end up influencing her.

I was curious, of course, to learn how she would define herself and the six years she had experienced thus far. I was able to hear it, loud and clear, during the performance she and her classmates gave at the end of the week.

338 Choosing Single Motherhood © Mikki Morrissette

What made it into her poem were not profound things like "who do you most admire?" (her delightful answer: *the women in our family because they're so smart)* or "who would you most like to meet?" *(God)*, or the American Idols concert I had just taken her to as our special (pricey) date, or that she was mad at her biological father for not being around, or that her Mom was too busy writing a book to play dolls.

Rather, her poem defined herself in the context of her own simple connect-the-dot moments: her growing skills and strength in *capoeira*, family time (months earlier!) spent bowling, the lefse-making tradition with Dave's family at Thanksgiving, the special Fourth of July cake she and I made together.

If she'd been a few years older, and able to read complex sentences, I would have wondered if she'd been reading my book. I had just days before finished writing about how the simple moments of connection with others sustain us.

The Eloquence of Choice Motherhood

Back in 2003, one of the Choice Mothers I've never met but long admired for her eloquent postings on the Single Mothers by Choice website, wrote an excellent encapsulation of this life we lead. I thank Melissa for sharing her thoughts, online and in this book (and thank Jane Mattes, founder of the SMC network, for agreeing to let me excerpt the post here):

I am totally and completely in love with and astonished by my child. And I have been, all through the times I've hated her behavior and been amazed at how angry such a small person can make me feel. I really love being a mother.

Yes, there are bad times, sometimes a lot of them. But there are so many good times that I literally can't count them. Like one day during Winter Break when we just lounged around in our pjs all day, playing games and drawing pictures and cuddling and reading and watching TV and playing dolls and having a "beauty day."

I can't begin to tell you how much more I laugh since I became a mother. I watch my kid flying around the apartment dressed as Wonder Woman, complete with fake boobs, and I crack right up. And she makes jokes! Sometimes they are moronic kid jokes, but sometimes they are totally unexpected one liners that lay me on the floor.

I have made new friends since becoming a parent—people I would never have met otherwise, who have become important parts of my life. I have a renewed interest in my faith and ancestry. I live each day more aware of the world around me because I see it with fresh eyes—my daughter's eyes—because experiences are so new to her.

I have become a better person in myself—stronger, more self-reliant, able to stand up for what's important to me and for my child. I'm more well-rounded than I used to be—my life is no longer mostly about my work. I always had a good relationship with my parents, but becoming a parent myself had improved that. My extended family in general treats me differently—as a person with a family, not as the spinster adjunct.

It is impossible to adequately convey the joy I feel when I pick up my daughter at the end of the day and she comes flying into my arms. To know that I am loved as fiercely as I love. I'm lucky to have a physically affectionate child; she tells me in a thousand non-verbal ways how deeply we are connected. I try to do the same. We never part without saying "I love you."

I take the responsibility of shaping her morals and ethics very seriously. When I see my daughter applying the principles of equality and justice and compassion that I have tried to teach her, I feel that I am doing my part to improve our collective future.

I look at the joy and involvement my daughter has given to me, to her grandparents (she's their only grandchild), to my brother, who is still tickled at the thought that he's an uncle, and I can't imagine my life without her as being anywhere near as rewarding and invigorating as my life with her.

Do I worry? You bet! How am I going to afford college? What if I get hit by a bus? What if the teacher thinks I did all the work on this school project? Did I do all the work on this school project? Does she say she loves me when I'm angry as a manipulative tactic? How will she react when I tell her I won't be home for Halloween this year? If I take off a day in one week to do something at school, and the kid gets sick the following week, will my boss be really pissed when I take time off again? Is she going to hate me when she's a teenager because she has no father? Is she going to grow up thinking that she's responsible for my happiness?

Nonetheless, this was the right choice for me. The payoff's been hugely positive, and gets more so every year.

Choosing Single Motherhood © Mikki Morrissette

Coming Full Circle

As I wrote at the beginning of these Final Thoughts, I had dipped into a bout of loneliness, while sitting in yet another sandbox during a return trip to the New York City of my younger, childless days. A serendipitous chat with a Choice Mom I met helped lift me out of the dip I had taken, and reminded me how essential it is to surround yourself with a network of people who can support you and your child— emotionally, logistically—throughout the Choice Motherhood journey.

Later during that sandbox day, I was sharing pizza and wine with a single friend I used to club-hop with in my childfree days. We were sitting in a back room I never knew existed, where kids were free to be, in a restaurant where I had years earlier flirted over drinks with a short-lived beau. Sophie was excitedly making her own pizza, wearing a plastic chef's apron supplied by the staff. Dylan seemed intent on chewing a hole into a large purple balloon.

"You're really digging being a mom," my friend exclaimed. And I acknowledged that yes, with all the different lives I had experienced in the 25 years since high school, in the 21 years since I had moved to New York as a naïve but ambitious young career girl, in the 18 years since I had married (and 12 since I had divorced), I had played with many interesting roles—and this Mom title was definitely suiting me better than I ever imagined.

Sometimes it is difficult to be a Choice Mom. Some days I think I'm doing a great job at it, and other days I know I'm not.

It is never my intent to encourage women to take this step lightly. While I believe everyone can, I recognize that many should not. Yes, there are issues of finances, fatherlessness, biological identity, energy, and ability to offer basic, quality parenting skills: open communication, authoritative discipline, respect, and effective stress management. But what it boils down to is whether each one of us has the heart to raise a child.

To be a responsible parent, quite simply, requires the capacity to love. If your heart is open, and you have the good judgment required to be responsive to someone else's needs, as well as the capacity to set limits, then you have the ingredients needed to build a Choice Home filled with the simple, connect-the-dot moments that every child needs.

NOTES

INTRODUCTION

1 — Based on "Fertility of American Women: June 2002," by Barbara Downs, Current Population Reports P20-548, U.S. Census Bureau, issued October 2003. Note that birth certificate information collected by the U.S. National Center for Health Statistics reported that in 2002 there were 83,000 births to unmarried women over the age of 35.

2 — "The living arrangements of new unmarried mothers," by W. Sigle-Rushton and S. McLanahan, *Demography*, 39 (3), 2002.

3 — "Unmarried With Children," by Barbara Kantrowitz and Pat Wingert, *Newsweek*, 28 May 2001

4 — "The Adopting Single Mother: Four Portraits of American Women Adopting from China," by Valerie S. Mannis, *Adoption Quarterly*, Vol. 4 (2), 2000

5 — "Baby Makes Two," by Cindy Rodriquez, *Boston Globe*, 17 October 2002

6 — "The XY Files: Forgoing a trip down the aisle, our correspondent heads straight to the sperm bank," by Lori Gottlieb, *Atlantic Monthly*, September 2005

CHAPTER 1

1 — "Juggling Congress, Adoption Not Easy: Single white mom raises black baby," by Malia Rulon, The Associated Press, 29 May 2005

2 — "Single Mothers By Choice," by Valerie S. Mannis, *Family Relations*, Vol. 48 (2), April 1999

3 — *In Praise of Single Parents: Mothers and fathers embracing the challenge,* by Shoshana Alexander (Houghton Mifflin), 1994

4 — *The Myths of Motherhood: How Culture Reinvents the Good Mother,* by Shari Thurer (Penguin Books), 1994

CHAPTER 4

1 — "The Adopting Single Mother: Four Portraits of American Women Adopting from China," by Valerie S. Mannis, *Adoption Quarterly*, Vol. 4 (2), 2000

2 — See Mannis, *Adoption Quarterly*, Vol. 4 (2), 2000

3 — "Doing the Right Thing: Single Mothers by Choice and the struggle for legitimacy," by Jane Bock, *Gender & Society*, Vol. 14 (1), Feb. 2000

4 — "Family Matters: Single Orthodox Mothers," by Rochelle Furstenberg, *Hadassah Magazine*, Vol. 86 (7), March 2005

5 — *From Father's Property to Children's Rights: The History of Child Custody in the United States*, by Mary Ann Mason (Columbia University Press), 1994

CHAPTER 5

1 — "Dan Quayle Was Right," by Barbara Dafoe Whitehead, *Atlantic Monthly*, April 1993

2 — "Nostalgia as Ideology," by Stephanie Coontz, *American Prospect*, Vol. 13, 8 April 2002

3 — Quayle addressed the Commonwealth Club of San Francisco on 19 May 1992

4 — *Life Without Father: Compelling new evidence that fatherhood and marriage are indispensable for the good of children and society*, by David Popenoe (The Free Press), 1996

5 — *Mothering the Race: Women's Narratives of Reproduction, 1890-1930*, by Allison Berg, (University of Illinois Press), 2001

6 — *Single Mothers and Their Children*, by Sara McLanahan and Irwin Garfinkel, (Urban Institute Press), 1988

7 — As reported in *Second Chances: Men, Women, and Children a Decade After Divorce*, by Judith Wallerstein and Sandra Blakeslee (Houghton Mifflin), updated edition 1996. A subsequent book by Wallerstein, Blakeslee and Julie Lewis was *The Unexpected Legacy of Divorce: A 25-Year Landmark Study*, (Hyperion), 2000

8 — Psychologist Nicholas Zill conducted The National Survey on Children, which interviewed children aged 7 to 11 in 1976, again in 1981, and in 1987.

9 — Whitehead spoke before the Committee on Health, Education, Labor and Pensions Subcommittee on Children and Families, on 28 April 2004

10 — "Bergen: Dan Quayle Was Right About Murphy," reported by The Associated Press, 11 July 2002

11 — As reported in "Quayle 10 Years After Murphy Brown," by Tobin Beck, United Press International, 9 May 2002; and "Murphy Brown Redux: Quayle Looks Back on the Big Speech," by Bob Costantini, evote.com.

12 — "Why I Think I'm Still Right: Since the flap over 'Murphy Brown,' American families have come under even more pressure," by Dan Quayle, *Newsweek*, 28 May 2001

13 — "The History of Private Life: An Overview," by Steven Mintz, Digital History website. (Retrieved 2005 from http://www.digitalhistory.uh.edu/historyonline/plife_overview.cfm)

CHAPTER 6

1 — Including "Intergenerational Consequences of Family Disruption," *American Journal of Sociology*, Vol. 94 (1), 1988

2 — *Growing Up With a Single Parent: What Hurts, What Helps*, by McLanahan and Gary Sandefur, (Harvard University Press), 1994

3 — *For Better or For Worse: Divorce Reconsidered*, by E. Mavis Hetherington and John Kelly, (W.W. Norton), 2002

4 — As Whitehead reported in "Dan Quayle Was Right," *Atlantic Monthly*, April 1993

5 — "Solo mothers and their donor insemination infants: follow-up at age 2 years," by C. Murray and S. Golombok, Family and Child Psychology Research Centre, City University, Northampton Square, London

6 — "Children raised in fatherless families from infancy: a follow-up of children of lesbian and single heterosexual mothers at early adolescence," by Fiona MacCallum and Susan Golombok, *Journal of Child Psychology and Psychiatry*, Vol. 45 (8), November 2004

7 — "Dispelling Myths and Creating Opportunity: A comparison of the strengths of single-parent and two-parent families," by Marilyn Ford-Gilboe, *Advances in Nursing Science*, Vol. 23 (1), September 2000

8 — "The Scarlet Letter Revisited: Single Mothers by Choice," by Leslie Talmadge, master's thesis, completed at Columbia University Graduate School of Journalism, 2003

9 — "Gender Role Differences in College Students from One- and Two-Parent Families," by Michael Slavkin, *Sex Roles: A Journal of Research*, January 2000

10 — *The Myths of Motherhood: How Culture Reinvents the Good Mother*, by Shari Thurer (Penguin Books), 1994

11 — "Moral parent, moral child," by Richard Weissbourd, *The American Prospect*, Summer 2002

CHAPTER 7

1 — See Child Trends Data report "Family Structure," as based on calculations of U.S. Census Bureau, Current Population Survey, 2004 Annual Social and Economic Supplement, "America's Families and Living Arrangements: 2004"

2 — *Real Boys: Rescuing Our Son From the Myths of Boyhood*, by William Pollack (Owl Books), 1999. Quoted in "Solo With a Son: Single moms face challenges in raising sons, but with a little help, boys do just fine," by Jennifer Wolcott, *The Christian Science Monitor*, 13 September 2000. See also "Single Mothers: What women need to know about raising their sons," on ABCNews.com.

3 — *Boys Will Be Boys*, by Myriam Miedzian (Lantern Books), 2002

4 — Some of Michael Gurian's several books include: *The Wonder of Boys: What Parents, Mentors and Educators Can Do to Shape Boys into Exceptional Men* (Jeremy P Tarcher/Putnam Books), 1996; and *The Good Son: Shaping the Moral Development of Our Boys and Young Men*, 1999

5 — See *Young, Poor and Pregnant: The Psychology of Teenage Motherhood*, by Judith S. Musick (Yale University Press), 1993. Blankenhorn also cites "Effects of Father Absence on Personality Development in Adolescent Daughters," by E. Mavis Hetherington, *Developmental Psychology*, Vol. 7 (3), 1972

6 —*Life Without Father*, by David Popenoe (The Free Press), 1996

7 — *Fatherneed: Why Father Care is as Essential as Mother Care for Your Child*, Kyle D. Pruett (The Free Press), 2000

8 — See also *The Two Sexes: Growing up apart; coming together*, by Eleanor E. Maccoby, (Harvard University Press), 1999

9 — Head Start Bureau, Administration on Children, Youth and Families, U.S. Department of Health and Human Services, as prepared by the National Head Start Training and Technical Assistance Resource Center, 1000 Wilson Boulevard, Suite 1000, Arlington, VA 22209

10 — *How Fathers Care for the Next Generation: A Four Decade Study*, by John Snarey (Harvard University Press), 1993.

11 — As reported in *America's Fathers and Public Policy: Report of a workshop*, edited by Nancy A. Crowell and Ethel M. Leeper, Commission on Behavioral and Social Sciences and Education, National Research Council (National Academy Press), 1994

12 — Richard Weissbourd is author of *The Vulnerable Child: What really hurts America's children and what we can do about it*, (Addison-Wesley Publishing), 1996

13 — See, for example, "Violence and Today's Youth," by Felton Earls, *The Future of Children: Critical health issues for children and youth*, Vol. 4 (3), Winter 1994

14 — Findings presented by University of Maryland School of Medicine at the Pediatric Academic Societies and American Academy of Pediatrics Conference in Boston, Massachusetts, on 13 May 2000. The results also were published in the August 1999 issue of *Child Development.*

15 — "Children's Object Representations of Anonymous Donor 'Fathers' and Impact on Self-Concept," by Elizabeth E. Groisser, dissertation for doctorate, Ferkauf Graduate School of Psychology, Yeshiva University, New York, May 2003

16 — "Elective single mothers and their children: The missing fathers," by M.K. Rose, *Child and Adolescent Social Work*, Vol. 9 (1), 1992

17 — As reported in Pruett's book. Also: *Father and Families: Paternal Factors in Child*

Development, by Henry B. Biller (Auburn House), 1993; "The Effect of Child-Rearing Practices on the Development of Differential Cognitive Abilities," by Ellen Bing, *Child Development,* Vol. 34, 1963; "Father-Child Interaction and the Intellectual Functioning of Four-Year-Old Boys," by Norma Radin, *Developmental Psychology* , Vol. 6, 1972; Biller's "The Father and Personality Development: Paternal Deprivation and Sex-Role Development," in Michael E. Lamb, ed., *The Role of the Father in Child Development* (Wiley & Sons), 1981

18 — "The Family Origins of Empathic Concern: A Twenty-Six Year Longitudinal Study," by Richard Koestner, Carol Franz, and Joel Weinberger, *Journal of Personality and Social Psychology,* Vol. 58, 1990

19 — "The Father Factor and the Two-Parent Advantage: Reducing the Paternal Deficit," by Henry B. Biller, presented to the father-to-father working group meeting with White House advisor William Galston, 17 December 1993 and 15 April 1994

20 —*The Troubled Journey,* by Peter L. Benson (Minneapolis: Search Institute), 1993

21 — *Reviving Ophelia: Saving the selves of adolescent girls,* by Mary Pipher (Ballantine Books), 1995

CHAPTER 8

1 — "The Father as an Idea: A Challenge to Kinship Boundaries by Single Mothers," by Rosanna Hertz, *Symbolic Interaction,* Vol. 25 (1), 2001

2 — As reported in "Sperm donor fights order to support two children," by Barbara White Stack, *Pittsburgh Post-Gazette,* 20 May 2005; and "Case Could Freeze Sperm Donation," by Wendy McElroy, 31 May 2005, for FoxNews.com

3 — *Being Adopted: The Lifelong Search for Self,* by David M. Brodzinsky, Marshall D. Schechter, and Robin Marantz Henig (Anchor Books), 1993

4 — Quoted in "What does it mean to be a donor offspring? The identity experiences of adults conceived by donor insemination and the implications for counseling and therapy," by A.J. Turner and A. Coyle, *Human Reproduction,* 2000, Vol. 15 (9)

5 — Turner and Coyle, *Human Reproduction,* 2000

6 — Hertz is currently working on a book about this and broader issues about single motherhood in a book that will be published by Oxford University Press in Spring 2006

7 — "Single Mothers by Choice: Deciding on a Known or Unknown Donor," by Karen Kessler, thesis for a Master of Science in Nursing, completed at the University of Wisconsin–Madison, 1987

8 — "A gay man reflects on his decision to become a known donor," by Andrew Berg, *Alternative Family,* retrieved from website in 2005

9 — "Lesbians and gay men having children together," conference keynote address delivered by Jennifer Firestone, 1 December 2001

Choosing Single Motherhood © Mikki Morrissette

CHAPTER 9

1 — As reported in *Helping the Stork: The choices and challenges of donor insemination,* by Carol Frost Vercollone, Heidi Moss, and Robert Moss (Wiley), 1997

2 — According to "Sperm donors' offspring reach out into past," by Judith Graham, *Chicago Tribune,* 19 June 2005

3 — "When Dad is a Donor," by David Noonan and Karen Springen, *Newsweek,* Vol. 138, (7), 13 August 2001

4 — See Judith Graham, *Chicago Tribune,* 19 June 2005

5 — "Donor insemination: a comparison of lesbian couples, heterosexual couples and single women," by Claire I. Wendland, Francis Byrn, and Cynde Hill, *Fertility and Sterility,* Vol. 65 (4), April 1996

6 — "Choosing Between Anonymous and Identity-Release Donors: Recipient and donor characteristics," by Joanna E. Scheib, Maura Riordan, and Phillip R. Shaver, *Reproductive Technologies,* Vol. 10 (1), January 2000

7 — "Choosing Identity-Release Sperm Donors: The parents' perspective 13–18 years later," by J.E. Scheib, M. Riordan, and S. Rubin, *Human Reproduction,* Vol. 18 (5), 2003

8 — See *Reproductive Technologies,* Vol. 10 (1), January 2000

9 — See *Reproductive Technologies,* Vol. 10 (1), January 2000

10 — According to California Cryobank's medical director, Dr. Cappy Rothman, as reported by *Chicago Tribune,* 19 June 2005

11 — "Adolescents With Open-Identity Sperm Donors: Reports from 12–17 year olds," by J.E. Scheib, M. Riordan, S. Rubin, *Human Reproduction,* Vol. 20, 2005

12 — As reported by *Chicago Tribune,* 19 June 2005

13 — "Identity-Release Sperm Donors 10–16 years later," by J.E. Scheib, M. Riordan, S. Rubin. Manuscript in preparation 2005.

14 — "Runs in the Family," by Scott Duke Harris, *Los Angeles Times,* 4 July 2003

15 — "The Father as an Idea: A challenge to kinship boundaries by single mothers," by R. Hertz, *Symbolic Interaction,* Vol. 25 (1), 2002

16 — "Plural Perspectives on Lesbian Artificial Insemination," by Jenifer Firestone, delivered at MIT panel discussion, 14 March 2003

17 — "Identity-Release Sperm Donors 10–16 years later," by J.E. Scheib, M. Riordan, S. Rubin. Manuscript in preparation 2005.

18 — "Recruitment of Semen Donors Still Possible Under Open System," *Human*

Reproduction, by Ken Daniels, Vol. 20, 2005

19 — "Choosing Identity-Release Sperm Donors: The parents' perspective 13–18 years later," by J.E. Scheib, M. Riordan, and S. Rubin, *Human Reproduction,* Vol. 18 (5), 2003

20 — "Intrauterine insemination with frozen donor sperm. Pregnancy outcome in relation to age and ovarian stimulation regime," by I. Ferrara, R. Balet and J.G. Grudzinskas, *Human Reproduction,* Vol 17 (9), 2002

21 — "Psychosocial adjustment among children conceived via donor insemination by lesbian and heterosexual mothers," Raymond W. Chan, Barbara Raboy, and Charlotte J. Patterson, *Child Development,* Vol. 69 (2), 1988

22 — "Planning a family on your own: a letter from Emily to single women," published by Donor Conception Network (www.dcnetwork.org)

CHAPTER 10

1 — *Adopting on Your Own: The complete guide to adopting as a single parent,"* by Lee Varon (Farrar, Straus and Giroux), 2000

2 — See "Adopting Smart: How Adoption Works and How Much It Costs," by Lois Gilman and Susan Freivalds, available on AdoptiveFamilies.com website. Also *The Adoption Resource Book,* by Lois Gilman (Harper Perennial), 1998

3 — See "Shifting Gears: The adoption option," on TheAFA.org website (www.theafa.org/faqs/afa_shifttoadoption.html)

4 — Per U.S. Department of Health and Human Services, Administration for Children and Families, Administration on Children, Youth and Families, Children's Bureau

5 — See: "A Fresh Look at Genealogical Bewilderment," by Michael Humphrey, *British Journal of Medical Psychology,* 1986, Vol. 59. For early research on genealogical bewilderment, see: "Genealogical bewilderment in children with substitute parents," by H.J. Sants, *The British Journal of Medical Psychology,* 1964, Vol. 37. Also: "Children without genealogy: A problem of adoption," by E. Wellisch, *Mental Health,* Vol. 13 (1), 1952

6 — Pavao was quoted in "Telling the Whole Truth to Adoption and Foster Care Children," a paper presented by Jayne Schooler to the 12th Annual Statewide Adoption Training Conference, May 2001, Albany, New York. Schooler's paper was adapted from work by Lois Melina and Dr. John Powell Young.

7 — See Schooler's paper cited above (www.nyscc.org/Conferences/Conf2001/whytell.html). See also *Telling the Truth to Your Adopted or Foster Child: Making Sense of the Past,* by Betsy Keefer and Jayne E. Schooler (Bergin & Garvey), 2000

8 — See *Raising Adopted Children: Practical reassuring advice for every adoptive parent,* by Lois Ruskai Melina (Collins), 1998

9 — See: "Families and Adoption: The pediatrician's role in supporting communication," by Deborah Borchers and the Committee on Early Childhood, Adoption, and Dependent Care," *Pediatrics,* Vol. 112 (6), December 2003. "Adoption Losses: Naturally occurring or socially constructed?" by I.G. Leon, *Child Development,* Vol. 73, 2000. "Adolescent Search for Birthparents: Who moves forward?" by Gretchen Miller Wrobel, Harold D. Grotevant, and Ruth G. McRoy, *Journal of Adolescent Research,* January 2004.

10 — *Being Adopted: The Lifelong Search for Self,* by David M. Brodzinsky, Marshall D. Schechter, and Robin Marantz Henig (Anchor Books), 1993

11 — "Openness in Adoption: Outcomes for adolescents with their adoptive kinship networks," by Harold D. Grotevant, Yvette V. Perry and Ruth G. McRoy, to appear in D. Brodzinsky and J. Palacios (Eds.), *Psychological Issues in Adoption: Theory, research and application* (Greenwood Publishing), submitted November 2003

12 — "The Impact of Openness on Adoption Agency Practices: A Longitudinal Perspective," by Susan M. Henney, Ruth McRoy, Susan Ayers-Lopez and harold D. Grotevant, *Adoption Quarterly,* Vol. 6 (3), 2003. See also: "Adoption Options: Thinking about adoption but not sure which kind is right for you? Here's an overview of options—how they work and what they cost," by Lois Gilman and Susan Freivalds, from *Adoptive Families 2005 Adoption Guide.*

13 — "How Many Children Were Adopted in 2000 and 2001," U.S. Department of Health and Human Services, National Adoption Information Clearinghouse, published 2004

14 — See: "Single parent adoption," by W. Feigelman and A. R. Silverman, as appears in *The Handbook for Single Adoptive Parents* (National Council for Single Adoptive Parents), 1997. "Single parents and their adopted children: a psychosocial analysis," by V.K. Groze and J.A. Rosenthal, *The Journal of Contemporary Human Services,* 1991. "Solo mothers and their donor insemination infants: follow-up at age 2 years," by C. Murray and S. Golombok, Family and Child Psychology Research Centre, City University, Northampton Square, London. "Children raised in fatherless families from infancy: a follow-up of children of lesbian and single heterosexual mothers at early adolescence," by Fiona MacCallum and Susan Golombok, *Journal of Child Psychology and Psychiatry,* Vol. 45 (8), November 2004

15 — The interview "Five Questions With Cheri Register" was featured July 2005 on the website for As Simple As That (www.simpleasthat.com)

CHAPTER 11

1 — As reported in "The Adopting Single Mother: Four Portraits of American Women Adopting from China," by Valerie S. Mannis, *Adoption Quarterly,* Vol. 4 (2), 2000

2 — *Raising Your Spirited Child: A guide for parents whose child is more intense, sensitive, perceptive, persistent, energetic,* by Mary Sheedy Kurcinka (Harper), 1998

3 — *The Explosive Child: A new approach for understanding and parenting easily frustrated, chronically inflexible children,* by Ross W. Greene (Harper), 2001

4 — *The Caregiver's Book: Caring for another, caring for yourself,* by James E. Miller, (Willowgreen), 1996. Available from www.willowgreen.com, or 206-490-0000.

CHAPTER 12

1 — "Sharing information with donor insemination offspring: A child-conception versus a family-building approach," by Ken R. Daniels and P. Thorn, *Human Reproduction,* Vol. 16 (9), 2001

2 — "Out of the Dish: Talking to children about their IVF origins," online article prepared by American Fertility Association, 2004 (www.theafa.org/faqs/afa_talktoivfchildren.html)

3 — *Flight of the Stork: What children think (and when) about sex and family building,* by Anne C. Bernstein (Perspectives Press, 1994). See also: "Children's concepts of how people get babies," Bernstein and P.A. Cowan, *Child Development,* Vol. 46, 1975

4 — According to "Sperm donors' offspring reach out into past: But those searching for roots can run into rules and dead ends," by Judith Graham, *Chicago Tribune,* 19 June 2005

5 — "Family Vacation: Why would Raechel McGhee fly her two beloved children across the country to stay with a man they had never met? Because he is their father," by Michael Leahy, *Washington Post,* 19 June 2005, p W12. Online question-and-answer session took place 20 June 2005.

CHAPTER 13

1 — For more from adoption expert Dr. Joyce Maguire Pavao, author of *The Family of Adoption* (Beacon Press), 1999, see www.kinnect.org, website of Center for Family Connections

2 — *Being Adopted: The Lifelong Search for Self,* by David M. Brodzinsky, Marshall D. Schechter, and Robin Marantz Henig (Anchor Books), 1993. See also: "The meaning of the search," by Schechter and D. Bertocci, in D. Brodzinsky & M. Schechter (Eds), *The Psychology of Adoption* (Oxford University Press), 1990

3 — "Discovering Dad: At 18, Christina Hall introduces herself to Phillip, her sperm-donor parent," by Christina Cheakalos and Vicki Sheff-Cahan, *People,* 14 July 2003

4 — According to a paper presented by Jayne Schooler to the 12th Annual Statewide Adoption Training Conference, May 2001, Albany, New York. Schooler's paper was adapted from work by Lois Melina and Dr. John Powell Young.

5 — "What does it mean to be a donor offspring? The identity experiences of adults conceived by donor insemination and the implications for counseling and therapy," by A.J. Turner and A. Coyle, *Human Reproduction,* Vol. 15 (9), 2000. Their findings were based on questionnaires filled out by 16 participants, aged 26 to 55, who were recruited from donor

insemination support networks.

6 — The report provides an overview of a child's understanding of adoption and offers advice for parents and pediatricians who talk about adoption with children. The report is available at aappolicy.aappublications.org.

7 — "Children's understanding of adoption," Brodzinsky, Singer, Braff, *Child Development*, Vol. 55, 1984. See also "Children's conception of adoption: A preliminary investigation," by Brodzinsky, C. Pappas, L.M. Singer, and A.M. Braff, *Journal of Pediatric Psychology*, Vol. 6 (2), 1981.

8 — As suggested in "Strange Bedfellows? Reproductive technology and child development," by Kyle D. Pruett, *Infant Mental Health Journal*, Vol. 13 (4), Winter 1992, based on personal communication with Robert Abramovitz, March 1991

9 — For more on Erikson's stages of life, see the Child Development Institute's www. childdevelopmentinfo.com/development/erickson.shtml. For more on middle childhood and the stage of mastery, see articles such as "A View from the Middle: Life through the eyes of middle childhood," by Robin F. Goodman, based on Sesame Workshop research, 2001 (see online article at www.aboutourkids.org/aboutour/articles/middle.html)

10 — "Children's Object Representations of Anonymous Donor 'Fathers' and Impact on Self-Concept," by Elizabeth E. Groisser, dissertation for doctorate, Ferkauf Graduate School of Psychology, Yeshiva University, New York, May 2003

11 — "Nontraditional family romance," by Ken Corbett, *Psychoanalytic Quarterly*, Vol. 70 (3), 2001

12 — "Kids Need a Real Past: Children with donor parents suffer when those raising them downplay their origins," by Elizabeth Marquardt, opinion piece published by *Chicago Tribune*, 15 May 2005

13 — "Alternatives to the Stork: Fatherhood fantasies in donor insemination families," by Diane Ehrensaft, *Studies in Gender and Sexuality*, Vol. 1 (4) 2000

14 — "The father as an idea: A challenge to kinship boundaries by single mothers," by Rosanna Hertz, *Symbolic Interaction*, Vol. 25 (1), 2002

15 — "Out of the Dish: Talking to children about their IVF origins," online article prepared by American Fertility Association, 2004 (www.theafa.org/faqs/afa_talktoivfchildren.html)

16 — "Choosing to be open about donor conception: the experiences of parents," by Sharon Pettle and Jan Burns (Donor Conception Network)

17 — *Real Parents, Real Children: Parenting the adopted child*, by Holly van Gulden and Lisa Bartels-Rabb, (Crossroad Classic), 1995. See also: "The Family Book" by Todd Parr (Megan Tingley), 2003. "Waiting Adoptive and Foster Families and Lifebooks," by Beth O'Malley, 2001, available on www.adopting.org, or check www.adoptionlifebooks.com

18 — See also "Positive Adoption Language," a fact sheet available from www. adoptivefamilies.com, as reprinted from *Ours* magazine, May/June 1992

19 — "Adopted Children and Stepchildren," U.S. Census Bureau, Census 2000 special report, issued October 2003.

19 — "Raising a Child of Another Race: Deliberate parenting can make a difference," by Jana Wolff, available at www.adoptivefamilies.com/articles.php?aid=155 (which also features an excellent resource list)

20 — "Making Sense of New Conceptions...in a Family Way," by Anne Bernstein, *Family Therapy News*, Vol. 26 (1), February 1995

21 — Dr. Elaine R. Gordon is author of *Mommy, Did I Grow in Your Tummy: Where some babies come from* (E.M. Greenberg Press), 1992, available at www.elaingordon.com. See the website also for her article "Talking to children about their adoption."

22 — See also articles available at www.adoptivefamilies.com, such as "Dear Teacher," "What Your Child's Teacher Needs to Know," "Tips for Helping Your Child Cope with Intrusive Questions," "Becoming an Advocate at School," "The Family Tree," and much more.

23 — "Study finds international adoptees better adjusted," reported by Reuters, 24 May 2005

24 — "Behavior problems and mental health referrals of international adoptees: A meta-analysis," by Femmie Juffer and Marinus H. van Ijzendoorn, *Journal of the American Medical Association*, Vol. 293 (20), 25 May 2005

CHAPTER 14

1 —Kurcinka's books include: *Raising Your Spirited Child: A guide for parents whose child is more intense, sensitive, perceptive, persistent, energetic*, 1998; *Kids, Parents and Power Struggles: winning for a lifetime*, 2000

2 —Pruett's publications include: *Fatherneed: Why Father Care is as Essential as Mother Care for Your Child*, 2000; *Me, Myself and I: How children build their sense of self 18 to 36 months*, *1999*

3 — Gurian's many books include: *The Wonder of Boys: What Parents, Mentors and Educators Can Do to Shape Boys into Exceptional Men*, 1996; and *The Good Son: Shaping the Moral Development of Our Boys and Young Men*, 1999

4 — Weissbourd's publications include: "Moral parent, moral child," by Richard Weissbourd, *The American Prospect*, Summer 2002; *The Vulnerable Child: What really hurts America's children and what we can do about it*, 1996

5 — See "Just the Two of Us: Parent-Child Relationships in Single Parent Homes," by Barbara Risman with Kyung Park, *Journal of Marriage and the Family*, November 1988

6 — *You and Your Adolescent: A Parent's Guide for Ages 10-20*, by Laurence Steinberg and Ann Levine, (Collins), 1997

7 — *The Intentional Family: How to Build Family Ties in Our Modern World,* by William Doherty (Perseus), 1997. Or: *The Intentional Family: Simple rituals to strengthen family ties* (Harper), 1999

8 — *Loving Your Child Is Not Enough: Positive Discipline That Works,* by Nancy Samalin with Martha Moraghan Jablow (Penguin), 1998

CHAPTER 15

1 — For more on international regulations in the insemination industry, see InfertilityNetwork.org. For ongoing regulations in adoption, see AdoptiveFamilies.com

2 — "Screening practices and beliefs of assisted reproductive technology programs," by Drs. Andrea D. Gurmankin, Arthur L. Caplan, and Andrea M. Braverman, *Fertility and Sterility,* Vol. 83 (1), January 2005

3 — "Parenthood: How old is too old?" by Carey Goldberg, *Boston Globe,* 5 April 2005

4 — "Wanted: Scientific reason for FDA's gay sperm ban," by Aubrey Noelle Stimola, posted 23 May 2005 to the Health Facts and Fears section of the American Council on Science and Health website (www.acsh.org/factsfears/newsID.556/news_detail.asp)

5 — "Who's Your Daddy?" opinion piece by David Plotz, appeared in *The New York Times,* 19 May 2005. Plotz is author of *Genius Factory: The Curious History of the Nobel Prize Sperm Bank.*

6 — "Single mothers-to-be face bias, race ticking clock," by Molly M. Ginty, *Women's E-News,* 18 June 2004

7 — "Lesbians protest rules on donors: Regulations seen causing unsafe self-procedures; approvals needed for gay, older men called unfair," by Tracey Tyler, *Toronto Star,* 15 February 2005. See also: "Jane and Sue make two in battle for sperm access," 27 April 2005.

8 — Per Steven S., Plaintiff and Respondent, v. Deborah D., Defendant and Appellant, Cal. App. 4th, [No. B175996. Second Dist., Div. Four], 3 March 2005

9 — Per Jhordan C., Plaintiff and Respondent, v. Mary K., Defendant and Appellant; Victoria T., Intervener and Appellant, 179 Cal.App.3d 386 , 224 Cal.Rptr. 530 [No. A027810. Court of Appeals of California, First Appellate District, Division Five], 28 March 1986

10 — Diane L. Johnston et al., Petitioners, v. The Superior Court of Los Angeles, Respondent; California Cryobank, Inc., et al., 80 Cal.App.4th 1050 , 95 Cal.Rptr.2d 864 [No. B137002. Second Dist., Div. Two], 18 May 2000

11 — Robert B., Plaintiff and Respondent, Denise B., Plaintiff and Appellant, v. Susan B., Defendant and Appellant, 109 Cal.App.4th 1109, Cal.Rptr.2d [No. H024926. Sixth Dist.], 13 June 2003

12 — "Surrogate Mother Wins Custody of Triplets: Pennsylvania judge awards custody to surrogate mother who gave birth to triplets," by Associated Press, 7 January 2005, as appeared on ABCNews.com. Also by AP: "Surrogate mom, biological dad battle over triplets," as appeared in *St. Petersburg Times*, 1 May 2005, and "Surrogate mom perseveres in battle against biological father," as appeared on www.observer-reporter.com, 13 May 2005

13 — "Recruiting egg donors after the removal of anonymity," by Alan Thornhill and Ian Craft, of London Fertility Centre, as appeared on www.BioNews.org.uk, 14 March 2005

14 — See: "Plea from sperm donor children," as reported on BBCNew.com, 22 May 2002. Also: Press release for Liberty, "Liberty wins contact register for children of sperm donors," 9 October 2003

15 — For up-to-date state adoption laws, see naic.acf.hhs.gov/laws/infoaccessap.cfm

16 — "Lesbian wins full co-parenting rights to partner's newborn daughter," by Wayne Parry, Associated Press, 26 May 2005

17 — As reported by CBS Radio News, "Adoption Becoming Easier for Gays," 29 October 2003. See also: "Adoption by Gays and Lesbians: A National Survey of Adoption Agency Policies, Practices and Attitudes," released by the Evan D. Donaldson Adoption Institute, 29 October 2003

18 — "Lesbian and Gay Parenting: A Resource for Psychologists," review, released 1995 by American Psychological Association, co-published by APA's Committee on Women in Psychology, Committee on Lesbian and Gay Concerns, and Committee on Children, Youth, and Families. See also, by Charlotte J. Patterson: "Children of lesbian and gay parents," *Child Development*, 63, 1992; "Families of the lesbian baby boom: Parent's division of labor and children's adjustments.," *Developmental Psychology*, Vol. 31, 1995; "Lesbian mothers, gay fathers, and their children," in A. R. D'Augelli and C. J. Patterson (Eds)., *Lesbian, gay, and bisexual identities over the lifespan: Psychological perspectives* (Oxford University Press), 1995.

19 — See "U.S. Supreme Court sidesteps gay adoption case; conservatives cheer decision," by Gina Holland, Associated Press, January 10, 2005.

20 — Another source for up-to-date state laws is the Human Rights Campaign website at www.hrc.org

21 — "Deconstructing the Essential Father," by Drs. Louise B. Silverstein and Carl F. Auerbach, *American Psychologist*, Vol. 54 (6), June 1999

22 — "Lesbian, single-mother families still face hurdles," by Shauna Curphey, *Women's E-News*, 14 January 2003

23 — "Driven by costs, fertility clients head overseas," by Felicia R. Lee, *The New York Times*, 25 January 2005. On the other hand, see also: "Reproductive tourism: Foreign moms flock to USA for in vitro procedures," by Suzanne Leigh, *USA Today*, 2 May 2005

24 — For up-to-date state laws, see the Resolve website at www.resolve.org

25 — Whitehead's testimony before the Committee on Health, Education, Labor and Pensions Subcommittee on Children and Families, U.S. Senate, took place 28 April 2004

26 — See the Healthy Marriage Initiative, Administration for Children and Families, U.S. Department of Health and Human Services (www.acf.hhs.gov/healthymarriage/index.html)

27 — From "Beyond Marriage Licenses: Efforts in states to strengthen marriage and two-parent families," by Theodora Ooms, Stacey Bouchet and Mary Parke, Center for Law and Social Policy, April 2004 (www.clasp.org). See also: Testimony of Theodora Ooms before the Committee on Finance Subcommittee on Social Security and Family Policy, U.S. Senate, hearing on "The Benefits of a Healthy Marriage," 5 May 2004.

28 — "Nostalgia as Ideology," by Stephanie Coontz, *American Prospect*, Vol. 13 (7), 8 April 2002

Chapter 16

1 — See *Gender Vertigo: American Families in Transition*, by Barbara Risman, (Yale University Press), 1998

2 — "The Marrying Kind: Why Men Marry and Why," by David Popenoe and Barbara Dafoe Whitehead, of the National Marriage Project, Rutgers University, 2004

3 — "…Finding a Village," by Rahel Musleah, *Hadassah Magazine*, March 2005

RESOURCES

In addition to the sources cited in Notes, these books, journal articles and websites may be of interest to readers who want to do more detailed research.

CHILDFREE LIVING

www.nokidding.net — helps people form and join support groups with others who are childfree

www.resolve.org — includes a helpful childfree section

The Childless Revolution: What it means to be childless today, by Madelyn Cain, 2001

Women Without Children: The Reasons, The Rewards, The Regrets, by Susan Lang, 1996

Reconceiving Women: Separating Motherhood from Female Identity, by Mardy Ireland, 1993

Sweet Grapes: How to stop being infertile and start living again, by J. Carter & M. Carter, 1989

The Parent Test: How To Measure And Develop Your Talent For Parenthood, by Ellen Peck and Dr. William Granzig, 1978.

USING A DONOR

Having Your Baby Through Egg Donation, by Ellen Sarasohn Glazer and Evelina Weidman Sterling, 2005

The Ultimate Guide to Pregnancy for Lesbians, by Rachel Pepper, 2005

Mommies, Daddies, Donors, Surrogates: Answering tough questions and building strong families, by Diane Ehrensaft (The Guilford Press), July 2005

Experiences of Donor Conception Parents, Offspring and Donors Through the Years, by Caroline Lorbach, 2003

But I Don't Feel Too Old to Be a Mommy: The complete sourcebook for starting motherhood beyond 35 and after 40, by Doreen Nagle, 2002

Helping the Stork: the choices and challenges of donor insemination, by Carol Frost Vercollone, Heidi Moss and Robert Moss, (MacMillan), 1997

Taking Charge of Your Fertility, by Toni Weschler, 2001

Having Your Baby by Donor Insemination, by Elizabeth Noble, 1988 (used copies on Amazon)

Choosing Single Motherhood © Mikki Morrissette

Building a Family with the Assistance of Donor Insemination, by Ken Daniels (available from Infertility Network)

Choosing to be Open about Donor Conception: The Experiences of Parents, by Sharon Pettle and Jan Burns (available from Infertility Network)

Having a Baby Without a Man, by Susan Robinson, 1985 (used copies on Amazon.com)

Author Buying Dad: One Woman's Search for the Perfect Sperm Donor, by Harlyn Aizley (available at www.harlynaizley.com)

Children, Lesbians, and Men: Manual useful to both lesbians and heterosexual women considering the idea of becoming pregnant by a donor, dealing with deciding between using a sperm bank and a private donor, and between having a known donor or an anonymous donor. Stories have helped women talk with possible donors. Includes the experiences of men with different degrees of involvement with their biological children, and what their relationships are like as the children get older. (68 pages. $12.50, incl. postage. Men's Resource Center, 236 N. Pleasant St, Amherst, MA 01002)

Websites

FertilityPlus.org — good layman's source for sperm banks and fertility procedures, including home insemination

FertilityNeighborhood.com — information on "how to choose a fertility clinic," etc.

InfertilityNetwork.org — offers an impressive library of information and support

SpermCenter.com —helpful guide to banks and donors, created by a Choice Mother

InfertilityTimes.com —online magazine covering topics such as insurance, adoption, treatment options, childfree living, donors, testing and procedures

DCNetwork.org — website of the UK-based Donor Conception Network

PerspectivesPress.com — books about fertility and adoption

MaiaMidwifery.com — offers phone consultations about donor negotiations and more

Human Rights Campaign (www.hrc.org) — offers excellent information about politics, policy and alternative family building, including (under Family: Parenting) sample agreements to use with known donors and valuable information about the process

Scholarly research

"Lesbians Choosing Motherhood: Legal Implications of Donor Insemination, Second Parent Adoption, Co-Parenting, Ovum Donation and Embryo Transfer," 1996 — *written for lesbians but applicable to anyone especially considering the use of a known donor* (available at www.nclrights.org/publications/pubs/lcm.pdf)

Benward, J. (1998) Donor registries in reproductive medicine. In *Advanced Counseling Issues:*

Third Party Reproduction. American Society for Reproductive Medicine 31st Annual Post-Graduate Course, San Francisco

Blyth, E. (2002) Information on genetic origins in donor-assisted conception: is knowing who you are a human rights issue? *Human Fertility,* 5

Golombok, S., Cook, R., Bish, A., & Murray, C. (1995). Families created by the new reproductive technologies: Quality of parenting and social and emotional development of children. *Child Development,* 66

Golombok, S., Murray, C., Brinsden, P. & Abdalla, H. (1999). Social versus biological parenting: Family functioning and the socioemotional development of children conceived by egg or sperm donation. *Journal of Child Psychology & Psychiatry & Allied Disciplines,* 40 (4)

Golombok, S., MacCullum, F., Goodman, E., & Rutter, M. (2002). Families with children conceived by donor insemination: A follow-up at age twelve. *Child Development,* 73 (3)

Golombok, S., Brewaeys, A., Giavazzi, M.T., Guerra, D., MacCallum, F. and Rust, J. (2002a) The European study of assisted reproduction families: the transition to adolescence. *Hum. Reprod.,* 17

Hewitt, G. (2002) Missing links: identity issues of donor-conceived people. *J. Fertil. Counselling,* 9

Klock, S.C., Jacob, M.C. and Maier, D. (1996) A comparison of single and married recipients of donor insemination. *Hum. Reprod.,* 11

Leiblum, S.R., Palmer, M.G. and Spector, I.P. (1995) Non-traditional mothers: single heterosexual/lesbian women and lesbian couples electing motherhood via donor insemination. *J. Psychosom. Obstet. Gynecol.,* 16

Vanfraussen, K., Ponjaert-Kristoffersen, I. and Brewaeys, A. (2001) An attempt to reconstruct children's donor concept: a comparison between children's and lesbian parents' attitudes towards donor anonymity. *Hum. Reprod.,* 16

Wendland, C.L., Byrn, F. and Hill, C. (1996) Donor insemination: a comparison of lesbian couples, heterosexual couples and single women. *Fertil. Steril.,* 65

Sperm Banks

This is not an all-inclusive list, but is a guide to reliable sperm banks known to be friendly to lesbians and single women. Many of them offer an increasing number of open-identity donors.

BioGenetics Corp. *(ethnically diverse),* Mountainside, NJ. 908/654-8836, www.sperm1.com

California Cryobank Inc. *(large selection),* Los Angeles, CA, 800/231-3373 or 310/443-5244, www.cryobank.com

Cryobiology Inc. *(offers donor essays),* Columbus, OH, 614/451-4375, www.cryobio.com

Cryogenic Laboratories Inc. *(donors from any geography)*, Roseville, MN, 800/466-2796 or 651/489-8000, www.cryolab.com

Genetic and IVF Institute *(high tech)*, Fairfax, VA, 800/552-4363, www.givf.com

Idant Laboratories *(high tech)*, New York, NY, 212/244-0555, www.idant.com

Fairfax Cryobank *(good donor info)*, Fairfax, VA, 800/338-8407, www.fairfaxcryo.com

New England Cryogenic Center *(ships worldwide)*, Brookline, MA , 800/991-4999 or 617/244-4447, www.necryogenic.com

Pacific Reproductive Services *(self-insemination and known-donor friendly)*, San Francisco, CA, 888/469-5800 or 415/487-2288, www.hellobaby.com

Rainbow Flag Health Services and Sperm Bank *(gay and lesbian friendly)*, Alameda, CA, 510/521-7737, www.gayspermbank.com

Scandinavian Cryobank *(eclectic donors)*, Seattle WA, 866/366-6777, www.scandinaviancryobank.com

Sperm Bank of California *(non-profit, research-oriented, pioneering)*, Berkeley, CA, 510/841-1858, www.thespermbankofca.org

Xytex Corp. *(full service)*, Augusta, GA 30904, 800/277-3210, www.xytex.com

Zygen Laboratory *(anonymous or directed donor)*, Tarzana, CA, 800/255-7242 or 818/705-3600, www.zygen.com

ADOPTION

Adopting on Your Own, by Lee Varon, 2000

Adoption Nation: How the Adoption Revolution is Transforming America, by Adam Pertman, 2001

Raising Adopted Children, by Lois Ruskai Melina, 1998

The Whole Life Adoption Book: Realistic advice for building a healthy adoptive family, by Jayne Schooler, 1993

Being Adopted: The Lifelong Search for Self, by David M. Brodzinsky, 1993

The Adoption Resource Book, by Lois Gilman

Websites

www.adoptivefamilies.com — excellent, comprehensive resource naic.acf.hhs.gov/index.cfm — National Adoption Information Clearinghouse offers fact sheets, resource lists and information about everything from state laws to transracial adoption

www.angelfire.com/journal/adoptionhelp/adopthelp.html — excellent guide to covering adoption expenses

fwcc.org/financing.htm — useful 2003 article about financing adoption, written about Chinese adoptions but applicable to anyone; includes other financing resources

www.irs.gov— search "adoption" for up-to-date tax benefit information and forms

www.everychildinc.org— specializes in special needs adoption and foster care

www.davethomasfoundation.org — specializes in North America's foster care system

www.adoptionattorneys.org — source for finding lawyers specializing in adoption

www.adoptUSkids.org — features photos of U.S. children awaiting adoption

www.adopting.org — good source for support

www.adopting.com — good guide to resources

www.nacac.org — education and advocacy

Scholarly research

Bernstein, Anne C. (1994). "Talking with Children about Adoption," Chapter 10, in *Flight of the Stork: What Children Think (and When) about Sex and Family Building*, Perspectives Press

Rosenberg, E. & Horner, T. (1991). Birthparent romances and identity formation in adopted children. *American Journal of Orthopsychiatry*, 61(1)

Singer, L. M., Brodzinsky, D. M., & Braff, A. M. (1982). Children's belief about adoption: A developmental study. *Journal of Applied Developmental Psychology*, 3

Transracial

Beyond Good Intentions: A Mother Reflects on Raising Internationally Adopted Children, by Cheri Register, 2005

I'm Chocolate, You're Vanilla: Raising Healthy Black and Biracial Children in a Race-Conscious World, by Marguerite Wright, 1998 — Suggestions to help develop a positive sense of self-esteem and deal with racial prejudice

Pact: An Adoption Alliance (www.pactadopt.org) — Offers a 400-page manual, *An Insider's Guide to Transracial Adoption*, with strategies for dealing with the challenges of multiracial family life, including issues for single parents and those with special-needs children, and information about the predictable stages when children address particular racial issues.

Choosing Single Motherhood © Mikki Morrissette

As Simple as That (www.simpleasthat.com) — excellent resource that educates and entertains multicultural families, particularly those with children ages 3 to 8

Eastern European Adoption Coalition (www.eeadopt.org)

Families With Children From China (www.fwcc.org)

Our Chinese Daughters (www.ocdf.org/ocdf/)

Families for Russian Ukranian Adoption (www.frua.org)

Latin American Parents Association (www.lapa.com)

FOR THE KIDS

DonorSiblingRegistry.com — assists individuals in mutual consent contact with biological relatives conceived through sperm or egg donation

The Red Blanket (2004) — Sweet picture book for preschool children about a mother and her adopted child.

Families Are Forever (2003) — Prepares all children for the increasingly diverse, multiracial face of adoptive families.

The Best Single Mom in the World: How I Was Adopted (2001) — Picture book for ages 4-8.

W.I.S.E. Up! Powerbook (2000) — Good empowering guide to help children learn how to handle comments and questions about being adopted; includes parent guide.

Do I Have a Daddy? (1999) — Useful picture book for children ages 4-8 whose biological father left, including a special section for single parents about addressing the questions of preschool children.

A Mother for Choco (1996) — Heart-warming animal story useful for young children in multiethnic families.

How It Feels to Be Adopted (1988) — Personal stories from children about their feelings on being adopted, for kids ages 9-12.

How I Began: The Story of Donor Insemination — Explanation for kids ages 5-8 about basic human anatomy, conception, insemination and birth. (available from Infertility Network)

Mommy, Did I Grow in Your Tummy? Where Some Babies Come From — Author's view is that children are not born with a primary need to be from one particular type of family, but with a basic need to belong, to be wanted, to be loved and understood. Helps tell the story to young children of their creation in an open and honest way. (available from www.elainegordon.com)

Our Story — Illustrated storybooks for young children. Separate books for children conceived through egg donation, into single-parent families or into lesbian-parent families. (available from Donor Conception Network)

Sometimes It Takes 3 to Make a Baby: Explaining Egg Donation to Young Children — An illustrated guide explaining in simple language the process of egg donation; a workbook for the child to complete, including their own personal photos, mementos and drawings; advice for parents on how to talk to young children. (available from Infertility Network)

Truth & the Child 10 Years On: Information Exchange in Donor Assisted Conception — Essays by donor offspring, egg donors, a DI mother, a mother through surrogacy, a family through adoption, as well as counselors, researchers and lawyers, on the rights and needs of those born from assisted conception about their genetic origins. (available from Infertility Network)

SINGLE MOTHERHOOD

The Complete Single Mother, by Andrea Engber and Leah Klungness, 2000

On Our Own: Unmarried Motherhood in America, by Melissa Ludtke, 1999

The Single Parent Resource, by Brook Noel with Art Klein, 1998

Single Mothers by Choice, by Jane Mattes, 1994

In Praise of Single Parents, by Shoshana Alexander, 1994 (used available on Amazon)

Operating Instructions: A Journal of My Son's First Year, by Anne Lamott, 1994

Websites

groups.yahoo.com/group/choicemoms/ — author's new online discussion site for Choice Moms, with an emphasis on news and resources rather than chat

SingleMothersByChoice.com — support network for Thinkers, Tryers and Choice Moms

Singlemothers.org — good resource by author Andrea Engber

Single Rose.com — support site, although emphasis is with divorced single parents

www.makinglemonade.com — support, especially for single parents of teens

IS IT FAIR TO THE CHILD?

These are relatively recent scholarly articles—from all angles—that I did not use in this book, but might be useful to readers who want to do further research.

Choosing Single Motherhood © Mikki Morrissette

Madeleine Stevens, Susan Golombok, Michael Beveridge (2002), "Does Father Absence Influence Children's Gender Development? Findings From a General Population Study of Preschool Children" *Parenting*, 2:1

Judy Dunn, et. al. (June 2001), "Family lives and friendships: the perspectives of children in step-, single-parent, and nonstepfamilies," *Journal of Family Psychology*, 15: 2

Erin Calhoun Davis and Lisa V. Friel (August 2001), "Adolescent sexuality: disentangling the effects of family structure and family context," *Journal of Marriage and Family*, 63:3

Teresa Tsushima and Viktor Gecas (April 2001), "Role taking and socialization in single-parent families," *Journal of Family Issues*, 22:3

Maureen Perry-Jenkins and Sally Gillman (2000), "Parental Job Experiences and Children's Well-Being: The Case of Two-Parent and Single-Mother Working-Class Families," *Journal of Family and Economic Issues*, 21:2. [Single mothers' more positive evaluations of their work environments were linked to sons' reports of greater restraint of aggressive tendencies.]

Ronald P. Rohner and Robert A. Veneziano (2001), "The Importance of Father Love: History and Contemporary Evidence," *Review of General Psychology*, 5.4

Paul R. Amato and Fernando Rivera (1999), "Paternal Involvement and Children's Behavior Problems," *Journal of Marriage and the Family*, 61

M.K. Rose (1992). "Elective single mothers and their children: The missing fathers," *Child and Adolescent Social Work*, 9:1

HISTORY OF FAMILY LIFE

Stephanie Coontz, *The way we really are: coming to terms with America's changing families* (Basic Books, 1997), and *The way we never were: American families and the nostalgia trap* (Basic Books, 1992)

Judith Stacey, *Brave New Families: Stories of Domestic Upheaval in Late Twentieth-Century America* (University of California, 1998). Vivid descriptions of the new kinds of familial relationships not defined by biology or traditional gender roles.

Rima D. Apple and Janet Golden, Eds., *Mothers & Motherhood* (Ohio State University, 1997). A collection of essays examining the social, cultural, demographic, medical, and political factors that have shaped the definition and experience of motherhood.

Elaine Tyler May, *Barren in the Promised Land* (Basic Books, 1996). Examines changing attitudes toward childlessness, compulsory sterilization, and adoption.

Steven Mintz and Susan Kellogg, *Domestic Revolutions: A Social History of American Family Life* (Free Press, 1988). Argues that the only constants in the history of American family life have been diversity and change.